# Women, Culture, and Politics in Latin America

# Women, Culture, and Politics in Latin America

Seminar on Feminism and Culture in
Latin America

Emilie Bergmann, Janet Greenberg, Gwen
Kirkpatrick, Francine Masiello, Francesca
Miller, Marta Morello-Frosch, Kathleen
Newman, Mary Louise Pratt

UNIVERSITY OF CALIFORNIA PRESS
Berkeley   Los Angeles   Oxford

University of California Press
Berkeley and Los Angeles, California

University of California Press
Oxford, England

Copyright © 1990 by The Regents of the University of California

Library of Congress Cataloging-in-Publication Data

Women, culture, and politics in Latin America/Seminar on Feminism
and Culture in Latin America (University of California-Stanford
University).
    p.    cm.
   Includes bibliographical references.
   ISBN 0-520-06552-2 (alk. paper).—ISBN 0-520-06553-0 (pbk.:
alk. paper)
   1. Feminism—Latin America—Congresses.  2. Women in politics—
Latin America—Congresses.  3. Women—Latin America—Intellectual
life—Congresses.  4. Feminism in literature—Latin America—
Congresses.  5. Women in literature—Latin America—Congresses.
6. Women and literature—Latin America—Congresses.
HQ1460.5.W624  1990
G05.42'098—dc20                            89-77866
                                           CIP

Printed in the United States of America
1 2 3 4 5 6 7 8 9

The paper used in this publication meets the minimum requirements of American
National Standard for Information Sciences—Permanence of Paper for Printed
Library Materials, ANSI Z39.48–1984

# Contents

*v*

# Preface

This book is about the history of women in politics, letters, and intellectual life in Latin America. Its authors are scholars in literary criticism, history, and cultural studies working mainly at research universities in the United States. The collection by no means attempts a comprehensive account of the topics named in its title. Rather, it takes the form of a series of case studies that examine particular dynamics and raise questions that ultimately will prove essential to a more comprehensive account. The intention here is decidedly to open rather than conclude discussion.

The overall corpus of research on women in Latin America shows little focus on women's intellectual, literary, political, and pedagogical activity. In part owing to its very important links with policy studies, research on women has been oriented toward topics such as health, reproduction, migration, demographics, and development. When women's participation in politics is discussed in this context, often only grass-roots and local activity are considered. When the question of culture is raised, the term is often taken to encompass everyday life, domestic activity, manual work, religious practices, marriage, the body.

Feminism has taught us the immense importance of these dimensions of women's being and activity. At the same time, the tendency to restrict culture and politics in these ways with respect to women reinforces a male elitism that claims serious intellectual, artistic, and political work as exclusive preserves of men. Women now striving for legitimacy and equality in these arenas (such as ourselves) must contend with such prejudices every day. We must know our predecessors and the history of their struggle, and make them known to others.

The eight authors published here make up a study group, the UC-Stanford Seminar on Feminism and Culture in Latin America, which has met monthly for the past seven years to discuss feminist theory and Latin American women's history and literature. In our reading and discussion we have examined women's literary and journalistic production and their participation in national and international political life; we have undertaken bibliographical projects; we have worked together to design new courses and made a number of panel presentations at regional and national conferences. At all such events, we have encountered other women scholars working in related areas, often in considerable isolation. Their enthusiasm for our project, and for the collective nature of our work, has been a vital source of encouragement.

While all of our members had at some time participated in feminist study groups or in women's studies programs, the decision to seek institutional support as a research group was without precedent among us. Some members had participated in an earlier group of California women Latin Americanists, which organized itself informally to counteract the marginalization of women and women's issues in mainstream scholarly meetings. This group's effectiveness, and the solidarity it promoted, inspired us to reconstitute it into the present seminar. The increasing legitimacy of feminist inquiry made it possible for us to seek institutional support from the Stanford-Berkeley Joint Center for Latin American Studies. We appreciate the funding and logistical support the center has provided over the years.

The essays included in this volume represent only a part of the seminar's work. The group remains a forum for discussion (most recently on issues of gender and state) and a setting where members can present their own work in progress and share new findings. Given the history of women in the academy and the continued resistance to feminist scholarship in most academic departments, one of the group's essential functions has been to guide and support individual members as they meet the challenges of the profession. Since our members represent a wide range of career situations, from graduate student to part-time lecturer to full professor, this support function has proved to be an important priority.

We have also sought continuously to shape our work along lines of feminist collective practice. The seminar retains a fundamental commitment to collaborative intellectual activity, with its particular ability to mediate among areas that benefit from mutual understanding. We see collective practice as the key to our efforts to mediate among literary studies, history, politics, area studies, feminist theory, and Europe and the Americas. To our great benefit, the group's activities have brought us into contact with information and research networks of feminist scholars in the United States and Latin America. It is clear that new forms of research and criticism are meeting the challenge of integrating women into the scholarly picture of Latin America. We hope to continue to participate in this vital and exciting project.

We are indebted not only to the Stanford-Berkeley Joint Latin American Studies Center, which provided us with subsistence support for several years, but also to the Hewlett Foundation, the UC Berkeley Women's Studies Program, and the Beatrice M. Bain Research Group for grants to do bibliographical projects and to the Stanford Humanities Center for logistical support in the preparation of the manuscript.

# Notes on Contributors

Emilie Bergmann is a specialist in Spanish Golden Age literature in the Department of Spanish and Portuguese, University of California at Berkeley.

Janet Greenberg holds a Ph.D. in comparative literature from the University of California at Berkeley. She is an executive associate of the American Council of Learned Societies in New York.

Gwen Kirkpatrick teaches Latin American literature in the Department of Spanish and Portuguese at the University of California at Berkeley.

Francine Masiello teaches Latin American and comparative literature at the University of California at Berkeley.

Francesca Miller teaches inter-American relations and women's history at the University of California at Davis.

Marta Morello-Frosch teaches Latin American literature at the University of California at Santa Cruz.

Kathleen Newman teaches Latin American film and mass communications theory at the University of Iowa.

Mary Louise Pratt teaches comparative literature and literary theory at Stanford University.

# ONE

# Introduction

*Seminar on Women and Culture in Latin America*

The history of women's participation in literary culture and political life in Latin America is a history still in the making. The partial and often biased record of women's thought and activity in that cultural region has limited our historical perspectives and our understanding of feminist contributions. For example, Sor Juana Inés de la Cruz has been seen as a unique phenomenon, an iconographic feminist presence, rather than as one of many women involved in a long tradition of engagement in Latin American culture. As recent investigations in women's history show, the activities and achievements of women have not been restricted to the celebrated appearance of rare genius, such as Sor Juana. By the latter half of the nineteenth century, numerous women in lettered culture had advanced the issues of women's rights, especially with respect to civil status, family, and participation in literary life. The typical forum for these ideas was not the public podium, but the political journal, where the arguments for women's equality were cast in terms of progressivism and the hope of a better life in the New World. Latin American intellectuals, male and female, were well aware of the women's movement in Europe and the United States; the international exchange of ideas was particularly important for the earliest proponents of women's rights in Latin America. However, the acknowledgment of the influence of international intellectual currents should not be allowed to obscure the fact that a feminist critique of society arose out of the distinctive experience of the Latin American women themselves.

Of necessity, our book examines the work of Sor Juana, who questioned her own self-presentation and the representation of herself and other women by the patriarchal culture. We then turn to the decades between 1910 and 1950 as the focus of our study on feminism and culture in Latin America. It is in this era that the first generation of urban, literate women appeared in

*1*

Buenos Aires, São Paulo, Rio de Janeiro, Santiago de Chile, Montevideo, Mexico City, and Havana. The emergence of women novelists, poets, journalists, and political activists and the development of a shared feminist consciousness in the early twentieth century in certain nations of Latin America are directly linked to the trends of modernization. Major social upheavals took place in Mexico and Cuba, but women intellectuals first found their strongest voice, and audience, in Argentina, Uruguay, Chile, and Brazil. Our studies concentrate to a great extent, then, on this second regional grouping.

Gender in modern societies is a fundamental social category that shapes every dimension of human existence. Its interaction with class is dynamic and highly varied. On one hand, class hierarchies and relations of exploitation are reproduced within the gender system—for example, in relations between upper-class women and their female domestic employees. On the other hand, gender creates inevitable and significant instabilities in class hierarchies. It creates difference within class boundaries (upper-class women do not participate in society or culture in the same ways as upper-class men do), while it creates sameness across class boundaries (the experiences of upper-class and lower-class women have points in common). Official high culture has tended to suppress both these dimensions. The essays in this collection mainly explore the first dimension—that is, the struggle of women to participate in public culture, and the particularities of their participation, especially in print culture.

Motivated by their sense of social injustice or by the way in which they understand their social and cultural privileges, the women studied in this volume ally themselves with wide-ranging political issues that transcend their class and gender. The case of Alfonsina Storni is exemplary of this class transformation. Coming from humble beginnings in a working-class family, Storni took advantage of democratic reforms in the educational codes in Argentina to pursue a career as a poet, teacher, journalist, and dramatist. Thus, the figure of the *maestra* is of interest not only as a transmitter of class culture but also as an actor across class boundaries and a frequent transgressor of her own class culture. Gabriela Mistral, the celebrated poet who emerged from desperate rural poverty in Chile, was later recognized, like Storni, for her pedagogical commitments, while she engaged in national debates about the destiny of her country. Victoria Ocampo was born into the Argentine oligarchy, yet she also challenged tradition by setting an independent course for herself as editor, publisher, and memorialist. The common thread that binds these writers is their perception of the inadequacies of the traditional spaces from which they were allowed to speak and act and their search for strategies that would relieve them of the burden of patriarchal tradition and fulfill the need for reform. It is from this perspective, with its specific historical context, that we perceive these writers as cultural innovators.

It was female schoolteachers drawn from different classes who formed the nucleus of the first women's group to articulate what may be considered a feminist critique of society. That is, they were the first to protest against the pervasive inequality of the sexes in legal status, access to education, and political and economic power. Two factors are of great importance. First, the teachers represented a new group in Latin American society—the educated middle sector—which included skilled workers, clerks, and government employees as well as educators, who were well aware of their precarious social economic and legal status. Second, these women were in touch with one another through their institutions of learning and through professional associations, forums in which they could share their common experience. Many who lived in the most cosmopolitan centers of Latin America were aware of local issues and ideas, as well as national and international politics. Furthermore, as the essays included here explore, it is this moment of self-conscious reassessment of roles that is crucial to our understanding of a new function of women writers in Latin America.

The first decades of the twentieth century were of great significance for changes in women's status and political and cultural participation. The political and intellectual environment of the Western world in the first decades was volatile. The Mexican Revolution, which broke out in 1910, was the first great social revolution of the twentieth century, preceding both the Chinese Revolution (1911) and the Russian Revolution (1917). Moreover, cosmopolitan Latin Americans, especially South Americans, were closely attuned to European events, a factor that was intensified by the thousands of emigrating Italians, Spanish, Germans, and Greeks who settled in Argentina, Brazil, Chile, and Uruguay during the period. In the 1930s, the earlier immigrants were joined by thousands of Jews seeking refuge from the rising influence of National Socialism in Germany, Italy, Austria, Poland, and Romania. In that same decade, Mexico took in over thirty thousand refugees from the Spanish Civil War. The political movements that shook Europe were not far removed for readers of *La Prensa* in Buenos Aires, *El Nacional* in Mexico City, or *La Lucha* in Havana; those movements were present in the political spectrum of the major states of the hemisphere: Brown Shirts in Brazil, followers of Leon Trotsky in Mexico, anarcho-syndicalists in Montevideo.

Within the American community of nations, the hegemony of the United States in the Caribbean and Central America posed a new diplomatic configuration. Criticism of United States policy was increasingly vociferous, and by the 1930s the interventionism of the early years of the century gave way to a diplomacy of inter-American reconciliation. While the Western Hemisphere was spared the devastation of the world war, numerous armed conflicts marked the era. In Mexico, the smoldering struggle between church and state erupted in the Cristero Rebellion (1926–1929). In Nicaragua, Augusto Sandino's troops fought Anastasio Somoza, the National Guard, and United States Marines, in a conflict that ended in the treacherous assassination of

Sandino (1934). In South America, the dispute between Bolivia and Paraguay over control of the vast Chaco territory, a dispute that opened with a few armed skirmishes in the late 1920s, flared into a bitter and bloody war in which nearly 100,000 lives were lost and both countries nearly bankrupted before a truce was reached in 1935.

The Great Depression had a profound effect on the export-oriented economies of Latin America and exacerbated political divisions. One of the most significant political forces to emerge was the *indigenista* movement, especially in the Andean region. At the same time, the pressure to transform traditional structures to respond better to the needs of the rapidly changing society resulted in the passage of protective labor legislation, the revision of the civil codes that regulated spousal and parental rights (in Mexico, Cuba, and Argentina), and the promulgation of new constitutions that incorporated labor laws and female suffrage (in Brazil and Uruguay, 1934). However, the legislative reforms found weak adherence, owing to financial constraints and governmental indifference. Women, whatever their economic and social milieu, continued to be at a disadvantage in securing and holding jobs for pay, in their familial relationships, and in the political arena.

Women intellectuals worked and fought side by side with men for independence in Cuba, for revolutionary change in Mexico, and for profound social reform in Argentina, Uruguay, and Brazil. But by the 1920s the women activists shared a collective realization that issues of primary concern to them—economic, social, and legal equality—were considered secondary to the general movements for social and political change: the Sáenz-Peña Law of 1912, which granted universal suffrage in Argentina, excluded women; the Mexican Constitution of 1917, hailed as the most radical social and political document of its time, did not include women in the definition of citizen, nor did the Cuban Family Code. The tension between women's struggle to be included as equals and their alienation from the essential patriarchal structure of the nation-state had its analogue in the revised consideration of gender and women's literary production in the era.

The first half of the century had special significance in Latin America both for the openings witnessed in the political arena and for the expansion of modern culture. It marked the consolidation of liberal reformist movements and the rise of an urban middle class. At the same time, with the introduction of United States capital in Latin American cities, a new consciousness of the neighbor to the north permeated cultural life and found expression, on one hand, in the form of a growing Pan-Americanist movement and, on the other, in heated objections to the policies of Yankee expansionism. Within the growing urban sectors of Latin America, where the work force was redefined, men and women for the first time worked together in the metropolitan city. In this period the gender system showed signs of flux and contradiction; the categories of masculine and feminine began to be redefined within the space of the city. In particular, the presence of women in the work force and in the cultural salons brought a heightened sense of urgency to the process of social reform. Women thus struck alliances with the men of anarcho-syndicalist, socialist, and even right-wing movements; they participated in political activities to alter the status of divorce laws; they organized suffragist movements and encouraged juridical recognition of women within the state. Simultaneously, women also formed part of a new reading public, which was expanded in the course of urbanization and increased literacy for the masses. This new readership, stratified by ideological and class differences, consumed a variety of publications ranging from sentimental romance and mystery stories to socialist-realist pamphlets. Gender, we would add, is the other fundamental factor that accounts for differences in reading and literary taste.

Together these factors contributed to a peculiar form of the modernist adventure, separate from cultural activities in Europe and distinctly marked along gender lines. Against the monolithic facade of its European counterpart, the modernism of the 1920s in Latin America (not to be confused with the movement of *modernismo* led by Rubén Darío) signaled an opening of cultural possibilities. It is not new to explain modernism in Europe as a break from traditional realism, a severing of linear discourse in art, and a fragmentation of the whole. Cultivating new technologies in science and philosophy, the modernist project was supported by the epistemology of rationalism, a questioning of the symbol, and a prolonged search for meaning. In Latin America, however, modernism also witnessed the consolidation of a new class of professional writers, who defended the autonomy of their craft while drawing a portrait of themselves in quest of legitimacy and power. By exercising control over his or her text and the institution of letters, the artist presumed to control history as well. Against this background, women writers engaged in a struggle to create a different voice.

We have isolated the feminine response to the modernist project outlined above as a discourse that does not necessarily follow the paradigms identified with the literature of this period. Participating in the cultural events of the day with a consciousness of their individual condition, women writers voiced a simultaneous concern for national questions and for aesthetic innovation and change. At the same time they reconsidered their own situation within the estate of letters. While often pursuing different aesthetic and political strategies, they found resounding unity in their efforts to construct alternative frameworks and outlets for literary production. It behooves us, then, to follow their path and determine how the modern canon was opened wide as women in Latin America embarked upon a distinctive course to find their own voice.

Revising the canon involves two interconnected and reciprocal activities: looking at the traditionally consecrated texts from new angles and giving

serious attention to little-known texts in a way that changes the contours of
the body of consecrated texts. The change in direction of our gaze toward
these previously marginalized texts changes our perspective on the texts traditionally considered central and the questions we ask of them. This change
in perspective reveals accepted distortions of human reality along familiar
binary oppositions such as active/passive and public/private. In some texts,
these divisions and the systems of social oppression that they support are
exposed by the text's resistance and subversion. Our research has examined
the objectification and distortion of women and women's lives resulting from
the operation of these categories in literary representation and in the political
and social roles of women.

Francesca Miller's research into the historical roles of women from the
1880s to the 1940s has revealed a world of activism across national boundaries, in a Pan-American context in which women could confront global
problems despite their disenfranchisement at home. Feminist research in the
history of women's movements in Latin America is essential to a transformation of our view of women in this period. If it is accepted that women's space
is only interior and private, the reality of women's work outside the home
is obscured, and the role of women schoolteachers, an important element in
the formation of generations of citizens in Latin America, is ignored. If we
go further to examine what is meant by "interior" and "private," we find
that these terms do not necessarily imply women's exclusion from cultural
and political processes, regardless of their exclusion from voting booths
or elected office. Nor has women's activity been tied specifically to interior
spaces: women operate in the open space of the marketplace, in some influential spheres in the public space of churches, and in the practice of journalistic
writing, an emphatically public arena instrumental to women's international
organizing efforts. Likewise, much male-dominated political decision-making
is done in enclosed, exclusive spaces. The assumptions attached to traditional images are challenged by the historical evidence.

Similarly, the related commonplace that women speak from indoors, from
womblike spaces, does not hold as an absolute: in relation to the land and
landscape, women's writing differs from the masculinist tradition by abandoning the terms of conquest and domination, which seek to label and
classify according to the known and thereby to control the mystery of the
unknown. Our collective work led us to examine how women poets write
nationalist epics. If feminists were concerned more with Pan-Americanism
than with loyalties to individual countries, and women's relationship to the
land was circumstantially different from men's because of inheritance and
ownership laws, then we could expect a different kind of "epic," which, in
turn, would change the way we read traditional nationalist epic poetry.
Mary Louise Pratt's study of travel literature illuminated her reading of
Gabriela Mistral's *Poema de Chile*: the poetic voice is not the unified, dominat-

ing voice that names, lays claim to landmarks, and legitimizes authority. It is a rootless wandering and a dialogue in which a mother attempts to answer a child's questions; it does not narrate consecrated historical events or "explain" the national geography. Not only is Mistral's familiar canonical image as frustrated mother challenged but the position of nationalist epic is also necessarily shifted from the center to another position on a sphere.

If Mistral's "epic" changes not only the way we read Mistral but also the way we read epic and position it in a literary hierarchy, then rereading other women authors and other genres has similarly wide-ranging effects. Alfonsina Storni's political writings have been neglected in traditional analyses, which see her poetry as desperate, frustrated, and focused on the male lover. Gwen Kirkpatrick's rediscovery of Storni's journalistic writings permits her to be seen as a working woman, acting autonomously for change in the social status of women. She no longer represents the woman seeking her reflection in the mirror of male desire. Her poetry is a different kind of statement, not simply speaking to the male lover but also speaking to her readers about the way in which male-female relationships are articulated in poetic imagery. Marta Morello-Frosch's reading of the profound irony in "Tú me quieres blanca" illustrates this challenge to the traditions of love poetry. The poem involves not only the apostrophe to the ostensible "tú" but also an indirect, strong address to a listener who overhears a criticism of the one-sided and previously acceptable demand for female purity and innocence.

Francine Masiello's reevaluation of the novel of family relationships in the 1920s and 1930s casts new light on the representation of family structures in the novel: how this representation conforms to or deviates from current political exigencies. Expanding the range of novels to include popular fiction exposes attitudes toward the changing social structure and the changing role of women during this period. An awareness of the vitality of women's movements in Latin America reveals the view of women as potentially disruptive to be a reaction to women's growing sense of autonomy. If women were in fact working and active in some public spheres, and some women writers were working and traveling on an international scale and living independently of stable homes dominated by husbands and fathers, the traditional family had to become a literary convention instead of a social reality based on natural laws. The rereading of the canon is a reexamination of the relationship of those texts to historical contexts, as instruments of social control challenged by some devalued texts and exposed by the exaggerated reproduction of these conventions in some popular novels.

Kathleen Newman exposes another aspect of the public role of woman in her study of the media images of women between 1916 and 1926, as they reflect political anxieties of a changing society. She examines the modernization of femininity in relation to the historical context of social unrest and the entrance of women into the work force. The possibility of a public, but not political, image of femininity in the film star once again complicates these traditional categories.

Literary scholarship influences the ways in which a work may be read: the scholarship we and other feminists have been doing is meant to expand the possibilities. Feminist analysis of the literary-historical situation of Sor Juana Inés de la Cruz (1648–1695) exposes the internal contradictions of the poetic canon and the effect on women's writing of the patriarchal definitions of public and private spheres. The three mythic female figures of Mexican Colonial history—the Virgin of Guadalupe, La Malinche, and Sor Juana— represent modes of inscription of the feminine in the theological and political discourse of colonization; the process of inscription recasts each one in the cultural coinage of successive regimes. The most popular image of Sor Juana sets the stage for the role of the woman writer as passionate, self-destructive heroine. Until very recently, book-length studies of Sor Juana centered on scrutiny of the personal life of the nun and speculated on her sexuality, rather than on Sor Juana's highly praised poetry and prose. Like Storni and Mistral, whose public work in journalism and political activism was obscured in the process of anthologizing and canonizing their work to conform to cultural norms, Sor Juana is a writer whose place in her context is important to our understanding of women's writing in her own time and after.

Recent feminist scholarship has opened the possibilities for rereading the personal to reveal its political implications. Sor Juana and Storni, for example, represent the female body and the consequences of the male gaze in women's lives and women's creation of woman-centered art. Storni, in "Hombre pequeñito" or "Tú me quieres blanca," is confronting the way in which the male gaze is enshrined in poetry. This is the same gaze that Sor Juana cleverly mocks as she instructs the observer in the proper viewing of her portrait. Our research has not been directed toward establishing Sor Juana or other poets more solidly as precursors, as cultural "mothers," or as models for Latin American women poets. Rather, we have sought to recover what has been left out of the processes of canonization: works, writers, genres that do not fit a male model of women's lives.

Our research, by restoring the aspects left out of some conventional images, shows why these works, writers, and genres are omitted: with all their aspects included, the lives and works of women writers take full form in areas that disregard the artificial boundaries of public and private. Sor Juana's intellectual speculation in her *Sueño* and her appreciation of the beauty of a female friend and patron are inextricable from her precarious political situation. As social representation, what can be more public than a nun's renunciation of her previous individual identity in the interest of serving the Church? Likewise, in subsequent centuries, when single mothers, schoolteachers, and orphaned children as well as traditional families are represented in fiction as metaphors for the state and its perceived enemies, the domestic is no longer the domain of the private, but its use in sexual politics is indicative of social insecurities.

Sor Juana chose the apparent impersonality of the philosophical poem, a marginal literary genre. Janet Greenberg's reading of Victoria Ocampo's autobiography has exposed neglected aspects of the writings of an important figure in Argentine literary history. Autobiography has been described as another marginalized genre, and precisely for that reason it has been a genre available to women from the early mystics to the present. Ocampo's journalistic writing and activity had an important impact on twentieth-century literary movements in Latin America, but a distorted view of her has been perpetuated by critics. To reevaluate her writing is ultimately to replace the trivializing gossip surrounding her name with the reality of an influential woman and a complex writer in the context she was instrumental in creating.

Our research in women's journalism has been essential to our awareness of the social and historical context of women's roles and women's writing. Each of us in her area of interest has been led to pursue research in periodical literature produced by, for, and about women. Literate women have not been isolated from one another, but the scope of their dialogue has often been hidden. Feminist historians have shown the importance of magazines published as early as the eighteenth century as resources for studying the history of women. This material clarifies the evolution of feminist theory and its relationship to action throughout modern history; it also provides a strong base from which to build contemporary feminism. In the presentation of Greenberg's working bibliography of women's periodicals we make a contribution toward the reconstruction of women's dialogue about and relationship to public debate and private life. The examination of this multifaceted debate opens another route to information about the ideas, strategies, goals, and accomplishments of women's movements.

To read what was previously unread or to read familiar texts in a new way always offers the possibility of discovery. We have examined not only the relationships between literature and social realities but also the impact of neglected or critically misrepresented works upon their literary and social contexts. This perspective rearranges the canonical view of art as an unbroken tradition representing dominant views of class, race, and sex with negligible voices of dissonance on the margins. Instead, we find a varied and conflictive field of activity in which the judgments of critics do not represent the response of readers or the dialogue among writers. For the members of our group, this work has been a process of discovery and reevaluation that has widespread effects on the way we read and think about history and culture.

# TWO

# Latin American Feminism and the Transnational Arena

*Francesca Miller*

In the early twentieth century, feminists from North and South America took their agenda to the tables of the International Conferences of American States. The history of Latin American women's participation in the inter-American conferences suggests that the transnational arena held a particular appeal for Latin American feminists. There are a number of reasons this was so. Within their national communities, they were disfranchised; and, as elsewhere, the national social and political arenas were characterized by androcracy. Moreover, Latin American female intellectuals were particularly alienated from politics as practiced within their countries, excluded from leadership positions by the forces of opposition as well as by their governments.

The inter-American arena in the first half of this century proved to be an important domain for feminist activity, one in which women activists from throughout the Americas pursued a number of the longstanding goals of international feminism. Two of the themes that emerge in the examination of women's concerns in this period are the push for resolutions that would commit the signatory governments to pursue legal and civil reform and the search for international peace.

## ESTABLISHING A PRESENCE: 1898–1928

Venezuelan novelist Teresa de la Parra, speaking before a conference of Latin American women novelists and authors in Bogotá in 1930, described "la influencia de las mujeres en la formación del alma americana."[1] Teresa de la Parra posited a spiritual empathy among women of "Catholic and Spanish America"; she recalled Isabella I of Castile and Sor Juana Inés de la Cruz as spiritual precursors of the assembled women poets and writers. De la

Parra would not have described herself as a feminist; however, in her assumption that Spanish-American women had made a different contribution to the *alma americana* than their male counterparts, she implicitly subscribed to the thesis that the historical experience of women is not perfectly analogous to that of the men with whom their lives are linked.[2]

For de la Parra, women were not only different but also, in matters of the spirit, superior. In consonance with her belief in the uplifting moral influence of women on the American soul, de la Parra insisted that "History and Politics are a banquet for men alone." To her, the realm of politics was a corrupt masculine realm from which women should abstain, and history a record that excluded "the young, the people [*o povo, el pueblo*], and women."[3]

Consider, however, the inherent conflict between what de la Parra was doing and what she was saying: while advising women to abstain from politics, she herself was giving a public speech that was explicitly critical of political practice in states governed solely by men, a fairly universal condemnation but specifically aimed at the nation-states of the Western Hemisphere; surely this was a political act in itself. The conflict between her action and her message vividly demonstrates the ambiguity felt by many of de la Parra's colleagues in, on one hand, their alienation from politics as practiced in their own national governments and, on the other, their desire to effect social, political and economic reform—reform that would bring "the young, the people, and women" into social and political equity and, in so doing, transform the essential patriarchal character of the state.

By 1930 the discussion of whether women should enter the political fray was a moot one: women, and issues of special concern to women, were fully in the arena of public debate. However, the history of Latin American women's participation in and contributions to international feminist discourse in the early twentieth century has been shrouded in historiographic assumptions about the nature and extent of feminist thought in Latin America, assumptions that imply that feminist thought in Latin America is derivative and not sui generis. More concretely, it has been assumed that the creation of the Inter-American Commission of Women at the Sixth International Conference of American States in Havana in 1928 was not a collaborative effort by North and South American women but a response to the pressure tactics of the National Woman's Party of the United States and thus another example of North American hegemony, female-style.

The historical record belies these assumptions. Latin American women's participation in and contributions to international feminist discourse are well illustrated in the proceedings of inter-American conferences held between 1880 and 1948. The examination of the inter-American conferences is of particular significance in the study of Latin American women's contributions, because the precedent for using the international congresses of American states as a forum for the debate of feminist issues was established at the Latin

American Scientific Congresses, first sponsored by the Sociedad Científica Argentina, which met in Buenos Aires in 1898, Montevideo in 1901, Rio de Janeiro in 1905, and Santiago in 1908. Their purpose was to discuss "scientific, economic, social and political issues," and, as a later chronicler wrote, "women of the Latin American countries have been identified with these congresses since the first."

The majority of women participants came from Argentina, Chile, Uruguay, and Brazil, and the topics they addressed came under the rubric of "social problems": hygiene, child care, nutrition, maternal welfare. All these topics meshed comfortably with traditional feminine interests within their societies and were matters of concern to scientists and educators of both sexes.

For the Santiago meeting in 1908, the Latin American Scientific Congress was expanded to become the First Pan American Scientific Congress. Over two thousand members gathered from throughout the hemisphere; it was observed by W. R. Shepherd of Columbia University that "women school teachers constituted a large part of the audience, and it must be said that they express their opinions, as well as their difference in opinion, from those held by the other sex, with a freedom and frankness which is quite surprising."[4] It was on the issue of access to education for women that these Latin American female intellectuals found themselves divided from their male counterparts. However, discussion of the education issue was appropriate to the forum and does not represent the breadth of feminist social critique in the Southern Cone republics at the turn of the century.[5]

On May 10, 1910, over two hundred women from Peru, Chile, Uruguay, Paraguay, and Argentina convened in Buenos Aires for the first Congreso Femenino Internacional. The sponsoring groups included the Asociación Nacional Argentina Contra la Trata de Blancas, Asociación Nacional del Profesorado, Centro Socialista Femenino, Escuela Normal de Maestras de Tucumán, Grupo Femenino Unión y Labor, Liga Nacional de Mujeres Librepensadoras, and many more.[6] Dr.Cecilia Grierson presided; the topics discussed ranged from international law to health care to the problems of the married working woman, and reflected the participants' conversance with the international reformist and feminist dialogue of the day.[7] Among the resolutions was one commending the government of Uruguay for passage of a bill of divorce and of one demanding equal pay for equal work: "trabajar porque en la igualdad de circunstancias el trabajo de la mujer no sea menos retribuido de que lo del hombre."[8]

What is of significance of the examination of the inter-American congresses is that the women who spoke at the Congreso Femenino Internacional in Buenos Aires formed the nucleus of the South American women who attended the scientific congresses. The scope of their interests, their feminist perspective, and their critical stance vis-à-vis the status quo in their respective societies are well illustrated in the record of the Buenos Aires meeting. Furthermore, in their talks, many of the speakers foreshadowed the rhetoric that came to characterize the arguments put before the International Conferences of American States in the 1920s, as María Samame did in her speech "Democracy and the Political Personality of the Woman." After citing a number of examples from antiquity, she pointed out that Isabella I of Spain deserved the greatest credit for the discovery of the New World, the birthplace of democracy, and concluded, "In the old monarchies perhaps it would have been unnatural to recognize the right of woman suffrage; but in the democratic republics of America it is an inexcusable anachronism not to do so."[9]

The Second Pan American Scientific Congress was held in Washington, D.C., in 1915–1916. The Washington congress took on far more significance within the context of inter-American relations than the previous scientific congresses had done. In 1915, Europe was at war, and in North America, Mexico was in the throes of revolution. The United States Department of State, aware that the audience of the scientific congress would include the diplomatic representatives of the states of the Western Hemisphere resident in Washington, took the opportunity to put forth its interpretation of hemispheric security and the need to build up defensive power. Thus, the character of the meeting was altered from a collegial exchange of professionals to a facsimile of a full-dress inter-American diplomatic conference. One of the consequences was that, unlike the Congresses that had been held in South America, the Washington congress did not include women among the "savants, scientists, and publicists" invited. The women were relegated to the balconies.

Thus began the second phase of women's efforts to focus attention on issues of their special concern. In response to their debarment from the official Washington meetings, a number of Latin American women, among them educators and other professionals, diplomats' wives and daughters, foregathered with their North American counterparts to form an auxiliary meeting—a meeting that attracted so many participants that the women overflowed the small room they had originally been allotted and were moved to the ballroom of the Mayflower Hotel (this fact was carefully noted in the minutes).[10]

In these early phases of women's involvement at the international level, the women participants were of the same social and economic background as their male counterparts. However, the women had a different agenda. On issues of social welfare, their program often intersected with that of reform-minded males; the split came when the women sought to have equality of rights for their own sex, such as equal access to education and to the ballot box and equality within marriage. It is also significant that the women acting at the international level at this time were not, as the men were, professional diplomats, paid commercial agents, or subsidized scholars. The women were involved because they had issues about which they could agree, despite great diversity in background and personal political orientation.

The agenda drawn up at the Mayflower Hotel in 1916 stated that the purpose of the meeting was not only to "exchange views of the subjects of special interest to women," which included "the education of women, training of children, and social welfare," but also to discuss subjects of Pan-Americanism. In the words of the keynote speaker, "We the women of North and South America, which possess similar conceptions of individual rights and constitutional government, possess a common duty to mankind which we must not ignore."[11]

In the 1920s the early efforts of the women bore fruit in a series of well-attended Pan-American women's conferences. One in Baltimore in 1922 began with the intention of emphasizing the importance of suffrage, but concluded with a platform calling for international peace through arbitration; abolition of the white slave trade; access to education at all levels; the right of married women to control their own property and earnings and to secure equal guardianship; the encouragement of organizations, discussion, and public speaking among women and freedom of opportunity for women to cultivate and use their talents and to secure their political rights; and, finally, the promotion of friendliness and understanding among all Pan-American countries, with the aim of maintaining perpetual peace in the hemisphere.[12] Bertha Lutz, founder of the Federação Brasileria pele Progresso Femenino and one of the Brazilian delegates to the Baltimore conference, contrasted the atmosphere there with her experience in trying to bring the women's programs before the League of Nations:

> We were received in the United States, not as if we were representatives of unimportant countries as happens at the international congresses of the Old World, but with a frank cordiality and with the same consideration that has marked the relations of women of the Americas since the days of our pioneering foremothers.[13]

By 1922, the essential components for an effective, formal international exchange among women of the Americas were in place. A continuing organizational structure with an accumulated history of international activity was established; funding sources had been identified; a communications network was in place. Leaders were emerging. Of the Latin American women, some, like Amanda Labarca of Chile and Flora de Oliveira Lima of Brazil, were veterans of the scientific congresses; others, like Bertha Lutz, Clara González of Panama, and Elena Torres of Mexico, represented a new generation. A political platform had been enunciated and agreed upon; it was a distillation of the issues which had been raised over the past two decades. To the prewar concern for social problems and the belief in the need for education had been added the appeal for peace and for equal rights and, as a means to these ends, the desire for inclusion at the diplomatic council tables.

The sympathetic atmosphere and reformist zeal of the Pan-American women's conference described by Lutz were hardly characteristic of the pre-war International Conferences of American States. The early Pan-American meetings, convened between 1881 and 1910, had been primarily devoted to establishing conventions that would enhance inter-American commercial opportunities and exhibited little of the fiery idealism expressed by Simón Bolívar, who had dreamed that "the assembling of a Congress of Panama composed of diplomatic representatives from independent American nations [would] form a new epoch of human affairs," or the hopes of Henry Clay, who in 1828 called Bolívar's proposal the opportunity to establish "a human-freedom league in America."[14]

The invocation of the ideals of Pan-Americanism by the feminists working at the international level added a new dimension to the inter-American con-ferences of the 1920s. The Fifth International Conference of American States, held in Santiago in 1923, which was the first convened since the onset of World War I, took place in an atmosphere of controversy. The desire of the women to insert feminist issues and matters of broad social reform into the program of the conference paralleled the desire of many in both North and South America, male and female, to use the conferences to challenge United States imperialist activities in Central America and the Caribbean—a polit-ical position that was, in turn, fully supported by feminist leaders through-out the hemisphere.[15] A sizable number of "unofficial" female delegates attended the Santiago meeting, which passed a resolution recommending that women be appointed as official delegates to future inter-American con-ferences.

The next International Conference of American States met in Havana in 1928. There were no official women delegates; nevertheless, women from throughout the hemisphere had traveled to Havana for the conference. And they were not there as interested individuals or spouses. They spoke for the Consejo Feminista Mexicana, the Women's International League for Peace and Freedom, the Federação Brasileira pelo Progresso Feminino, the Nation-al Woman's Party of the United States, the Ligue Feminine Haitienne, the Club de Madres of Buenos Aires, and many, many more. They were hosted by the Alianza Femenina Cubana and the Club Femenino de Cuba.

By the end of the conference, these "unofficial" delegates had secured an audience before a plenary session, presented an Equal Rights Treaty for the consideration of the governments of the hemisphere, and successfully lobbied for the creation of an officially designated body, the Inter-American Commis-sion of Women, which was charged with the investigation of the status of

women in the twenty-one member states. The IACW was "the first governmental organization in the world to be founded for the express purpose of
working for the rights of women."[16]

The Equal Rights Treaty,[17] which was strongly opposed by the United
States diplomatic delegation, was eventually ratified by only four member
countries and was relegated to obscurity. Nevertheless, the choice of the Pan-
American meetings as a forum for the discussion of women's and feminist
issues proved politically astute: women had indeed succeeded in bringing
"women's issues" to the center of political debate within the hemisphere.
The leadership of the Latin American women is clearly illustrated not only in
providing the precedent of using inter-American congresses as a forum for
the debate of feminist issues but also in the insistence on the inclusion of
issues of social justice in the first Pan-American women's platforms, which
directly reflected the dominant concerns of Latin American feminists.[18]

In addition to their domestic agenda, through which they hoped to influence their respective national governments to enact laws that would bring
women into civil and legal equity with men, the feminists active at the inter-
American congresses took strong stands on international issues, supporting
the principles of nonintervention, the resolution of conflict through arbitration, and the rights of small nations. In Havana in 1928, the women demonstrated against the United States' occupation of Nicaragua and protested the
dismissal of the Haitian representatives.[19]

Many of the Latin American women who attended the Fifth International
Conference of American States in Santiago in 1923 and the North and South
American women who met at the Sixth IAC in Havana in 1928 were members of the Women's International League for Peace and Freedom. The positions the WILPF took in matters of hemispheric politics are discussed in the
report of the Comité de las Américas de la Liga Internacional de Mujeres de
la Paz y Libertad:

> La Sección . . . ha trabajado por muchos años contra el imperialismo norte-
> americano, y ha cooperado con resultados favorables por los siguientes fines:
> Declaración del Gobierno de los Estados Unidos que nunca volverá a interve-
> nir en países extranjeros para proteger la propriedad norteamericana;
> . . . retiro de los marinos de Haiti, Nicaragua, y la República Dominicana;
> derogación de la Emienda Platt en la Constitución de Cuba. Desde 1926 ha
> contribuído a mejorar las relaciones entre los Estados Unidos y Mexico.
> . . . Ha tratado de descubrir y aminorar la explotación de trabajadores en
> Cuba, Bolivia, Chile y otros países.[20]

> [The Section . . . has worked for many years against North American imperial-
> ism, and has cooperated with good results to the following ends: The Declara-
> tion by the Government of the United States that it would never again inter-
> vene in foreign countries in order to protect North American property; . . . the

retirement of the Marines from Haiti, Nicaragua, and the Dominican Republic, and the removal of the Platt Amendment from the Constitution of Cuba. Since 1926 [the Section] has contributed to the improvement of relations between the United States and Mexico . . . and has worked to reveal and ameliorate the exploitation of workers in Cuba, Bolivia, Chile and other countries.]

The members of the first IACW were Flora de Oliveira Lima (Brazil); Aida Parada (Chile), Lydia Fernández (Costa Rica), Gloria Moya de Jiménez (Dominican Republic), Clara Gonzáles (Panama), Elena Mederos de González (Cuba), Irene de Peyre (Guatemala), Margarita Robles de Mendoza (Mexico), Juanita Molina de Fromen (Nicaragua), and Teresa Obrogoso de Prevost (Peru). Doris Stevens (USA) was chair. The IACW took up the task of collecting material on the legal status of women from every country in the hemisphere:

> The commission, created in the Sixth Pan American Conference for the purpose of dealing with the Conflict of Laws and Uniformity of Legislation . . . took into consideration the resolution adopted in the plenary session of February 18, 1928, for the constitution of an IACW charged with the duty of preparing information, which it might consider useful, of a legal and other nature, to the end that the Seventh International Conference should take up the study of the civil and political equality in the continent.[21]

The first meeting of the IACW was held in Havana, February 17–24, 1930. In addition to the commissioners listed above, Colombia was represented by Alicia Ricode de Herrera, Haiti by Mme Fernand Dennis, El Salvador by proxy, and Venezuela by Cecilia Herrera de Olavarría. The commission drafted a resolution to establish equality in nationality for presentation to the World Conference for the Codification of International Law, to be held at The Hague in March, 1930. The resolution stated, "The contracting parties agree that from the going into effect of this treaty there shall be no distinction based on sex in their law and practice relating to nationality."[22] Other resolutions requested the American governments to appoint the IACW commissioners as plenipotentiaries to The Hague conference, asked financial support for their work, and thanked the Carnegie Endowment for International Peace for its initial grant of five thousand dollars.

The women did their own secretarial work; they had secured a small office space in the Pan American Union building in Washington only after dealing with numerous harassment tactics—when they arrived at their office in the first few months of their existence, they often found that their two desks had been "borrowed" or that all the chairs were missing. Nevertheless, they succeeded in gathering a substantial amount of legal information from throughout the hemisphere, all of which was carefully collated, hand-labeled, and placed in black leather three-ring notebooks.[23] The intention was to be able to have access to the information pertinent to particular issues as they arose. The first of these was the issue of the nationality of married women.

The earliest opportunity to present the Resolution on the Nationality of Women to an international body came at the meeting of the council of the League of Nations at The Hague in 1931. As the women had no official status within the league, the resolution was put forth by male diplomatic representatives from the Americas: Matos of Guatemala, Barreto of Peru, and César Zumeta of Venezuela. The IACW draft urged the American states

> to consider the question of whether it would not be possible 1) to introduce into their law the principle of the equality of the sexes in matters of nationality, taking particularly into consideration the interests of children, and especially 2) to decide that in principle the nationality of the wife should henceforth not be affected without her consent either by the mere fact of marriage or by any change in the nationality of the husband. It is to be noted that there is a clear movement of opinion throughout the world in favor of a suitable settlement of this question.[24]

No action resulted; the resolution was taken under study. James Brown Scott, editor of the published collection of resolutions, added this comment to the document: "In the interest of historical accuracy, it is necessary to record that the initiative of the Council's action came from the IACW. The League's Commission of Women, when created, will concern itself with, and report to, the 1931 Assembly upon a single point: nationality and the status of women."[25] Scott's comment underscores the achievements of the IACW. Not only had the American women been successful in creating an officially recognized commission that became a model for the creation of the Commission of Women at the League of Nations but the IACW was endowed from the beginning with a far broader mandate for action than was the League Council.

## EQUAL RIGHTS AND PEACE: 1928–1938

From the early twentieth century, Latin American feminists, like their North American colleagues, were deeply commited to the idea of peace. At the Pan American Women's Auxiliary meeting in Washington in 1916, the Pan American Association for the Advancement of Women's conference in Baltimore in 1922, the International Conference of American States in Santiago in 1923 and in Havana in 1928, the women reiterated their commitment to "maintaining perpetual peace in the hemisphere."[26]

In the decade between 1928 and 1938, the Inter-American Commission of Women operated as an autonomous body within the inter-American organization. The themes of equal rights and peace, both of which were believed to be within the special province of women, mark their efforts. In the words of Nelly Merino Carvallo, who edited the international woman's journal *Mujeres de América* in Buenos Aires from 1930 to 1935: "From its inception, *Mujeres de América* has been dedicated to peace. Yes: it is through the woman that peace will be secured in the world."[27] The idea that women have a special role as peacemakers is persistent, despite evidence that men have in fact been the diplomats who have arbitrated peace agreements and sought international concord. Certainly the male representatives to the International Conferences of American States saw themselves as working toward peace in the hemisphere. But there are a number of factors that differentiate the attitudes and expressions of men and women in the transnational discourse of the period. First, the male diplomatic community recognized force as a legitimate diplomatic tool; they were not pacifists. Second, the male diplomats and representatives to the inter-American conference tables were speaking for their governments, not of their personal convictions. Only a handful of women were members of national delegations. From the beginning, the constituency of the IACW was drawn from women's organizations. The original members of the commission were, in effect, self-appointed. During the 1930s, the IACW solicited, and received, confirmation by individual governments of the women who already were on the IACW.

There is evidence that another factor was crucial, particularly for the Latin American women. In this era, the women active at the international level had little tradition of identifying with the nation-state. To the contrary, they had historically articulated their position as other within the home, the society, and the nation, and looked to the transnational arena as the space where they could find mutual support from one another and publicize their agenda. We are not speaking of all women—some were patriotic, and most were indifferent. We are not speaking of the women of the Liga Patriótica, or of the women who embraced their disfranchisement and inequality as badges of femininity, but of feminists who articulated their position of dissent from the prevailing order and sought change.

The 1930s were a period of powerful nationalist movements in Argentina, Mexico, and Brazil. The iconography of those movements was overwhelmingly masculine, the ideal national figure being a male head of state, who, if not himself a general, a hero of the revolution, or a gaucho, was certainly surrounded by military power. Although women worked for reform and change at home, they had few effective channels for garnering support, and their programs were often dismissed as irrelevant by both government and opposition leaders. Alienation from the political process within the national community should not be construed as obviating love of homeland, of place, of one's historical family; rather, it should be understood as part of the meaning that the transnational arena held for Latin American feminists in this era.

The Seventh International Conference of American States, held in Montevideo in 1933, marked the first inter-American conference at which women had an official presence, both within the Inter-American Commission of Women and as members of national delegations.[28] At that meeting, the Convention on the Nationality of Women was presented to the conference by the Inter-American Commission of Women. The convention stated, "There shall be no distinction based on sex as regards nationality." It was signed by twenty American countries, becoming the first convention on the rights of women to be adopted at an international conference. It served as the model for the Convention on the Nationality of Women that was subsequently adopted by the League of Nations.[29]

The women's work for gender equity did not diminish their commitment to the cause of international peace. Of central concern in the Southern Cone in this period was the conflagration in the Gran Chaco. The dispute between Bolivia and Paraguay over the vast territory of the Chaco, which stretches from the eastern slopes of the Andes to the Paraguay River, began with isolated armed skirmishes in the late 1920s. The conflict flared into a bloody war that ultimately took nearly 100,000 lives and bankrupted the treasuries of the participants before a truce was reached in 1935.

During the war, nationalist passions were high. In this unsympathetic atmosphere, *Mujeres de América* ran a petition initiated by the Círculo Argentino "Pro Paz"[30] and addressed to the delegates at the Montevideo conference. The petition called for arbitration and denounced the participants in the war as tools of international capitalist interests; but most telling of the sentiments of the publication and its audience was the dedication of the July–August 1933 issue to the women of Boliva and Peru, "reviving the spirit of the glorious days of Independence" when the two nations were one.

> En la dolorosa tragedia que conmueve las soledades del Chaco, un corazón de americana y defensora de la paz a toda costa, llora de dolor y de inquietud fraternales. Y, ante la impotencia de detener esta cruenta tragedia, aspiro por lo menos que *Mujeres de América* vaya formando un nuevo concepto de "patria" que es progreso; "patria" que es paz; "patria" que es unión.
>
> Sí, mujeres bolivianas, amigas mias, unámosnos todas. Trabajemos con fé, con amor, para que en no lejanos días tengamos la patria grande, la patria sin fronteras; la patria fundada en el mejoramiento espiritual.[31]

[In the unhappy tragedy that breaks the solitude of the Chaco, a heart of America and defender of peace at all costs, weeps full of pain and broken brotherhood. And, confronted with the impossiblity of halting this cruel tragedy, I hope that at least *Mujeres de América* may help to form a new concept of "patria" that is progress; "patria" that is peace; "patria" that is unity.

Yes, women of Bolivia, my friends, we are one. We are working with faith, with love, for the time where we will be one great country, a "patria" without frontiers; a country founded on spiritual betterment.]

The idea of a "patria" without boundaries is a specifically nonnational vision.[32] The ways in which feminists in Latin America talked and wrote about peace, as but one aspect of their transnational activities, illuminates the ways in which they viewed the nation-state. The idea of sisterhood, of an imagined community of interests based on gender, of the women's insistence on the commonality of the human experience, undermines the idea of nation. This is well illustrated in the subsequent history of the women's platform.

The Eighth International Conference of American States met in Lima in 1938; the main business of the conference was the effort, led by the United States, to unite the hemisphere in the event of war. In the Declaration of Lima, the American republics reaffirmed their continental solidarity and "determination to defend themselves against all foreign intervention."[33] The Inter-American Commission of Women succeeded in putting forth its resolution that "women have the right to the enjoyment of equal civil status,"[34] but the Lima conference was also the scene of an attempt to disestablish the Inter-American Commission of Women as an autonomous entity. The Inter-American Commission of Women had never enjoyed the support of the United States diplomatic corps, and under the Roosevelt regime, it became a particular target of Eleanor Roosevelt.[35] Its feminist stance had made it a target for attack throughout its existence, and in the atmosphere of the late 1930s the women's platform was seen as secondary to the efforts to unite the hemisphere. The feminist leaders were advised to turn their efforts to the defense of democracy, not to raise divisive issues. Over the protests of the members of the commission itself, the opposition, which came principally from the United States delegation, succeeded in recasting the Inter-American Commission of Women from an independent women's commission to a subsidiary unit of the inter-American apparatus.[36]

Despite its diminished status, the IACW continued its work, and its legacy is readily apparent in the next decade. At the Chapultepec Conference on the Problems of War and Peace in Mexico on March 8, 1945, the wording of the Lima resolution was directly incorporated into the plans for the United Nations; in October, 1945, in San Francisco, Inter-American Commission of Women representatives Bertha Lutz of Brazil, Minerva Bernadino of the Dominican Republic, and Amalia Caballero de Castillo Ledon of Mexico used the precedent inter-American resolutions on the status of women to insist that the opening paragraph of the Charter of the United Nations include the phrase "the equal rights of men and women." It reads, "We the peoples of the United Nations, determined . . . to reaffirm faith in fundamental human rights, in the dignity and worth of the human person, in the equal rights of men and women and of nations large and small."[37] In Bogotá in 1948, again with the leadership of Amalia Caballero de Castillo Ledon, the Comisión Interamericana de Mujeres was established as part of the Organization of American States.

### THE GUATEMALA CONFERENCE

Legal rights and the appointment of women to the diplomatic tables were
only a part of the Latin American and North American feminists' agenda in
the pre-World War II period. The women's concerns and those of their like-
minded male colleagues on issues of social welfare, education, and the need
for economic change were incorporated in the Chapultepec Charter, the
Charter of the United Nations, and the newly organized Organization of
American States. Women themselves were now part of governmental delegations, and much of their agenda was incorporated into the international
agenda.

A number of questions arise. Did women as the counter-voice at the
international conferences vanish after 1945, only to reemerge during the
United Nations International Year of the Woman in 1975? Did women,
once they were the official representatives of their governments, cease to
function as a pressure group for change? Did the historical antinationalist
position of the first generation of Latin American feminists disappear in the
1940s? Or is there evidence of the continuation of a separatist, explicitly feminist, political strategy within the context of inter-American relations?

By 1947 the attention of the inter-American diplomatic community had
shifted from social and economic reform to a focus on opposition to commu-
nism, a position embraced by governments throughout the hemisphere. An
extraordinary meeting of American foreign ministers and heads of state
was convened at the Inter-American Conference for the Maintenance of Continental Peace and Security, in Petropolis, near Rio de Janeiro, from August
15 to September 2, 1947, at the instigation of the Latin American states.[38]
The delegates drew up the Treaty of Reciprocal Assistance, known as the
Rio Pact, which put into effect the principle that an attack upon one American state would be considered an attack upon all. The emphasis on arming
the nation-states of the Western Hemisphere, which has formed the bulk of
inter-American assistance in postwar history, dates from this agreement.[39]

Between August 21 and August 27, 1947, the Primer Congreso Interamericano de Mujeres convened in Guatemala City.[40] Women from
fifteen American nations attended. They came not as representatives of their
governments but as delegates from women's clubs throughout the hemisphere: Zonta International, Sociedade Civica Feminina de Santos, Brasil;
Unión Femenina de Colombia; Movimiento Pro Emancipación de las Mujeres de Chile; Asociación Puertorriqueña de Esposas de Masones; La Cruz
Blanca de la Paz (Cuba); Federación Argentina de Mujeres Universitarias;
Ateneo Femenino (Bolivia); Asociación de Mujeres Tituladas del Uruguay;
Alianza Femenina Colombiana; Comités Populares Femeninos de Guayaquil; Sociedad Unión de Costureras (El Salvador); Ligue Feminine d'Action

Sociale (Haiti); Unión Democrática Femenina Hondureña; Ateneo Mexicano de Mujeres; Sección Femenil del Sindicato Nacional de Trabajadores de la Educación (Mexico); Cruzada de Mujeres Nicaragüenses; and Asociación Continental de Intelectuales de América (Panama). Most of the representatives from the United States—who hailed from cities from Minneapolis to San Francisco to Boston to Brooklyn—were members of the Women's International League for Peace and Freedom, as were the Canadian women.[41]

These women were not politically radical within their national communities, but they believed strongly in the need for women to speak out on issues of social and political equality, human welfare, and peace. Their first press release stated:

> The First Inter-American Congress of Women meeting in Guatemala, representing mothers, wives, daughters of our Continent, has resolved in plenary session to denounce the hemispheric armament plan under discussion at the Rio Conference, asking that the cost of the arms program be used to support industry, agriculture, health and education for our people.

The women declared their right to speak on international issues: "We consider that interamerican political problems deserve particular attention on the part of women of the Continent. . . . We resolve to ask the Pan American Union and all Pan American associations to enact the following resolutions in the inter-American conferences." Their first concern was that the "American governments meeting in conference in Rio de Janeiro comply in good faith with the Final Act of Chapultepec, which is an instrument of peace, and not give it a militaristic interpretation."[42]

In those weeks of August 1947, the proceedings of the Rio conference were headlined in the world press; *The New York Times* carried daily page-one coverage. The Primer Congreso Interamericano de Mujeres was also noted in the press. In a number of Latin American papers, including the opposition press in Guatemala, it was accused of communist sympathies. On August 19, *The New York Times* carried a story—on page 21, in the Food Section of the Women's Pages.

The women were not successful in staying the arming of the Americas, but it is apparent that in the immediate postwar period the women of the Americas continued to look beyond the nation-state to the transnational arena for community, for empowerment, for the opportunity to articulate their ideas and to be heard. The women who met at Guatemala City in 1947 to counter the Rio Pact came together not to buttress the position of their respective nation-states but to protest the aggrandizement of national power through arms at the expense of the citizenry, an issue they saw as within their traditional purview. Nor was their petition based upon an imagined equation between dollars for arms and dollars for aid; the Latin American women, especially, clearly perceived the probability of arms' being used not in defense of the hemisphere but against the populace by the state.[43]

The women were acting within the historical context of a half century of a feminist, pacifist tradition, established by the women of the Americas from the Latin American Scientific Congresses of the 1890s to the Primer Congreso Femenino in 1910 to the creation of the IACW in 1928. In the immediate postwar period, when the formal inter-American community refused to respond to the women's historical commitment to peace and disarmament, the women again looked to a separatist transnational strategy.

## NOTES

1. Teresa de la Parra, *Tres conferencias* (Bogotá: 1930).

2. Karen Offen, "Toward an Historical Definition of Feminism" (Paper presented for the Western Association of Women Historians, May, 1985); Francesca Miller, "Problems and Concerns of Women in Latin America: Historical and Contemporary Perspectives," *Conference Group in Women's History Newsletter* (Winter 1976).

3. De la Parra, *Tres conferencias*.

4. Francesca Miller, "The International Relations of Women of the Americas," *The Americas: A Quarterly Review of Inter-American Cultural History* (Fall 1986): 174.

5. Asunción Lavrin, "The Ideology of Feminism in the Southern Cone, 1900–1940," Latin American Program Working Papers 169 (Washington, D.C.: Wilson Center, Smithsonian Institution, 1986).

6. *Congreso Femenino Internacional* (Buenos Aires: 1910).

7. Teresa González Fanning, "Educación doméstica y social de la mujer," *Congreso Femenino Internacional*, 280.

8. Ibid.

9. J. María Samame, "La democracia y la personalidad política de la mujer," *Congreso Femenino Internacional*, 374.

10. "The Second Pan American Scientific Congress," *Bulletin of the Pan American Union* 45, 8 (December 1915): 762.

11. There is good reason for this ideological diversity, which within the Pan American Women's Central Committee in the 1920s ranged from Wilsonian democrat to Trotskyite. I suggest that it is inherently related to the historical development of a feminist critique of society in the American states. For example, María del Carmen Feijóo writes of the Argentine feminists, "Puede considerarse con certeza que es a partir de 1890 cuando se empiezan a desarrollar de manera sistemática los esfuerzos dirigidos al esclarecimiento de la cuestión femenina y los primeros intentos organizativos. En nuestro pais, son las anarquistas quienes se anticipan en las discusión sistemática del problema" (*La Vida de Nuestro Pueblo* 9, *Las Feministas* [1982]: 7). See also K. Lynn Stoner, "From the House to the Streets: Women's Movement for Legal Change in Cuba, 1898–1958" (Ph.D. diss., University of Illinois, 1983); Shirlene Soto, *The Mexican Woman: A Study of Her Participation in the Revolution*, 1910–1940 (Palo

Alto, Calif.: R&E Research Associates, 1979); Alicia Moreau de Justo, *El socialismo y la mujer* (Buenos Aires: Editorial La Vanguardia, 1931).

12. "Delegates to the Pan American Conference of Women," *Bulletin of the Pan American Union* 54, 4 (April 1922): 350–351. See also "A Permanent Pan American Association of Women" (n.p., n.d.), Alice Park Collection, Archives of the Hoover Institution on War, Revolution, and Peace, Stanford University.

13. Bertha Lutz, *Homenagem das Senhoras Brasileiras a Illustre Presidente da União Inter-Americana de Mulheres* (Rio de Janeiro: 1926).

14. James Brown Scott, *The International Conferences of American States, 1889–1928* (New York: Oxford University Press, 1931), vii.

15. Papers of the Comité de las Americas de la Liga Internacional de Mujeres de la Paz y Libertad, 1947, Archives of the Hoover Institution.

16. *CIM Inter-American Commission of Women, 1928–1973* (Washington, D.C.: General Secretariat, Organization of American States, 1974), 1.

17. The Equal Rights Treaty was drafted by Alice Paul of the National Woman's Party of the United States and presented to the Havana Conference by Doris Stevens.

18. "Declaration of Lima in Favor of Women's Rights, 1938," *CIM Inter-American Commission of Women*, 1928–1973, ID.

19. Alice Park, 1928 diary, Alice Park Collection, Archives of the Hoover Institution.

20. Papers of the Comité de las Americas.

21. Scott, *International Conferences*, 507.

22. Ibid.

23. Uncollated MS, Doris Stevens Collection, Arthur and Elizabeth Schlessinger Archives of the History of Women, Radcliffe College.

24. Scott, *International Conferences*, 507.

25. Ibid.

26. "The Second Pan American Scientific Conference," *Bulletin of the Pan American Union* 45, (December 1915): 762.

27. Nelly Merino Carvallo, editorial, *Mujeres de América* 1, 5 (September–October 1933). ix. I am grateful to Gwen Kirkpatrick for providing me with a number of copies of this journal.

28. Three women were members of national delegations.

29. Scott, *International Conferences*, 507.

30. Pro Paz was organized by "asociaciones femeninas y estudantiles" in Argentina; the signatories of the petition included many men's and women's associations, as well as individuals. Ibid.

31. Ibid.

32. Mary Louise Pratt, "Women, Literature, and National Brotherhood," this volume. Pratt addresses the ideas put forth by Benedict Anderson in *Imagined Communities: Reflections on the Origin and Spread of Nationalism* (London: Verso, 1983). Anderson proposes viewing the nation as "an imagined political community, imagined both as inherently limited and sovereign."

33. "Declaration of Lima," cited in *CIM Inter-American Commission of Women 1928–1973*, 10.

34. The declaration was drawn up and presented by the Mexican delegation to

the Inter-American Commission of Women. Ward M. Morton, in his study, *Woman Suffrage in Mexico* (Gainesville: University of Florida Press, 1962), states that in anticipation of their victory in securing suffrage "the jubilant [Mexican] feminist organizations urged the delegation to the Eighth Pan American Conference in 1938 to take advantage of Mexico's progress toward women's rights by submitting a declaration on the subject" (37). The Mexican women's hopes were to founder as Congress buried the amendment that would have given them suffrage; it was not secured until 1953.

35. Doris Stevens Collection, Radcliffe College.

36. Ibid.

37. Charter of the United Nations.

38. Inter-American Conference for the Maintenance of Continental Peace and Security, Petropolis, Brazil, 1947.

39. The Rio Treaty served as the blueprint for NATO (North Atlantic Treaty Organization).

40. Papers of the Primer Congreso Interamericano de Mujeres, 1947, Collection of Alicia Moreau de Justo, Montevideo, Uruguay. I am grateful to Janet Greenberg for providing this document.

41. Ibid.

42. Ibid.

43. The reason the Guatemalan government particularly welcomed the women was in celebration of the overthrow of the Ubico dictatorship and establishment of civil liberties, including freedom of speech, under the administration of Juan José Arévalo.

# THREE

# Women, State, and Family in Latin American Literature of the 1920s

*Francine Masiello*

Latin America in the 1920s faced a menacing crisis of modernization. Beset with the problems of nation building and rapid urbanization, its leading critics and intellectuals sought to rationalize these dramatic changes occurring in society by generating a theoretical construct to explain new American ideas. Conservatives and liberals alike studied the merits of progress and the price the more established social classes would have to pay for the growth of the modern city. Creative writers also participated in the quest for self-definition, responding to the modernization program in three different registers.

In the first instance, a highly patriotic literature defended state ideology. Faced with the question of representing Latin America to its readers, or better, of creating a social subject resistant to modern realities, conservative authors of the 1920s tried to preserve the authority of tradition. Writing of this kind was informed by a desire to protect the status quo and reiterated the symbols and ideas that enforced the rights of those in power. These authors strove to create a myth of an organically unified America, in which the civilizing leadership of the elders might bring order and harmony to the nation.

In the second instance, a more skeptical band of writers challenged the validity of the emerging state, but far from looking to the past as a model of successful nation building, they emphasized fragmentation and disruption as key features of modern times. Doubt was cast on the possibility of forming any enduring project of state organization. While some responded to this perception of disorder with nihilism and despair, others reveled in what was seen as the chaos of modernity. From this latter group, a host of new writers emerged to carry the banner of avant-garde aestheticism. Not to be confused with members of the European cultural movements of the time, writers of the Latin American avant-garde incorporated selected elements of their national or regional conditions in their works while looking to contemporary Spain or

France for novelty of literary form. Modernity, with all of its force, was celebrated by these youthful authors, who rushed to the innovation of form and
ideas as a way to break from the elders; thus, they staged a generational
rebellion against audience, tradition, and institutions.

Finally, a highly politicized, left-wing political program emerged in the
1920s to provide an alternative to bourgeois politics and literatures. Rooted
in the new social movements that emerged with urban growth, social realist
literature took as its focus of study the plight of marginals in society.

While these diverse literary experiences may be defined in part as a challenge to aesthetic *modernismo*, the turn-of-the-century movement identified
with the poet Rubén Darío, Latin American writing of the 1920s exhibited a
rich complexity of expression, incorporating the radical impulses of the
experimental avant-garde while also addressing the crisis of modernity that
beset the nations of the Southern Hemisphere. Writers demonstrated a range
of interests extending from political reformism (of both left- and right-wing
tendencies) to a fervent defense of the autonomy of the work of art.

Among these possibilities, a feminine literary discourse emerged, assessing both aesthetic and nationalist projects to forge a different system of writing. As such, women's literature of the 1920s provided a new framework for
the reception and interpretation of masculine symbols of identity. It also
offered terms for rereading the deployment of power. For this realization it
depended upon the strategies of disruption produced by the avant-garde,
but it also came into obvious debate with the nationalist tendencies of
Latin American literature as if to reevaluate the programs of the modern
state from a distinctively female perspective.

## THE POLITICS OF WOMANHOOD

The status of women in the early twentieth century may be analyzed in the
context of political programs for national reform and modernization. Rapid
economic growth was matched by a vast migration to the capital cities; at the
same time, the unionization of labor created suspicion and fear among Latin
America's ruling classes.[1]

Through this period of massive social upheaval, when anarchism
threatened the state and democratic impulses shook the foundations of the
oligarchy, women became at once subjects and pawns of the emerging texts
of resistance. Indeed, in cities such as Buenos Aires, whose population was
radically transformed by these events, working women—and foreigners
especially—were suspected of destroying the basis of modern society. In
particular, these working women of the early twentieth century were singled
out for their affiliations with anarchist movements and were accused of sub-
versive activity. Not only did women in Buenos Aires establish their own
anarchist newspapers but they also spoke freely against the repressive struc-

tures of the family and the authoritarian-paternalist model of government.[2] In addition, they freely questioned the juridic rights of women in civil society and investigated the strictures of marriage as a barrier to women's progress. Women's sexuality and free control over their bodies were of deep concern to these anarchists as they sought to protect females from public and domestic abuse.[3] Accordingly, in much of the literature and propaganda pamphlets, even the prostitute is depicted as a martyr of the new age.[4]

Aside from the declarations found in pamphlets of the time, women were quite active in organized strikes and acts of sabotage. One historian notes that women in lower-class neighborhoods of Buenos Aires organized the largest strike in Argentina before the decade of the 1920s.[5] This strike, perpetrated by women tenants who demanded rent stabilization in poor neighborhoods, represented one of the most successful grass-roots urban movements of modern times.

Meanwhile, in a less strident tone and usually at variance with anarchist platforms, socialist parties argued for equal rights for women, universal suffrage, reform of the civic codes, and better education for all.[6] Feminist unions, journals, and international symposia devoted to improving the legal status of women were common in the first two decades of the twentieth century.[7] Women in Cuba demanded legalized divorce; Pan-Americanists sought union among the women of the Americas; Argentine socialist feminists demanded a reformed civic code granting rights of emancipation to women.[8] Clearly, a significant number of Latin American women had much to gain by identifying with these feminist movements.

Because of feminist activities in turn-of-the-century Latin America, women were often perceived as straying from the family unit. In a society where the family was equated with the national good, women who left the private sphere and moved into the public domain were often considered saboteurs of the unified household, promoting activities that undermined larger state interests.[9] In addition, they often came to be equated with the tendencies of anarchism itself. As such, their presence in the modern nation-state posed some contradiction. After all, women were necessary for the pronatalist policies of the state; their work outside the home was often necessary for the economic survival of the working-class family; and their public engagements as teachers or supervisors of beneficent groups generally received official support.[10] In spite of these positive factors, the feminine was often regarded with suspicion by intellectuals in Latin America.

In the early years of the twentieth century, there was considerable popular and scientific concern for the monitoring of women's bodies. This concern is evident in the contents of the penny dreadfuls and the women's weekly magazines, in the hygiene manuals designed for women, and in the almost xenophobic emphasis on keeping immigrant women from the nationalist domain. The hygiene movement, for example, which was generated by a concern among men for their safety from venereal diseases, encouraged women to look after their bodies to safeguard their reproductive functions and maintain a code of cleanliness.[11] The many hygiene manuals by Latin America's most prominent publishers read more like pornography than like any form of advice for women.[12] Similarly, the women's magazines issued warnings to women to maintain their bodies clean from disease and to ensconce themselves in the safety of the family.[13] These texts suggest, interestingly enough, a series of double discourses in competition for the attention of women: insofar as they advise a female audience, they are also designed to keep those readers in their place. The woman's body became embarrassingly public, less through her own volition than through the schemes of those in authority.

These popular lessons for women were accompanied by pseudoscientific discourses; even the weekly magazines published clinical diagnoses of love or positivistic analyses of erotic relationships. *Caras y Caretas, Plus Ultra,* and the *Almanaque Hispanoamericano* in this period provided many such explorations of eros. At the same time, certain intellectuals of the Centennial period in Latin American history attempted to organize a theory of the feminine in order to preserve the integrity of the nation. In 1910, for example, José Ingenieros delivered a series of lectures on the topic of love (later assembled in a volume titled *Tratado del amor*), a psychologizing attempt to distinguish passion from marital obligations and commitment. He denounced the restraints that marriage imposes upon individual freedom and sensuality; indeed, he asserted, insofar as it generates a concern for legal order, propriety, and convenience, marriage appears to threaten the very possibility of romantic love.[14] Ironically, Ingenieros went on to argue, it is love that spurs marriage in the first place; therefore, he urged men to be wary of entering in legal contracts with women. Love and marriage were to be regarded as separate matters; the first was a question of instinct, the second a matter of household management and ultimately of the continued efficiency of the state apparatus. Restraint in love was thereby advised for those preoccupied with matters of organization and progress; in the interest of moral affirmation and domestic peace, love and marriage were to be kept apart.

A concern for the efficiency of the family also informed the pedagogical programs of the Argentine school system. Thus, in the introduction to his multivolumed *La literatura argentina*, Ricardo Rojas denounced the impoverished values of the modern nuclear family and its failure to meet the needs of children.[15] He insisted, therefore, on the usefulness of public institutional education, which clearly would wrench children from the hands of their ill-trained parents and compensate for the ignorance evident in the home. The real *paterfamilias* was to be found in the academy. Rojas had in mind a retraining of Argentine children born to immigrant families, but his message pointed to the shortcomings of mothers in general. Unable to adapt to a symbolic mode of thinking, women, Rojas argued, should at least be given a minimum of training in order to equip them for responsibilities in the home.[16]

These efforts were part of a state program to enforce homogeneity on the various social projects upon which modern women had embarked. At a time of ebullient multiplicity in mass cultural practices, the state tried to impose and retain hierarchical order over its subjects; in a period when the feminine was equated with the unmanageable, women became the specific target of such disciplinary action.

This programmatic endeavor to exercise control over women is seen in creative literary endeavors as well, where it was largely held that the advancement of nationalist interests constituted a moral mission. Manuel Gálvez, for example, in an essay of 1912, described Argentine nationalism as coextensive with a moral mandate. Referring in particular to the impact of this ideology on creative production of the period, he explained:

> Yo veo que la producción literaria argentina va a entrar en una nueva era. He hablado del nacionalismo. Esta tendencia va a dominarlo todo. Ella será el motor que nos mantenga en perpetua acción, la impulsadora y transformadora de nuestra poesía, la creadora de nuestros ideales. Pronto los escritores argentinos han de ser leídos en todas las naciones de habla española; tal sucederá cuando nuestro predominio se establezca y consolide en la América española y cuando sobre toda ella se extienda gigantescamente nuestro gobierno moral.[17]

> [I see that Argentine literary production is about to enter a new age. I'm speaking about nationalism. This tendency will dominate everything. It will be the motor that keeps us in perpetual action, the generator and transformer of our poetry, the creator of our ideals. Soon Argentine writers will be read in all Spanish-speaking nations; this will happen when our predominance is recognized and consolidated in Spanish America and when our moral governance looms gigantically over the continent.]

Gálvez was correct in anticipating a rise in nationalist sentiment, which was destined to be carried over into the social programs and literary texts of the time. In addition, this discourse on nationalism was clearly marked by considerations of gender, prompting some curious disquisitions by men of both left- and right-wing persuasions.

Men of fiercely nationalistic convictions and even those who argued for a democratic alternative used the image of the feminine to defend their respective programs of action. In the 1920s, two prominent literary journals in Spanish America offered noteworthy cases of left- and right-wing discourses that exploited the image of women. Promoting a specifically nationalist discourse, *Inicial* (1923–1926), an Argentine periodical supported by intellectuals of literary culture, defended a return to traditional values and an unambiguous defense of the state. In the prefatory statement of this review, the editors of *Inicial* declared war on subversives, advocating serious reprisals against those who threatened the state with modern liberal ideals. As part of this denunciation, *Inicial* specifically protested

> contra las aspiraciones, sentimentales y romantizantes, con que los fuertes engañan a los débiles y los débiles se consuelan de su impotencia; . . . contra los apologistas del sufragio universal, del parlamentarismo y la democracia de nuestros días. . . contra los afeminados de espíritu que ponen en verso el gemido de las damiselas y hacen ensueños sobre la ciudad futura; en fin, contra todo lo que hay, en arte, en politica, de engaño, de impotencia y de feminidad.[18]

> [against the aspirations, both sentimental and romantic, with which the strong deceive the weak and the weak console themselves with their impotence; . . . against the apologists for universal suffrage, for parliamentarianism, and democracy in our time. . . against the effeminate of spirit who put in verse the cry of ladies and build dreams about the city of the future; in short, against all [traces] in art, [and] in politics, of deception, impotence, and femininity.]

Here, the editors draw unabashed comparisons between acts of national perfidy and feminine behavior; the traitors of the nation are clearly aligned with women. Thus, in this highly gendered text, a masculinist discourse upholds virtue and patriotism while the vile elements of society are singularly debased to the sphere of the feminine. It follows then that the feminine is a threat to the stability of the state; universal suffrage, modernization, and revolutionary ideals form part of a program of subversion.

The identification of the feminine with an oppositional consciousness in Latin America is broadly suggested in the decade of the 1920s and is evident even in the texts of progressive advocates. For example, the *Revista de Avance* (1927–1930), a Cuban literary magazine whose editors included some members of the newly founded Cuban Communist Party, represents the most radical avant-garde achievement in Latin America in the period and offers a paradigmatic evaluation of feminist practice within a nationalist context. Praising the work of the Alianza Nacional Feminista, a suffragist group active in Cuba in the 1920s, the *Revista de Avance* links feminism with democratic process, as the following citation reveals:

> Un grupo de nuestras mujeres, oficialmente constituido bajo el rótulo de "Alianza Nacional Feminista," se dispone a la conquista del voto en los precisos momentos en que nuestros hombres comienzan a prescindir de él como de una molestia ciudadana sin objeto. Esta falange de mujeres puede significar una oportuna reserva de fuerzas para nuestra diezmada democracia. Cuando los hombres, usurpadores de un exclusivismo democrático esencialmente antidemocrático, más aún, antihumano, nos sentimos ganados por la desilusión *y* lloramos un poco boabdilescamente [sic] los principios que no supimos defender, las mujeres, menos escépticas, menos maliciadas en las manos de la politiquería al uso, más henchidas de fe en los destinos del pueblo, acuden a cubrir la vanguardia y afirman enfáticamente su fe en los ideales de la democracia.[19]

[A group of our women, officially constituted under the rubric of "National Feminist Alliance," is getting ready to win the vote at the very moment in which our men begin to set it aside as a purposeless citizen's nuisance. This phalanx of women can represent an opportune reserve of strength for our weakened democracy. When as men, usurpers of a democratic exclusionary practice that is essentially antidemocratic, and even more, antihuman, we feel beaten by disillusion and we cry somewhat foolishly over principles that we did not know how to defend, women—less skeptical, less apprehensive in the face of common politics, more filled with faith in the destiny of their people—run to the vanguard position and emphatically affirm their faith in democratic ideals.]

Following a course of resistance to state authoritarianism, the *Revista de Avance* relied upon the image of the feminine to organize a program of opposition. Here feminine practice is perceived as a behavior available to all progressive individuals to compensate for the abusive political projects traditionally embraced by Cuban men. Less cynical and less corrupt, women, in the eyes of the editors of *Revista de Avance*, have the potential to introduce a genuinely democratic reform in society.

It is interesting, at the same time, to contemplate the uses of women in Cuban projects of modernization. In this period, women lobbied actively for divorce legislation and claimed a voice in congressional proceedings to demand suffrage and equal compensation.[20] But their demands were not necessarily perceived as unsound or without basis in reason; rather, the feminist activity of these years provided an example of civic engagement from which society as a whole might benefit. Thus, if in the parlance of the right women were situated among the adversaries who threatened the stability of official institutions, in the rhetoric of the left the feminine was equated with democracy and the possibility of reform. Undoubtedly, women played an important symbolic and active role in civil society of the 1910s and 1920s.

Like the texts of political movements, with their heated polemic about the merits of nationalist programs, positioning the feminine within a discourse of opposition, literary texts of the 1920s aligned women in counterpoint to the state; concomitantly, the family was perceived as a unit in hopeless disarray. This is consonant with a long history in Latin American letters, where traditionally the role of women and the family had been cast in debate with nationalist interests.

Elizabeth Kuznesof and Robert Oppenheimer have noted that alliances between family and state power were characteristic of nineteenth-century nationalism in Latin America.[21] Indeed, theorists of family and state relations have often drawn an equivalence between the two.[22] Max Horkheimer, for example, has observed that the clear imperative of the bourgeois family was to enforce a sense of duty among all of its members to the father; by extension, the blind obedience to the patriarch would be continued in the individual's unquestioned submission to the state.[23]

Latin American literary texts of the nineteenth century give a different interpretation of the family, picturing it as headed toward irreversible destruction when managed by an irrational father, a metaphor for state authority. In this condition, the woman saves her family by taking charge of the household; in the process, she becomes a figure of opposition to the state. One can observe, beginning in the post-Independence period, a clear interest in the feminine figure in this kind of adversarial role; this occurred especially at moments when the dissolution of the family in literature was read as a challenge to political regimes.

Argentine literary history is especially rich in examples of this image of the feminine, particularly in the nineteenth century, when liberal men of letters voiced their opposition to the tyrant Juan Manuel de Rosas and used his daughter, Manuela, to show the fragmentation of the family qua state (see Mary Louise Pratt's essay, this volume).[24] Manuela thus became the protagonist of a variety of liberal literary texts, from ballads and short stories to seminal novels in the Latin American tradition, in which often she was made a figure of resistance, showing moral indignation in response to the actions of the Argentine strongman. This example takes us beyond Christopher Lasch's definition of the family as a "haven in a heartless world," for in nineteenth-century representations we see that the repressive family, as a microcosm for the state, often exhausts itself due to the efforts of women.[25] Thus, in much Argentine literature of the post-Independence period, woman offers the possibility of an oppositional consciousness while men are forced into silence; yet she also suggests the decay of the patriarchal family whose control she manages to elude.

The creative literature of the 1910s and 1920s confirms this perception of women as adversaries of nationalist interests. In this period, however, female characters lack the heroic fortitude to challenge the injustice of tyranny; clearly, they are not recommended for public service, nor do they serve the interests of democratic reform. Rather, they are revealed as sinister agents of subversion. Their behavior is informed by irrationality and misguided eros, so that the only solution for them is found in a controlled domesticity. Thus, in the conservative texts of the early twentieth century, women are cautioned against excess and eliminated from the public realm; they are then returned to the domestic sphere, where they are supervised by a benevolent spouse.

The naturalist novel, which survived in Latin America well into the decade of the 1920s, reinforced these paradigms of domesticity. In this kind of fiction, women were representative of the forces of disruption, or often were identified with the uncivilized land insofar as both are objects of masculine conquest and domination. In Gálvez's first novel, *La maestra normal* (1914), inspired by the Centennial celebration of 1910 and by the influential presence of the normal-school movement in Argentine life, he represented woman as a victim of evil ideologies.[26] Here, in a broad critique of the educational policies of the normal-school teachers, Gálvez attacked the lay school system for its challenge to religion, tradition, and the unified family, and he demonstrated the system's failure particularly in reference to provincial women. The fall of Raselda, the protagonist of *La maestra normal*, is attributed, by Gálvez's logic, to the ideologies of liberalism in which she was formed. Had she been under the tutelage of her parents with appropriate discipline and guidance, she would not have fallen prey to corruption or lost her sense of virtue.

In this scheme of things, women bear no responsibility for the larger questions of ideology and institutions, nor should they be allowed access to untested ideas. Accordingly, women like Raselda had no business in the education of youth. Furthermore, in this novel, with its abundant erotic passages and explicitly detailed abortion, all images converge on a single objective: the monitoring of women in civil society. The body of woman is to be controlled at any cost in a period of social decadence, for unattended she succumbs to the barbarous extremes of undisciplined sensuality. In the literatures of nationalist and avant-garde tendencies, women are often presented as subverting family harmony. Since domestic peace is a goal lust and desire must be contained. But Gálvez's novel is also about the dangerous intersection of public and private spheres, for when women escape the domestic realm and enter the public workplace they show a marked incapacity for making rational decisions. Raselda, the heroine, suffers in love and work because she cannot properly separate these antagonistic realms, and she lacks sufficient clarity to separate work and passion. Finally, she is expelled from civil society and condemned to solitude. Far from consolidating a nationalist project, the woman was used in Centennial texts to show disruption and chaos, while she indicated the cause for the failure of any program of social reform.

In short, in an age when women were considered antagonistic to national interests, it was common to exercise control over them, suppressing their passions unsparingly. Control was then reasserted in literature by the representation of a unified household. Within this context, men were to fulfill the role of paterfamilias, imparting wisdom and rule to their flock, while women were destined to serve as housekeepers, devoted to domestic labor and motherhood; but this plan always met with resistance. In the organization of family roles in fiction of the realist, *mundonovista* mode, the feminine was thus identified as the center of contradiction. Accordingly, in the great sagas of the South American frontier, the theme of civilization versus barbarism—the dichotomy that sums up the thinking of writers and statesmen who tried to understand Latin America from the time of the mid-nineteenth century— women were equated with barbarism, which had to be curbed by men of reason. It is also important to observe the absence of any great matriarch or woman of intuitive magic in these novels: there is no Ursula Buendía, in the manner of Gabriel Garcia Márquez's fiction, no character equivalent of La

Maga in Julio Cortázar's *Rayuela*. Instead, the women in the novels written by men of the 1920s were depicted as uncontrollable and often evil, inclined to wanton aggression or irrational, perilous endeavors. The women in these novels had two courses available to them: either they accepted the domestic calling and resigned themselves to a life of subservience or they found themselves eliminated from the scene of narration. Such is the case in adventure novels like Ricardo Güiraldes's *Don Segundo Sombra* (1926), where the bonding among men constitutes the only civilizing influence on the community at large, and in Rómulo Gallegos's *Doña Bárbara* (1929) where the protagonist is banished from the novel and only her innocent daughter survives, through alliance with the civilized master.

Finally, the avant-garde literatures, as an independent activity of the 1920s, also broached the debate on women with overt hostility. In general, practitioners of the avant-garde insisted on a culture of masculinity; forceful, isolating, arrogant, the search for power that informed this movement was abusive of women. This is true of the Argentine Oliverio Girondo, who describes women's bodies as fragmented limbs or objects to be contemplated by the tourist-poet, and of the Chilean Vicente Huidobro, whose ironic prose poems express an extravagant violence against women.[27] Not unlike modernists such as Wyndham Lewis, Filippo Tommaso Marinetti, and Ezra Pound, these Latin American writers engaged in a brutal yet gratuitous subjugation of women, so that the exertion of power over subalterns almost seemed synonymous with the institutionalization of modernism itself.[28] This attitude was also shown consistently in the abundant little magazines of the period, in the many jokes and limericks that served as gestures of male camaraderie, and in the anonymous doggerel that celebrated a bonding among men to the exclusion of women.[29] The few women writers present in these circles were recognized in their roles as literary doyennes, companions of the major author, or occasionally eccentric artists and poets whose works were sometimes included in minor spaces of the little reviews. Clearly, in this lively confraternity of men of the 1920s there was little space for women.

## LITERARY WOMEN

Artistic and intellectual production by women of this period repudiates these perceptions and gives evidence of transforming the tradition of nationalist literature. In the prose fiction of the 1920s and 1930s, a new social body was produced in which women refused their status as "other" and challenged their domestic assignments. As such, this literature initiated a reevaluation of traditionally perceived gender roles while it situated women's activity in opposition to authority. Its goal, then, was to produce an autonomous female subject, one that escapes the deadening effects of a repressive nationalist discourse, and one in which woman resists her status as an object within the abstract rhetorical programs of men. Literature of this kind provided a clear alternative to avant-garde movements in Latin America and to the masculinist discourse they produced; it challenged the dominant voices of experimental authors such as Girondo and Huidobro. It also answered the nationalist program contained in the *mundonovista* novels, in which heroes of near-epic stature laid claim to the vast American terrain.

As the salient examples of this kind of modern sensibility in Latin American women writers dating from the 1920s, María Luisa Bombal, Norah Lange, and Teresa de la Parra subverted patriarchal discourse and the ruling logic of traditional writing. Intrinsic to their project, lived experience guides the premises of their narrative fiction. As itinerant intellectuals who embarked upon the traditional grand tour and traveled frequently between Europe and America in search of a better life, these women participated in the life common to Latin American *vanguardistas*. De la Parra, for example, left her native Venezuela to study and travel in Europe and sustained active transcontinental communication with writers such as Gabriela Mistral. Lange, the "damisela" of the Argentine avant-garde, wife of Oliverio Girondo, friend of the cosmopolitan circle known as the "Florida Street poets," was born into special privilege in Europe before moving to Latin America. Throughout her lifetime, she engaged in dialogue with international elites. Also a writer uprooted, Bombal was, like Lange, privileged. She left her native Chile and spent many of the vanguard years in Argentina and in Europe, where she became an intimate friend of Lange and other women writers.

Together, the fiction of these women reflects the constant displacement or homelessness of the female intellectual, as much as it voices an opposition to the masculinist avant-garde programs. What we see, then, are women who used their status as exiles to resist the containment of an encroaching nationalist rhetoric. They refused the unifying discourse that maintains the female body in place, limiting woman to reproductive functions or domestic labor. Indeed, almost as a correlative of the anarchist activities described earlier, women writers engaged in a series of deconstructive challenges in which discourses were multiplied and the sites of meaning released from their compartmentalized frames, no longer anchored by male prerogatives in the literary or social domain.

Accordingly, in the writings of these women, narrative situation, structure, and the position of character disregard the masculine attention to birthright, inheritance, and linear order and clearly repudiate the nationalist program. Multiple voices participate in the structuring of fiction, until finally characters find themselves dismissing any identity as unified subjects. In order to sustain this rebellion, feminine heroines, first of all, repudiate any fixed point of origin. Female migration, travel, and orphanhood or abandonment thus provide the motivation for women's fiction of the 1920s. Alone or on the road in search of adventure, the new heroine renounces family and starts life anew. Like their authors, who traveled extensively between Europe and America, the female protagonists of Latin American avant-garde fiction use homelessness to their advantage and finally unleash themselves from domestic constraints by refusing any heterosexual commitments.

The novel of orphanhood is particularly interesting in the feminist context. It has been suggested frequently that family relationships and particularly the role of the father stand at the center of all activity in fiction.[30] Marthe Robert has observed that the modern novel is in fact a tale about orphans, of lost heroes in search of their parents or surrogate figures of authority.[31] In this respect, the question of the father is essentially one of absence, in which the hero or heroine sets about the task of relocating the missing parent. To put it more directly, the dead father initiates society in the novel; his true status is revealed in the trace of his absence. As such, the novel seeks to piece together fragments of reality in order to strive toward a coherent whole, a unified vision of reality in which the hero finds his destiny by reconstructing his past. The *mundonovista* narrative that I have described in earlier pages indeed attempts to replicate that quest for a coherent text. Fabio Cáceres, at the close of *Don Segundo Sombra*, learns of his true identity and brings order to his life through an identified father; Santos Luzardo eliminates Doña Bárbara and marries Marisela in the end, thus suggesting a parallel between the romance mode in fiction and the renewed possibility of an improved and civilized "family of man."

The feminine example, however, is designed to repudiate all models of authority, to unleash the heroine from the bondage of rules and the constraints of romance. Moreover, the feminist model for fiction decidedly strays from the paternal search. No longer is the father a model who asserts his symbolic authority in fiction; in fact, the daughters in these novels of orphanhood repudiate his influence. Accordingly, the family replacements and surrogates who are sought are drawn not from hierarchical or vertical relationships but from the peers of the protagonist. In this respect, the demise of a father-child relationship calls an end to a certain kind of entrapment registered in the signifying experience; as a discursive act, it ends a clearly repressive gesture and disperses stable meanings or associations throughout the text.

Thus, a new symbolizing mode was inaugurated in fiction. Endowed with fewer stable meanings and now replete with contradictions and echoes, the texts produced in the feminized mode announce their own ambiguity. They register plural narrative voices that challenge all linearity, they insist on a self-referential vagueness, which consumes all marks of difference. As if to challenge the authority invested in a single, hierarchical bond between father and child, the feminine mode in narrative disperses all centralized power. In the modernist texts under consideration, this project has consequential importance, observable in the reformulation of female identity, in the reconstruction of an inherited symbolic tradition, and finally in the defiance of canonical literary order.

In the novels of Bombal, Lange, and de la Parra, nameless heroines wander about bereft of parental protection while also lacking the burden of children who might inhibit their freedom of activity. Disinherited from any family properties, they encounter a new freedom that permits them to restructure their social world along with their worlds of discourse. Their frequently described anonymity, moreover, allows them to escape the burden of official sanctions or formal institutions that might constrain their activities. But orphanhood also supplies a vantage point outside of history from which one may evaluate questions of genealogy and the laws that govern the family. Thus, if the history of the traditional family is unilinear and without disruption, in these feminist novels the heroines elect disorder. They reject the discipline of the family along with its structures of repression and choose, instead, a less clearly defined course of action. This new space, along with a revised definition of the traditional family, allows them to challenge the rule of the paterfamilias and to initiate an independent path as literary creators or artists. The "portrait of the artist" novel, so important to the modernist tradition, acquires an interesting twist in the hands of women writers, as they situate all artistic work of their heroines beyond the economic circuits of exchange. Neither compensated financially nor publicly recognized for their achievements as artists or writers, the protagonists of these feminist texts withdraw their artistic production from the exchange system controlled by men.

This is especially evident in de la Parra's novel *Ifigenia*, where the protagonist, orphaned in the world, attempts to make sense of her rights of inheritance.[32] Some have commented on the curious autobiographical element in de la Parra's work, insofar as it reflects the life of wandering preferred by the author, who traveled between Europe and America on countless intellectual adventures. Her contacts with other women intellectuals from Latin America, among them Gabriela Mistral and Lydia Cabrera, created a secure world of letters, nurtured by thoughtful debate and dialogue.[33] In her fictions, de la Parra reproduced the female bonding that characterized her own intellectual life. In *Ifigenia*, for example, the heroine, fresh from Europe, joins with other women characters in the novel to test the dominant rules that qualify male privilege. The protagonist thus abandons Paris after the death of her father and takes up a new life in America in the custody of her grandmother and other female relatives. It becomes clear that the women characters are of different persuasions, the elders representing domestic tendencies while the young protagonist, María Eugenia, struggles for her freedom. Yet the independent spirit of these women, all left without an inheritance, elevates the spirit of the novel and provides the nucleus of narrative development.

Life without father, although his death is the source of María Eugenia's initial despair, provides the impulse for a first creative liberation. It allows her to come to terms with herself and to challenge symbolic authority in art and life; equally important, this challenge is realized through her experiments in writing, observable in her journals and acts of her imagination. These artistic impulses are made possible through her female alliances, especially in the case of the journal annotations, which are first prompted by an intimate friend.

But what, in fact, is the social status of this artistic production? The election of the epistolary tradition creates a curious effect upon the modern reader, who realizes that the letters presented are not organized for public distribution or for a market of exchanges. They are meant only for a single reading, as intimate confidences shared with another friend. Consequently, as a privatized text, a minor expression in the field of print culture, the journal survives as a document that will refuse to engage in society. In addition, this diary, which stands as a testimonial to self, provides a curious contrast to the ironically omniscient narration that introduces each chapter of the book, thus inserting hybrid readings into the novel as a whole. A halfway house between fiction and reality, the journal invites us to investigate the boundaries that separate fantasy and lived experience within the space of narration.

It might be possible to regard *Ifigenia* as an unsuccessful bildungsroman if we consider María Eugenia's failure to marry as a sign of her arrested maturation.[34] But I take this as the author's refusal to engage in the consequences of linear narrative. In that way, the story stands in defiance of the common expectations of the life stories of women. Indeed, as a novel that inserts irreparable conflicts in the strategy of the bildungsroman. *Ifigenia* announces a resistance. In the first place, the bildungsroman is never completely realized: *Ifigenia*'s heroines abandon romance to pursue their own identity interests; they upset both the linear structure of narrative and the constancy of accumulation. Problems in the early sections of the novel never find resolution in the end. In addition, de la Parra's work represents an overlapping of genres. It is hardly a quest novel, for its objectives are never fully achieved. Nor is it clearly within the structure of romance, for *Ifigenia* collapses the programs of differing genres by refusing to supply a neat conclusion. There is a conflict between dominant discourse and the feminized discourse of the novel. Feminized novels like de la Parra's fiction are imbued with a language of refusal. Prolonged, nondiscursive pauses permeate the text; madness, silence, and nonverbal spaces offer a challenge to linearity.[35]

Similarly, other fiction works by Spanish American women of the period intersperse discursive narration with musically oriented texts; white noise permeates conversation, while gossip and banal exchanges undermine authoritative narration; a constant, irreducible mist occludes the space of narration. This kind of activity in fiction creates a timeless zone in which narration, sequential order, and logical association are momentarily brought to a halt. It also serves as a specific challenge to the reigning logic of bourgeois perception. In this way, feminist modernism undermines the social ideology of the 1920s without falling into the gratuitous challenges that so often mark the avant-garde experiment.

In novels of this kind, the domestic sphere is never left intact; in fact, the space of the home is subject to constant erosion. This is apparent, for example, in Bombal's *La última niebla*, which begins with a description of the invasive rain that leaks through the roof of the protagonist's country estate.[36] Nature erodes the home that has held the heroine captive; throughout the novel, the family is seen as an adversary of the peaceful tranquillity of nature. Indeed, in *La última niebla*, as in the life of the author herself, there is no desired "room of one's own"; rather, the protagonist seeks to escape the house that has inhibited her freedom. Fantasy, then, assists her in her flight from the domestic sphere. Seen in this way, Bombal's novel suggests that liberation may exist for those who can step outside the constraints of the real. Other writers have shared this view: the Argentine Raquel Adler described the fantasies of mystical experience; the novelist Sara de Etcheverts described her character's interludes away from home in images reminiscent of the futurist appeal to flight and movement.[37]

The heroine who successfully escapes from the home finds fulfillment in female bonding, a camaraderie established among women to the exclusion of the masculine sphere. Even more than the novels of de la Parra, those of Bombal emphasize this same-sex bonding as a form of freedom for women. In the novels where Bombal emphasizes marriage and heterosexual fantasy, she still insists that the only plausible relationship is the bonding between female friends. Once again, *La última niebla* communicates this strategy insofar as the protagonist seeks the support of her secret comrade, Regina. Because of its strength as a secondary text, this clandestine relationship manages to undermine the heterosexual dynamic of the novel. It provides the heroine a source of identity, encoded by reference to musical notation or the visual fantasy of dreamlike experiences. Moreover, this gesture toward a symbolic system that escapes linearity provides an alternative to the historically determined relations of submission and domination which the women have sustained with their husbands.

Female friendship of this kind is often the subtext of women's modernist fiction. This is noted in the prose of British and North American writers— Djuna Barnes, Gertrude Stein, and Virginia Woolf principal among them— for whom an authentically feminist version of modernism is constructed by doing away with the presence of men. Rarely celebrated by critics of literature, this feature of modernism nonetheless offers the real possibility of structural subversion in the modern novel by destroying the stability of the family unit, which often passes as a metaphor for the novel itself.

The case of de la Parra's novel *Las memorias de Mamá Blanca* is interesting in this respect for, although the family described in the novel is organized by an authoritarian father, the scene of writing and the dialogue that gives the novel its structure are controlled exclusively by Mamá Blanca and the young, anonymous raconteur.[38] The spiritual affinities among the women are given special privilege in the novel in contrast to the masculine world, which invokes questions of inheritance and social prestige. In addition, a pact is established among these two women which draws connections between teller and listener, between the logic of an imagined discourse and the authority of narrative fiction in general.

It has been noted often that in Woolf's novel *To the Lighthouse* the real relation of value is not that of Mrs. Ramsey and her husband but that of the protagonist and Lily Briscoe, the artist, in their secret dialogue.[39] This bond between characters stirs the discursive situation to emphasize the visual mode of Lily over the linear, philosophical mode of Mr. Ramsey. The shift in emphasis from verbal to visual discourse is similarly enacted in Latin American feminist texts, which often represent the bonding among women as part of a revolt against the logic of language.

The Argentine writer Lange in her novel *Los dos retratos* offers a useful example of this kind of narrative problem.[40] In this novel, the heroine, orphaned from her natural parents, seeks the consolation of distant aunts, who provide her with a controversial account of her inherited family history. Not having lived through these experiences, she is obliged to reconstruct family traditions through the hearsay of older relatives, who provide an element of distortion and misrepresentation to the narrative. These women guide her through a series of family portraits, so that the visual element in narrative provides an alternative to family lore. The paintings insert the possibility of a double reading in fiction and multiply the temporal markers with which we come to terms with any narrative history. Drawing a comparison between interior and exterior spaces, between framed and unlimited visions, the paintings create a double vision of reality that cannot be reduced to a single image. By extension, the heroine becomes freed from her traditional view of self as a coherent subject within history. Thus, the search for a "room of one's own"—indeed, for a space in the family—begins with a reconstitution of the domestic scenario that emphasizes the feminine impulses toward community.

Lange's literary experiments against stable forms of authority also have a peculiar structural correlative. As I argued earlier, *Los dos retratos* is about the reproduction of portraiture and the questioned stability of the past. The author tests the static limitations of any form of representation by invoking a hallucinatory realm, or a descriptive sphere without recourse to linear order. By this act of disruption, the portraits call a halt to the family romance in progress; paradoxically, they cancel the search for the father that might have motivated the fiction in the first place. In this manner, the novel simultaneously questions the symbolizing process and breaks open the cluster of meanings and images previously fixed in a unified manner.

The family, the home, and the logos of patrimonial authority are all suspect in the avant-garde fictions of Latin American women. Because these structures served to hamper their freedom rather than offer them solace, women writers used these themes and images to question traditional restrictions imposed by society. At the same time, this challenge to the legal status of the female self involved a reevaluation of conventional definitions of the body. Thus, the female body described in feminine avant-garde fiction is not a vehicle of reproduction or an object of masculine desire. Rather than representing the female body as victim of the destructive effects of patriarchy, these writers celebrated the woman's body for its independence. In fact, their protagonists are usually childless and without male companions. Their bodies, moreover, bespeak fragmentation and exuberant disorder. In short, they refuse to collaborate with the demands of the masculine imagination. Consequently, the body of woman is often presented with an attention to minute detail, such that the composite form is all but lost to the reader.

In de la Parra's *Las memorias de Mamá Blanca*, for example, detailed attention is given to the hair and clothing of characters in order to emphasize the contrived artificiality of women's sphere. Far from corroborating the mythical schema in which women reproduce nature, de la Parra's novel offers the feminine as an alteration of nature, a forceful transformation of the presumably untainted realm of women's beauty. In other cases, the female figures described in the fictions of the 1920s are presented as ill and lymphatic, and at physical odds with their environment. The only way in which their bodies are restored to salubrious integrity is through a successful liberation from their conventional roles with men. Even in *La última niebla* by Bombal, the doublings and mirror reflections of the heroine's body upon the body of her alter ego challenge the single-lens optics with which woman is traditionally regarded. The pluralized body thereby comes to represent an act of creative resistance; in its fractures or mirror reflections, it eludes a single source of identity. Consequently, in the avant-garde novels of Bombal, Lange, and Parra the female body is reclaimed as an independent presence.

Women's fiction of the 1920s is marked by these countless acts of narrative resistance as if to offer a challenge to the symbolic traditions within literary history. The domestic sphere is exploded with new possibilities for representation; symbols of the feminine are inverted, and the discursive-arrangements in narrative are restructured. In Bombal's short story "El árbol," included in *La última niebla*, the tree that serves as a central metaphor for the regeneration of life ceases to stand in alliance with the world of women; nature, as a traditional analogue of the feminine, is viewed here as a hostile, unsympathetic adversary. And while Bombal strives to break the analogy between woman and nature, she simultaneously removes her female characters from the repression of any dominant logos. In *La útima niebla*, for example, the mist that enshrouds the protagonist bears no real relationship to any identifiable signifying system. Alternately described by critics as an invitation to a surrealist dream state and a withdrawal by the heroine from her milieu, the mist nevertheless stands as an ambiguous, undecipherable blind spot in Latin American narrative; it breaks all attempts at linearity and refuses to accommodate itself to any binary logic. Like the music, dream states, and visual discourses of the fictions mentioned earlier in this essay, the mist described by Bombal refuses a single interpretation; it inserts heterogeneity into the novel, as if to unravel the neatened fabric of any single pattern of meaning. As such, it creates a new locus for the activities of the imagination.

This ambiguity and multiplicity in fiction by women carries rich suggestions for writing. Literature by women of the 1920s provides a new definition of gender within the structure of the family; and, insofar as equivalents had been drawn previously between the family and the national good, women's literature challenges nationalist discourse as well. Put another way, the feminine in literary discourse now stands in opposition to conventional treatments of the domestic sphere and the patriotic mandate. In addition, as these writers propose new definitions of the feminine—seeking an autonomous subject relieved of the weight of tradition—they invite serious speculation about the possibility of a feminist version of modernism. Insofar as writers like Bombal, Lange, and Parra question the process of representation in fiction, they also engage in the major challenges of the avant-garde. But the feminist response goes further by responding to the assumptions of writing in the masculine tradition. Their writing opens narrative space for radically new discursive practices; by identifying alternative forms of disruption that modify the symbolic tradition in letters, women's writing thus brings into question the problematic status of gender hidden in the texts of the canonical avant-garde.

## NOTES

1. David Rock treats this period most succinctly in *Politics in Argentina, 1890–1910: The Rise and Fall of Radicalism* (Cambridge: Cambridge University Press, 1975).

2. On this topic, see Maxine Molyneux, "No God, No Boss, No Husband: Anarchist Feminism in Nineteenth Century Argentina," *Latin American Perspectives* 14, 1 (Winter 1986): 119–145. Asunción Lavrin also addresses some of the problems surrounding women in the anarchist movements in *The Ideology of Feminism in the Southern Cone, 1900–1940, Latin American Program Working Papers 169* (Washington, D.C.: Wilson Center, Smithsonian Institution, 1986).

3. On women's activism in this period, see Donna J. Guy, "Women, Peonage,

and Industrialization: Argentina, 1810–1914," *Latin American Research Review* 16, 3 (1981): 65–89.

4. The exaltation of the prostitute comes in part from anarcho-socialist protests over the white slave trade and the traffic of women. For a detailed discussion of this, see Molyneux, "*No God*," 135.

5. On the social organization of women, see Sandra McGee Deutsch, *Counterrevolution in Argentina, 1900–1932: The Argentine Patriotic League* (Lincoln: University of Nebraska Press, 1986), especially chapters 1 and 2. On women's participation in labor, McGee states: "In 1914, females were 22% of the labor force over fourteen years of age. As many as 30% of all industrial and manual laborers were female, as were 52% of instructors and educators. And 84% of those providing personal services. . . . The fact that women tended to work longer hours under worse conditions for less pay than men led some of them to participate in the labor and feminist movements" (15).

6. On the feminist demands for democratic reform, see Cynthia Jeffress Little, "Education, Philanthropy, and Feminism: Components of Argentine Womanhood, 1860–1926," in *Latin American Women: Historical Perspectives*, ed. Asunción Lavrín (Westport, Conn.: Greenwood Press, 1978), 235–253.

7. See Lila Sosa de Newton, *Las argentinas de ayer a hoy* (Buenos Aires: Zanetti, 1967), especially chapter 3.

8. On Pan-Americanism, see Francesca Miller, this volume. On women in Cuba, see Karen Lynn Stoner, "In Defense of Motherhood: Divorce Law in Cuba During the Early Republic," *Journal of Third World Societies*, 15 (March 1981): 1–32. On the women's movements demands for reform of the Argentine civic code, see Catalina Wainerman and Marysa Navarro, *El trabajo de la mujer en la Argentina: Un análisis preliminar de las ideas dominantes en las primeras décadas del siglo XX*, Cuadernos del CENEP 7 (Buenos Aires: CENEP, 1979), 111–114.

9. Even the socialist movement, though supportive of women's rights, clearly urged women to celebrate their roles as mothers and cherish the family nest.

10. In Argentina, for example, a Society of Beneficence was established in the early nineteenth century in which women were invited to participate actively in the administration of a public school system for girls and, later, in social welfare programs. Women were charged with the management of the society and the administration of programs. On this topic, see Cynthia Jeffress Little, "The Society of Beneficence in Buenos Aires, 1823–1900" (Ph.D. diss., Temple University, 1980).

11. On the hygiene movement and legal restrictions on women see Donna Guy, "Lower Class Families, Women, and the Law in Nineteenth-Century Argentina," *Journal of Family History*, 10, 3 (Autumn 1985): 318–322.

12. See, for example, the advice manuals printed by the Argentine Antonio Zamora through his publishing firm, Claridad. Although supposedly representing the interests of women, these manuals were clearly pornographic.

13. Even in the Pan-Americanist women's journal *Mujeres de América*, the column on health and hygiene advised women to serve their husbands. Beatriz Sarlo has commented on the representations of women's bodies in popular fiction in her *El imperio de los sentimientos* (Buenos Aires: Catálogos, 1985).

14. José Ingenieros. *Tratado del amor*, ed. Anibal Ponce (Buenos Aires: Ramón J. Roggero, 1950).

15. Ricardo Rojas, *La literatura argentina* (Buenos Aires: Librería La Facultad, 1924), vol. 1.

16. Rojas, "Los modernos," in *La literatura argentina* 7: 767. See also his *La restauración nacionalista: Informe sobre educación* (Buenos Aires: Ministerio de Justicia e Instrucción Pública, 1909), in which he describes the moral crisis of modern Argentina.

17. Manuel Gálvez, "La literatura argentina contemporánea," in *La vida múltiple* (Buenos Aires: Nosotros, 1916), 210–211.

18. "Protestamos," *Inicial* 1, 1 (1923): 5–6.

19. "Directrices: feminismo y democratización," *Revista de Avance* 3 (1929): 36.

20. See Stoner, "In Defense of Motherhood."

21. Elizabeth A. Kuznesof and Robert Oppenheimer, "The Family and Society in Nineteenth-Century Latin America: An Historiographical Introduction," *Journal of Family History* 10, 3 (Autumn 1985): 215–234.

22. See Ricardo Rodríguez Molas, "Sexo y matrimonio en la sociedad tradicional," *Todo Es Historia* 16, 187 (December 1982): 8–43.

23. Max Horkheimer, "Authority and the Family," in *Critical Theory: Selected Essays*, trans. Matthew J. O'Connell (New York: Seabury Press, 1972), 99.

24. I have also written about the evolution of the literary treatment of Manuela Rosas in "Nationalism and the Discourse on Gender" (Paper delivered at the Seventh Berkshire Conference on Women's History, Wellesley College, June 1987). On the representation of women in nineteenth-century Argentina, see my "Between Civilization and Barbarism: Women, Family and Literary Culture in Mid-Nineteenth Century Argentina," in Hernán Vidal, ed., *Cultural and Historical Grounding for Hispanic and Luso-Brazilian Feminist Literary Criticism* (Minneapolis: Institute for the Study of Ideologies and Literature, 1989), 517–566.

25. Christopher Lasch, *Haven in a Heartless World: The Family Besieged* (New York: Basic Books, 1977).

26. Manuel Gálvez, *La maestra normal* (Buenos Aires: Tor, n.d.).

27. See, for example, Oliverio Girondo, *Espantapájaros*, in *Obras completas*, ed. Enrique Molina (Buenos Aires: Losada, 1968), or Vicente Huidobro, *Temblor del cielo*, in *Altazor/Temblor del cielo*, ed. René de Costa (Madrid: Cátedra, 1981).

28. I have addressed this question in my *Lenguaje e ideología: Las escuelas argentinas de vanguardia* (Buenos Aires: Hachette, 1986).

29. See "Parnaso Satírico" in *Martín Fierro* magazine (Buenos Aires, 1924–1927), a page of limericks and expressions of mutual admiration by the avant-garde poets of the 1920s. Of interest also is the publication of poetry in a female voice about prostitutes involved in Argentine white slavery. This poetry, which poked fun at the travails of women of the streets, was authored by César Tiempo under the pseudonym Clara Béter in a volume called *Versos de una . . .* (1926). It inspired a series of critical discussions by Tiempo's male colleagues, who knew of the false authorship but preferred to express mock horror about the trade of prostitutes for the purpose of literary fun. For details of the controversy, see César Tiempo, *Clara Béter y otras fatamorganas* (Buenos Aires: Peña Lillo, 1974).

30. These critical discussions are generated from Freud's essay "The Family Romance," in *The Standard Edition of the Complete Psychological Works of Sigmund Freud* (London: Hogarth Press, 1959), 9: 237–241. Lacanian readers of literature have emphasized the missing father as the principal generator of fiction. See, for example,

Robert Con Davis, ed., *The Fictional Father: Lacanian Readings of the Text* (Amherst, Mass.: University of Massachusetts Press, 1981).

31. Marthe Robert, *Novela de los orígenes u orígenes de la novela* (Madrid: Taurus, 1973).

32. Teresa de la Parra, *Ifigenia: Diario de una señorita que escribió porque se fastidiaba* (Paris: Casa Editorial Franco-Iberoamericana, 1924).

33. Elizabeth Garrels, in *Las grietas de la ternura: Nueva lectura de Teresa de la Parra* (Caracas: Monte Avila, 1986), makes note of de la Parra's exchanges on the topic of women's position in the world of letters.

34. Cynthia Steele has suggested that much of the fiction by Latin American women fits the category of "failed bildungsroman," in her article. "Toward a Socialist Feminist Criticism of Latin American Literature," *Ideologies and Literature* 4, 16 (1983): 327.

35. As a discussion relevant to my argument, it is worth considering Margaret Homans's essay, "Her Very Own Howl: The Ambiguities of Representation in Recent Women's Fiction," *Signs* 9, 2 (1983): 186–205, in which she studies the uses of nonverbal utterances in women's fiction.

36. María Luisa Bombal, *La última niebla* (Buenos Aires: Andina, 1981).

37. I have commented on the uses of female irrationalism and flight in the two writers mentioned in "Sara de Etcheverts: The Contradictions of Literary Feminism," in *Women in Hispanic Literature: Icons and Fallen Idols*, ed. Beth K. Miller (Berkeley: University of California Press, 1983), 243–258.

38. Teresa de la Parra, *Memorias de Mamá Blanca* (1929; reprint Buenos Aires: EUDEBA, 1966).

39. Elizabeth Abel addresses the subtext of female bonding in "Narrative Structure(s) and Female Development: The Case of *Mrs. Dalloway*," in *The Voyage In: Fictions of Female Development*, eds. Elizabeth Abel, Marianne Hirsch, and Elizabeth Langland (Hanover, N.H.: University Press of New England, 1983), 161–185.

40. Norah Lange, *Los dos retratos* (Buenos Aires: Losada, 1956).

# FOUR

# Women, Literature, and National Brotherhood

*Mary Louise Pratt**

## WOMEN AND *LA HISTORIA OFICIAL*

The reader who picks up Javier Ocampo López's encyclopedic *Historia de las ideas de integración de América Latina*[1] encounters a rich and ambitious survey of three centuries of Spanish American political history and thought, encompassing the problematics of colonialism, independence, nation building, and transnational identity. In this impressive panorama, a lone woman makes her appearance: the cigarette seller Manuela Beltrán, who on March 16, 1781, in Socorro, Nueva Granada, tore down a tax edict imposed by the Spanish colonial government. Her act, cheered on by an angry crowd, triggered an insurrection (the *conjuración de los alfaiates*) that then spread throughout the provinces, a prelude to Spanish American independence. The figure of Beltrán in Ocampo's book in many ways typifies the position women have occupied with respect to the official histories of modern times. For the most part they have been simply absent. When they are present, they are isolated figures, and they have no voice—one cannot help but notice that it is not Beltrán's "ideas de integración" that mark her place in history. Though she clearly did have the "right idea" at the time, it was never a question of recording her thoughts or words for posterity, only her gesture, as a prelude and metonymy for the larger drama.

For present purposes, it is of particular interest that this lone woman is a late-eighteenth-century popular revolutionary figure, a Marseillaise *avant la lettre*. She is conspicuously not a member of the criollo elites who claimed the American revolutions as their own and went on to fashion themselves into national bourgeoisies. While women have never been well represented by official histories in any age, it is worthwhile to recognize how particularly limited and repressive the bourgeois republican era has been in producing

48

and imagining women as historical, political, and cultural subjects. As Joan Landis put it, the democratization of politics in the nineteenth century brought with it the domestication of women, and the elision of women (along with most other people) as subjects of history.[2] Such elisions are part of the hegemonic project of the official story—as the Argentine film of that title (*La historia oficial*, 1985) reminds us. Indeed, that film exhibits some of the complexities and compromises involved in trying to insert women, especially women of privilege, into modern narratives of national history. At the same time, *La historia oficial* bears witness to the current emergence of new female political and historical subjects in Latin America, in mothers' movements and other powerfully innovative, often cross-class forms of female activism. The discussion to follow is offered in deliberate relation to these extraordinary contemporary developments.

After some general considerations of how women are situated and symbolized by masculinist ideologies of nation, this essay looks at how such ideologies are played out in some key Spanish American literary texts by men and women writers. Though somewhat loosely related, the examples all undertake to focus interest on the ways Spanish American women writers and intellectuals have symbolized themselves in this "socio-semantic field," and how they have problematized masculinist ideologies of nationhood and citizenship. Of necessity, the focus is on times and places for which texts by women are available to contemporary researchers, but also on times and places in which questions of national definition and identity are especially pressing. Thus, writings by José Mármol and Juana Manuela Gorriti from the Argentine independence period provide an initial comparative case; the second half of the essay is devoted to the period of the 1920s and 1930s, a time of rapid modernization, social and ideological upheaval, and national redefinition. Two rather different examples are considered: first the early women collaborators of the Peruvian *Revista Amauta*, and second the renowned Chilean poet Gabriela Mistral, specifically in her unfinished, and widely unread, *Poema de Chile*.

## THE NATION AS "IMAGINED COMMUNITY"

In the previous section reference was made to the limitations within bourgeois republicanism for creating or imagining women as subjects of history. The term "imagining" is introduced here as it is used by Benedict Anderson in his stimulating book *Imagined Communities: Reflections on the Origin and Spread of Nationalism*.[3] Anderson explores the idea of the nation as an *imagined* political community whose totality can never be experienced concretely: "The members of even the smallest nation will never know most of their fellow-members, meet them, or even hear of them, yet in the minds of each lives the image of their communion" (15). In fact, Anderson argues, all human communities tend to be imagined entities. Communities differ, he argues, "not by their falsity/genuineness, but by the style in which they are imagined" (15). Anderson introduces three useful terms to characterize the style in which the modern nation is imagined:

> The nation is imagined as *limited* because even the largest of them . . . has finite, if elastic boundaries beyond which lie other nations. . . . It is imagined as *sovereign* because the concept was born in an age in which Enlightenment and Revolution were destroying the legitimacy of the divinely-ordained, hierarchical, dynastic realm. . . . Finally it is imagined as a *community*, because, regardless of the actual inequality and exploitation that may prevail in each, the nation is always conceived as a deep, horizontal *comradeship*. Ultimately it is this fraternity that makes it possible, over the past two centuries, for so many millions of people, not so much to kill, as willingly to die for such limited imaginings. (16)

Anderson's analysis of the character of modern nationalism is of particular interest to Latin Americanists. One of his most radical, though not entirely convincing, suggestions is that the modern nation as a political idea arose not in Europe but in the Americas, in the republicanist movements that fought for independence. (Hence perhaps the stress on autonomy and sovereignty in ideologies of the nation.) As the nation-states of continental Europe sought to consolidate themselves and define national destinies in the nineteenth century, Anderson argues, it was to the American republics that they looked for guidance and example. Anderson's analysis is of considerable interest to literary scholars as well, because he singles out print culture, notably the novel and the newspaper, as the necessary condition for creating the invisible networks that form the basis of the imagined national community. This factor is of particular interest with respect to women.

The language of fraternity and comradeship used in the passages just quoted displays (without commenting on) the androcentrism of the modern national imaginings. Indeed, Anderson's three key features of nations (limited, sovereign, fraternal) are metonymically embodied in the finite, sovereign, and fraternal figure of the citizen-soldier. Anderson goes on in the book to discuss cenotaphs and tombs of the unknown soldier as some of the "most arresting emblems of the modern culture of nationalism" (17). Military service and electoral politics, domains originally limited to males, have been obvious central apparatuses for producing the imagined community of the modern nation-state, along with mass print culture, in which women have participated.

Though he does discuss the ways ethnic, racial, and class subgroups are incorporated into national self-understandings, Anderson does not take up the question of gender. His own terms make clear, however, that the issue is not simply that women "don't fit" the descriptors of the imagined community. Rather, the nation by definition situates or "produces" women in permanent instability with respect to the imagined community, including, in very particular ways, the women of the dominant class. Women inhabitants of nations were neither imagined as nor invited to imagine themselves as part of the horizontal brotherhood. What bourgeois republicanism offered women by way of official existence was what Landis and others have called "republican motherhood," the role of the producer of citizens. So it is that women inhabitants of modern nations were not imagined as intrinsically possessing the rights of citizens; rather, their value was specifically attached to (and implicitly conditional on) their reproductive capacity. As mothers of the nation, they are precariously other to the nation. They are imagined as dependent rather than sovereign. They are practically forbidden to be limited and finite, being obsessively defined by their reproductive capacity. Their bodies are sites for many forms of intervention, penetration, and appropriation at the hands of the horizontal brotherhood.

In the case of Europe, Landis argues that such gender asymmetries were sharply resisted by late-eighteenth-century feminists as bourgeois challenges to absolutism unfolded. Ultimately, however, their resistance was either defeated or co-opted. In England, this historical shift is neatly borne out in the writings of the famous mother-daughter pair Mary Wollstonecraft and Mary Shelley. In 1792 Mary Wollstonecraft wrote her famed *Vindication of the Rights of Woman* in a clear revolutionary spirit in which a much fuller recognition of women in society was an imaginable possibility. Thirty-some years later, in her daughter's book *Frankenstein*, what has become imaginable is a nightmarish world in which women are elided altogether as the man of science obsessively seeks, and finds, a way to reproduce on his own. In Shelley's story, it is the monster (associated often in the story with the wild Americas) who reasserts a "primitive" need for female companionship; the idea of female citizenship is nowhere to be found.

As bourgeois democracy consolidated itself, so the argument goes, women's legitimate political sphere was narrowed down to the home (regardless of where women were actually spending their time). The agenda of nineteenth-century feminism can be seen as both reflecting and resisting this domestication. Obviously, one cannot assume that this Europe-based argument holds identically for Spanish America; however, it is illuminating at certain points, as I hope the discussion below will show.

The fundamental instability accorded to women subjects may be one of the features that most distinguishes the modern nation from other forms of human community. But, of course, to say that women are situated in permanent instability in the nation is to say that nations exist in permanent instability. Gender hierarchy exists as a deep cleavage in the horizontal fraternity, one that cannot easily be imagined away. While subaltern ethnic and class groups can sometimes be contained as separate regional entities or as distinct genetic kinds, women cannot readily be dealt with in these ways. They are, after all, expected to cohabit with men, not to live in separate parts of the city or national territory. The efforts of Dr. Frankenstein aside, it is through women that the horizontal brothers reproduce themselves. At the same time, the reproductive capacity so indispensable to the brotherhood is a source of peril, notably in the capacity of those nonfinite, all-too-elastic female bodies to reproduce themselves outside the control of the fraternity. It was no accident that modern nations denied full citizens' rights to illegitimate offspring, and that women's political platforms continuously demanded those rights.

Women remain especially anomalous with respect to the one right that for Anderson sums up the power of the imagined community: the right to die for one's country. On one hand, women have mainly been excluded from this privilege; on the other hand, and perhaps more important, they have never as a group sought it. In the face of their exclusion from the national fraternity, as the work of Francesca Miller has shown (this volume, for example), women's political and social engagement became heavily *inter*nationalist, and often *anti*nationalist. Elite women activists established a long-standing presence and commitment in such spheres as the Pan-Americanist movement, international pacifism, and syndicalism, and in transnational issues of health, education, and human rights. Perhaps it is the vociferous, relentless pacifism of these activists that expresses most clearly their dissociation from the fraternal, soldierly imaginings of nationhood.

Other ambiguities emerge in the domain of culture. In the eighteenth century, women of privilege had gained access to the all-important networks of print culture that "underwrote" the imagined national communities. As writers, readers, critics, salon-keepers, and members of literary circles, they were legitimate, though far from equal, participants in the sphere (republic?) of letters. In the nineteenth century, despite pressures toward domesticity, women retained their foothold in lettered culture (though they were constantly obliged to defend it). Hence, though lacking political rights, they remained able to assert themselves *legitimately* in national print networks, engage with national forms of self-understanding, maintain their own political and discursive agenda, and express demands on the system that denied them full status as citizens. To a great extent, this entitlement was anchored in class privilege, which the women of letters shared with their male counterparts. One might suggest four elements then, that in part came to define the conflicted space of women's writing and women's citizenship: access to print culture (class privilege); denial of access to public power (gender oppression); access to domesticity (gender privilege); and confinement to domesticity (gender oppression).

## WOMEN AS NATIONAL ICONS: MÁRMOL, GORRITI, AND MANUELA ROSAS

The uneasy coexistence of nationhood and womanhood is played out in that paradoxical republican habit of using female icons as national symbols. For every Unknown Soldier there is a Statue of Liberty, a Britannia, a Marseillaise, a national virgin—in the Americas, the indigenous figures of La Malinche, Pocahontas, the violated Indian woman. In patriotic speeches, in sculpture, in poetry, novels, and plays, female icons are used to symbolize the nation—symbolizing, often enough, that which is at stake between warring groups of men. Such symbolizations played a conspicuous role in the extraordinary drama of national self-fashioning that took place in Argentina following independence from Spain. In its cultural and literary dimensions, that drama provides a vivid instance of the modern ideological tangle of nationalism, militarism, republicanism, fraternity, and womanhood.

In a configuration that has some points in common with the American Civil War, the battlelines in Argentina in the 1830s and 1840s were drawn between two camps, the *unitarios* and the *federales*. Roughly speaking, the *unitarios* were led by Buenos Aires-based, Europe-oriented liberal republicans advocating free trade and a centralized, secular, progressive republic centered in Buenos Aires. The *federales* who opposed them are generally seen as constituting an alliance of two groups: first, traditional land-based elites of the interior, defending local autonomy, traditional economies, trade protectionism, and church power; and second, a new wave of capitalists who had entered the cattle industry in Buenos Aires Province much more recently, after other forms of commerce with Europe failed to expand. Following independence from Spain, the *unitarios* had formed a centralized Argentine Republic, consecrated in the Constitution of 1826. The effort was short-lived, however. By 1830, power had been lost to the *federales*, and the two groups remained locked for twenty years in a devastating civil war. The *unitarios* called the *federales* barbarians, and the *federales* called the *unitarios* savages (both terms highly charged in the context of decolonization).

Until the victory of the unitarians in 1852, the dominant historical figure was the now-legendary federalist leader Juan Manuel de Rosas. Having become leader of the federalists (in part by assassinating the opposition), the politically talented and ruthless Rosas ruled Argentina from 1838 to 1852, with an iron hand and a secret police force that sent scores of Argentinians to their deaths or into exile. Debate still goes on in Argentina regarding whether Rosas was a crude leftover from the colonial era or the first great Argentine nationalist, but there is no question how the *unitarios* saw him. The *unitario* leaders were urban intellectuals deriving from the colonial bureaucracy and the colonial universities. They were prolific writers, passionately devoted to

the project of decolonizing their culture, of creating a enlightened republic of
letters. Lacking control of the economy, one form of production they did
control was print, and during the Rosas period they produced an immense
body of writings, mainly journalistic, including a corpus devoted to Rosas
himself, which must be one of the great literatures of denunciation of all time.

In 1844 José Mármol, a key unitarian intellectual, began publishing the
serial novel *Amalia*, which became and has remained a canonical testimonial
to the period. The title character is a young and beautiful upper-class Buenos
Aires woman. Through family ties and her love for a unitarian militant,
she becomes embroiled in political intrigue and exposed to Rosas's reign of
terror. When an attempt to overthrow the dictator fails, she and her lover
arrange to marry and flee the country. The novel ends minutes after the
marriage, when Rosas's henchmen invade Amalia's house, killing her lover
and leaving her in the hands of a benevolent, but federalist, uncle. Mármol's
novel is not at all simplistic, but the national symbolics are clear. Amalia's
initial situation allegorizes the moment of Spanish American independence:
when she was a young woman, her father died and her mother married her
to an old family friend for protection. After a year of passionless union, the
friend dies, as does the mother, leaving Amalia (alias Argentina) a young,
beautiful widow (a near virgin) of considerable resources, including her own
house. At the end of the novel, Amalia is still an unexchanged woman, the
frustration of her marriage reflecting the failure of the unitarian national
project. The sexual and the domestic are homologous with the political and
the military. No new national family has been founded to replace the already defunct colonial patriarchy. The entire drama takes place, of course,
among the criollo elite.

Though republican ideals remain unfulfilled in the novel, they are not
unexpressed; the language with which Mármol's characters describe their
political aspirations echoes Anderson's account of the modern nation. In this
passage from near the end of the novel, the hero, Daniel Bello, calls for a
"spirit of association" and attributes the unitarian defeat to

> nuestros hábitos de desunión, en la parte más culta de la sociedad; nuestra falta
> de asociación en todo y para todo; nuestra vida de individualismo; nuestra
> apatía; nuestro abandono; nuestro egoismo; nuestra ignorancia sobre lo que
> importa la fuerza colectiva de los hombres. . . . Aquel que sobreviva de noso-
> tros, cuando la libertad sea conquistada, enseñe a nuestros hijos que esa libertad
> durará poco si la sociedad no es un solo hombre para defenderla, ni tendrán
> patria, libertad, ni leyes, ni religión, ni virtud pública, mientras el espíritu de
> asociación no mate al cáncer del individualismo, que se ha hecho y hace la
> desgracia de nuestra generación.[4]

> [the habits of disunion among our cultured class; our want of association every-
> where and in everything; our life of individualism; our apathy; our neglect; our
> selfishness; our ignorance regarding the value of the collective strength of

men. . . . Let him who survives among us when liberty has been won teach our children that this liberty will last for a very short time if the nation does not unite as one man to defend it; that they will have neither a country, nor liberty, nor laws, nor religion, nor public virtue until the spirit of association shall have destroyed the cancer of individualism, which has made and which still makes the misfortune of our generation.]

Since we are talking about a civil war, it is no surprise to find that Amalia, the unitarian national symbol, has a federalist counterpart in Mármol's novel. She was a real person—Manuela Rosas, daughter of the hated dictator. A woman the same age as Mármol himself, she too has been the subject of a sizable literature of praise and condemnation. Historically, Manuela Rosas became her father's confidante and a chief political agent after her mother's death in 1838. In Mármol's novel, she appears as a competent, appealing person victimized by her father's crude tyranny. Like Amalia, she remains an unexchanged woman at the end of the novel (as she did in real life, marrying in her thirties only after her father went into exile in England).

Apart from her fictionalization in *Amalia*, Manuela Rosas turns up elsewhere in Mármol's writings, as the pretext for prescribing the future of women in the new republic. In 1851 Mármol published an essay on Manuela Rosas analyzing her life and character.[5] It reads as a fairly straightforward exhortation to domesticity and republican motherhood. Mármol sees Manuela as "la víctima de esa imposición terrible de vivir soltera" [the victim of that terrible imposition to live unmarried]. With "otra educación y otro padre" [a different upbringing and a different father] she would become capable of falling in love with a suitable man and would no longer be found attending orgies, dancing "hasta con negros" [even with Negroes], or, in a particularly unladylike lapse, serving to an English naval officer the salted ears of a unitarian colonel. Thus, as I will suggest more fully below, Mármol's writings portray elite women as both symbols and historical agents in the ongoing drama of nation building; at the same time, their absorption into domesticity will be the very sign that the nation has indeed been born.

Juana Manuela Gorriti was also the same age as Mármol, and as engaged as anyone with the future of the emergent Argentine nation. She too left Argentina during the Rosas period, and around 1850 she wrote a very popular story about the civil conflict, titled "El guante negro" ("The Black Glove").[6] In this story, too, the drama of nation building is played out in love relations, and women are important both as symbols and agents in that process. Gorriti's story, however, presents a much less orderly symbolic structure than does *Amalia*. Here, the sexual and the domestic do not operate homologously with the political and the military. Love, politics, patriotism, and militarism tangle in complex fashion.

Like *Amalia*, "El guante negro" embodies the national conflict in two women, a unitarian named Isabel (note the courtly name) and Manuela

Rosas. They are in love with the same soldier, a young federalist named
Wenceslaus (another courtly name), whose sincere affection for Manuela has
been overwhelmed by a newfound passion for Isabel. Unlike Amalia, Isabel
does not espouse her lover's political cause as her own. Rather, she places her
politics above love and demands that Wenceslaus prove his faith to her by
enlisting in the unitarian army. Placing love above family and politics, he
does so. His father, a federalist colonel, hears this news and, placing his
politics above family, arranges to murder his son for disloyalty. Wenceslaus's
mother, placing family above politics and motherhood above marriage, mur-
ders her husband to prevent him from killing her son. Wenceslaus hears of
his mother's deed and, reversing his earlier choice, decides that her sacrifice
obliges him to return to the federalist army and the arms of Manuela Rosas.
He does so and is promptly killed on a battlefield. The story ends with the
unexchanged, unfulfilled unitarian Isabel—alias the still unformed nation—
standing on the battlefield in the midst of a tangled pile of male corpses,
among which she has found that of her beloved Wenceslaus. She loses on two
counts: the unitarians have lost the battle, and her federalist lover has been
killed. Manuela reaps a Pyrrhic victory, and it remains unclear in whose
hands the national future ought to rest. The men in the story are all dead.

While in *Amalia* it is clear that the heroine's happiness and her lover's life
have been sacrificed to the tyranny of Rosas, no such clear conclusion can be
drawn from "El guante negro." Love, politics, and family weave in, through,
and around one another in unpredictable ways. In *Amalia*, women characters
are embedded in family structures that are weak, parentless, sometimes per-
verse; in "El guante negro," the family has disintegrated even further. Isabel
and Manuela are without visible family ties in the story; for example, both
are presented traveling alone to Wenceslaus's bedside. Wenceslaus's mother,
far from being sheltered by her family men, finds herself murdering one to
protect the other. While Amalia is often called upon to heroically defend the
sentimental/domestic sphere of her house from political violence, in "El
guante negro" *both* the house and the battlefield are sites for *both* sentimental/
domestic and political action, by either sex.

It should be emphasized that I am presenting what one might call "preferred readings" of these texts—that is, I am for the most part interpreting
them in the terms in which they seek to be interpreted. Deconstructive and
other skeptical approaches give rise to different and more textured readings;
these go beyond my present purpose, which is simply to introduce literary
uses of national iconographic conventions. In *Amalia* and "El guante negro,"
the abandoned fiancée left standing after the final shoot-out symbolizes the
failure to consolidate the republic. At the same time, in neither text can the
women be said to function solely as national symbols. They are also active
protagonists in the political drama. They have not been domesticated;

republican motherhood has not been consolidated (though the stage is seemingly set for it). *Amalia* and, to an even greater extent, "El guante negro" support the suggestion that at least in some sectors of Spanish American society this postrevolutionary period marked a historical aperture for women, an experimental moment in which they could be imagined as players in the drama of nation building.

### THE 1920S AND 1930S: THE COUNTRY AND THE CITY

Like the 1830s and 1840s, the decades following Europe's first world war were a period of intense nationalisms and debates on nationalism in many parts of Latin America, this time in the context not of independence but of modernization (see Francine Masiello, this volume). Many countries had experienced internal economic expansion through the challenge of meeting Europe's needs during the war. Internal markets and small industry developed, creating in some countries national business classes and middle sectors strong enough to challenge land-based oligarchic interests. Urbanization and industrialization created conditions for the emergence of the first modern mass political movements. Industrial working classes developed and became a political force in some places. Challenges to traditional oligarchic orders were often expressed as internationalism, urban cosmopolitanism, Latin American continentalism, and a critique of nationalism. At the same time, in response to changing demographic and political landscapes, nationalist visions were formulated both by those seeking change (in Peru, for instance, the indigenous majority leaped into the foreground of national concern) and by those opposing it (in Argentina, Rosas was revindicated, for example).

Print culture, as Benedict Anderson's argument predicts, was active in formulating dramas of modernization and competing national self-understandings. In every capital city, cosmopolitan avant-garde movements undertook to create modern, urban high cultures. At the same time, regionalist literatures emerged, seeking to consolidate urban-based discourses about the countryside, affirming, rejecting, or parodying visions of rural progress. It is a symptom of the time that both regionalist and avant-garde movements operated to the complete, and often aggressive, exclusion of women. The great women poets of these decades—Alfonsina Storni, Juana de Ibarbourou, Gabriela Mistral—were widely acclaimed but not accepted in avant-garde circles. Today they are benignly classified in literary typologies as *posmodernistas* distinct from the avant-garde. The experimentalism of their writing goes largely unrecognized by the literary establishment.

While the male avant-garde often combined a critical perspective with an eager radicalism and enthusiasm for modern urban life, equally cosmopolitan women writers tended to depict modern urban life as a source of confinement, fear, or despair. While for some male poets the mobile figure of the urban *flâneur* became a vehicle for elaborating a vigorous aesthetic of the city, such an aesthetic seems to have lacked plausibility for many women writers. A critique of domesticity and suburban boredom emerged, consolidating itself in the 1940s in the work of such writers as Chilean María Luisa Bombal.

No women writers appear in the canons of regionalist literature either. This is not to say, however, that women did not write about rural life. No contrast could be more revealing than that between the two classic Venezuelan texts that appeared in 1929: Rómulo Gallegos's *Doña Bárbara* and Teresa de la Parra's *Las memorias de Mamá Blanca*. Gallegos's novel became Venezuela's canonic epic of modernization, in which an enlightened, urban-educated man returns to the countryside, takes over a ranch owned by a crude and powerful woman rancher, and tames and marries her daughter, thus securing the future for reason, progress, and the patriarchal family. De la Parra, through the reminiscences of an elderly woman city-dweller, nostalgically depicts elite rural life as a feminocentric paradise of girls, women, and servants, still identified with the colonial era. Modernization is represented by a catastrophic move to the city, where the young female protagonists experience a drastic loss of liberty in the name of a highly repressive urban femininity.[7]

The schematic contrast between *Doña Bárbara* and *Mamá Blanca* should not obscure their common ground. Symbolically, gender operates similarly in the two works, though with contrasting value signs: both Mamá Blanca and Doña Bárbara stand for preindustrial social structures inherited from the colonial period and now seen to be passing. Both represent forms of female power and entitlement destroyed by modernization. Both remind us that, from a purely socioeconomic standpoint, the development of urban centers of power and elaborate state apparatuses threatened to deprive women heirs and property owners of an economic base for which there was no urban or industrial equivalent. Elite men could leave family estates to become lawyers, bankers, or businessmen, but the city held few such new beginnings for their female counterparts. Transposed to the house in the suburbs, class privilege realized itself in new ways that perhaps seemed narrow and small in comparison with the *hacienda* or the *fundo*. As literary creations, *Doña Bárbara* and *Las memorias de Mamá Blanca* register in contrasting ways the impact of feminism on the lettered imagination. De la Parra seeks to revindicate a lost oligarchic mother, while Gallegos feminizes and "barbarizes" a traditional figure in order to dispel it from the national landscape. In Peru at this same time, a very similar fate was being dealt to another traditional icon, the figure of the indigenous woman, to which I now turn.

## *INDIGENISMO*, THE *MADRE INDÍGENA*, AND
## THE WOMEN OF *AMAUTA*

One of the oldest and most durable myths of self-definition in Spanish America is that of the sexual appropriation of the indigenous woman by the European invader. It is a true narrative of origins, dating back to the tale of Cortés and the princess la Malinche (or, in North America, to Pocahontas and Captain John Smith). Endless repetitions and variants have mythified this figure, simultaneously victim and traitor, as the mother of the American mestizo peoples. At the same time, she has stood for all the indigenous peoples conquered (feminized) and co-opted (seduced) by the Spanish. Nowhere have such symbols been more active than in the Andean region.

In 1924 the Peruvian writer and francophile Ventura García Calderón published a short story, almost a vignette, titled "Amor indígena,"[8] which grotesquely reenacts the classic American drama of conquest as rape. Three Spanish (i.e., non-indigenous) Peruvians—a landowner, a businessman, and an anonymous but educated narrator—are traveling together on horseback in the Peruvian sierra. They stop for a midday meal in a town that is celebrating the feast of its patron saint. They spot a beautiful young Indian woman in the procession and playfully flip a coin to decide "whose she will be." The narrator wins the toss. Led by the feudal landlord Don Rosendo, the trio amuse themselves terrorizing the town at gunpoint and laughing at the desolation of the inhabitants as their prized possessions are destroyed. "Éramos ya los dueños de aquel poblado solitario, y la vida tenía el color dorado de las mañanas de otoño en tierra bárbara," exults the narrator [Now we were masters of that lonely village, and life had the golden color of autumn mornings in barbaric lands]. Deciding it is "a matter of duty" that they fulfill their intentions toward the young Indian woman, Don Rosendo with his horsewhip disperses the crowd of relatives around her and brings her by force to the narrator. The pair are left alone in the *tambo* (tavern). "Aquello fue salvaje," reports the narrator, "como en las historias de la Conquista" [It was savage, as in the times of the Conquest]:

> Me encerré, despedí al chino aterrado, y la indiecita fue mía, sollozando palabras que yo no acertaba comprender. Estaba primorosa con su alucinado temor y su respeto servil al hombre blanco. Me alentaba por vez primera esa alegría de los abuelos españoles que derribaban a las mujeres in los caminos para solaz de una hora y se alejaban ufanos a caballo, sin remordimiento y sin amor. La linda niña me miraba sumisa como a su dueño.

> [I shut myself in, dismissed the terrified mestizo, and the Indian girl was mine, sobbing words that I could not understand. She was exquisite in her hallucinated fear and her servile respect for the white man. For the first time I was animated by the joy of the Spanish forefathers who would knock over the

women on the road for the pleasure of an hour and ride off proudly, feeling neither love nor remorse. The lovely girl looked up at me submissively as if at her master.]

The group saddles up and leaves town, only to hear footsteps behind them. The narrator turns around to find "his little girl" ("mi chiquilla") following him, looking up "con tan desamparada súplica de esclava, que sentía un vuelco de orgullo en el corazón" [with such a helpless, slavish pleading, that I felt a burst of pride in my heart]. The narrator picks her up and places her on the back of his horse, concluding that he has found the best woman society will ever afford him:

> ¿Quién iba a quererme así, pisando las huellas de mi caballo, en busca del Amado por los caminos, como en el excelso cantar de Salomón? ¿Cuál otra me perseguiría también, desmelenada, olvidando a los suyos y entregándose para toda la vida? Resucitaban en mi sangre los abuelos magníficos, y obedecí a su atavismo.

> [Who else would love me like that, following the hoofprints of my horse, searching the pathways for the Beloved, as in the holy song of Solomon? What other woman would follow me, disheveled, forgetting her family and giving herself for life? My lordly forefathers were reawakening in my blood, and I obeyed their atavism.]

As in *Doña Bárbara*, a stereotype of the rural, uneducated woman is presented as an erotic ideal for the urban, educated man. Again, one is justified in seeing such images in part as reactions to the feminist images of sexual equality to which these urban writers (García Calderón lived nearly all his life in Paris) were inevitably exposed.

García Calderón's contemporary version of the rape story is startling precisely because of the mechanical exactitude with which it simulates the ideology of conquest (right down to the guns and horses). It is as if nothing at all had happened in the nearly four hundred years between Pizarro and himself. Conscious but not critical of the drama's anachrony, the narrator sees himself as recuperating a lost self, and at the same time regards the contemporary colonial figure, Don Rosendo, with a parodic distance. It is this combination of conscious anachrony and a touch of parody that marks this brief text as the reactionary document that it is. García Calderón reaffirmed the image of the conquest precisely at the moment in which both were being intensely questioned in Peru. The "problema del indio" was coming to occupy the center of the political agenda, and a reworking of Peruvian national imaginings was in the making.

The status of the indigenous population in Peru fueled one of the great national dialogues of the 1920s and 1930s. Intensely exploited under semifeudal conditions or withdrawn into marginal regions, the indigenous inhabitants had never been integrated into the imagined national fraternity—

despite the fact that they formed the great majority of the population, of the work force, and of the army. Indeed, it is usually argued that Peru's military defeat by Chile in the Guerra del Pacífico (1879–1884) first called attention to the need to make full-fledged citizens of the indigenes: the defeat was blamed on their lack of national identity and purpose. (One recalls Anderson's view of military sacrifice as the ultimate test of nationalist imaginings.)

Modernization in Peru produced great pressures on the semifeudal structure of the agricultural economy, based on exploitation of the indigenous labor force. Progressive urban middle sectors made it their goal to challenge the political hegemony of the landowning oligarchy, develop industrial and commercial potential, and further integrate and democratize the country. It was with these items at the top of the agenda that socialism took root in Peru in the 1920s, under the leadship of José Carlos Mariátegui. Again, literature and journalism were actively engaged in the ideological project of reformulating national self-understanding. Discussion of nationalism, the national future, and the "problema del indio" flourished on the pages of the magazine *Amauta*, founded by Mariátegui in 1926. *Indigenismo* became a full-fledged literary movement as urban-educated writers sought to engage imaginatively with the subaltern majority of which they were so woefully ignorant.

Writings about the Indian in this period display several kinds of ideological momentum. On one hand, there is a sincere effort to come to grips with the reality of indigenous life and incorporate it into national self-understanding. On the other hand, an exoticist tendency distances, objectifies, and dehumanizes the indigenous peoples in a decidedly nonfraternal way. At best they are seen as a national "problem" that new urban elites are called upon to solve. Yet in the symbolic realm a fraternal appropriation also occurs: the new intellectuals often identify with indigenous tradition, adopting a strong cult of authenticity toward Incaic culture and language. The very title of the magazine *Amauta*, for example, is a Quechua word that in Inca times referred, as the magazine tells us, to "un sabio que al ejercer función de maestro socializaba en cierto grado sus conocimientos y, formando así a los funcionarios que el imperio requería, se había convertido en pivote de la administración" (*Amauta* 1: 10) [a wise man who, in his capacity as teacher, socialized his knowledge to some extent and, as educator of the public servants required by the empire, had become the pivot of the administration]. And it is of course this iconic male figure who adorned the cover of the magazine when it first appeared (should one speak here of republican fatherhood?).

This elite intellectual in the service of the state readily sums up the *Amauta* group's aspirations for themselves. The "problema del indio" in their writings is a terrain on which the group works out its own self-identification as a national political force. It becomes a mirror for the self-understanding of a young, oppositional sector of the bourgeoisie committed to transforming a national social structure and economy dominated by the landed oligarchy. Thus, at a time when nationalism itself was often questioned as retrogressive and provincial, the preoccupation with the Indian seems to operate as a kind of displaced nationalism. In identifying with the interests of the Indian, the new intellectuals identified themselves as authentic Peruvians, while distinguishing themselves from other sectors of Peruvian society and of their own class.

As an iconic figure, the *amauta* radically displaced the traditional icon of the indigenous woman violated by the Spanish conqueror. This displacement is often vividly dramatized in the *indigenista* poetry and fiction of the period (for which *Amauta* was also an important mouthpiece). One particularly memorable example is found in a story titled "El campeón de la muerte" by Enrique López Albújar. López Albújar was one of the early progressive *indigenista* writers, and this story was published in 1920 in a collection titled *Cuentos andinos*, which according to one critic "convulsed the literary scene" when it appeared.[9] As this story opens, an indigenous father is trying to locate his only daughter, who has been carried off by a renegade *indio malvado*. As he chews his coca, seeking a vision of her whereabouts, he hears a voice behind him. In the dark there appears the hand of the renegade, holding a bloody sack whose contents are dumped out on the ground. It is the dismembered corpse of the violated daughter, who has not appeared alive in the story. This almost allegorical scene of horror inaugurates a long tale of revenge in which the grieved father hires a mestizo professional gunman to join him in hunting down and methodically killing the rapist-murderer one bullet at a time.

Several key transformations occur here. First, the point of origin is an indigenous father, not a mother. Second, the rape is transferred from a gun-toting European conqueror to a knife-wielding (i.e., premodern) Indian. Third, the symbol of the raped woman is literally disposed of, in the most aggressive and misogynist fashion. It is substituted by a fraternal pair (the father and the hired gunman) who suggest a new masculinized and militarized symbolic space. This new fraternal pair is explicitly modern: they bear guns; their relation is horizontal; it is mediated by professionalism and cash. More important, they represent an alliance of mestizo and indigenous individuals, long-standing enemies in Andean society. López Albújar is credited as being one of the first Andean writers to create complex indigenous characters, literary candidates for full membership in the imagined national fraternity. At the same time, his narratives inaugurate an intensely masculinized universe in which images of female power and agency are virtually absent.

Given the masculinist thrust of nationalist and indigenist imaginings of the period, it is hardly surprising that women writers and intellectuals in this period seem not to join in them. For example, the early women collaborators in the *Revista Amauta*, notably Dora Meyer de Zulen, Blanca Luz Brum, Magda Portal, and María Wiesse, tended to write on contemporary politics, art, and everyday life. Their lack of engagement with the "problema del indio" contrasts, however, with the activism of the previous century, when race was very much a women's issue. Antislavery movements were heavily female, for example, while in the literary sphere, Gertrudis Gómez de Avellaneda's *Sab* (Cuba, 1841), Clorinda Matto de Turner's *Aves sin nido* (Peru, 1889) and Harriet Beecher Stowe's *Uncle Tom's Cabin* (United States, 1852) attest the engagement of women intellectuals with issues of racial oppression. In Peru, the torch apparently passed into the hands of men, and into mainstream politics. Indeed, this shift is explicitly ritualized in the opening issue of the *Revista Amauta*. The issue includes an article by Dora Meyer de Zulen, cofounder of the Asociación Pro-Indígena, one of the first public lobbies for indigenous rights. At the request of Mariátegui, she wrote the history of the organization, including its demise in 1915. Her article has the effect of an act of closure on the older movement and an acknowledgment that the initiative now lies elsewhere.

Gender equality has an important place in Meyer de Zulen's view of both Incaic society and her organization. Speaking of the superior civilization of the Incas, she notes that while most peoples furnish themselves with myths of a founding father, the enlightened Incas have a founding couple, Manco Capacc and Mama Occllo. She goes on to draw a parallel with herself and her spouse as the founding couple of the Asociación Pro-Indígena. One wonders whether she was trying to caution the new *indigenistas* against their own androcentrism.

When the women writers of *Amauta* did engage with the issues of identity, authenticity, and the indigenous majority in Peru, their work often contested conventional *indigenista* paradigms and located national problematics along lines other than race. One striking example is a text by short-story writer María Wiesse that appeared in issue 11 of *Amauta* magazine. The story, titled "El forastero" ("The Outsider"), opens on the figure of an aged indigenous woman receiving with joy the news that that young white aristocrat whom she cared for from birth is returning to the *hacienda* after a ten-year absence in Europe. The woman, so the genre might lead one to suspect, will represent a pole of cultural authenticity through which the Europeanized surrogate son might recover his true Peruvian identity. The story takes quite another turn, however. The maternal icon is invoked, only to be quickly moved offstage, and the problem of national identity is articulated in quite another set of terms. Conflict breaks out between the European-educated son, who indeed expected to return home to the "authentic" *hacienda* of his youth, and his "authentic" Peruvian brothers, whose way of life has been transformed by imported European goods and practices. The nostalgic returnee is heart-broken at the presence in the paternal home of English furniture and English

food, the change to single-crop agriculture, and the abandonment of pater-
nalism in favor of intensified, rationalized exploitation of indigenous labor.
The brothers have no patience with the returnee's longing for old, uncomfortable, and inefficient ways. The story ends on a bizarre but very real contradiction: the traveled, cosmopolitan brother aligns with colonial tradi-
tionalism and questions modernization, while the narrow provincials are
the ardent partisans of the foreign and the modern.

Wiesse's story broaches a set of contradictions the *indigenista* discourse
begs: what exactly can national identity be if the "authentic" values and
practices of the dominant class are imported from outside? Is attachment to
nonindustrial lifeways simply alienated nostalgia of the kind Europeans
thrive on, or are things of real value being lost? Wiesse adroitly moves in on
these questions from within conventional *indigenista* thematics, embodied in
the figure of the Indian surrogate mother. This figure is invoked almost as a
gesture, only to be declared anachronistic and irrelevant. Wiesse locates the
problem of authenticity and national identity not in the indigenous majority
but squarely within the nonindigenous ruling classes, within the national
brotherhood long divided regarding issues of modernization and identity.

A similar contestation of *indigenista* discourse is made by the socialist
writer and activist Magda Portal in the first issue of *Amauta*, where she published an avant-garde prose poem titled "Círculos violeta." Taken from a
collection with the chilling title *El derecho de matar* [the right to kill], the
poem follows the thoughts of an impoverished, infirm young woman bear-
ing an unwanted pregnancy. Even today (or especially today), the poem
sounds radically explicit: "¿Para qué, pues, el hijo? ¿La prolongación de las
lágrimas mudas del abandono, del extravío? ¡La prolongación de las miserias
der mundo!" [Why, then, the child? To carry on the mute tears of abandonment, of wandering? To carry on the miseries of the world!]. In this mood of
despair, the woman gives birth to a girl. Carrying the newborn child through
the streets, she passes by the orphanage but rejects it as an "incubador de
esclavos y de asesinos" [incubator of slaves and murderers]. She walks on till
she reaches the river:

> Después envolvió a la niña en su amplio abrigo, y sencillamente la arrojó.
> El rio se abrió en un punto para dejar pasar a la huésped—y se volvió a cerrar.
> Sólo un instante se quebraron las estrellas en sus ondas revueltas.
> La MADRE tomó el regreso a su posada—bañada de indiferencia,—
> Se insinuaba la aurora—como en los ojos de la niña.
> Todos los pájaros lloraban.
>
> [Then she wrapped up the child in her roomy overcoat, and simply threw her in.
> The river opened itself in a spot for the guest to enter—then closed again.
> Only for an instant did the stars break their rolling waves.
> The MOTHER headed back to her lodgings—bathed in indifference,—
> Dawn began to break—as in the eyes of the little girl.
> All the birds wept.]

So ends the poem.

The scene of infanticide by drowning in a river is a commonplace of *indigenista* narrative and its antecedents, a scene often used to suggest either pathos or a brutal indifference to life. Portal appropriates and radically reworks this trope in her poem. Most noticeably, though the infanticide would suggest to any Peruvian reader an indigenous protagonist, the woman in Portal's poem is never identified by race. The issue of infanticide is posed in terms of gender and economics rather than ethnicity. Moreover, the setting in the poem is manifestly modern and urban rather than preindustrial and rural—the woman is even identified as suffering tuberculosis and neurasthenia, the two great urban diseases of the time. Thus the equation of infanticide with primitivism is rejected. The colonial figure of the violated indigenous woman is merged with that of the deracinated and impoverished urban worker. Among other things, the result implies a brutal indictment of the national iconography and of republican motherhood: here is a mother who has produced a new citizen nobody wants, not even herself, a citizen for whom the protection of the state consists only in the anomie of an orphanage and domestic servitude. Unlike many *indigenista* portrayals, Portal's poem contains complex emotional dynamics. On one hand, the woman is portrayed as "indiferente" to the death of her baby rather than brokenhearted; the river welcomes the child as a guest and not a victim. At the same time, the event is billed as tragic—the birds weep like a chorus—and as the result of social injustice.

In an uncanny but probably coincidental way, Portal's ending echoes and revises another mother/infant death scene from a half century earlier. In Zorrilla de San Martín's long narrative poem *Tabaré* (Uruguay, 1888, though the author's definitive edition appeared only in 1923), Tabaré's mother, a Spanish captive of the Charrúa Indians, dies weeping over her mestizo baby:

> La madre le estrechó, dejó en su frente
> Una lágrima inmensa, en ella un beso,
> Y se acostó a morir. Lloró la selva,
> Y, al entreabrirse, sonreía el cielo.[10]

> [The mother held it, left on its forehead
> An immense tear, and on that a kiss,
> Then she lay down to die. The jungle wept,
> And peeking through, the sky smiled.]

Here, the raped woman is a Spaniard, and as Bonnie Fredrick has pointed out,[11] having been contaminated by the Indians, she must die, in a paradigmatic and culturally threatening reversal of conquest. Again, Portal's protagonist makes no such sacrifice, nor will her offspring live, as Tabaré does, to become a hero who dies in the name of criollo hegemony.

Portal's poem takes the scene of infanticide out of the indigenist-nationalist-criollo context and relocates it in the context of patriarchy, class struggle, and the modern state. The symbolics of *indigenismo* and republican motherhood are invoked, only to be substituted by the politics of gender and reproduction and the concrete figure of the female citizen. A rather similar substitution occurs in the final text to be examined here, Gabriela Mistral's *Poema de Chile*.

## GENDER, RACE, AND NATION IN THE *POEMA DE CHILE*

Gabriela Mistral's *Poema de Chile*[12] is a collection that Mistral began in the 1920s and worked on for twenty years, much of the time living in Brazil and traveling widely as an international intellectual figure and educator. It is perhaps in keeping with the problematic relation between women and nation, and between women writers and nationalist writing, that the collection was never finished. It was edited posthumously by Doris Dana and is not always included in summaries and anthologies of Mistral's work. Though a work of major proportions (seventy-seven poems in 250 pages), the collection is quite marginalized in the critical legacy on Mistral. The *Poema de Chile* is problematic for patriarchal criticism in a way other writings of Mistral are not. Most of Mistral's writing has been subjected to the common critical strategy of reading women's texts as autobiographical or "personal," contained in a private sphere that is an appendage of the domestic. Nationalist or patriotic writings by women tend to confound this strategy. They cannot easily be read back into the domestic sphere, for they take as their very subject matter the impersonal entity of the nation-state; their authorial voice is that of the citizen. What follows is not an attempt to "rescue" the *Poema de Chile* from obscurity or to nominate it for admission into the poetic canon. Rather, it is an attempt to think about this remarkable and problematic work in connection with gender and traditions of nationalist and patriotic discourse.

From this perspective, one of the most conspicuous features of the *Poema de Chile* is that its author opts entirely out of a long-standing heroic tradition of patriotic poetry that celebrates official history, singing the glories of battles, generals, sons in service of the motherland, and the like. This is the tradition of such canonical works as Alonso de Ercilla's *La Araucana* or José Joaquín Olmedo's *La victoria de Junín*, revived in a radical, counterhegemonic guise by Pablo Neruda in his *Canto general* (1950).[13] In contrast with this historical, often militaristic tradition, Mistral writes about Chile exclusively as nature. The *Poema de Chile* consists entirely of titles like "Cobre" ("Copper"), "La chinchilla" ("The Chinchilla"), "Luz de Chile" ("Light of Chile"), and "Manzanos" ("Apple Trees"). The official or public history of Chile plays no role in the work; patriotism and nationalism in their political guise, affirming the imagined community, are absent. Rather, following another powerful criollo tradition, love of country is expressed through a passionate engagement with ecology and geography, America as primal paradise.

At first glance, one might see Mistral's focus on nature as a straightforward "feminine" choice. But to do so is simply to insert her poem into patriarchal meaning systems and to fail to see it also as an intervention in those systems. Within modern patriarchal forms of knowledge, nature is female and history male. With respect to the normative male subject, nature/woman is an Other, and the object which that subject appropriates. Nature is the woman-object on which men sow the deeds of history; on which men bestow the nomenclatures of science; which the explorer discovers and the colonizer develops or tames. In the case of the neo-Romantic poetic tradition, nature is that which the poet contemplates and appropriates as a correlate of his inner state. Men's dominance over nature in such writings is often expressed symbolically by the speaker's position on a high point or promontory (the "promontory poem" is recognized as a lyric subgenre) and through fantasy in which the landscape is transformed in the poet's imagination. One thinks of José Heredia at Niagara or atop the Teocalli; of Alexander von Humboldt's influential writings which sought to merge the poet and scientist into a single speaker-seer surveying the American landscape. This traditional configuration of the (male) poetic subject inspired by contemplation of the (female) landscape impinges heavily on Mistral and is one she reorganizes in her poem.

Though passivity is most often associated with the woman-landscape on which the male acts, it is important to note the equal passivity and immobility of the contemplating man-poet in neo-Romantic nature poetry. It is precisely this immobile observer that Mistral abandons. In a highly original gesture, she substitutes a mobile poetic voice and a narrative configuration. The speaking subject in the *Poema de Chile* is a woman who returns to Chile as a spirit after many years of absence and travels through the country on foot in the company of an Indian boy. In many respects Mistral's discourse abandons the dominance over nature that is traditionally expressed in the elevated stance of the promontory poem. The rejection of such a stance is explicit in the dramatic opening poem of the collection, titled "Hallazgo" ["Discovery"]. Here is its first stanza:

> Bajé por espacio y aires
> y más aires, descendiendo,
> sin llamado y con llamada
> por la fuerza del deseo,
> y a más que yo caminaba
> era el descender más recto
> y era mi gozo más vivo
> y mi adivinar más cierto,
> y arribo como la flecha
> éste mi segundo cuerpo
> en el punto en que comienzan
> Patria y Madre que me dieron.

Literally translated, this reads:

> I came down through space and air
> and more air, descending,
> without calling, but being called
> by the force of desire,
> and the more I walked
> the straighter was my descent
> and the greater my joy
> and the straighter my aim,
> and like an arrow I land
> this my second body
> at the point where they begin,
> Fatherland and Mother I was given.

The poetic "I" uses her strength to descend into the landscape rather than to climb up to a promontory from which an immutable, totalizing vision might be claimed. The play on grammatical gender ("sin llamado y con llamada") may be intended to foreground this choice as a female one. Yet the erotics of the stanza are intensely male—the phallic arrow impelled by its own desire, heading for its mark, its pleasure ("gozo") intensifying as it approaches. Conspicuously, the arrow's target is neither simply the fatherland nor the motherland, but the doublet Patria y Madre, a reverse of the conventional epithet "la madre patria." The speaker's desire is aimed at a parental couple; it is thus markedly not oedipal in character (one is reminded of de la Parra's figure of a founding mother and of Dora Meyer de Zulen's identification with the Inca founding couple).

The contrast between Mistral's practice in this opening and that of her contemporary Neruda is striking. Early in the *Canto general*, Neruda's famed "Alturas de Macchu Pichu" begins with a descent, but it is a descent into death, self-disintegration, and absence of desire, from which the poet emerges in the famous line "Entonces subí hasta ti, Macchu Picchu" [then I ascended to you, Macchu Picchu]. Neruda then recovers the traditional promontory stance in the heights of the Incaic ruins, from which he contemplates an overwhelmingly masculine march of history.

The traditional subject-object relation between man-poet and woman-landscape is substituted in Mistral's poem with an intersubjective one, the mother-child relation between the poetic "I" and the adoptive Indian child who accompanies her on her trek through Chile. Nearly all the poems in the collection are addressed to the child or are dialogues with the child. The speaker's project in many of the poems is to pass on her everyday knowledge of Chilean nature to her offspring, a mentoring activity quite distinct from both romantic self-expression and scientific classification. Indeed, the verb *mentar*—"to name" or "to mention"—is a key term throughout the work, as Mistral's "I" names the world for the accompanying child (see, for example, "El Mar" or "Salvia").

Historicity is thus present in the *Poema de Chile* not in the form of canonical history (battles, treaties, dates to be commemorated) but in the "micropractices" of social reproduction through which one generation continually shapes the next. Indeed, masculine heroics are explicitly set aside in poems like "Perdiz," ["Partridge"] where the poet-mother admonishes the child for wanting to catch birds:

> —¡Ay, tienes tiempo sobrado
> para hacer la villanada!
> Los hombres se sienten más
> hombres cuando van de caza.
> Yo, chiquito, soy mujer:
> un absurdo que ama y ama
> algo que alaba y no mata,
> tampoco hace cosas grandes
> de ésas que llaman "hazañas."

> [—Ah, you have plenty of time
> to make mischief!
> Men feel more
> manly when they go hunting.
> I, little one, am a woman:
> an absurdity who lives and loves
> something that praises and does not kill,
> nor does great things
> of the kind they call "deeds."]

Equally, Mistral's engagement with Chile in the poem is not played out in any of the fraternal imaginings Anderson identifies with nationalism. There is no imagined community in Mistral's poem, only the national territory naturalized as an ecological entity, and a concrete maternal (not fraternal) relation. Though there is patriotism in the work, then, there are no politics, at least in conventional senses of that term.

Though Mistral's relation with her child interlocutor is one of dominance in which the poet-mother has authority, her addressee is anything but the silent recipient of her words. Their relation is dialogic, conflicted, continuously challenged—as in the poem just quoted—by the contentious, querying child. At times, it is quite unclear who is leading whom (see, for example, "A veces, Mamá, te digo" or "Boldo"). Mistral's mother-child dyad is in many ways true to life, capturing vividly the experience of women who move through their days from task to task in the company of a small child. At the same time, Mistral's dyad contrasts markedly with stereotypes of the mother-child pair: the silent motionless icon of Mary and the baby Jesus, both parties looking outward with no possibility of dialogue between them; the endlessly mobile Llorona, who, unlike Mistral's ghost mother, is moving in search of, not in company with, her children. In effect, Mistral puts republican motherhood in motion, generating an unusual apolitical citizen-building project. Like Portal in the poem discussed earlier, Mistral pulls the mother-child dyad out into the street and makes it into a locus of social agency, power, and consciousness. Unlike Portal's poem, however, criollo racial hierarchy remains in place in the *Poema de Chile*, in the infantilized Indian dependent on the Euro-american for knowledge and understanding. This is an aspect also shared by Neruda's *Canto General*.

In addition to reworking established poetic stereotypes, Mistral in the *Poema de Chile* explicitly challenges the identification of women with the domestic. Hatred of houses is a recurrent theme in the collection, developed at greatest length in the poem "Flores" ["Flowers"]. This text opens with the child challenging his mother's habit of avoiding houses:

> —No te entiendo, mamá, eso
> de ir esquivando las casas
> y buscando con los ojos
> los pastos o las mollacas
> ¿Nunca tuviste jardín
> que como de largo pasas?

> [I don't understand you, mama, this
> thing of avoiding houses
> and searching with your eyes
> for pastures or groves
> Did you never have a garden
> so that you pass them right by?]

The mother replies at length: "No es que deteste las flores / es qe me ahogan las casas" [It's not that I hate flowers / but I am suffocated by houses]. Like the sinner, she says, she both loves and hates houses: "Me las quiero de rendida / las detesto de quedada" [I love them to rest in / I hate them to stay in]. She prefers "cerros y montañas" [hills and mountains] to "rosas y claveles" [roses and carnations], because "los cerros cuentan historias / y las casas poco o nada" [mountains tell stories / and houses few or none]—a clear, ironic inversion of established identifications of history with the human world.

This theme is picked up in a number of the poems, such as "A dónde es que tú me llevas" ("Where are you taking me"), in which the child wonders,

> O es, di, que nunca tendremos
> eso que llaman "la casa"
> donde yo duerma sin miedo
> de viento, rayo y nevadas.

> [Or is it, tell me, that we will never have
> this thing they call "home"
> where I can sleep without fear
> of wind, lightning or snow?]

The mother's reply is that what she seeks for her son is not a house, but racial justice and land:

> Te voy llevando a lugar
> donde al mirarte la cara
> no te digan como nombre
> lo de "indio pata rajada,"
> sino que te den parcela
> muy medida y muy contada.
>
> [I am taking you to a place
> where looking at your face
> they do not call you
> "split-footed Indian"
> where they give you a piece of land
> fully measured and reckoned.]

What she seeks for herself, however, is never stated. The "I" of this remarkable work remains a deracinated, dispossessed ghost in a national limbo, and at the same time a spokesperson with a sense of national identity and entitlement. Urbanization and industrialization, the realities of modernization, play no role in that mission. Not a single city, or even a town, is encountered by the wandering pair. No smokestacks or slag heaps besmirch the landscape. Modernization has no role in the future Mistral's "I" projects.

In sum, the *Poema de Chile* reorganizes the literary patrimony in a poetry of movement and action which is not, however, a poetry of heroics or transformation. Nationalism and *amor patrio* are deployed in the private domains of mother-child relations and personal reminiscence; yet these private domains are explicitly dissociated from a domestic sphere. They are transposed into an idealized outdoor world through which woman moves with freedom and authority in relations that are vertical and maternal, not horizontal and fraternal. The Chile Mistral celebrates contrasts to an extreme with Anderson's model of the modern nation. In her heart there lives no image of fraternal communion (to paraphrase Anderson), only a commitment directly to the national territory as a concrete and "natural" thing. In her Chile there is no fraternity, and in fact there are no men. It is an escapist vision of whose limits Mistral was perhaps aware when she abandoned the project in the 1940s. The image of a fully empowered female citizen was as inaccessible then as on the day she was born—more inaccessible, perhaps, than a hundred years before, when Gorriti's virgin Isabel stood up alone among the corpses of the fratricidal national brotherhood.

## CONCLUSION: LITERARY HISTORY AS DIALOGUE

This essay has sought to read a discontinuous series of texts, somewhat as if they were moments overheard in an ongoing dialogue among women and men writers—Mármol and Gorriti in mid-nineteenth-century Argentina; in the 1920s and 1930s, de la Parra and Gallegos in Venezuela; Wiesse, García Calderón, López Albújar, and Portal in Peru; Chileans Mistral and Neruda in the 1930s and 1940s. A variety of instances have been taken up: the identity crisis of the Argentine Independence period; the reviewing of *hacienda* society from the perspective of modernization in Venezuela; the "nationalizing" of race problematics in Peru; the search for epic in Chile. All involve moments of crisis in nationhood and national self-understanding. The aim has been to observe the participation of women writers and intellectuals in these moments, placing them in dialogue with the dominant male voices of their contemporaries. All these writers and these instances have their own deep complexities, which discussion here has necessarily oversimplified. The goal in this essay has been less to elucidate the dialogue than simply to observe it, to establish that it existed.

Literary history can be told in many ways, of course, and to construct it as a dialogue across lines of gender and power is only one way. But it is a valid and important way: critical understanding, and literature itself, are impoverished and distorted when all is reduced to a monologue, or to a conversation exclusively among men. The principal strategy in this paper has been to read writings of the less powerful as contesting and reworking those of the more powerful. The challenge that remains is to achieve the reverse as well—that is, to understand the writings of the dominant as constituted by and in relation to the voices of subaltern groups that the dominant often like to think of as silent.

## NOTES

*The work presented here has been shaped by discussions with many people. My colleagues in the UC-Stanford Seminar have been an ongoing source of guidance and inspiration. I am also indebted to many graduate students in the Department of Spanish and Portugese at Stanford, who have been vital interlocutors on issues of gender and literary history over the past several years. In particular, this paper has benefited from discussions with Magali Roy (on women and nationalism), Nina Menéndez (on Gorriti), Marcela Prado (on Mercedes Marín del Solar), Elena Feder (on de la Parra), Efraín Kristal (on *indigenismo*), and Linda Koski (on Brunet and Bombal).

   1. Javier Ocampo López, *Historia de las ideas de integración de América Latina* (Tunja: Editorial Bolivariana Internacional, 1981).
   2. Joan Landis, "Women and the Public Sphere: A Modern Perspective," *Social Analysis* 15: (1984): 20–31.
   3. Benedict Anderson, *Imagined Communities: Reflections on the Origin and Spread of Nationalism* (London: Verso, 1983).
   4. José Mármol, *Amalia*, ed. Teodosio Fernández Rodríguez (Madrid: Editora

Nacional, 1984), 738–739. English translation by Mary J. Serrano (New York: E. P. Dutton, 1919), 366–367.

5. José Mármol, "Manuela Rosas," in *Asesinato del Sr. Dr. D. Florencio Varela/ Manuela Rosas*, ed. Juan Carlos Ghiano (Buenos Aires: Casa Pardo, 1972), 101–126.

6. Juana Manuela Gorriti, "El guante negro," in *Sueños y realidades* (Buenos Aires: Biblioteca de la Nación, 1903): 91–127.

7. For extended commentary, see Elizabeth Garrels, *Las grietas de la ternura: Nueva lectura de Teresa de la Parra* (Caracas: Monte Avila, 1986).

8. Ventura García Calderón, "Amor indígena," in *Obra Escogida*, ed. Luis Alberto Sánchez. (Lima: Ediciones Edubanco), 420–424.

9. Enrique López Albújar, "El campeón de la muerte," in *Cuentos andinos*, 4th ed. (Lima: J. M. Baca, 1965), 27–40.

10. Juan Zorrilla de San Martín, *Tabaré* (Montevideo: Barreiro y Ramos, 1888). The quotation is from book 1, canto 2. For an introduction to this work, see Enrique Anderson Imbert, *Análisis de "Tabaré"* (Buenos Aires: Centro Editor de América Latina, 1968).

11. Bonnie Frederick, "The Unwilling Traveler: The Journey of the Captive Woman" (Paper delivered at the Rocky Mountain Modern Language Association, October 1987).

12. Gabriela Mistral, *Poema de Chile*, ed. Doris Dana (Santiago: Pomaire, 1942).

13. This "official" mode has, of course, not always been completely inaccessible to women. One is reminded, for example, of Mercedes Marín del Solar's "Canto fúnebre a la muerte de don Diego Portales" (1837), considered to be one of the founding texts of the Chilean lyric. In the twentieth century, women poets have participated, like Neruda, in the oppositional, protest-oriented branch of this militant tradition, though perhaps not in the epic dimensions of the *Canto general*. One thinks, for instance, of the militant socialist poetry of Magda Portal written in the context of Peruvian labor struggles of the 1930s and 1940s, or of Violeta Parra as the voice of Chile in the 1960s and 1970s.

# FIVE

# The Modernization of Femininity: Argentina, 1916–1926

*Kathleen Newman*

In 1926, the year in which Argentine women gained their civil rights, *Plus Ultra*, the glossy monthly supplement to the then leading national weekly *Caras y Caretas*, published a special issue in homage to Argentine women. This special issue (June 30, 1926) paid its homage principally through briefly captioned photographs or reproductions of paintings, edifying quotations, and poetry in praise of what the editors called "exquisite national femininity." The photographs ranged from quarter- to full-page studio portraits of the young women of Buenos Aires high society to "album pages" with some fifty small photographs of leading women writers, painters, intellectuals, doctors, and feminists of the period. The potential female reader of the issue could browse from nineteenth-century president Domingo Sarmiento's comments on the importance of the education of women, to captions reminding her that "a woman at the swimming pool, more than a charming decoration, is also a brilliant promise of the vigor and excellence of the race." She could contemplate notes on women journalists, aristocratic women of the Colonial period, leaders of charitable societies, nurses, women in "humble labors," sportswomen, ballerinas, or seamstresses. On facing pages she could read an Alfonsina Storni prose poem about golf (and female despair) and poems by Ricardo Gutiérrez on the serenity of women, Héctor Pedro Blomberg on *Amalia*, and Horacio Rega Molina on "la mujer," assuring the reader that only for her do men "desire life." Finally, perhaps after noticing with appreciation the elegant layout of the magazine, with its curlicued cursive titles and page frames, the feminine reader could peruse at leisure equally elegant ink-drawing advertisements for rugs, perfume, clothing, gas appliances, Studebaker cars, medicine, corsets, crystal, cooking oil, linen, jewelry, furniture, and Standard bathroom fixtures.

*Plus Ultra* was in its tenth year when it published this issue; it was founded in 1916, the same year of the first national election in which there was universal male suffrage (for Argentine citizens, not immigrant males), the election ending the oligarchy's longtime overt control of government and bringing to power the more middle-class Radical Party. Not surprisingly, the images of the Argentine woman that graced the inaugural pages of 1916 are not the same as those of 1926. In the second decade of the century, from the 1910 Centenario onward, the national print media conveyed the intensity and headiness of social change—from the sense of innovation created by political change at the national level and the spread of new cultural forms such as cinema, to the sense of danger associated with labor and feminist struggles and the sense of despair produced by World War I. Ten years later, in the mid-1920s, the pace of change was different. Though the problems of urbanization and modernization were no less pressing and no less serious, *Plus Ultra* carefully eschewed *all* portrayal of conflictive social change in its 1926 special issue on women. Though their photographs are much smaller, the feminists and the intellectuals, who had a great deal to say about the social problems of the moment, coexist in these pages in decorous harmony with the ladies of society. In the year Argentine women gained their civil rights,[1] after much legislative debate and after decades of street agitation, *Plus Ultra* attempted to set a tone minimizing any imminent social changes that civil rights for women might portend. Political rights (and possibly votes for the socialists) and seemingly anarchist morals (divorce, sexual liberation, and the like) were still threatening the horizon. But the differences between the 1916 and 1926 issues of *Plus Ultra* are not only those of the representation of political or sociological change. In ten years the magazine's visual preoccupations had changed. In 1916, *Plus Ultra* and *Caras y Caretas* were much taken with the "new urban woman" and with a new photographic image, the female film star portrait. In 1926, significantly, there are no female film stars in *Plus Ultra*'s homage to Argentine women, but the photographic portraiture of the elegant young aristocracy is, in every shadow and highlight, read against film star modernity even as these stars' "exquisite femininity" is rejected.

What *Plus Ultra* registered in 1926 by its attempted omission of filmic images of Argentine women was an ongoing modernization of femininity. Postcentennial Argentine society had perceived itself to be a modernizing nation on its way to a preeminent position in the twentieth-century world economy, and in terms of the gender system this would have required, at the very least, a female labor force, intelligentsia, and aristocracy equal to Argentina's "modern times." Yet the elite, as well as portions of other classes, generally also desired the maintenance of a hierarchal gender system in which women would never be truly coequal with men, and certainly not coequal as national political figures. Modern times, yes, but controversial new women, no; what were needed were examples of a mindful modern woman. Thus, from the end of the nineteenth century onward, the presence of women in factory and labor struggles, the entrance of women into the professions, and the incursion of feminism into the public sphere together foretold a modern but less obedient Argentine woman. Yet at the same time a new discursive nexus was created: a "position available" for a modern woman who still embodied "eternal" (i.e., nineteenth-century) femininity.

With the introduction of film and its rapid institutionalization in national life, Argentina as a national society did gain exactly this woman, an idealized referent (or nexus of meanings) for its struggling *real* "new urban women": the female film star was public but not political, daring without threatening the social order, national yet international. She was also beautiful, far distanced from any "ugliness" of everyday life, and therefore "attractive" to all sectors and classes of a national audience. To the extent the silent screen star's image synthesized modernity and ideals of femininity, it was imitated and circulated throughout the mass media; but to the extent this image synthesized modernity and democratic or feminist ideals, it did not reach the national press. In *Caras y Caretas* and *Plus Ultra*, the film star image has an interesting trajectory: it is an image embraced in 1916, fervently displayed in 1919, and, in the latter magazine's case, eschewed in 1926. It is a trajectory that has much to tell us about related changes in the gender system and the nation as a State in these ten years.

To review this "gender modernization" process it would be best to return to 1916, to look more closely at how *Plus Ultra* presented women and femininity in its opening pages. *Plus Ultra*'s first issue in March, 1916, included a glossy page of three sonnets framed by three photographs of elegant women, women with heads slightly inclined, eyes glancing upward and the slightest of smiles. The title across the top reads, "The Argentine Woman, Homage of the Poet." The first two stanzas of the top sonnet, by Eugenio Díaz Romero, read:

> Blanca carne de lirio, *ojos ígneos de estrella*
> En que arden fulgurantes las llamas de amor;
> Boca fina y purpúrea donde la gracia sella
> Su encanto capitoso de roja rosa en flor.
>
> La sangre de las razas más nobles puso en ella
> Sus rasgos dominantes de belleza y valor
> Ungiéndola en el mundo mirífica doncella,
> Promesa del destino, *Varona en Dolor.*
>
> [Lily-white skin, *volcanic eyes of a star*
> in which burn resplendent the flames of love.
> A dark and fine mouth where grace seals
> the enchantment of a flowering pink rose.

> The blood of the most noble races are in her.
> Her dominant characteristics are beauty and valor,
> anointing her a surprising woman in this world,
> A Promise of Destiny, *Masculine in Suffering*. (emphasis mine)]

It is an interesting combination: in 1916 this all-inclusive "Argentine Woman" has the volcanic (igneous) eyes of a star—surely these must be smoldering, earthly, Hollywood volcanos—and is almost male in her ability to bear pain or sorrow—the unusual word "varona" is "*varón*" (male) made feminine by adding an *a*. She is physically very feminine, having all the appropriate (and then standard) poetic features of the perfect criolla: lily-white skin, a fine roselike mouth. She is a perfect woman in terms of her class, having the requisite oligarchic grace and nobility beyond beauty. She is more sensual than a nineteenth-century symbolic ideal of woman: the white flesh is swiftly juxtaposed to burning love in the first two lines, and thus it is worldly love the poet describes (taking advantage of the relatively recent *modernista* reintroduction of explicit sensuality into Latin American poetry). But she has inherited from "the most noble races" (i.e., nonimmigrant/upper-class stock) a masculine strength that makes of her femininity a promise for the future, a modern woman. Her literary foremothers, the Amalias of the previous century, had themselves a near masculine strength in the face of adversity, but their strength did not have the same suggestion of gendered independence to it: here in 1916 to juxtapose "Varona en Dolor" with "Promesa del Destino" is to suggest, beyond an established feminine endurance and suffering, a stalwart and *independent* modern woman.

In fact, the real "promise of Argentine destiny" was less likely to be a "surprising woman." The director of the Commission of the Third National Census in 1914 wrote (as Catalina H. Wainerman and Marysa Navarro noted in their original study):

> Hoy la mujer presta servicios en la municipalidad, en el correo, en la aduana, en el telégrafo y en diversas reparticiones públicas. Tiene, además, casi exclusivamente a su cargo el servicio de los teléfonos. Todo este censo fue también compilado por manos femininas. Aparte de su misión de maestra, para la que se encuentra admirablemente preparada, la mujer se abre cada día más camino en las industrias, en el comercio, en las profesiones. El empleo de dactilógrafa está casi reservado para la mujer. . . . Existen mujeres médicas, masajistas, traductoras, abogadas, doctoras en letras, contadoras, notarias, etc.[2]

> [Today women work for the city, the post office, customs, the telegraph company and in diverse public areas. The telephone service is almost exclusively their responsibility. This whole census was compiled by feminine hands. Beyond their mission as teachers, for which they are admirably prepared, women are each day making progress in industry, commerce, the professions. The job of typist is almost reserved for her. . . . There are women doctors, masseuses, translators, lawyers, professors, accountants, notaries, etc.]

What these women endured, and what their presence in the labor force promised, was indeed a change in gender roles: what was *varona* would come to be merely modern.

There are four topics interwoven in the stanzas of the poem cited above: nationality—Argentine, of course; film stars—passionate, of course; beauty—gendered, of course; and health—in terms of vigor and strength, which, as will be shown, was not a matter of course. The emphasis on health subtly underlies much of the poem: in the final stanzas, in fine poetic form, this exemplary Argentine woman's voice is associated with purity of the sea, and "her brow like a temple breathes hope." The weave of these four topics creates (or draws upon) a kind of politicized or civic sexuality—a strong, active, passionate new woman in homology with a vital nation, a "pure breath of hope"—but the repertoire of meanings against which the topic of health was read would have created a conflicted, even anguished view of the "health" of the nation and of modern womanhood. Not surprisingly, these four topics recur constantly in the pages of *Plus Ultra* and *Caras y Caretas* all the way through to 1926, so it is important to break them down and look at each closely, to find the rub of anxiety in this weave.

The most complex repertoire of meanings for these topics is the gender system itself: the topics of film stars and beauty depend directly upon the specific gender system in place at the time. By 1916, when this poem was published, the gender system of Argentina was under visible attack by the Argentine feminist community and visible stress by the changes of class structure brought about by immigration.[3] Strikes of women workers were part of the closure of the nineteenth century, from the domestics' strike of 1888 to the women factory workers' strikes of the early years of the twentieth century. The activism of feminist leadership also dates from the turn of the century. For example, Dr. Cecilia Grierson, Argentina's first woman doctor, attended the 1899 Second International Women's Congress in London and established an affiliate organization upon her return; Adela, Fenia, and Mariana Chertkoff and Raquel Camaña, among others, founded the Centro Feminista Socialista in 1901; Julieta Lanteri-Renshaw's *La mujer librepensadora* was published in 1908; Gabriela Laperrière de Coni, a tireless reformer, presented for the Centro Feminista Socialista the law protecting women and children workers in 1903 (which was passed in 1907).

Indeed, the list of feminist organizers and activities from 1900 to 1926 is quite extensive. According to sociologist María del Carmen Feijoó by 1910, the *centenario*, feminism in Argentina had two clearly defined tendencies: one, more militant, that worked for improved work conditions, the vote, and the liberation of women (from what would now be called patriarchy), and the other, more cautious, that worked for an improved feminine role but not a change in female social status. Noting that these tendencies were part of the movement from the very beginning, she cites feminist organizer Carolina de Muzzili:

Yo llamo feminismo de diletantes a aquel que sólo se preocupa por la emancipación de las mujeres intelectuales. . . . Es hora de que el feminismo "spor-
tivo" deje paso a aquel verdadero feminismo que debe encuadrarse en la
lucha de clases.[4]

[I call dilettante feminism that which is only preoccupied with the emancipation of women intellectuals. . . . It is time that "sportive" feminism give way to
the true feminism that joins in class struggle.]

Feijoó also observes that while the First International Feminist Congress,
organized by the Association of University Women, proposed a week before
the 1910 Centenario celebration a factory reform law called "la ley de la
silla" (which was finally passed in 1919), the leading newspaper *La Nación*
gave the nod of approval to a less militant women's gathering, the Patriotic
Congress and Centennial Exhibition, for its measured good sense. Fortunately, in a demonstration of a lack of "good sense," in 1919 an international delegation of feminists attended the plenary session of the League of
Nations, and then in 1920 women in the United States gained the vote. The
impact of these gains was felt in the Argentine feminist community, if not in
Argentina at large.

In response to the women workers, the feminist, socialist, and anarchist
female organizers, the women intellectuals, the philanthropic-minded sector
of upper-class women, and, finally, the numbers of immigrant women moving into the work force (and increasingly, as the 1914 census shows, into the
service sector), the gender system necessarily reworked itself in the first two
decades of the century into a configuration that could tolerate to a certain
extent the lessening of overt male authority. Though motherhood and a
homebound life might still be the ideal and every thread of social life steeped
in patriarchal gender relations, it was time for a new patriarchal configuration. Shop girls rode the streetcar to work, and women ran for office, even if
their candidacy was only symbolic; thus women in public life were no longer
the equivalent of "public women" (i.e., prostitutes or "fallen" women). The
gender system reconfigured the public/private split in Argentine patriarchy
and simultaneously reworked the concept of feminine beauty. Public beauty
was now film beauty: a certain tilt of the head, a slightly mischievous expression in the eyes, a worldliness, a determination of spirit, a seductive
smile, a framed face that was more than photographic, a framed human
image out of *moving*, modern time. This beauty, the female film star, had in
Argentina much the same history as her counterparts in other national film
industries.

The first public film showings of the Lumière brothers in France was in
December, 1885; the first film showing in Argentina was six months later, in
July, 1886, and was organized by Eustaquio Pellicer, who later founded *Caras
y Caretas*.[5] Eugenio Py and Max Glucksmann initiated much of the film experi-
mentation, and soon thereafter Mario Gallo and José A. Ferreyra distin-

guished themselves as national film directors. In 1910, the Centenario was celebrated with numerous newsreels and documentaries, and the first full-length feature was shown, the historical film *El fusilamiento de Dorrego*. Among the many films of the day were *Amalia* and *Nobleza gaucha*, shown in 1914 and 1915 respectively, the latter of which was a great commercial success. European and American films were imported and viewed with great interest, but it was the female film star who, in terms of the cultural representation of film, eventually overshadowed in the mass print media all other aspects of film culture. In the second issue of *Plus Ultra* (May, 1916), there is a full-page commentary on the police-suspense movie *La mano que aprieta*, heralded as an international success, shown by "la casa Max Glucksmann, en los cines Petit Palace y Palace Theatre." In the upper right corner is a photograph of a menacing hand; just below it and in the left lower corner are two smaller shots of the actors, Percy Bennet and Walter Jameson. But in the center of the page, drawing the reader's eye, is a high-contrast photo of actress Elaine Dodge: her face framed by a dark beret, a dark bow at her neck, and a half-smile on her lips, she is glancing slightly upward, not at the menacing hand, but past it to that point in some other world that only film stars can see.

It is not only historical hindsight that reveals the importance of this new but unattainable public beauty; it was a matter of contemporary comment. In 1919 *Caras y Caretas* initiated a column of film criticism titled "Los estrenos cinematográficos." It is one of the footnotes of literary history that the author of this column, generally credited with being Argentina's first film critic, was none other than writer Horacio Quiroga. In his very first column, December 6, 1919, under the interesting signature "the Husband of Dorothy Phillips," Quiroga asked whether the beauty of the film stars was the source of their particular "encanto," observing at the same time that all around the men of Buenos Aires were women of inexpressible beauty. He wrote:

> ¿Por qué, pues, la profunda ola de amor por las estrellas mudas en que se ahoga y continúa ahogándose el alma masculina de las salas del cine?
> Por esto, y he aquí la razón: porque la hermosa chica que toma el tranvía se lleva con ella el *tiempo* que hubiéramos necesitado para adorarla. . . . Pero la estrella de cine nos entrega sostenidamente su encanto, nos tiende sin tasa de tiempo cuanto en ella es turbador: ojos, boca, frescura, sensibilidad arrobada y arranque pasional. Es nuestra, podemos admirarla, absorberla cuarenta y cinco minutos continuos . . .

> [Why, then, this profound wave of love for the silent stars in which the masculine soul drowns and continues being drowned in the movie theaters?
> Because—and here is the reason—because the beautiful girl who takes the streetcar carries away with her the *time* we would have needed to adore her. . . . But the film star gives over to us her sustained attraction, she provides

without measure of time all that in her is disturbing: eyes, mouth, freshness, enrapturing sensibility, passionate impulses. She is ours, we can admire her, absorb her forty-five minutes continuous . . . ]

Quiroga ends with a wry comment, that were any Argentine woman to afford a masculine admirer such full contemplation he would know happiness far sooner than in any movie theater. Still, the import of his comments is that there now circulated in Argentine culture an imaginary woman who was beyond real women, but who was also the standard to which real women were compared. Indeed, nearly every week in *Caras y Caretas* in 1919 there was a page for the column "Teatro del silencio," which featured, for example, "beautiful" backlit studio shots of Mary Pickford, Alice Brady, Marion Davies, Constance Talmadge, or Billy Burke,[6] accompanied by paragraph-length commentary on their lives and films. However, Quiroga notes the factor of time, seeing the irony that it is the *moving* image that is more available to the observer than people themselves in the hustle and bustle of the modern city. The measure of time has become such that it is an event (still) seemingly outside the routine of everyday life, a film, that affords a modern aesthetic of gender its development. That event, in that it is repeated in film theaters all over the city and around the world, becomes a national cultural referent in an international context. The feminine face Quiroga admires in the darkened theater now bears on much more than the question of beauty he raised.

By 1919 the pages of both magazines reveal the four topics of nationality, film stars, beauty, and health to have a more complex weave, to have in fact a new double twist: the association of feminism and State crisis. Politically the year is significant: January marks the Semana Trágica, the week in which an ongoing metallurgic workers' strike came to be a citywide, violent street confrontation between workers, police, and an oligarchic paramilitary, and the week in which an anti-Semitic, post-Russian Revolution hysteria was released. The play of meanings on any historical conjuncture can never be reduced to one master set of oppositions, but it is possible to detect that the anxieties of 1919 circulated around and through a sense of an opposition between foreign dangers and native strengths. In January of 1919 this sense of the foreign and the national was particularly acute. It was the upper-class, "native Argentine" fear of the foreign—specifically, an exaggerated idea of the potential for a Bolshevik or Maximalist revolution, in combination with an anti-Semitic xenophobia—that produced the attack on the Russian Jewish communities by upper-class vigilante groups. The violence began with a sudden hour-long violent confrontation on January 7 at the Vasena factory between uniformed guards and a group of workers and their wives and children. Four or five were killed and twenty to forty wounded. The metallurgic workers called a work stoppage for January 9, and other unions responded.

On the afternoon of the 9th, an estimated 200,000 joined the funeral cortege for the victims of the shooting two days before. Near the cemetery, they were fired upon, and rioting broke out. The city in effect shut down, and the Radical government, facing the prospect of its own downfall due to charges of inaction, decided on the tenth to deploy the army alongside the police against the workers and any other "suspicious" people in the streets.[7] Sporadic violence and "peace negotiations" continued until the fifteenth. Rumors circulated in the national and international press that the violence had been instigated by a Bolshevik cell in Buenos Aires.

The *Caras y Caretas* treatment of the week is revealing as to the political climate and the discourses in circulation. The cover photograph of the January 18 issue is of the team of doctors and medical assistants who treated the victims, and our entrance into the story is therefore focused on questions of health and medical emergencies. The story of the week's events is told in some thirty pages of photographs (and a few drawings), four to eight on a double page, beginning with a shot setting the scene of the street corner where the violence broke out and a dramatic shot of the bullet holes in the wall of the house where one of the victims died. In fact, the entire photoessay has the narrative structure of a film documentary. On the first double page, the upper right quadrant is a shot of the caskets and dark-suited workers in the funeral cortege. The lower right quadrant seems a redundant shot, showing more dark-suited workers; but the caption reads, "Workers who accompanied the funeral cortege and a group of women of the 'Feminist Committee.'" The figures in the photos are small, but it can be seen that two women are carrying banners or fronds; behind them, at a distance, are marching arm-in-arm rows of women in light-colored dresses. There are few other pictures of women in the photographic narration of events, and what is not said in the various captions leaves the impression that the week was the result principally of worker violence and lower-class aggression. Near the end of this photoessay, after shots of the police dispersing suspicious groups and army patrols on duty, again in the bottom right corner, is a small shot of armed civilians—men in suits with boater hats and two policemen with rifles—with the caption, "Commissions of young men belonging to the 'Patriotic Committee of Youth' covering the streets of the city in automobile with the mission of maintaining order." It seems that, like the feminists of the first pages, these young men, who no doubt joined the soon-to-be-formed Patriotic League (part of what David Rock has characterized as "the crystallization of a new Right with authoritarian and proto-fascist tendencies"[8]), did not need comment further than photographic portrayal. This is the discursive range of danger: foreign-influenced feminists and workers in the streets moments before violent disorder versus armed native-born, higher-class men in the streets maintaining order.

The intensity of this danger is signaled metonymically by a short story included in the same *Caras y Caretas* issue. The story, by Conrad Casenave, is "De la mente enferma" [from the unsound mind]. It is the story of a medical student who, on duty late one night in the morgue, sees on the table before him two cadavers, a young man and woman who have committed suicide together and are locked in a final gruesome embrace.[9] He observes that the dead woman is "celestialmente bella" [celestially beautiful] and wonders, "¿Actuaría el amor sobre los cuerpos aun más allá de la muerte misma?" [would love act upon bodies after death itself?]. So he opens up the bodies to examine both hearts and brains. Finding no evidence for his theory, he angrily throws her heart onto the table, where it comes in contact with her lover's heart. The two seem then to beat together. The story ends with the medical student terrified and haunted by his discovery. Though the girl in the story is not a film star, her beauty is at least "celestial." Both the characters of the suicide pact and the medical student have lived agitated, driven lives and have been antisocial in their acts. Juxtaposed to the photoessay of the violence of the Semana Trágica, the physical destruction of the two cadavers in the story becomes a macabre intensification of recent events. The two stories are similar: the rational mind and the rational society cannot tolerate young women committing suicide for love (her death is foregrounded in the story as somehow more important than her lover's), and thus a surgical intervention and investigation is required; the rational and orderly society cannot tolerate mass "antisocial behavior," and thus a police intervention and an investigation of "foreign agents" is required. Gender and national identity, filmic beauty and social health are once again recombinant.

*Plus Ultra*, in its glossy pages, never dealt with politics, but what it did run after the Semana Trágica suggested another kind of danger. In January, it ran material most likely prepared before the violence, including an essay by Quiroga on women's smiles. In February, after double-page wide-angle photos of the summer vacationers on the boardwalk at the seaside resort Mar del Plata, it included a column titled "Feminismo norteamericano," headed by a photo of two women in dull dress—long, masculine jackets and matching long skirts of a heavy material, plain, full-brimmed hats—the uniform of the National Army of Women, mentioned in the article in admiring tones for having aided the male war effort. The two women, president and vice-president of the organization, are said to have "worked without rest to achieve such a *beautiful* result" (emphasis mine). In the same issue is a small, bottom-corner article by Argentine feminist leader Elvira Rawson de Dellepiane on women's rights, both civil and political. In April, the ongoing discursive juxtaposition of meanings around feminism, politics, and beauty becomes all too transparent. There is a page divided between upper and lower half: the upper half bears the title "Women Farmers" and a photo of five American women sitting on a wagon; the bottom half is filled by an article giving "practical advice to conserve beauty." The women farmers are wearing broad-

brimmed hats, a makeshift sort of working uniform with heavy-material
bloomer-pants, dark stockings, and boots. The five are sitting in a somewhat
relaxed fashion, hands folded, legs hanging over the side of the wagon. Two
have ankles crossed, two have knees and feet together, and the woman in the
middle sits with her knees apart, a jolly smile on her face, with just a hint that
at any moment she might start swinging her legs. The "frescura" [freshness]
of these healthy women would not have enraptured Quiroga. Though theirs
is the story of a 1918 agricultural prize for having set a women's record for
number of acres cultivated, the beauty article below their picture suggests
that they are ugly, or at least not working to conserve their femininity, and
their frumpy dress and "masculine" activity aligns them with the army-
feminists of the previous issue. In the next issue, July, the four topics explicitly converge. The title above the photograph of an American woman farmer
reads, "Las mujeres en el arado" [women under the yoke]. The column beside it explains that the "bitter title of the Italian film here is an appropriate
commentary on the picture," which shows again a healthy, smiling American
woman in odd dress harnessed to a plow, that the woman took up farm work
as part of the war effort, and that her efforts "redeem her enslaved sisters,"
who will now escape the yoke of male tyranny. However, the family group in
the background was caught in the photograph staring unsmilingly at the
woman, as if her actions were improper and deserving of censure. Despite the
magazine's brief words of support for feminism, there is a sense that all this
gender change is dangerous and undermines society.

The overall implication of these months of *Plus Ultra* is that on the negative list of social matters are American, feminist, ugly, antifamily, mule-
healthy women who will never be film stars. On the positive side might be, as
a December issue of *Caras y Caretas* suggests, that Argentine feminist leaders
are different from the Americans. A commentary with small, formal photos of
Elvira Rawson de Dellepiane and Alicia Moreau states that the former, the
president of the Asociación Pro Derechos de la Mujer, "is of unimpeachable
moral authority and a person against whom the detractors of feminism cannot argue because she offers her double condition as wife and mother, who
directs and cares for her 'home' [the word 'home' is in English] that is for
her, like for other women, the center and altar of the most generous and
elevated sentiments." The statement is followed by reproductions of hand-
written cards by the two women, seeming notes of decorum.

To the 1919 enchantments of the star of the "teatro del silencio," the
alleged refined sentiments of Argentine feminist leaders, the dangers of drab,
coarse American feminism, the alleged foreign-inspired violence, and the just
national order, one further discursive referent concerning health must be
added. A series of advertisements for an admirably all-purpose medicine
called Iperbiotina Malesci ran in both *Plus Ultra* and *Caras y Caretas* in the
ten-year period 1916–1926. In *Plus Ultra*'s first year, Iperbiotina Malesci had

a new full-page advertisement for each issue. The first issue, for example, showed two photos, a cinematic side-shot of a mother with a rose, which was placed beneath a shot of her sweetly posed daughter and son; the caption read, "La felicidad más grande de la mujer, consiste en saber que su hogar está libre de padecimientos físicos, y que, tanto ella misma, como cuantos la rodean, están sanos" [a woman's greatest happiness is knowing that her home is free of physical suffering, and that she herself, as well as those around her, are healthy]. Though an exhortation to the maintenance of the traditional home, the caption suggests a brisk urban household run by a modern woman. Other Malesci ads in this year spoke more abstractly of Samson-like strength, prolonged youth, and "Health, Beauty, Happiness"; but by 1919, the need for Iperbiotina Malesci was made more explicit. In this year it explicitly cured women of nervous attacks and "ailments peculiar to the feminine sex," and men of "character-souring body pains." This was modern urban life with modern anxieties—like State crises and shootings in the streets. In the pages of *Plus Ultra* and *Caras y Caretas* in 1919 the images of modern life brought into play specific oppositions. Some were internal to the nation: feminine physical weakness versus native criollo strength, or a cautious, home-based health versus modern urban hysteria. Others were based on the opposition between national positivity and foreign threat: delicate Argentine feminine beauty versus hearty American feminine health, decorous Argentine feminism versus unbounded international feminism, native security versus foreign destruction. Interestingly, in all these oppositions, even in the dangerous discursive mixes of the Semana Trágica, film beauty is still positive. By 1926, even that would change.

In a 1926 issue of *Caras y Caretas* there is a story titled "Retrato de mujer"; one of its striking lines reads, "Amar y confiar son palabras antagónicas en esta triste etapa de los mundos" [love and confidence are antagonic words in this sad stage of the worlds]. This gendered angst, however, seems less important when compared to the anxieties to which Iperbiotina Malesci must address itself in 1926:

> Un militar sin energías, sin voluntad y sin el arma que defiende su autoridad, está al igual que cualquier ciudadano que dejó caer su organismo en una pobreza absoluta de salud, energía y vigor. Es prudente entonces armarse contra todos los males que ataquen los sistemas del cuerpo humano.

> [A military man without energy, without will, and without the weapon that defends his authority is in exactly the same circumstances as any citizen who lets his organism lapse into an absolute poverty of health, energy, and vigor. It is prudent then to arm oneself against all of the evils that attack the systems of the human body.]

The copy runs next to an ink sketch of a military figure—not a modern general, but wild-eyed, disheveled *prócer*, a father of the Independence. The first coup of the twentieth century was four years away, but the anxiety of an anemic body politic and a depleted military unable to defend its authority was already circulating in Argentine society.

Though the military now circulated in the modern anxieties, the female stars of silent film no longer had even a page dedicated to them in each issue—perhaps because silent film was now at its height. The novelty of cinematic narration—its new juxtaposition of images—had been transformed into the familiar. It is an interesting historical note that D. W. Griffith's *Intolerance* (1916), a narratively complex film with four parallel historical plots and many new cinematic techniques that would later become standard, played in Buenos Aires in the turbulent year of 1919. The cinematically most complex film of the silent era—a film whose style can be seen as the document of a society's "modern" capacity to handle radical narrative juxtaposition—played at the same moment as a critical internal realignment of the national social formation. By 1926, a time of an emergent state (re)-structuration, images of female film stars in *Caras y Caretas* were reduced, literally, to small photos in advertisements for beauty products: Renee Adoree and Kathleen Key, for example, endorsed the ever-present Polvo Graseoso Leichner; Virginia Valli endorsed Crema Dental Kolynos (on a page opposite an ad for a Hocking Valley corn-shelling machine). There were, however, many more of the cinematic-style photoessays, in the form of "crime pages" with titles like "Drama pasional" and "Suicidio espectacular," and formulaic plots of the cinema had their repercussions in everyday life, as the following *Caras y Caretas* filler shows:

> ¡SIGUEN LOS FILMS!
> . . . Como en pleno Far-West . . . en Buenos Aires nos está tocando una película que, según parece, va a tener numerosas partes. Los aficionados al crimen espectacular, a los robos vistosos, ingeniosos y sangrientos, deben estar encantados. . . . No así las víctimas inocentes y sus familiares, que pagan tan caro el espectáculo. Mas reciente parte de la película ha tenido un defecto: la falta total de autoridades policiales en San Martín.

> [THEY'RE FOLLOWING THE FILMS!
> . . . Like in the Westerns . . . in Buenos Aires we have a film that, it seems, will have various parts. The fans of spectacular crime, with brilliant, ingenious, bloody robberies, must be overjoyed. . . . Not so the innocent victims and their relatives, who are paying a lot for the show. But recently the film has had a defect: the total absence of police in San Martín.]

The film metaphor to explain city violence indicates that film narrative had become a commonplace. Once films had become unremarkable activities of everyday life and minor stars were doing commercial endorsements, the distance between citizen and star lessened, save for those few Hollywood idols whose image would exceed earthbound humanity. These still-celestial

women from time to time would grace the pages of the newer women's magazines, but they were not promoted with the same intensity as a desirable
feminine standard as in 1919.

However, changes in kinds of mass publications and the increasing institutionalization of film culture do not explain what happened to the film
star in the 1926 special issue of *Plus Ultra*. In this issue, the silent screen film
beauty was eschewed: by 1926 her class status was too ambiguous, her sexuality too obvious, her internationalism questionable. She did get a group re-
placement: "La aristocracia porteña." However, every studio photo of the
upper-class women employed a standard photo-manual pose with flat light-
ing, and, ironically, this anachronistic display of the beauty and the silk
flapper dresses of the "cream" of Argentine society only serves to make it
seem as if these women were trying to exceed filmic beauty. The women's
expressions are more reserved than those of their Hollywood sisters, their
body language stiffer, their gowns perhaps more expensive, but they are completely modern women. Though their photos are not artistically "beautiful"
(and are militantly lacking in photographic technique), these women's gaze
assumes an admiring observer who will be able to distinguish them as both
similar to and *better than* the film star. *Their* modernized femininity no longer
needs the stellar agent of the first years of transition:

> *Plus Ultra* que siempre consagró sus mejores páginas a las manifestaciones
> de la exquista feminidad nacional desea ahora rendir entusiasta homenaje a la
> mujer argentina, a su belleza, a sus virtudes, a sus trabajos. Las madres y las
> esposas contribuyeron, desde la gestación de la libertad, al engrandecimiento
> del país. . . . Por la Fe, por el amor feminino, se intensificó la cultura. A esa
> constancia en el esfuerzo femenil dedicamos hoy el presente número.
>
> [*Plus Ultra*, which has always dedicated its best pages to the declarations of
> [our] exquisite national femininity, wishes now to render an enthusiastic hom-
> age to the Argentine woman—to her beauty, her virtue, her work. Mothers and
> wives have contributed since the gestation of liberty to the greatness of our
> country. . . . Faith and womanly love have intensified [our] culture. To this
> constancy of feminine effort, we dedicate this special issue.]

Exquisite national femininity is now everything but openly cinematic: it is to
be modern/traditional, no longer changing and rushing forward like the shop
girls on the streetcar or the provocative ladies of silent screen. Even the layout of the issue is static, as if a denial of the movement, through a denial of
the photoessay form, would stay the social changes wrought by modernity.

In 1926, the year in which women gained their civil rights in Argentina,
*Plus Ultra* and *Caras y Caretas*, in the discursive mix of the four topics examined here—nationality, film stars, beauty, and health—found the national
more often than the foreign, a modern domestic beauty more often than an
unmindful international femininity, and a disturbing national malaise, a

body politic in need of a conservative tonic. The patterns of changing images of the new urban women in their pages reveal that the representation of gender is intimately tied to that of the State. When all male citizens received the vote in 1916, on the brink of national chaos in 1919, and when women gained their civil rights in 1926, the danger of these changes was each time registered in a discursive remix of gender and State in the mass print media. The moving image of a modernizing femininity flickered in the theaters in these ten years, and women pressed for their civil and political rights. It is clear that by 1926 a gender modernity, which had previously been felt to be in the national interest, was sensed to be a threat by those who served either oligarchy or patriarchy, or both.

It may have been a self-fulfilling prophecy. The cover of the second issue of *Plus Ultra* in 1916 is a shaded line-drawing that looks either traced from or imitative of a photograph. The "camera" sees the Avenida de Mayo entrance to the Plaza del Congress, and the dome of the Congress is visible in the distance. To the left, in the shade of a great tree, is a kiosk with all the newspaper and mass magazines of the day displayed, and passing by the kiosk in the street is a man in what appears to be a motorized buggy. There are a few people entering the plaza—two men, several boys. Dead center is a woman walking toward the Congress. She is in a direct line with the dome, and her shadow lengthens behind her. We see her from the back. Her dress and hat are the dark, practical sort preferred by matrons and feminists. She is striding toward the Congress, past the modern publications, into the sunlight. The left-hand caption reads, "Revelaciones del objetivo"—which can be translated as either "developments from the lens" or "revelations of the objective." The right-hand caption reads, "Aspectos nuevos de cosas conocidas" [new aspects of known things]. In 1916, the real modern woman was walking straight past the images of her modernity and her femininity, into the public space of nationality and politics. Did she have time in 1926 to read *Plus Ultra*'s special issue in homage to Argentine women?

## NOTES

1. Civil rights for women included, for example, the right to enter into contracts without a husband's consent for a married woman and parental authority for a widow. See, for greater detail, Marifran Carlson, *¡Feminismo!: The Women's Movement in Argentina from Its Beginnings to Eva Perón* (Chicago: Academy of Chicago Publishers: 1988), 166.

2. Catalina H. Wainerman and Marysa Navarro, *El trabajo de la mujer en la Argentina: Un análisis preliminar de las ideas dominantes en las primeras décadas del siglo XX*, Cuadernos del CENEP 7 (Buenos Aires: CENEP, 1979), 16.

3. For an overview of feminist history in Argentina, see María del Carmen Feijoó, "Las luchas feministas," *Todo Es Historia* 2, 128 (January 1978): 6–23.

4. Feijóo, "Las luchas feministas," 12–14.

5. For an overview of Argentine film history, see Jorge Miguel Couselo, et al., *Historia del cine argentino* (Buenos Aires: Centro Editor de América Latina, 1984).

6. For the importance of these actresses in film history, see William K. Everson, *American Silent Film* (New York: Oxford University Press, 1978).

7. For a detailed commentary on the events of this week, see Hugo del Campo, "La semana trágica," in *La clase media en poder*, ed. Haydeé Gorostegui de Torres, Historia integral Argentina 6 (Buenos Aires: Centro Editor de América Latina, 1971), 63-84.

8. David Rock, *Argentina 1516–1982: From the Spanish Colonization to the Falklands War* (Berkeley, Los Angeles, London: University of California Press, 1985), 202. See also Sandra D. McGee's articles and book on La Liga Patriótica.

9. The bound edition I consulted placed this story one page before photos of the cadavers from the Semana Trágica; I do not know whether this was the page sequence in the original issue.

# SIX

# Alfonsina Storni: The Tradition of the Feminine Subject

*Marta Morello-Frosch*

translated by

*Michael Bradburn-Ruster*

*The existing monuments form an ideal order among themselves, which is modified by the introduction of the new (the really new) work of art among them.*
T. S. Eliot, *"Tradition and the Individual Talent"*

If we take as our starting point the definition stated in the epigraph, tradition could be categorized as the space wherein a consensus is developed between the works of the past and of the present, a space in which modern readers reformulate and reinterpret—in short, read—what is received.[1] It is from such readings that the transformations that renew and modify the cultural production of the present arise. In this transforming activity the function of reading prevails, anticipating the formulation of a new writing.

Women writers must add to these functions that of making problematic literary past that has been bestowed on them already made by others, one in which their only possible participation has been as passive receivers. Thus, under the weight of an alien and exclusionist tradition, yet molded by that very tradition, they often maintain an ambiguous relationship with this past, which, if they do not in fact acknowledge it as their own, has to a great extent shaped them both socially and culturally. For if on one hand woman has often been identified as the maintainer of tradition, as opposed to man's eminently historical, consciously renovative character, she has had to maintain practices that were not her own. Moreover, she has often been obliged to defend this alien corpus diligently, since the private sphere, recognized as specifically feminine, was governed by essentially traditional norms and customs, a *doxa* affected but little by historical ocurrence. Yet this preassigned function was not always assumed in a passive manner. Ever since Sor Juana Inés de la Cruz, feminine literary production in Latin America demonstrates that women writers have known how to reelaborate tradition, to appropriate its most effective weapons, and often to demonstrate the social and historical arbitrariness of its premises and the imminent obsolescence of many of its configurations.

It should be clarified that any woman writer has an initial advantage when she confronts the tradition, for precisely the reasons mentioned: she does in fact regard the tradition as an alien discourse, as a nonorigin, and for this very reason she can approach it in an iconoclastic manner—ironize it, modify it, deconstruct it in order to expose its imperfect functioning. The question is not, as Roland Barthes might say, that the reader—in this case a woman—has no history, biology, or psychology.[2] Rather, it is that women, precisely as a result of having been marginalized from history and its production, have not developed their subjectivity exclusively in terms of participation in or in relationship to authorized origins.[3] Therefore, having been systematically deinstitutionalized, marginalized, de-authorized, they have a relationship to this tradition-text that differs radically from that of men. It is a discourse of omissions, pressures, and prior denials that can be, and indeed often are, assumed affirmatively, inasmuch as these leave the feminine subject "free of baggage," at liberty to formulate what is her own and to celebrate her difference not as an aesthetic phenomenon—a function sometimes accorded her even by hegemonic masculine discourse[4]—but rather as a project of resistance and realignment. Out of necessity, then, and in reaction to the presumed universality of the tradition, the feminine response will be partial and provisional, will adopt representations of a collective nature[5]—since it will speak for all women, even literary archetypes—and will take stock of the possible approaches or alternatives to proclaimed tradition. This plural and exploratory impulse will also allow the inclusion of diverse forms of difference, giving voice to a multiple succession of voices as opposed to the univocal nature of manifest tradition.

For man to rebel against tradition as well—to de-authorize it while de-authorizing himself in the process—would almost be suicide, for he would thereby deny his identity as a possible follower or inheritor of remote and transmittable origins in order to become different from them. Woman, however, simply becomes herself, asserts her identity, authorizes herself, and assumes her own destiny in separating herself from this tradition, in declaring that it is not and never has been hers.

The woman writer, furthermore, with this break undertakes her long journey toward attaining a genuinely feminine and consciously feminist voice and discourse. In this study, then, we shall refer to the break with a hegemonic tradition, a break we detect in many Latin American women writers of the 1920s. It is not the case that these writers had no identifiable literary precursors—some of whom were mentioned in the new texts—but rather that these precursors had not yet formed an alternative tradition. This is evident in the work of women in the 1920s, with its attempt to question the masculine tradition: to modify, complete, and criticize it. The women writers faced representations of themselves which they did not recognize. In the traditional discourse of the Other the woman writer did not discover "un sujet à aimer,"[6] but rather a distorted, grotesque image of what she felt herself to be. The woman writer, then, had to reconstitute her subjectivity in terms of her own gender and sex, and to do so she gave *her* reading of the received tradition.

As the object of this study we have selected two poems of Alfonsina Storni which belong to the tradition of the love lyric. In them the poet appraises and modifies this genre, which had been rigidly codified as much by literary precept as by literary history, even in its most significant and authorizing association: that conferred by the divine origin of the amorous impulse and the literature that shapes it. We shall contrast two poems that designate traditional archetypes: the Don Juan figure in "Divertidas estancias a Don Juan" and the figure of the "untouched" and hence perfect beloved in "Tú me quieres blanca."[7] In analyzing these two poems we intend to explicate the author's position with regard to both the literary tradition she consciously invokes and her new feminist propositions. The latter are the product of a new and very active reading of the tradition as sociocultural artifact, and the options suggested reveal historical conditions different from the traditional ones, therefore requiring a shift in the discursive boundaries and a redefinition of the spaces thus created. In this way the author seeks to constitute her identity within the boundaries that the culture offers her at a specific moment, and that she identifies as a given present (in "Don Juan") or an attainable future ("Tú me quieres blanca"). Both instances register transformations and change, and testify to the provisional nature of the new discourse at the same time that they question the immovability of the old. In opposition to the fixed concept of tradition, the reformulation insists on this destabilizing process, on the new possibilities ushered in by the change, and especially on a new awareness that results in new identities.

Some of the conditions that make this revision of tradition possible have to do with Storni's life, her personal and social experiences. The relationship between these experiences and the discourse she adopted served to shape both the kind of feminism she articulated and her unique vision of the tradition. It would be fitting, then, to note some of these personal circumstances before analyzing the text.

Certain dramatic circumstances in Storni's private life—in particular her position as an unwed mother and as an immigrant of the poor middle class, and finally her suicide—have been generative keys in many readings of her poetry. Much less studied have been her journalistic, pedagogical, and theatrical works; in short, her public activity during that era.[8]

Storni began to publish at the time the First World War was declared.[9] An abundance of material testifies to her participation in newspapers and the public sphere on behalf of democratic forces, as well as to her work in schools for disadvantaged children.[10] Her activities coincided with workers' movements and proposals for social change in both national and international spheres.[11]

Storni's labor during the 1920s represents the emergence of a class of professional women, of recent immigrant origin, who joined with groups of workers and feminists of the era in search of solutions to the problem of marginality. Like other intellectual women of her age, Storni—a journalist, teacher, actress, and activist writer—exemplifies the labor of this new class—a product, to a large extent, of the *normalista* culture, as she herself remarks: "They come partly from the *normalista* culture: the majority of South American women writers are teachers and, as a result of intellectual ferment, oppose their social milieu more than they serve its traditional forms."[12]

In the title of the first poem we shall analyze, "Divertidas estancias a Don Juan" [amusing stanzas to Don Juan], the great lover is perceived as an object of mockery rather than one who mocks, as tradition has defined him.

> Noctámbulo mochuelo,
> Por fortuna tú estás
> Bien dormido en el suelo
> Y no despertarás.
>
> Si tu sombra se alzara
> Vería a la mujer
> Midiendo con su vara
> Tu aventura de ayer.
>
> La flaca doña Elvira,
> La casta doña Inés,
> Hoy leen a Delmira,
> Y a Stendhal, en francés.
>
> Caballeros sin gloria,
> Sin capa y sin jubón,
> Reaniman tu memoria
> A través de un salón.
>
> No escalan los balcones
> Tras el prudente aviso,
> Para hurtar corazones
> Imitan a Narciso.
>
> Las muchachas leídas
> De este siglo de hervor
> Se mueren aburridas
> Sin un cosechador.
>
> Más que nunca preciosas,
> Oh gran goloso, están.
> Mas no ceden sus rosas.
> No despiertes, don Juan.

> Que no ha parado en vano
> La aventurera luna:
> Hoy tu castigante mano
> No hallaría fortuna.
>
> Y hasta hay alguna artera,
> Juguetona mujer,
> Que toma tu manera
> Y ensaya tu poder.

The first verse continues the belittlement of the figure of the great seducer by calling him "noctámbulo mochuelo" [little night owl], preferring the reference to the predatory but diminutive bird of night, a character from popular proverbs, as opposed to the falcon or hawk of traditional amorous pursuit. If indeed the poem describes to us a dead Don Juan, "bien dormido en el suelo" [fast asleep on the floor], the vision of the great lover recumbent is utterly devoid of the activity and the terror that his condition might arouse. His ghost would see not the great commander, but rather a woman, who judges his adventures with a masculine staff, not as a victim. It is precisely those victims, transformed now by reading—the experience of other discourses—who are no longer subject to an eternal, passive waiting for the lover. The men, too, appear transformed; diminished, "sin gloria, sin capa y sin jubón" [without glory, without cape or doublet], they merely mill about the salons, a narrow field for heroic endeavor, a cramped but appropriate stage for the superficial activities of these narcissistic gallants.

It is important to observe that the women's new experience is reiterated as being a product of reading (they are "muchachas leídas"—well-read girls), which has transformed their behavior: they are waiting for a harvester, but not for Don Juans. Whoever harvests has cultivated; he does not steal roses as Don Juan would do. In vain the seducer raises an angry hand to defend himself, for his previous good fortune has run out. The times have obviously changed; chance is no longer his accomplice in deception, a tactic perhaps befitting the woman who is his cunning ("artera") disciple. This possible reversal of roles is characterized negatively by the adjective "cunning," which defines the seductress as a practitioner of wicked ways and as frivolous ("juguetona," or minx). It is thus a question of discursively reducing the figure of the seducer to that of a recumbent or sleeping trickster who has been outwitted, perhaps chastened, whose example no longer holds sway for vigorous masculine models or for dreaming women. The latter have now transformed themselves, by virtue of reading, into subjects of their own destiny ("no ceden sus rosas"—they do not surrender their roses), even when they choose to become flagrant imitators of Don Juan.

Noteworthy is the fact that in contrast to Don Juan's constant amorous activity, his sudden shifts, his incessant self-indulgence in the pursuit of victims, the poem opposes a conceptual world of reflective women who read, who judge the conduct of the man-seducer, who decide for themselves to whom and in what circumstances they will grant their reward. The reference to roses evokes the traditional bestowal of the reward by the woman to the knight, the fortunate harvester who has previously had to prove himself worthy in jousts or lyrical competitions. Roses, the traditional prize of poetry contests, again show a preference for poetic practice, for the intellect over other forms of activity.

Thus the poem presents Don Juan as an obsolete figure who no longer holds sway in a world of reading women. It is precisely this new occupation, reading, that annuls the possibility that the Don Juans of the salon might meet with luck.

If Storni notes with this poem the depreciation of *donjuanismo*, the aggressive and unbridled masculine erotic impulse, on the other hand she assigns an ambiguous function to the girls who read, who die of boredom ("se mueren de aburridas") in a world where man will be the laggard. In this way she points out a disparity between modern man and the new modern woman. Men equally transformed by new experiences are absent: the only models to appear in the poem are the stale gallants of the salon and a Don Juan fast asleep on the floor. On the other hand, the newly literate women—if through literature they have indeed broadened their frame of reference—could discover dubious liberating models in Stendhal, although perhaps they might well feel represented by Delmira Agustini's poetic discourse.

The position of the poetic voice is an ambiguous one, for if it does in fact cancel one tradition, it proclaims the need for another without defining it, yet notes the signs of its coming into being. Thus the poem accepts and addresses the contradictions, the partial meanings, the mistakes that are part of the process of transformation Storni depicts, of the new relationships between the subject—in this case, women—and the text, suggesting that this is a provisional configuration in which the new components of feminine subjectivity have not yet formed a homogeneous and congruent whole. Nevertheless, the poem bars all possibility of reversal or of binary structure by authenticating the gradual constitution of a new subject, who will be none other than the woman reader. She will not be, like Emma Bovary, a victim of a literary process of becoming unreal. On the contrary, by augmenting the referential capacity of women, reading transforms the nature of her previous and future experiences.

The book *El dulce daño*,[13] contains the poem "Tú me quieres blanca" ("You Want Me to Be White"). If this work has not in fact deserved the attention granted to "Hombre pequeñito" from *Irremediablemente*,[14] the earlier text proposes a rereading of the traditional aims of love poetry, a radical restatement of amorous discourse in terms of a new feminine subjectivity. Hence it is not simply a question of denouncing the "smallness of men" as in

the later poem, but rather of postulating a complete program for the reconstitution of the lover in terms acceptable to the enunciating feminine subject.
She does not protest her condition as victim by denouncing the victimizer,
but rather suggests new conditions for amorous dialogue which take into
account, modify, and annul the models established by cultural tradition.[15]

Starting from a notation of differences, in Michel Foucault's sense,[16] the
beginning of the text recites the definition of woman as opposite inscription of
the masculine:

> Tú me quieres alba,
> Me quieres de espumas,
> Me quieres de nácar.
> Que sea azucena
> Sobre todas, casta.
> De perfume tenue.
> Corola cerrada.
> Ni un rayo de luna
> Filtrado me haya.
> Ni una margarita
> Se diga mi hermana.
> Tú me quieres nívea,
> Tú me quieres blanca,
> Tú me quieres alba.[17]

Here it is a question of emphasizing the oppositional binarity woman/
man, from which a masculine subject has created the other. This strategy is
shared by most love poetry, the genre invoked by Storni's recitative, yet her
poem leaves no doubt that this is an *alien* construction. In speaking of genre,
and in order to establish a base from which the modifications proposed by
the poet may be observed, we have in mind the particular configuration of
terms, themes, modes, and symbols that, according to Northrop Frye,[18] can
give shape to a literary convention, once they have been generalized through
adoption and repetition to the point where they form a body of texts. It
should also be remembered that the issue here is not only one of noting how
the traditions of literary history operate but also, as Jurij Tynjanov
remarks,[19] how the mutations of such systems are formed in relation to cultural and social orders annexed to those systems, since the literary system
changes its relations to other systems that it tries to "translate" or to organize as knowledge.

It seems to us that this is precisely what Storni succeeds in doing with this
initial concept of the feminine as cloister, as a blank page to be inscribed by
the masculine subject.[20] Femininity is thus conceived as a project, a surface
smooth (like that of the blank page) and undifferentiated: sealed petals,
through which even moonbeams have not filtered (let us not forget that the
moon is traditionally associated symbolically or biologically with the femi-

nine). Most especially, femininity is alone, lacking affiliation even with flowers ("Ni una margarita / Se diga mi hermana"—not even a daisy may be called my sister), excluded and exclusory, devoid of all referentiality, closed to all self-significance except for whiteness—a metaphor of absence, color-lessness, lack of meaning. We should note that the syntax itself recreates a fixed object, not actualized, but of a nature absolutely predetermined by the masculine subject: "de espumas," "de nácar," "azucena," "de perfume tenue" [of foam, of nacre, white lily, of a rarefied perfume]. The passivity of this object, already formed but still lacking vital breath, unmarked, is inten-sified by the peculiar syntax of the first two strophes, in which she is a re-ceptacle neither penetrated by rays nor called sister. The dependency of this entity—which is immobile yet already defined with certitude by the enun-ciating subject—is substantiated by the particular verbal construction: ". . . Filtrado me haya. / Ni una margarita / Se diga mi hermana." [. . . has filtered through to me. Not even a daisy may be called my sister]. The passive constructions reiterate the inactivity of the concept "beloved" ("amada").

The dynamic by which the woman is construed as an object and the product of such an objectificaton are here the result of the authorial vision of a masculine subjectivity that invents her, desires her precisely thus: dis-tanced, isolated, untouched. Desirable precisely on account of these lacks, the woman is turned into an object that at once resists possession and refer-entiality and is desired, as the expression "you want me" reiterates. In this way the feminine is converted into a contradictory rhetorical figure, a kind of oxymoron, abandoning everything—including the man—outside of herself and defined by her lack of relation to the rest of the world. While this strophe is articulated around the dominance of the active verb "quieres" [you want], the amorous semantic component disappears from the verb, thereby yielding to the exercise of the will: the authority of the other and his de-eroticized desire. For it is a matter of his desiring something that has nothing, that does nothing, that is scarcely seen, and especially that has no voice of its own. The precarious status of this feminine object, according to the enunciation of the masculine subject, is revealed in its nature—unnamed, empty (in Lacanian terms),[21] unmarked, absent. It is rhetorically marked by the metaphors that compare its attributes to evanescent, perishable natural objects: unopened bud, foam, morning fog, white lily.

In this regard, the feminine image is conceived in terms similar to those of courtly love, in which the elaboration and expression of the poet's desires are structurally dependent upon the absence of the beloved. As one element in the possibility of versification, feminine nature is established in this tradition as eccentric to the poem: absent and inaccessible. In the poem, the poet articulates his desire for the distant other. The tension is based on the lack of correspondence at various levels between the lover and the desired object.

The other—the woman—enters only to share with the subject the same system in the poem, which is thus transformed into an attempt to capture or mediate a form of correspondence that cannot be attained in any other way. For that reason this type of poetry is often characterized by the impulse to recover or reconstruct an object that is absent, illusory, fleeting.[22] It should also be emphasized that this eccentricity of the amorous object is based on a manifest difference.

Storni gives us a new version of how this opposition to the masculine can be converted. For if indeed the first two strophes cited demonstrate the operative rules for the fabrication of the other—of the beloved by the masculine subject—through the invocation of figures that are inert, fixed, or drastically perishable (in other words, not subject to operations of transformation), she will propose another model, moving beyond the "you want me ivory fair" ("tú me quieres alba") of the last verse cited toward another "you" operating in another system:

> Tú que hubiste todas
> Las copas a mano,
> De frutos y mieles
> Los labios morados.
> Tú que en el banquete
> Cubierto de pámpanos
> Dejaste las carnes
> Festejando a Baco.
> Tú que en los jardines
> Negros del engaño
> Vestido de rojo
> Corriste al estrago.
> Tú que el esqueleto
> Conservas intacto
> No sé todavía
> Por cuáles milagros,
> Me pretendes blanca
> (Dios te lo perdone),
> Me pretendes casta
> (Dios te lo perdone),
> ¡Me pretendes alba!

Here Storni resorts precisely to the concept of difference—not to define the "other," however, but to expand a single term ("you") while codifying it in two utterly distinct systems: the "you want me" versus the "you who did." The repeated use of preterites evokes the historical and finite character of his actions and, as if in a negative mirror, contrasts the chromatic history of his gallant adventures (dressed in red, through black gardens of deceit) with her predetermined whiteness of the first strophe. Storni does not privatize the differentiation of gender, but rather exhumes it from a now more obviously

modernist tradition, to account for the sociohistorical character of the creation of gender, especially of the masculine subject (gallant). That "tú" is
converted into the image of the courtier who attends not love feasts but bacchanals in which he indulges the flesh; he is one who consumes honeys and
fruits and who in his ghostly aspect and function has more of the vampire
than the man about him: a totally devitalized vision, a presage of the death of
that skeleton who yearns for her to be white. He appears at the threshold of an
end that has been "miraculously" delayed, in an almost unnatural manner.
The end of the third strophe establishes the extraordinary comparison between this skeletal presence and his aspirations of whiteness and chastity
with regard to her. The bivalence of the phrase "May God forgive you that,"
between ironic and sympathetic, establishes rhetorically the distancing that
has already been conceptually stated. With this ambiguous expression a new
form of amorous *conceptismo* is introduced in which a new rule of exchange
arises: sorrow for the dissipated man? compassion for a ruined image of
being?

The rhetoric allows an isolation of the feminine subject, a distancing that
is not exclusion now but a new positionality that will facilitate a critical,
balanced, reasoned, and leveled vision, from which the new feminine subject
can formulate her model:

> Huye hacia los bosques;
> Vete a la montaña;
> Límpiate la boca;
> Vive en las cabañas;
> Toca con las manos
> La tierra mojada;
> Alimenta el cuerpo
> Con raíz amarga;
> Bebe de las rocas;
> Duerme sobre escarcha;
> Renueva tejidos
> Con salitre y agua;
> Habla con los pájaros
> Y lévate al alba.
> Y cuando las carnes
> Te sean tornadas,
> Y cuando hayas puesto
> En ellas el alma
> Que por las alcobas
> Se quedó enredada,
> Entonces, buen hombre,
> Preténdeme blanca,
> preténdeme nívea,
> preténdeme casta.

Now a new proposal is articulated through an exhortative, almost imperative program, which rhetorically assumes full authorial responsibility on the
part of the poet. In this new function, feminine subjectivity delineates a model for the man, in a project wherein a new form of sensuality is invoked for the
reconstitution of the lover. For if she had in fact been defined by a masculine
discourse that separated her from the cultural and even from the sensual, the
model she suggests locates the lover precisely in the realm that has been
assigned to her: in nature, not in culture.

Yet this new feminine subjectivity rejects the culturally defined binarity of
the two previous strophes, in which sexual difference appears as an obvious
construction codified in the social realm. The poet—the new subject—
abandons the patriarchies of culture and history, and from her own formerly
minimal referentiality, nature, dictates not merely a new program to reconstitute the masculine but also a new meaning of love, giving rise to a sort of
program of antiseduction. For what she proposes for this man who has lost
nearly everything is a future: to restore the body, to establish sensual contact
with the earth and the waters so as to be purified, and, like a modern Laz-
arus, to regain his lost flesh, which can only then be an abode for the soul.
If she was desired as a pure project, a sealed body, he is reconstituted as
a body-dwelling, as a possible receptacle of a soul that is at no point pre-
scribed, as he too is capable of being reborn, but in fresh terms of purity.

This new purity, then, will not be the product of ascetic practices, of isolation, of seclusion. On the contrary, it will result from a dynamic of contact
with the natural, from interaction, from drinking, touching, and being in the
world in the broadest sense, to become connected to ample and open spaces,
not pure yet without vitiations such as the courtly gardens, banquets, and
bedchambers that he once frequented and by which he was defined. Now
man-nature, he can at last aspire to her; he is pure by dint of contact, not
through isolation, nor owing to the purity of the "other" or to her desired
seclusion.

If traditionally he desired her to be without history, uninscribed, he himself, according to the cultural bipolarity of the genre, was the opposite icon.
But the poet refuses to be the inverted mirror of what he signifies, and she
proposes an active regimen of corporal and sensual integration by means of
which his soul will be able to anchor itself. She further refuses to be the
complementary or negative description of his identity, defining him in his
present and past in a direct discourse, with a minimum of totally transparent
cultural metaphors in which he appears as that which is finite, completed.
Thus she destroys the obvious binary construction established in the first two
strophes: she as project, he as the agent who grants life and speech, a little
god who can induce sealed petals to a significant unfolding. In this initial
bipolar premise we encounter a paradigm of a fixed nature, in which the
binary model implies the existence of a primordial masculine element and

a complementary feminine element, in a relation like that of signifier and signified. But the poet rejects as a cultural dogma this logic of binary oppositions and recreates the image of woman as a subject responsible for the production of culture and history, as well as a source of authority and of proposals for change and action in which male-female relationships are no longer predetermined by the separation culture/nature.

If the unfolding and completion of the body and soul are to be the medium of exchange between the sexes, as the image initially evoked suggests, the poet articulates her subjectivity in her desire for an other who is also complete in relation to the natural—repostulated, as we have seen, in terms of contact. Storni thus reverses the traditional conception of man as representative of culture and woman of nature, the latter ready to be provided with history by the man, who is the conqueror of the feminine and the natural. By doing so the poet disposes of the traditional dichotomy of feminine and masculine gender, a dichotomy that historically is based on the centrality and identity of the masculine subjectivity that describes, invents, utters the other, be this woman, slave, or colonized people.[23]

It seems to us that in addition to proposing a new model for the masculine, the latter's inherent character has been feminized. This new masculine "you" is now natural and purified—although not pure—and the poet casts away the specific cultural notation of absence and separation as signs of purity, while reactivating the concept of purification in direct relationship to contact with the environment. In this way she frees herself from obsolete models and puts an end to their dominance by suggesting a model that is not modernist or courtly or protean (of romantic provenance). Furthermore, the poet replaces the idea of completion through enclosure, proposing by contrast the reconstitution of a body emaciated by cultural and amatory excesses. Conceptually and rhetorically, then, she suggests a leveling of positions: she, too, can create models. Yet there is a difference in the operative rules, for while he wants, she exhorts; while he exercises his will upon her, she urges him to exercise it upon himself, and by inciting him to act upon himself she avoids the appropriation of the other which prevails in the original structure. She further suggests a new conception of the verb "pretender" [to solicit, desire, endeavor], which becomes dynamic in the dialectic of the one who appeals, who entreats. In short, we move from an initial system that is socially and culturally static, one to which he alone has access, through a devitalizing, moribund system of deceptive bacchanals toward a system that is open, active. This last phase is supported by the use of verbs—flee, go, feed, drink, sleep—which will be summed up in the synthesis of the restorative project: renew. Only then, renewed, will he be worthy of the qualifier "good man" ("buen hombre"), syntactically paired and conceptually balanced with "Desire me to be white" ("Preténdeme blanca").

Thus Storni suggests a new kind of exchange between equals: two complete beings, without either absences or lacks, who are related to their environment, rooted. In this manner she proposes an equitable exchange that in the poem disposes of obsolete models and an oppressive discursive rhetoric: the binary structure of opposites, in which the masculine subject invented the feminine as a signifier of himself and a locus of meaning for all his relationships of implicit domination. Actually, the poles were never equivalent, but indeed different and very unequal: one formed and the other needing to be formed, one present and one absent in relation to the already constituted speaking subject. For there exists a basic contract in this arrangement wherein the masculine has a central, starring role that is preassigned in the symbolic construction, apart from and excluding the feminine presence, silent and white. The preexistence of the man as the authority who utters, as already formed subjectivity, relegates the feminine to an imaginary territory of foam, mist, seclusion, to a prelinguistic zone, the limbo of subjectivity. In "Tú me quieres blanca" this masculine authorial vision and the tradition that validates it are in the end supplanted by another in which the feminine speaker enters to dictate her conditions, not only to propose a new model for the masculine but also to constitute herself as another subject within the natural.

The discursive realignment is carried out with certain tensions that are rhetorically marked by the phrases "you want me" ("tú me quieres," a factual quotation, a pure present from which he has spoken and has been culturally recognized) and "wish me, ask me" ("preténdeme"), the final point of persuasion, a verbal notation full of potentiality that connotes desire, appeal, entreaty, with the possibility—between comparable beings—but not the certainty that what is requested will be conferred.

That is the heart of the matter: an exchange under new terms, between equals, and in broad daylight. It is a new sort of contract, subverting the model of deceitful seduction as well as the one of the appropriation of assets presumed to belong to no one. Here the figure of Don Juan and that of the untouched beloved exemplify two external and opposite archetypes of traditional discourse which mythify masculine aggression and feminine passivity and, in so doing, authorize them. Alfonsina Storni's critical reading questions—in one case with irony, in the other with an alternative program—the possible modifications of the proposed models. Cautious about assuming a stance of opposition or reversal toward traditional poetic utterance, she designates new discursive spaces wherein a dialogue between equals should be able to take place.

## NOTES

1. For a detailed discussion of the theme of tradition and its manifestations, see Edward Shile, *Tradition* (Chicago: University of Chicago Press, 1981). See also San-

dra Gilbert and Susan Gubar, "Tradition and the Female Talent," in *The Poetics of Gender*, ed. Nancy Miller (New York: Columbia University Press, 1986).

2. Roland Barthes, "The Death of the Author," in *Image-Music-Text*, trans. Stephen Heath (New York: Hill and Wang, 1977), 142–148.

3. For a criticism of Barthes's position see Naomi Schor, *Breaking the Chain: Women, Theory, and French Realist Fiction* (New York: Columbia University Press, 1985), 187.

4. For this theme see Abdul JanMohamed and David Lloyd, "Introduction: Minority Discourse—What Is to Be Done?" in *Cultural Critique* (University of Minnesota) 2, special issue, "The Nature and Context of Minority Discourse" (Fall 1987): 13.

5. See Giles Deleuze and Félix Guattari, *Kafka: Toward a Minority Literature*, trans. Dana Polan (Minneapolis, University of Minnesota Press, 1986), chap. 3.

6. Barthes, "The Death of the Author," in *Image-Music-Text*, trans. Stephen Heath (New York: Hill and Wang, 1977): 142–148.

7. In *Ocre* (1925), compiled in Alfonsina Storni, *Obra poética completa* (Buenos Aires: Editorial Meridion, 1961). All references are to this edition.

8. We are familiar with an unpublished study by Gwen Kirkpatrick on the theme: "Alfonsina Storni: A Return to History" (Paper delivered at the Iberoamerican Congress of Literature, Stanford University, July 1985).

9. Her first book, *La inquietud del rosal*, appeared in 1916.

10. In 1914 she participated in a homage to Belgium, on the occasion of the German invasion.

11. Worthy of mention are the armistice signed in Compiegne in 1918, "the tragic week" ("la semana trágica") of the workers' strike and the ensuing repression at the Vasena Ironworks in Buenos Aires in 1919, the First Congress in Geneva (1920), which brought together workers and management, the Third International in Moscow in 1921, Mussolini's march on Rome in 1922, and the regulation of working conditions for women and children in Argentina in 1923.

12. Gwen Kirkpatrick, "Alfonsina Storni." Kirkpatrick also quotes an illuminating commentary on Storni by Gabriela Mistral: "knowledgeable about life as few are, offering the most apt comments on the most diverse subjects, a very cosmopolitan woman who has been in touch with everything and has integrated all of it."

13. Alfonsina Storni, *El dulce daño* (Buenos Aires: Sociedad Cooperativa Editorial, 1918).

14. Alfonsina Storni, *Irremediablemente* (Buenos Aires: Cooperativa Editorial, 1919). For a complete bibliography see Marta Baralis, *Contribución a la bibliografía de Alfonsina Storni* (Buenos Aires: Fondo Nacional de las Artes, 1964).

15. It is interesting to see a poet receiving and reformulating the very tradition with which she is identified, while not having contributed more extensively to its elaboration. The semantic reformulation of these concepts is what strikes us as most significant about this poem. On first reading it appears to be enunciated within traditional boundaries, and perhaps that is why it has not received much attention.

16. We are thinking here of the manner in which Foucault indicates how difference is enunciated from the sphere of power, in such a way that what is enunciated produces the limits within which difference can be transformed into discursive material. With regard to this see Michel Foucault, *El discurso del poder*, ed. Oscar Terán

17. Quotations of this poem are from Alfonsina Storni, *Obra poética completa* (Buenos Aires: Ediciones Meridion, 1961), 11–12.

18. Northrop Frye, *Anatomy of Criticism* (Princeton, N.J.: Princeton University Press, 1957).

19. Jurij Tynjanov, "On Literary Evolution," in *Readings in Russian Poetics*, ed. Ladislav Matejka and Krystna Pomorska (Cambridge, Mass.: MIT Press, 1971).

20. Here we are employing the concept elaborated by Susan Gubar in "'The Blank Page' and the Issues of Female Creativity," in *Writing and Sexual Difference*, ed. Elizabeth Abel (Chicago: University of Chicago Press, 1982), 73–94.

21. Jacques Lacan, *Feminine Sexuality: J. Lacan and the "École Freudienne,"* ed. and trans. Juliet Mitchell and Jacqueline Rose (New York: W. W. Norton, 1983).

22. We have in mind the conventions of *amour courtois* as exemplified in the poetry of Petrarch and Provençal poets, as well as Renaissance developments as seen in the work of Shakespeare, Sidney, and Spenser.

23. We are employing here a concept adapted from Teresa de Lauretis's proposal in *Alice Doesn't: Feminism, Semiotics, Cinema* (Bloomington: Indiana University Press, 1984), 5. In this work the author distinguishes between the concept "woman"—a fictive product shaped by congruent and dominant discourses in Western culture and construed as "different from man"—"women" as real, historical beings, who have not yet been defined outside of the discourses mentioned, yet whose material existence is undeniable.

# SEVEN

# The Journalism of Alfonsina Storni:
# A New Approach to
# Women's History in Argentina

*Gwen Kirkpatrick*

Few women writers in the history of Latin American letters can match the dramatic appeal of the life and career of Alfonsina Storni. The impact of her poetry and prose and the events of her life have given rise to a legend. With her immigrant beginnings, her early and widely publicized success as a poet, her status as an unwed mother and social rebel, her tragic suicide, and a body of poetry that touches on vital women's issues, her name has become a symbol for generations of Latin American women. The different stages in the creation of a mythic Alfonsina Storni also reflect stages of women's roles in society. Her name has been used in popular songs and has served as the bannerhead for various types of women's magazines in Argentina; her life has been the subject of many studies and of televison and film dramas.

Although the popular appeal of this legend has made famous some of her poetry, other aspects of her life and career have been ignored in the necessary shrinkage involved in mythmaking. As the following study of Storni will show, her activism was not limited to the message of her poetry and to the rebellious gesture. In her career as poet, journalist, teacher, and speaker, Storni exhibited an uncanny eye for social topics directly affecting women's lives and was able to publicize them through her prose writings.

As an inheritor of a vigorous feminist movement in Latin America, Storni used the "women's page" of major daily newspapers and magazines to set forth her own version of feminism. In many respects, her efforts exemplified the rise and decline of women's activism during her lifetime. More traditional than some of her feminist friends and associates, she nonetheless championed many feminist concerns of her day. On a more personal level, we can see her sense of social urgency wane as she received wider critical acclaim and was accepted into influential literary circles.

It is not surprising, given many of the facts of her life and the content of her work, that her public image draws its best-known images from certain aspects of her private life. Like so many women writers before her, Storni defined herself as a prisoner of her gender. Indeed, some of her most famous poems, such as "Hombre pequeñito" ("Little Man") and "Tú me quieres blanca" ("You Want Me White"), forcefully protest and subvert gender hierarchy in a male-dominated society. Her tortured love life (at least as it is presented in her poetry), her status as an unwed mother, her difficulty in supporting herself, and her suicide in 1938, following a long illness, have given dramatic shading to this myth.

Although Storni protested eloquently against the public insistence on her private life, she also collaborated to promote the private myth. While at the same time working for women's rights and other collective sociopolitical concerns, her own stance, as reflected in her poetry, popularized her image as a caged woman, trapped within society's domesticated view of women. Her suicide, for which she wrote a farewell poem to her friends and readers (which she mailed the day of her death to the major newspaper of Buenos Aires), has reinforced this image.

What is needed in the criticism of Storni's work is an effort to integrate both the public and the private versions. Given her symbolic role, it is not surprising that most studies on Storni separate her from the public sphere, choosing to examine her only in her role as an isolated and sentimentalized figure. Therefore, it is important to recognize that Storni was a woman involved in many of the wider social issues of her day and was an exemplary case of the thousands of middle-class women who were moving into the work force and into professional life in the early decades of this century. A study of some of her journalistic writings, heretofore unexamined, can help to move this legendary poet back into the context of her lived history.

One of the challenges of feminist criticism today is to offer new contextual readings of canonized literary figures. Placing their works within their historical and social context can add new dimensions to our understanding of the environment that shaped their literature. The resources of history (in this case, the rapidly developing field of women's history in Latin America) and the study of extraliterary writings offer different perspectives for situating literary works within a social context. Literary biography, often exaggerated in the case of women writers, tends to respond to society's needs to see woman in the private, not the public, sphere. In Spanish American literary history, one has only to remember the seemingly endless speculations concerning the love lives of female writers such as Sor Juana Inés de la Cruz, Delmira Agustini, and Gabriela Mistral in order to become aware of this phenomenon. The following study will examine some of the stereotyped critical evaluations of Storni and her work and will propose an outline of some different methods of evaluating Storni's work and impact. New contextual readings of her work, using Storni's own writings, previous studies and biographies, and recent research in women's history produce a very different image of the legendary Alfonsina Storni. Especially important in this project is the review of Storni's journalistic production, unexamined until now. The project of collecting and analyzing these writings is part of a more extensive study that will connect Storni and other women poets to a wider social matrix.[1]

A look at some of the appraisals by contemporaries of Storni can reveal some of the factors that have shaped the accustomed vision of her and her work. Baldomero Fernández Moreno's "seguidilla" of 1938, published in the influential journal *Nosotros* (to which Storni contributed from 1918 on), offers an emblematic image of the stereotypical groupings so often accorded to women writers. In his affectionate evocation of the three major female poets of the time—Gabriela Mistral, Juana de Ibarbourou, and Storni—he features them in diminutive terms:

> Chile y el Uruguay
>  y la Argentina
>  tienen tres pajaritos
>  de gorja fina.
> Que son Gabriela,
>  y Juana y Alfonsina
>  del mundo y nuestras.[2]
>
> [Chile and Uruguay
>  and Argentina
>  have three little birds
>  of finest warbling.
> They are Gabriela,
>  and Juana and Alfonsina;
>  they belong to the world and to us.]

Given that one of Storni's best-known poems, "Hombre pequeñito" (*Irremediablemente*, 1919), uses the image of the caged bird as a symbol of the woman's cry for greater freedom, Fernández Moreno's use of the diminutive "pajarito" to characterize the three poets is particularly infelicitous.

Jorge Luis Borges is especially harsh in his comments about Storni. On reviewing the work of Nydia Lamarque in 1925, he compares Lamarque to other women writers, dismissing in one blow the young Storni. According to Borges, Lamarque's work has neither "las borrosidades ni la chillonería de comadrita que suele inferirnos la Storni" [the vagueness nor the gossipy shrillness that this Storni tends to offer us].[3] In his section of the prologue to the important anthology *Índice de la nueva poesía americana* (1926), Borges singles out Storni for especially derisive criticism:

De la Storni y de otras personas que han metrificado su tedio de vivir en esta ciudá de calles derechas, sólo diré que el aburrimiento es quizá la única emo-ción impoética . . . y que es también, la que con preferencia ensalzan sus plu-mas. Son rubenistas vergonzantes, miedosos.[4]

[Of Storni and of others who have versified their tedium of living in this city of straight streets, I will only say that boredom is perhaps the only unpoetic emotion . . . and it is also the one with which they choose to sauce their pens. They are shameful and fearful "rubenistas."]

One can only guess why Borges chose Storni for attack amid other poets in a crowded literary scene, although his earlier cited remarks strongly suggest social class divisions.

Eduardo González Lanuza gives another perspective on her work at the time of her death. As a well-known literary journalist for newspapers and magazines such as *Sur* and *La Nación*, a poet, and a member of the avantgarde revolt of the 1920s, González Lanuza evaluates her work in the way that could be called the "canonized" view of Storni. While applauding her valiant struggles and courage within a hostile environment, he finds an "aesthetic impurity" in her work:

> Mujer inteligente y fuerte, no logró realizarse como poeta por no haber sabido superarse a sí misma. En sus mejores poemas aparece con regularidad fatal un elemento de impureza estética, un residuo inorgánico no asimilado, un prosaísmo que se enquista y resta vitalidad a sus versos.[5]

> [An intelligent and strong woman, she could not fulfill herself as a poet because she didn't know how to rise above herself. In her best poems, an element of aesthetic impurity appears with fatal regularity, an inorganic residue, a prosaic quality that invades and robs her verses of vitality.]

González Lanuza attempts to justify his criticism of Storni, and in doing so reveals the exclusivity of his aesthetic principles:

> Su sexo constituía una traba. Aun teniendo genio, las dificultades hubieran sido inmensas. . . . Aceptó el reto, y ése fue su mayor mérito y su irreparable error. Su mérito como mujer que supo tomarse los derechos que se le negaban; su error como poeta, porque la poesía no puede servir para nada ajeno a sus propios fines. Menos aun puede servir de válvula de escape para resentimientos personales: y en cada poema de la primera época de Alfonsina alienta, apenas reprimido, el resentimiento contra el hombre y la obsesión del eterno masculino.[6]

> [Her sex constituted an obstacle. Even while possessing genius, the difficulties would have been immense. . . . She accepted the challenge, and that was her greatest merit and her irreparable error. Her merit as a woman who learned to take for herself the rights denied to her; her error as a poet, because poetry cannot serve anything outside its own ends. It can serve even less as an escape valve for personal resentments: and in every poem of Alfonsina's first stage, scarcely repressed, there breathes a resentment against men and an obsession with the eternal masculine.]

These observations by a prominent literary critic, published in *Sur* shortly after Storni's death, remind us that literary judgments (as well as literary legends) are products of a given epoch's standards—in this case, those established by power groupings within a patriarchal society.

In reviewing the characterizations of Storni and her writings, it becomes clear that literary evaluations of her work are inextricably linked to the issues she addressed in her poetry and, even more directly, in her journalistic production. The previously reviewed criticism shows that many of her fellow writers and critics could not accept that women would bring their personal concerns to their writing. Women's issues, with their "aesthetic impurity," were not to appear in poetry, whether expressed as personal or as larger social issues. By regarding Storni's themes as purely personal complaints, and by separating her from her social context, many critics have seen the major themes of her writing as unique and unconnected to her participation in a wider cultural sphere.

The characterization of Storni by Gabriela Mistral is of a very different type, for Mistral stresses her active intelligence rather than her emotional nature:

> Informada como pocas criaturas de la vida, dando el comentario oportuno de las cosas más diversas, mujer de gran ciudad que ha pasado tocándolo todo e incorporándoselo, Alfonsina es de los que conocen por la mente tanto como por la sensibilidad, cosa muy latina. . . . Toda la fiesta de su amistad la hace su inteligencia. Poca emotiva.[7]

> [Informed as are few of life's children, giving witty commentary about the most diverse things, a woman of a great city who has lived touching and incorporating everything, Alfonsina is one who knows by her mind as much as by her sensibility, a very Latin trait. . . . She creates the entire festival of her friendship with her intelligence. Scarcely emotional.]

Juan Parra del Riego, who edited *Antología de poetisas americanas* in 1923, gives highly personalized and often astute accounts of the poets he selects. Like Mistral, he notes Storni's aggressive intellect, but with a difference: "ese aire de intensa melancolía intelectual, mejor dicho, de soledad intelectual un poco febril y agresiva que hace tan entrañable su poesía"[8] [that air of intense intellectual melancholy, or rather, slightly feverish and aggressive intellectual solitude, makes her poetry so intimate]. Unlike Mistral, however, he implies that this is a stance more masculine than feminine: "dolor intelectual, dolor de inteligencia, dolor más bien de hombres que dolor de mujeres"[9] [intellectual sorrow, a sorrow of intelligence, more like the sorrow of men than like that of women]. He compares her manner to that of

> esas estudiantes checo-eslovacas que llegan a París, menudas y ardientes. . . mujercitas sutiles y cerebrales, que fuman, que discuten con un calor de anarquistas temas de arte y filosofía y que se van llenando con el tiempo de esa cosa triste y ronca de los hombres del café.[10]

[those Czech female students who arrive in Paris, small and ardent . . . subtle
and cerebral little women who smoke, who discuss themes of art and philosophy with anarchist heat, and who in time are filled with that sad and harsh
quality of the men of cafés.]

The somewhat androgynous picture he describes could fit well with a scene
Storni herself might paint of a female "type" in her newspaper and magazine
articles. What is interesting here, however, is that one of the popular images
of her as nonconformist and marginalized was established early in her career.
It is an image fixed in popular consciousness and has provided a vantage
point from which most of her work has been read.

Storni's anthologized poetry is most often limited to highly personal
themes, and seldom are her other writings, many of which are different in
nature, brought to examination. Therefore an effort to return her to her historical epoch and to note her convergence and association with other working
and writing women of her times can reshape the vision of her work and its
impact.

Storni's life dramatically illustrates the rise of a new class of activist professional women, often immigrants or first-generation citizens, whose emergence in Argentina was affected by a growing feminist movement and by
labor movements in urban areas. These women often entered the public
sphere through the classroom, through journalism, or through community
organizing and service fields. Though hardly a typical case, given her extraordinary talent and energy, early recognition, and popular appeal, Storni
in many ways exemplifies the struggles and achievements of a new class of
women. From a Swiss-Italian immigrant family that settled in the provinces,
she, like a large group of women coming of age around World War I, was
educated as a *maestra*. She was to dedicate a great part of her working life to
the teaching profession, most notably in a school for the dramatic arts.

Storni herself noted the striking surge of middle-class women in intellectual life, and in 1936 she singled out the connection with the teaching profession. Calling many women writers "feministas a pesar suyo" [feminists in
spite of themselves], she pointed out the number of teachers among them:

Vienen en parte, de la cultura normalista: el mayor número de las escritoras
sudamericanas son maestras y más están, por vía de la fermentación intelectual, contra su medio social que sirviendo sus formas tradicionales.[11]

[They come, in part, from the schoolteacher culture, the greatest number of
South American women writers are teachers and, via intellectual ferment, more
are against their social milieu than are serving its traditional forms.]

This awareness of the antitraditionalism inherent in her class and gender
position constitutes an important thread running throughout all Storni's
writings and public activities.

The expressions of personal conflict in Storni's poetry have overshadowed other aspects of her career. A passionate defender of women's and children's rights, she took a visible position in feminist activities, especially in the early stages of her career. She used her assignments of the women's column in various periodicals, such as *La Nota* and *La Nación*, to make acerbic and penetrating commentaries in favor of social reforms, especially in the areas of women's legal status, workers' rights, the civil status of unwed mothers, and the role of the Church. Although the more overt political tone of such writings changed as Storni moved more completely into certain literary circles of Buenos Aires, the abundance and nature of the early journalistic writings may surprise the reader accustomed to a more private vision of her life.

Storni herself remarked on the limitations of the private focus, as in an interview of 1927:

> Siempre he pensado que iba a hacer un día un autoanálisis de mi obra; yo no soy una erótica, una desenfadada, una especie de esponja de la vida. Apasionada, ¿por qué no? Pero la pasión puede ser clara, espiritual, sin malicia. Soy un alma que gobierna un cuerpo, no un cuerpo que arrastra a tirones a un alma. Aquí sí hay confusión sobre mí, en parte del público y de la crítica, sin que falten espíritus sagaces que me vean como entiendo ser.[12]

> [I have always thought that I would one day make a self-analysis of my work; I am not an erotic, totally unconstrained, a sponge of life. Passionate, why not? But passion can be clear, spiritual, without malice. I am a soul that rules a body, not a body that yanks about my soul. Here there really is confusion concerning me, both by the public and the critics, even though there are some wise spirits who see me as I understand myself.]

Storni's response to the interviewer's question "¿Cómo reparte Ud. su tiempo?" [how do you spend your time?] reflects one of the facts of her life, the financial hardship that kept her busy with the effort to earn enough to support herself and her son. She answered, "Muy sencillamente. Trabajo, vuelvo a trabajar; trabajo de nuevo. ¡Divertidísimo!" [I work, I go back to work, I work once more. What fun!]. Such responses are revealing, for although perhaps exaggerated, they reveal her interest in deflating the image of the poet of the ivory tower, the writer dedicated to cultivating art for art's sake. And in this regard Storni shows her awareness of her links with working people, her impatience with the creation of the myth of the writer removed from mundane concerns.

The intense activity of Storni's life can be seen by the review of some vital facts. Born in Switzerland, she was brought at the age of four years (in 1896) to Argentina, where her family lived first in San Juan and then in the province of Santa Fe.[13] Storni studied in the *escuela normal* in Coronda and received the title of *maestra*, and in her early years she worked briefly as an actress. (She returned to the theater later in her career, writing full-length drama and children's theater.) In 1911 she took a teaching position in Rosario, where she began to publish some of her poetry and was active in a women's group. In 1912 she arrived in Buenos Aires, where her son was born.

The story of Storni's early life reflects many of the demographic trends of her place and epoch. Like so many other immigrant and native-born women, she began to work outside the home. Even her status as unwed mother was not as unusual as it may seem to later observers, for about 22 percent of the children born in Argentina between 1914 and 1919 were born to single mothers, with the rate being much higher in the provinces.[14] Yet while it may not have been an uncommon occurrence in general, it was not common in the circles in which Storni moved.

In Buenos Aires she first worked at various jobs, in a glove factory, as a cashier, and as an office worker in an importing firm.[15] Her first book, *La inquietud del rosal*, was published in 1916. In a speech given in Montevideo in 1938, sharing a platform with the two other major female poets of her time, Gabriela Mistral and Juana de Ibarbourou, Storni relates the beginnings of her literary career, with her first poems at the age of twelve years:

> Desde esa edad [12] hasta los 15, trabajo para vivir y ayudar a vivir. De los 15 a los 18, estudio de maestra y me recibo Dios sabe cómo. La cultura que en la Normal absorbo para en Andrade, Echeverría, Campoamor. . . .
>
> A los 19 estoy encerrada en una oficina: me acuna una canción de teclas; las mamparas de madera se levantan como diques más allá de mi cabeza; barras de hielo refrigeran el aire a mis espaldas; el sol pasa por el techo pero no puedo verlo; bocanadas de asfalto caliente entran por los vanos y la campanilla del tranvía llama distante.
>
> Clavada en mi sillón, al lado de un horrible aparato para imprimir discos dictando órdenes y correspondencia a la mecanógrafa, escribo mi primer libro de versos, un pésimo libro de versos. ¡Dios te libre, amigo mío, de *La inquietud del Rosal*! . . . Pero lo escribí para no morir.[16]

[From that age until 15, I work to live and to help others live. From 15 to 18, I study to be a teacher and graduate, God knows how. The culture I absorb in Normal College stops with Andrade, Echeverría, Campoamor. . . .

At 19 I am enclosed in an office: a song of keys taps out a lullaby, wood screens rise up like dikes above my head; bars of ice chill the air at my back; the sun passes through the roof but I can't see it; mouthfuls of hot asphalt enter through openings and the little streetcar bell calls out from a distance.

Stuck to my chair, beside a horrible apparatus that prints records dictating orders and correspondence to the typist, I write my first book of verses, an awful book of verses. May God spare you, my friend, from *La inquietud del Rosal*! . . . But I wrote it so I wouldn't die.]

Citing from the poem "Bien pudiera ser" from her third book, *Irremediablemente* (which she judged "también malo," or also bad), she contrasts the poem's message of the ancestral and silenced pain of women with the more personal nature of her early poems. Leaving the evaluations of collective versus personal inspiration to others, she does state that her presence at the gathering in Montevideo signifies

> un homenaje a la uruguaya y a la chilena; a Gabriela y Juana, y en ellas mi adhesión a la mujer escritora de América; mi fervor por su heroísmo cuya borra conozco y mi recuerdo inclinado para las mayores desaparecidas y las que, ausentes corporalmente en esta tribuna, están en ella por el valor magnífico de sus obras.[17]

> [A homage to the Uruguayan and the Chilean; to Gabriela and Juana, and my adherence to the woman writer of America; my fervor for her heroism, whose erasure I know, and my remembrance of the disappeared older ones, and those who, physically absent in this tribunal, are in it because of the magnificent value of their works.]

The solidarity with other women, especially women writers, is a constant trait often noted in histories and testimonies of Storni's life and work. Manuel Gálvez, an associate since her first contributions to *Nosotros* in 1918, applauded her active support of other women writers in his tribute of 1938:

> Una cosa que prueba la excelencia de su corazón es su generosidad para con las demás escritoras. Juzgó hasta con entusiasmo a las que pudieran ser rivales suyas en la poesía. . . . Prologó a tal cual escritora que se iniciaba. Y a otras las guió, las aconsejó, las vinculó a los medios literarios. El no tener envidias es propio de los grandes escritores, de aquellos que presienten la perduración de su obra.[18]

> [Something that proves the excellence of her heart is her generosity with other women writers. She even judged enthusiastically those who could be her rivals in poetry. . . . She wrote prologues for any writer who was just getting started. And she guided, advised, and connected them to the literary media. Not being envious is a trait of great writers, of those who sense the endurance of their works.]

Rachel Phillips, in her excellent study on Storni's poetry, points out that the years 1916–1925, when her first four volumes of poetry were published, "were the crucial years of establishing herself and fighting for a living."[19] Phillips also notes the apparent contradictions between the type of poetry that Storni wrote in this period and the activities of her life. She attributes the sentimentalism of the poetry to the exigencies of the commercial market and to Storni's impoverished circumstances. Whatever the reasons may have been (and Storni herself gives various reasons), it is clear that the poems do not reflect many of the concerns of the young Storni or the wide range of her public activities.

Storni's collaboration with other women in the public sphere began very early in Santa Fe, where she contributed to periodicals and was named vice-president of the Comité Feminista de Santa Fe.[20] In Buenos Aires in 1912, where she found work and began to publish her first articles in *Caras y Caretas*,[21] she also participated in feminist activities. One of her friends, Carolina de Muzzili (1889–1917), was director of the *Tribuna Femenina* one of Argentina's first feminist periodicals, and in 1914 Storni participated in a benefit recital for Muzzili's publication and her crusading work in behalf of working-class women and child laborers.[22] Muzzili, a self-taught socialist from the working class, was the first woman official of the Departamento Nacional del Trabajo, a position earned by her work in child labor and women's labor rights.[23] In 1916 Storni and Muzzili again appeared together in Rosario, where Storni spoke on women's education and gave poetry recitals, as she did in Buenos Aires at meetings sponsored by the Socialist Party.

María del Carmen Feijóo, in her studies of feminist movements in Argentina, divides the evolution of women's activism in the first half of the twentieth century in three cycles.[24] The first cycle, up to the beginning of World War I, centered upon the woman worker, especially the factory worker, whose struggle must be understood in the context of the ideological struggle between anarchists and socialists. The second period extends from the beginning of World War I until the military coup of 1930. During this period the women's movement focused on the civil and political rights of women. In the third stage, 1930–1947 (the year in which women gained the right to vote), the focus was more exclusively on women's suffrage. It was during the second period, when debates raged over the legal rights of women, that Storni established herself as a poet and wrote the journalistic pieces that so often reflect the debate over women's rights.

In Argentina, feminist organizations directed themselves to women's suffrage, especially after the first elections in 1916 under the Ley Sáenz Peña, which granted universal male suffrage.[25] The Argentine Socialist Party was a long-term ally of women's rights and since 1903 had included a platform supporting women's equality.[26] Alicia Moreau de Justo (1885–1986), a doctor, teacher, and founder and director of several organizations and magazines, was unquestionably the central figure in the women's movement within socialism, and her lifework became a symbol of intelligent and tireless leadership and service.[27] When the Socialist Party decided in 1918 to centralize the fight for women's suffrage, she served as president of the new Unión Feminista Nacional.

In 1919, the Partido Feminista Nacional came into being under the direction of Julieta Lanteri-Renshaw. Although without much hope of winning elections, this party did make an important symbolic impact by bringing women's suffrage, civil rights, and labor issues directly to the public's attention. In the same year, Storni published articles on both suffrage and civil rights, as will be examined later. The year 1919 also witnessed the first number of *Nuestra Causa*, a monthly journal founded by Alicia Moreau to serve as a forum for feminist groups and as the organ of the Unión Feminista Nacional. Storni participated in events sponsored by the journal and the organization; in 1921, *Nuestra Causa* recorded a program in her honor given by the Unión after she won the municipal prize for poetry.[28] Storni's efforts in the relief effort for victims of World War I in Europe led to an association with Moreau. According to Storni, World War I marked the end of an epoch for women, initiating radical changes in cultural and social values because of its revelations about the bankruptcy of patriarchal culture.[29] While she was not an active member of any political party, it is clear, given her participation in feminist activities and labor rights meetings, that she was fully aware of the political questions of her day and was outspoken in her support of these causes.

In 1918 Storni was one of the leaders of the Asociación pro Derechos de la Mujer, initiated by Elvira Rawson de Dellepiane (1867–1954), a physician, an educator, and one of the founders of the early Centro Feminista.[30] Among the goals of this group (whose numbers grew to eleven thousand) were the abolition of laws that established different standards for men and women, the advancement of women to directive positions in the educational system, the enactment of laws protective of motherhood, the eradication of prostitution, and equality of jobs and salaries. On this last issue Storni is especially vehement in her journalistic writings, often pointing out the reality of numbers of working women in the nation and their inequality in salary and in job opportunities. Some of these articles, such as "La perfecta dactilógrafa" [the perfect typist], in *La Nación*, 1920, and "¿Por qué las maestras se casan poco?" [why do few teachers marry?] in *La Nación*, 1921, use satire and humor to raise serious issues. For example, in "La perfecta dactilógrafa," Storni gives the "recipe" for the perfect typist:

Elíjase una joven de 18 a 21 años que viva en una casa de departamentos de cualquier apartado barrio. Píntesele discretamente los ojos. Oxígenesele el cabello. Púlasele las uñas. Córtesele un trajecito a la moda, bien corto. Comprímasele el estómago. . . . Póngasele un pájaro dentro de la cabeza (si es azul, mejor). Envíesela durante dos o tres meses a una academia comercial. (Hasta de cinco pesos por mes.) Téngasela luego pendiente de avisos comerciales durante uno, dos o tres años. Empléesela por poca cosa.[31]

[Select a young woman from eighteen to twenty-one years old who lives in an apartment building in any distant neighborhood. Discreetly paint her eyes. Bleach her hair. File her nails. Tailor her a fashionable little suit, quite short. Flatten her stomach. . . . Put a bird inside her head (better a blue one). Send her to a commercial academy for two or three months. (Up to five pesos per month.) Then keep her waiting on commercial ads for one, two or three years. Hire her for very little.]

In the 1920s, ironic articles like "La perfecta dactilógrafa" from the series "Bocetos Femeninos" in *La Nación* found space among the recipe columns, fashion photographs, society notes, church news, and items of general cultural interest. Without neglecting the constraints of this journalistic medium, she inserted a record of the less visible aspects of a large, low-salaried group of female employees. Reaching a group of readers who might not read specifically feminist publications, she presented her opinions. In this series for *La Nación* she wrote under the pseudonym "Tao Lao," while in the series of *La Nota*, "Femenidades," and in other publications, she signed with her own name.

By 1920, having published in some of the major periodicals of her day (*Caras y Caretas, Atlántida, La Nota, Nosotros*), Storni began to work as a regular contributor to *La Nación*, the major daily newspaper, where she continued to publish articles until her death in 1938. At the same time she was working as a teacher in public and private schools. Her journalistic production during this period calls attention to the major issues of the women of her epoch. As the following discussion of a selection of her journalistic writings shows, she was concerned with almost all areas of women's experience. Her articles often return to certain central issues: working women and their occupations, the relationship of women to national and cultural tradition, the role of the church, single mothers, marriage, good and bad models of motherhood, female poverty, migration to the city, fashion, and discussions of the "innate" characteristics of the female nature. Observations on class distinctions and references to the role of the teacher recur with regular frequency.

According to Storni, religion, poverty, and patriarchy are closely linked. For example, in "La carta al Padre Eterno" [letter to the Eternal Father] of 1919 she relates existing legal structures to church doctrines:

> Sabemos ya que desde el punto de vista moderno, filosófico, diré, las Sagradas Escrituras son anti-feministas, y las leyes por las que nos regimos, inspiradas en gran parte en aquellas, anti-feministas también.
>
> Pero toda mujer que entrara a considerarlas, en pro o en contra se volvería feminista, porque lo que por aquellas le está negado es pensar con la cabeza y por algunas de éstas, obrar con su voluntad.[32]

> [We now know that from the modern, what I would call philosophic point of view, the Sacred Scriptures are antifeminist, and the laws we rule ourselves by, inspired in great part by them, are also antifeminist.
>
> But every woman who might begin to consider them, either for or against, would become a feminist, because what they deny her is thinking with her head and, because of some of these laws, acting with her own will.]

The topic of patriarchy and moral standards returns in articles concerning women's poverty and the status of the unwed mother in "La complejidad femenina" [feminine complexity], in which she outlines the psychology of the roles of dominator and dominated.[33]

Other articles such as "En contra de la caridad" [against charity], in *La Nota*, 1919, and "Derechos civiles femeninos" [women's civil rights], in *La Nota*, 1919, are more straightforward in their vehement criticism of social norms and legal sanctions involving women. In "Derechos civiles femeninos" Storni calls for not only the vote for women but also equal protection under the law, so that such a vote might have practical worth. Both of these articles are related to women's struggle to reform the Civil Code—a major feature of Argentine feminism until 1926, when the reforms were won. Saying that women lead "una vida colonial" [a colonial life], she notes especially the necessary duplicity of the unmarried mother.

Sabido es que esta mujer, madre de un ser humano, que ha de servir a la sociedad en igual forma que los llamados hijos legítimos, no tiene protección alguna de la ley, ni del concepto público, ni de la tolerancia social.

La mujer en estas condiciones, si quiere educar al niño, mantenerlo a su lado, ha de usar de subterfugios, recurrir a falsedades, envilecerse de cobardía. . . . Para el hombre cómplice en la vida de un ser no hay sanción ni legal, ni moral. Hay más; ni siquiera está obligado económicamente a nada.

Esto es un resabio del Cristianismo mitificado.[34]

[We know that this woman, mother of a human being, who must serve society in the same way as the so-called legitimate children, has no protection whatsoever under the law, or of public regard, or of social tolerance.

The woman in these conditions, if she wants to educate the child, keep him at her side, has to turn to subterfuges and falsehoods, and vilify herself with cowardice. . . . For the accomplice male of this life of a human being there is neither legal nor moral sanction. Even more; he is not even obligated economically for anything.

This is a leftover of mythified Christianity.]

In another article of 1919, "El movimiento hacia la emancipación de la mujer en la República Argentina: las dirigentes feministas" [the women's emancipation movement in Argentina: the feminist leaders], Storni also points out that the Socialist Party was the only one that currently included the vote for women as part of its platform. Tracing the history of the feminist movement in Argentina, she describes the movement's leaders, outlines the goals of the different branches of the movement, and gives statistical evidence of women's participation in the labor force.[35] In her discussion of political support for the movement, she states that the Socialist Party has played an important role in spreading the suffrage movement throughout the working class.

Storni speaks out against the institutionalization of charity and the social structures that force the creation of such institutions in the article "En contra de la caridad": "Sabido tenemos que hay un concepto bien generalizado en las organizaciones sociales defectuosas: crear el pobre para darle la limosna"[36] [we know that in defective social organizations there is a well-generalized concept: create the poor so you can give them charity]. Storni called for wiser legislation that would oblige society to create means to provide for the needs of its citizens.

In "Un tema viejo" [an old theme] Storni calls feminism a collective transformation, a sign of the defeat of masculine directives, and a natural state of human evolution:

> Reírse del feminismo, por eso, me parece tan curioso como reírse de un dedo porque termina en una uña. Para llegar a lo que llamamos feminismo la humanidad ha seguido un proceso tan exacto como el que sigue el embrión para llegar a ser fruto o el fruto para transformar sus elementos en embrión, a pasos sucesivos.[37]

> [Therefore to laugh at feminism seems to me as strange as laughing at your finger because it has a fingernail. To arrive at what we call feminism humanity has followed a process as exact as the one an embryo follows to become a fruit, or for a fruit to transform its elements into an embryo, by successive steps.]

Arguing with those who attack feminism and who cite "authorities" such as classical precedents and biblical teachings, Storni counters that feminism is "una cuestión de justicia."

In her writings Storni claims that she is not a militant feminist, even though those same writings reflect her support of many proposed legal and social changes regarding women. The writings for *La Nota* (especially in 1918 and 1919), where she directed the column "Femenidades," as well as her other journalistic writings of that period, are notable for their partisan stance. Besides dealing with the civil status of women and other social issues, Storni gives ironic commentary on female fashion—the corset, "suicidal" high heels—in articles interspersed with sketches, poems, and short stories that generally reflect a more sentimental type of popular literature, with their intense appeal to "el desengaño en el amor" [disillusionment with love] and to elaborate backdrops of interior setting and dress.

With some striking exceptions, the column "Bocetos Femeninos" in *La Nación* responded to the demands of the commercial press. The form of the "sketch," which Storni often uses, makes few claims to permanence. These pieces are often impressionistic observations with highly personalized judgments. In a kind of urban adaptation of the travelogue, they record vignettes of daily life in Buenos Aires—the subway crowds, shoppers, female "types" (the domestic employee, the provincial, the secretary, the schoolgirl, the shopper, the mother)—in a chatty tone with frequent asides to the reader. The tone of these short essays varies widely. Some are breezy and humorous, while others are straightforward accounts of noteworthy topics concerning women, such as the recent census figures on occupational divisions for women or the marital status of the citizenry. They gain their appeal by mixing trite feminine stereotypes with issues of basic economic and social concern to women.

In some of these articles it is easy to see Storni's own personal issues, especially in her concern for the financial and professional insecurity of schoolteachers ("La maestra" and "¿Por qué las maestras se casan poco?"), the hypocrisy surrounding virginity ("La novia"), and society's excessive emphasis on female beauty ("La impersonal" and "Las crepusculares"). While she is often eloquent in her defense of women, she can be aggressively disparaging of many aspects of women's culture. Pretense, slavish imitation, and obsessive romanticism, specifically the fixation on marriage ("Las casaderas" [marriage brokers] and "El amor y la mujer" [love and the woman]), are targets of satirical exposés.

In "Las casaderas" (8 August 1920: 4) Storni calls for reader responses to her hypothetical marriage agency, which would solicit unmarried men (even from other planets) to match with husband-seeking women. Her reaction to the responses she received serves as the starting point for "El amor y la mujer" (22 August 1920: 6). With tongue in cheek, she salutes her readers as eternal romantics:

> Regocijáos por lo pronto, de ser todavía las celosas vestales del romanticismo (es muy lindo ser vestal; el tul blanco cae divinamente y lame el rosado pie con delicada gracia).
>
> Vuestra imaginación se interpone así entre la realidad y el sueño como un elástico de poderosa resistencia que apaga y suaviza los choques.
>
> [Rejoice, meanwhile, for still being the jealous priestesses of romanticism (it's very nice to be a priestess; white tulle falls divinely and licks your rosy foot with delicate grace).
>
> Your imagination inserts itself between reality and dream like a rubber band of powerful resistance that stops and softens blows.]

Storni uses the same article to respond to assertions by "malas plumas" [evil pens] that women are directed solely by instinct in their philosophy of love and that they lack the intellectual capacity to observe life objectively in its just equilibrium:

> Así comparan la condición voluptuosa de la mujer a la de ciertas razas inferiores que viven solamente para amar y satisfacer sus pasiones, y hasta pretenden que el alto sentimiento de la maternidad es instinto puro.
>
> [Thus they compare the voluptuous condition of woman to that of certain inferior races that live only to love and satisfy their passions, and they even claim that the lofty maternal sentiment is pure instinct.]

As in so many other articles, here Storni speaks from several different angles, using a highly embellished rhetoric common to many columnists. Addressing her female readers as "mis dulces amiguitas lectoras," "oh divinas," "adorables mujeres," and "pequeñas amigas," Storni as "Tao Lao" tackles many of the popular myths about women without, however, running too much risk of alienating the casual reader.

The column at times became the space for facetious debate, as in "El amor y la mujer," where she repeats the generalizations directed at woman's condition—"el lastre de la humanidad, la fuente, el pozo sentimental y básico" [the ballast of humanity, the fountain, the sentimental and basic well], in contrast to the lofty flights of masculine thought. She does not openly contest such generalizations, but immediately transforms the image of the soaring flight of the male into the indecorous plummeting of a "pollito mojado" [damp little chick]. Anticipating a defensive reaction from her readers, she states: "no os temo enojadas, sino mansas y suaves" [I don't fear you angry, but meek and gentle].

One of her favorite topics was fashion and women's devotion to it. In many articles on this topic Storni reveals contradictory impulses, or at least plays on those of her readers. While she denounces fashion's excesses and the often pathetic and ludicrous lengths to which women will go to serve this master, she shows a keen eye for details of dress and, more revealingly, what these details show about their wearers. Dress is the code to which she most commonly refers when discussing the ascent up the ladder of social class. Street scenes of Buenos Aires and commentary on social customs reveal her ambivalence toward Buenos Aires, as do many poems of her early period. References to the city's sacrifices to impersonal norms, its rapidity of movement, the rule of "vanity and pride," and a scale of values based on money and class—complaints registered by most urban observers of all periods— alternate with expressions of clear delight in the variety of human types and idiosyncrasies. The frequent idealization of provincial life is countered by depictions of the movement, color, and freedom of the city.

Storni's eye for the ridiculous and the pathetic often fastened on the cult of imitation that circulated in "la pequeña ciudad que de gran ciudad oficia" [the little city that acts as a big city], as in "La impersonal" (27 June 1920: 4). Here she scolds the female who is devoid of originality and "real sentiment":

Es la muchacha que imita a sus heroínas de novela, y se suicida por un fútil amorío, o lleva en verano sombrero de terciopelo, y en invierno zapato de seda; es la mucama que imita el peinado de su señora y la señora que imita a la esfinge desde un palco caro, y la empleada que quiere ser confundida con la niñabien, y la niñabien que se viste como su artista preferida, y la artista que se empeña en parecer una colegiala, y la colegiala que une a su cabello suelto los tacos desmesurados. . . .

Y si la impersonal es completamente pobre, caerá en la ridiculez de dar las formas más novedosas a telas viejas y ajadas, arrastrando así, sobre su propio cuerpo, la tristeza de su pobre alma expuesta a la mirada aguda del que pasa.

[She is the girl who imitates her novelistic heroines, and commits suicide because of a futile love affair, or who wears a velvet hat in summer, and silk shoes in winter; she is the maid who imitates the hairdo of the lady of the house and the lady who imitates the Sphinx from a theater box, and the shopgirl who wants to be taken for the rich girl, and the rich girl who dresses like her favorite actress, and the actress who strives to look like a schoolgirl, and the schoolgirl who wears her flowing hair with extremely high heels. . . .

And if the impersonal one is completely poor, she will be so ridiculous as to give the newest forms to old and worn-out fabrics, dragging along, on her own body, the sadness of her poor soul exposed to the sharp gaze of the passerby.]

In "Las crepusculares" she records the late afternoon pilgrimage to the downtown fashion stores in the Calle Florida. The "damitas" [little ladies] referred to by the synecdoche of their "zapatitos" [little shoes] cluster together, reverently awaiting a fashion show. Her use of diminutives is telling, as is her coy address to her feminine readers in the satirical articles— "oh divinas." Her sharp jabs at class and economic distinctions are hard to miss, and their juxtaposition to the society notes makes them especially acute. Alternating a highly embellished rhetoric with a spare, direct style, she usually makes her point in no uncertain terms.

In "La emigrada" Storni gives a sympathetic composite portrait of the young women who arrive alone in the city from the provinces to make their way "en las grandes ciudades como criada familiar o en los institutos de salud e higiene como mucama" [in the big cities as a domestic maid or in health and hygiene institutes as a maid] (*La Nación*, 1 August 1920: 2). She recounts a newcomer's growing awareness as the "María, Juana, Rosa, etc." begins to adapt to a new setting. In a short but richly detailed piece, she captures a scene so common to her day and to ours, the migration to Latin American cities of women alone or with their children. Such a young woman, reared in a rural setting without reading or writing skills, accustomed to turning her wages over to her elders, arrives in the city with a sealed envelope, whose contents she cannot read. The limitless possibilities of the city dazzle her:

La ciudad produce en la emigrada rápidos efectos: como una planta trans-plantada que no sabe qué hacer con la exótica savia que recibe, se resuelve de golpe por dar un estirón hacia arriba.

[The city produces rapid effects in the emigrant: like a transplanted plant that doesn't know what to do with the exotic sap it receives, she suddenly resolves to grow straight upward.]

The most common initial transformation of the transplant is superficial— fancy shoes, costume jewelry, and flashy clothes. The second phase is one of growing pains, as she begins to observe and to imitate not her peers (her roommates) but the family for whom she works. She learns to search not for the trappings of prosperity but for the means to a better income, and she asks for a raise. The "emigrada" learns the lessons of the city, unlearning the lessons of her place of origin, whose "árboles del camino podrían decir: la que pasa se llama María, o Juana, o Rosa, pero los árboles de Buenos Aires

sólo dicen que la que pasa es una libreta de ahorros" [trees along the road
could say: that one going by is María, or Juana, or Rosa, but the trees of
Buenos Aires only say she is a little bank book]. The marks of class and social
categories are nearly always present in Storni's journalistic writings. Even
though most of her articles focus on personality or character types, economic
and social status is the thread that unites her writings.

Occupational divisions among women are a frequent theme of her journalism, especially in *La Nación*. Based on census statistics in the capital ("Las
mujeres que trabajan," *La Nación*, 20 June 1920: 3), she records the percent-
age of women engaged in each occupation. Her statistics give some idea of
why women's rights groups were so active during this time, for almost half of
all salaried employees were women, "más mujeres de las que a simple vista
se sospecharía" [more women than one would imagine at first glance]. For
her it is no surprise that most domestic employees would be women, or that
the great majority of educators were women. Seventy thousand women
worked in industry, while the figures plummeted for the fine arts, letters,
and science, and even for commerce, where most were clerical workers.
In another article, "Las heroínas" (*La Nación*, 20 April 1920: 5), Storni adopts
a much more bantering style to describe the women who worked as the sole
representatives of their gender in certain occupations, such as furniture
polisher or coal deliverer.

Some occupations receive special attention in these articles, like the
secretary in the previously cited piece. The teacher, the doctor, the domestic
employee, and even the watercolorist (singled out for her irregularity of salary) constitute part of the gallery of contemporary portraits. Storni's own
profession through her adult life, that of teacher, receives special treatment.
She devotes two articles in *La Nación*, "La normalista" (13 June 1920: 1) and
"¿Por qué las maestras se casan poco?" (13 March 1921: 4), to this topic.
The first is a fanciful interview with the following interlocutors: a sheet of
paper, a Frenchman, a tree in the botanical garden, a public employee, the
popular masses, and the "normalista" herself. The latter is unequivocal in
her opinions:

> Opino sobre mí misma lo siguiente: que soy pobre. Que estudio con sacrificio
> para ayudar a los míos y quisiera obtener el puesto a que me da derecho mi
> título sin formar en este hilo interminable de postulantes. Afirmo que soy in-
> teligente y capaz.

> [I have the following opinion of myself: I am poor. I study at a sacrifice to help
> out my own family and I'd like to get a job my degree entitles me to without
> standing in that interminable line of candidates. I affirm that I am intelligent
> and capable.]

The *normalista* defends herself against her "cowardice" in bucking the system,
because she fears expulsion if she criticizes the educational administration.
As further justification of an apparent immobility, she ends with clear logic:

"Y por último: mi madre es viuda y mis hermanos están desnudos" [and finally, my mother is a widow and my brothers and sisters are naked].

Teachers are the one group that almost never provokes ironic commentary from Storni. It is clear that her own work as a teacher, and her admiration for other women teachers, is a matter of great pride. "¿Por qué las maestras se casan poco?" is another version of the traditional story of "la mujer que sabe latín," a topic still highly debated in contemporary society. Storni definitely sees this situation as a problem worthy of serious attention. Her analysis of economic, intellectual, social, and moral factors ends with no solution, but with a vindication of the superior qualities of the profession's members. Education marks a step up on the social scale, but offers little economic advancement or acceptance by more highly paid professionals. The serious discussion she devotes to the topic shows her concern for this emerging class of women, and perhaps a preoccupation with her own situation: "por lo que está en condiciones de leer, de adquirir, aspira a más de lo que su medio social le permitiría" [given that her condition allows her to read, to acquire things, she aspires to more than her social milieu will allow her].

In "La médica" (*La Nación*, 18 July 1920: 6), Storni reflects on some of the causes central to feminists of her day. In an article without apparent ironies, she notes the importance of women physicians as leaders in the women's movement:

Médicas son, en efecto, casi todas las mujeres que en nuestro país encabezan el movimiento de ideas femenino más radical, y médicas son las que abordan las cuestiones más escabrosas: problema sexual, trata de blancas, etc.

[Women doctors are, in fact, most of the women in our country who head the most radical women's movement and take on the most scabrous questions: sexual problems, white slavery, etc.]

She includes here a discussion of women's modesty, *pudor*, the type she calls "the same modesty of the slave," without free will or independent criteria, which limits women's abilities to care for themselves. The article, not really an examination of the world of the female physician, is a meditation on moral liberty. Here she asserts that "elasticidad ideológica" and tolerance are the marks of a highly evolved moral system. Physicians, therefore, by their direct confrontation with human pain and problems, represent a higher state that all women "will understand easily some day." Like many of the feminist arguments of the day, Storni's final statement appeals to motherhood as the basis for reclaiming equal rights: "y es por eso que, en nombre del derecho de la maternidad, un pequeño grupo de mujeres pide ya la igualdad moral para ambos sexos" [and that is why, in the name of the rights of motherhood, a small group of women calls for moral equality for both sexes].

While she is a staunch defender of women's rights, Storni is not always tolerant of all aspects of women's culture, nor does she accept wholeheartedly the idea of the equality of the sexes. More traditional in her approach to women's roles than some of her feminist colleagues and friends, she sees biological destiny as the major force for women. Instinctive motherhood, an innate sensitivity to human emotional needs, and a capacity for sacrifice are traits she attributes to her sex. Certain behavioral patterns associated with women, however, come under sarcastic attack. Sentimentalism and superficial rigidity in moral standards are two of her favorite topics. These two traits impede women from taking a "philosophical" view of their roles, inhibiting them in their search for self-development.

Articles from *La Nación* such as "La mujer enemiga de la mujer" (22 May 1921: 4) and "La mujer como novelista" (27 March 1921: 4) illustrate her position. Even though she was insistent about making a place for herself and for other women in literary circles in Buenos Aires (a fact never omitted from her biographies is that she was the first woman to attend literary banquets there, an action that met with no little resistance), she claims that women have not evolved sufficiently to be effective in certain spheres of action. As she so often does, she recurs to "principios filosóficos" to explain her position, although the basis of these philosophical premises is never presented. In both these articles she cites lack of experience as the determining factor in women's incapacities. In "La mujer enemiga de la mujer," she says: "A falta de educación del carácter, y a carencia de buena disciplina mental, hay que achacar tanta enemistad de mujer a mujer" [so much enmity from one woman to another must be attributed to a lack of character training, and to absence of good mental discipline].

Women's often-cited lack of generosity with one another could be remedied by attention to their training, by forming a type of sisterhood that would train them to uphold standards of virtue with more compassion and less harshness and hypocrisy. The price paid for rigid adherence to uncompromising standards indicates to her the female's greatest weakness, for "si la virtud ha costado tanto para conservarla que endurece el alma y la cierra para comprender cualquier error, entonces tanto valía no tenerla" [if virtue costs so much to conserve that it hardens the heart and closes it to understanding any error, then it is not worth having].

Despite the measured tone and appeal to reason that she creates, it is apparent that Storni speaks from the most acute personal awareness. Although she gained growing acceptance as a writer, was sought after as a speaker, and became known as a successful teacher, this kind of acceptance did not always transfer into the social sphere. As many of her contemporaries have recorded, she could not be welcomed into many "respectable" homes, even though she might associate with the same families in the public sphere. Her condition as unwed mother created barriers that not even her talents and energetic efforts could overcome.

"La mujer como novelista" is a troubling article for a reader who might search for a consistent and unequivocal defense of the woman artist in Storni's work. Her generalized remarks on the recent proliferation of novels by women lead to the conclusion that she saw a dubious future for women as novelists. Not only does she find women lacking the range of lived experience necessary "para observar el mundo con ojos claros y penetradores" [to observe the world with clear and penetrating eyes] but she also implies that the very sensibility that is their greatest gift can bring about their undoing as novelists: "si la sensibilidad femenina es rica, la sensibilidad pura no basta para la obra de arte" [even if feminine sensibility is rich, pure sensibility is not sufficient for a work of art]. Granted, women with fortune may be permitted to live the sort of life that permits them to break with expected norms and experiment more fully with other types of existence. Yet the same liberty robs them of their most treasured possession, their feminine nature: "Luego, una vida extraordinaria destruye en la mujer lo que la hace más preciada: su feminidad" [then, an extraordinary life destroys in woman the very thing that makes her most prized: her femininity].

In this article, Storni appears to go against many of the ideas she has established in other articles. Here woman is limited by her narrow range of experience, but breaking these limits makes her less womanly. In this respect the article is a notable link in her writings, forecasting some of the positions she would adopt later. Even more interesting, it reveals a link between her journalism, outspoken in defense of women's liberties, and her short prose fiction pieces of the period, which largely cling to the sentimental romantic plots that she finds to be the inescapable lot of the woman novelist.

Sentimentality, nonetheless, and an unrealistically romanticized view of reality (two of the main criticisms leveled at her early poetry) are targets of derision many times in these columns. "Confidencias populares" (*La Nación*, 20 March 1921: 4), a discussion of popular magazines, gives her an opportunity to examine the tone of this genre.

The image of woman as a mother and as the anchor of the family unit serves Storni as her rationale for the ethics of sexual equality. Such a position reflects that of many feminist activists during this period. She embraces the exaltation of motherhood, even though it leads her to some contradictory approaches. Many of her arguments find their logic by recalling women's importance and contributions in traditional roles, such as those found in rural societies. For instance, in "La selección de judías" (*La Nación*, 2 June 1920: 4), here referring to the common bean and not to a racial or religious group, she emphasizes the collective nature of women's work in an agrarian society. She reminds her readers of the "double day" involved in women's work:

Sabido es ya que las mujeres campesinas en todos los países y en todos los tiempos (antes y después del feminismo) han trabajado a la par del hombre en las más rudas tareas agrícolas y por veces con doble sacrificio, repartiendo su día entre las tareas maternales y caseras y la fuerte labor campesina.

[We already know that peasant women in all countries and all times (before and after feminism) have worked equally with men in the roughest agricultural tasks and often with double sacrifice, dividing their day between maternal and household tasks and hard field labor.]

Storni often refers back to a golden age of tradition where women were accorded their rightful place. In "Sobre nosotros" (*La Nota* 94, [May 26, 1917: 1865–1866) she proposes to analyze why the crowds of Buenos Aires are rude and why women suffer such discourtesy. Her thesis rests on the fact that, as a city of immigrants, Buenos Aires has not had time to develop a collective spiritual culture, because "la cultura colectiva descansa en el cariño a la tierra, a la historia, al hogar, a la ley, al porvenir" [collective culture rests on affection for the earth, history, the home, the law, the future].

Among other observations, she likens the development of a civic consciousness to the cohesion of the family unit:

¿Exigiríamos de él [el pueblo] las consideraciones espontáneas que las mujeres recibiríamos si tuviera cabal concepto de la familia como institución primera de la colectividad, como asiento y fundamento de la raza?

[Would we demand from the people the spontaneous considerations that women would receive if we had a full concept of the family as the first institution of collectivity, as the basis and foundation of the race?]

At the same time that the family unit serves her as the basic metaphor of a healthy society, it is an almost mythic family, one she finds hard to reconcile with the facts of a newly created society in constant flux and change.

In other articles the family in particular raises uncomfortable issues. The image of the mother can be a problematic one, especially when she drops the straightforward analytic tone and veers toward fictional recreation. In "La madre" (*La Nación*, 11 November 1920: 2) the narrator discovers her shallow values when she is reproached by her cousin, the mother of two young children. The narrator must explore her unexamined favoritism of the beautiful daughter over the unattractive boy child, when she is faced with the mother's compassionate, though understated, humility and fairness.

In "Una tragedia de reyes" [a tragedy of kings] (*La Nación*, 9 January 1921: 6), a child's move into self-awareness and his distancing himself from his mother provoke a strange and violent reaction. Seeking to preserve the magic of the myth of Christmas gifts from the Wise Men, the mother shields him from the knowledge that these gifts are really from the parents. When she discovers that he is already aware of the parental ruse but maintains silence in order to keep receiving the best gifts, the mother's reaction is sharp and troubling: "Sintió náuseas; empujó violentamente al hijo de su lado y le gritó amenazadora:—¡Vete! ¡Vete!" (she felt nauseated; she pushed the child violently from her side and shouted threateningly:—Get out! Get out!]. The story does not end with a summary of a moral lesson. As if in the dramatic end of a soap opera episode, the mother reacts to the fleeing, crying child by throwing herself on the bed: "lloró también, y sin sollozos, lágrimas lentas, frías, e interminables" [she also cried, soundlessly, slow, cold and interminable tears].

"La dama de negro" (*La Nota* 4, 191, April 4, 1919: 427–428) combines several features of Storni's journalism. A vignette of life in Buenos Aires joins with her moralizing on the mother's role and the baleful effects of a society obsessed with artifice and appearances. Here an excessively elegant lady with her five-year-old daughter is seated facing the narrator in the subway. On a second look, the narrator notices that the child has been transformed by her mother into a rather dirty and "cheap doll." With her bleached hair and painted cheeks, the child reflects a pathetic case of the vanity and dislocation of values the city so often presents. The scene brings to mind the case of a woman on trial who tried to commit suicide by flinging herself into the water with her two children; she succeeded in killing them but not herself. The narrator finds the attempted suicide more honorable than the subway child's deformation at her mother's hands. Like the obsession with matrimony, the relentless search for beauty and appearances, at great social loss, is highlighted constantly in Storni's articles. While the forms vary, from direct moralizing to sentimental tales with tragic endings, her aim is clear.

In reading the journalism by Storni, it becomes evident that these texts not only reveal unexplored facets of her personality and professional life but also cast light on the cultural and social milieu of her time. They give us an entrance into the coexistence of several versions of feminism and show the interrelationships among feminism, the popular press, literary movements, and the emergence of a middle-class female reader.

As Storni moved into the mainstream of intellectual life in Buenos Aires (or at least into certain sectors of that life), the topic of feminism became a less persistent theme in her journalism. Her writings in general reflect the tensions facing women of her class who found themselves in the midst of a rapidly changing society, where the realities of women's lives could no longer correspond to the reigning mythologies. These mythologies, so often reflected on the same pages of the newspapers and journals where Storni published her pieces, are brought into higher relief by their juxtaposition to Storni's articles.

Many of the women for whom Storni wrote came from a background like hers—children of immigrants who worked outside the home, some of whom were able to move into a growing middle-class sector via the teaching profession. And like her, many must have sensed the incongruities between their everyday realities and the weight of tradition. Although Storni herself is well known as a public figure and as a poet, her links to the history of women of her lifetime deserve to be explored. New approaches to history, biography, and literature, making use of the extraliterary writings of prominent women writers, can offer a way to return such isolated figures to a lived history. In doing so, we not only discover important neglected works of well-known writers but are able as well to rethink our canons of literary and social history.

## NOTES

1. For assistance with research in Buenos Aires, I am grateful to the staff of the Biblioteca Nacional of Buenos Aires; to Washington and Teresita Pereyra, who generously allowed me to use their private library; to Lea Fletcher; and to Susana Zanetti.

2. *Nosotros*, n.s. 3, 31 (October 1938): 276. All translations from Spanish are my own.

3. Jorge Luis Borges, "Nydia Lamarque," *Proa* 2, 14 (December 1925): 52.

4. Jorge Luis Borges, "Prólogo (III)," *Índice de la nueva poesía americana*, ed. Alberto Hidalgo et al. (Buenos Aires: Sociedad de Publicaciones el Inca, 1926), 15.

5. Eduardo González Lanuza, "Ubicación de Alfonsina," *Sur* 7 (November 1938): 55–56.

6. Ibid., 56.

7. Quoted in Alfredo Veivaré, *Alfonsina Storni*, Capítulo de la historia argentina 51 (Buenos Aires: Centro Editor de América Latina, 1980), 329 (originally published in *El Mercurio de Chile* in 1926).

8. Juan Parra del Riego, *Antología de poetisas americanas* (Montevideo: Claudio García Editor, 1923), 109.

9. Ibid.

10. Ibid.

11. Quoted in Rachel Phillips, *Alfonsina Storni: From Poetess to Poet* (London: Tamesis, 1975), 126.

12. "Como viven y trabajan las figuras descollantes del ambiente: En casa de la poetisa Alfonsina Storni," *La Razón*, 14 November 1927, 5.

13. For biographical information, see the chronology by Mabel Mármol in Conrado Nalé Roxlo, *Genio y figura de Alfonsina Storni* (Buenos Aires: Eudeba, 1964), 5–20. For more listings, see Marta Baralis, *Bibliografía argentina de artes y letras* (Buenos Aires: Fondo Nacional de las Artes, 1964), vol. 18.

14. Sandra F. McGee, "The Visible and Invisible Liga Patriótica Argentina, 1919–28: Gender Roles and the Right Wing," *Hispanic American Historical Review* 64, 2 (1984) 236. I thank Francesca Miller for this reference.

15. Fermín Estrella Gutiérrez, "Alfonsina Storni: su vida y su obra," in *Estudios literarios* (Buenos Aires: Academia Argentina de Letras, 1969), 305.

16. Alfonsina Storni, "Entre un par de maletas a medio abrir y la manecilla del reloj," *Revista Nacional* (Montevideo) 1, 2 (February 1938): 216–217.

17. Ibid., 214.

18. Manuel Gálvez, "Alfonsina Storni," *Nosotros*, n.s. 3, 32 (November 1938): 370.

19. Phillips, *Alfonsina Storni*, 6. See also 1–14. Mark Smith-Soto, in his *El arte de*

*Alfonsina Storni* (Bogotá: Ediciones Tercer Mundo, 1986), includes a study of the critical reception of Storni's work, as well as a chapter on her later poetry.

20. Carlos Alberto Andreola, *Alfonsina Storni: Inédita* (Buenos Aires: n.p., 1974), 98.

21. Nalé Roxlo, *Genio y figura*, 10.

22. Carlos Alberto Andreola, *Alfonsina Storni: Vida, Talento, Soledad* (Buenos Aires: Plus Ultra, 1976), 299.

23. Lily Sosa de Newton, *Las argentinas de ayer a hoy* (Buenos Aires: Ediciones Zanetti, 1967), 216.

24. María del Carmen Feijóo, "Las feministas," in *La vida de nuestro pueblo* (Buenos Aires: Centro Editor de América Latina, 1982), 5–6. For more information on the women's movements in Argentina and the Southern Cone, see also Feijóo, "Las luchas feministas," *Todo Es Historia* 128 ( January 1978): 6–23; Asunción Lavrín, *The Ideology of Feminism in the Southern Cone, 1900–1940*, Latin American Program Working Papers 169 (Washington, D.C.): Wilson Center, Smithsonian Institution, 1986); and Cynthia Little, "Education, Philanthropy, and Feminism: Components of Argentine Womanhood, 1860–1926," in *Latin American Women: Historical Perspectives*, ed. Asunción Lavrín (Westport, Conn.: Greenwood Press, 1978), 235–253.

25. Feijóo, "Las feministas," 14.

26. As both Asunción Lavrín and Cynthia Little point out in their previously cited studies, the Socialist Party was outspoken in its defense of women's rights, supporting suffrage, the right to absolute divorce, paternity investigations, and legal equality of both legitimate and illegitimate children. See Lavrín, 8, and Little, 243.

27. For biographical data on Alicia Moreau de Justo, see Mirta Henault, *Alicia Moreau de Justo* (Buenos Aires: Centro Editor de América Latina, 1983), and Sosa de Newton *Las argentinas*, 142–143, 148, 191.

28. In her review for *Nuestra Causa* of Storni's *Languidez*, Adela García Salaberry (teacher, journalist, and secretary of the Unión Feminista Nacional) defended Storni's work, calling her "uno de los más originales genios líricos de América" and "nuestra más genial poeta" (2, 22 [April 1921]: 230.) In the same year the magazine records an "Homenaje a Alfonsina Storni" presented by the Unión Feminista Nacional, on the occasion of her poetry prize in the municipal competition.

Mirta Henault states that Storni was also a contributor to *Nuestra Causa* (77). I have not, however, been able to examine those issues of the magazine.

29. Alfonsina Storni, "Un tema viejo," *La Nota* 4, 194 (April 25, 1919): 501.

30. Sosa de Newton, *Las argentinas*, 148–149.

31. "La perfecta dactilógrafa," *La Nación*, 9 May 1920, sec. 2: 1.

32. *La Nota* 4, 202 ( June 27, 1919): 682.

33. *Nuestra Revista* 4, 34 (April 1923): 45–47. The same article was originally published in *La Nación*, 14 November 1920: 9.

34. *La Nota* 5, 210 (August 22, 1919): 878.

35. *La Revista del Mundo* (Buenos Aires), August 1919: 12–19.

36. *La Nota* 5, 22 (November 14, 1919): 1173.

37. *La Nota* 4, 194 (April 25, 1919): 500.

# EIGHT

# A Question of Blood: The Conflict of Sex and Class in the *Autobiografía* of Victoria Ocampo

*Janet Greenberg*

Victoria Ocampo (1890–1979) was a trilingual woman of letters widely known in Argentina as a magazine editor and book publisher, essayist and autobiographer, salon leader and patroness of the arts. From the 1930s until her death, Ocampo was best known in international circles as the founder and sole director of *Sur*—the longest-lived literary magazine in South America, founded as an international vehicle for exchange between the Americas and Europe—and of a companion publishing house, Editorial SUR. An imposing beauty born into a first family of Argentina, she flaunted the privileges of her class, using her sizable fortune to finance her magazine and book-publishing enterprises and to publish the majority of her own works.

When Ocampo died in 1979, she left behind three generations of faithful followers and equally bitter enemies who have alternately glorified and vilified her in the popular and intellectual press for over half a century. Indeed, since the 1930s she has been the *bête noire* of the Catholic establishment, Peronist critics of the oligarchy, and left-wing critics of Peronism and cultural imperialism. She has also been championed as Argentina's first lady of letters and patroness of the arts and culture, while critics have juxtaposed her to Eva Perón as a symbol of that upper-class breed of feminist whose class interests invariably override allegiance to members of their sex. It is clear that both her ambiguous status in Argentine cultural history and the divided voice she manifests as director and contributor in her magazine find their source in her sexuality—her identity as a woman and a feminist. In her dual role as director of *Sur* and testimonial essayist, she was trapped between a defense of "permanent standards of artistic excellence"[1] and a lament about her own lack of artistry, even while she developed a formidable autobiographical persona and evolved as a sophisticated feminist critic in her context.

Though Ocampo is usually identified as the spokesperson for and driving force behind the editorial policies of her magazine, she has only recently been taken seriously as a writer.[2] Yet she was an accomplished essayist whose collected writings constitute a lifelong exploration in autobiographical form. Beginning in the 1920s and continuing until the late 1970s, she published ten volumes of collected *Testimonios* and a dozen other book-length works. Since her death in 1979, six volumes of *Autobiografía* have also appeared.[3] Probably the second most talked-about woman in Argentina—the first is Eva Perón— Ocampo seems also the second most mystified. Friends and foes alike have tended to attribute enormous powers of influence to her magazine, while there is almost total neglect of her *Testimonios* by scholars of the genre and little agreement (or serious discussion) about the quality of her writing or influence in *Sur*.

*Sur*, initially conceived as a vehicle for the exchange of ideas among South America, North America, and Europe, has been implicated in the most important debates about the politics of culture in Argentina in this century; its longevity is matched only by the polemic that still surrounds its role in shaping Argentine culture from the 1930s through the 1970s. Modeled on cultural magazines like the Spanish *Revista de Occidente*, the American *Partisan Review*, the English *Scrutiny*, and the French *Nouvelle revue française*, it is widely respected for quality translations by Ocampo and others of modern French- and English-language authors into Spanish—including Virginia Woolf, William Faulkner, Albert Camus, Jean-Paul Sartre, Rabindranath Tagore, and many others. Latin Americans such as Jorge Luis Borges first published much of their best work in its pages. Although the magazine changed editors-in-chief at several junctures, Ocampo alone directed and financed its publication continuously from 1930 until her death in 1979, making *Sur* exceptional among modern literary magazines for the coherence of its direction and length of continuous publication.

John King has noted that as director of *Sur*, Ocampo issued high-toned official statements that defended "the continuity of culture, the unchanging order, and the discipline of the intellectual even in troubled times,"[4] while she insists on *Sur*'s right to judge superior art and literature. Yet in her testimonial essays she is unable to reconcile the voice of personal experience as a woman and writer with the authoritative tone of a magazine director who defends the literary production of others.

Sympathetic and hostile critics alike have displayed a general inability to go beyond Ocampo's impressive public persona in order to analyze either the autobiographical form of her personal writings or her pivotal role as literary entrepreneur in *Sur* and Editorial SUR. Few have made more than cursory connections between the two contiguous aspects of her literary career. Her cultural influence extended beyond the sphere of publishing: she was a driving force behind numerous artistic and literary societies and cultural exchange programs linking Argentina to other continents. In 1975 she was the first woman ever invited to join the Argentine Academy of Letters as a full member, and she was honored by governments and universities in several countries over the decades. Historians of feminism in Argentina are similarly divided about her contributions to women's political and social liberation in general and the quality of her own feminist rebellion. The publication of the *Autobiografía* at regular intervals since her death in 1979 seems to have kept the range of conjectures about her life alive, but has not yet given rise to substantial critical debate over its content or import in the context of Ocampo's collected work.

The most prevalent image of Ocampo in the Argentine popular press is still that of the flamboyant, widely traveled collector of famous figures, both Argentine and international. From the 1930s through the 1970s, her social activities made news regularly in the cultural sections—and occasionally on the front pages—of the same daily papers in which she often published her essays. Her attraction to famous people—most often writers, but also philosophers, musicians, and statesmen like De Gaulle, Mahatma Gandhi, and Indira Gandhi—was acknowledged and defended by herself as often as it was disparaged by both critics of the liberal oligarchy and collaborators in *Sur*. In popular mythology, Ocampo is still at least as well known as an exotic femme fatale—the "amazona de la Pampa" (as Count Hermann Keyserling dubbed her) who flaunted her fortune and sexuality (to the titillation of some and the disgust of others) by driving alone with bare arms in Buenos Aires in the 1920s—as for her fifty-year commitment to publishing *Sur* as an international forum for ideas and literature.

Through all this, Ocampo is primarily considered as a woman and a public personality—not as an essayist, autobiographer, publisher, or magazine director. Yet her image is riddled with contradictions. Though she was a flamboyant public figure who enjoyed her celebrity, she apparently shrank from conversation in groups larger than two. José Bianco, her friend for over fifty years and editor-in-chief of *Sur* from 1938 to 1961, has noted that "Victoria era tan confidencial escribiendo porque lo era tan poco en la vida real" [Victoria was so intimate in her writing because she so lacked intimacy in real life]. Yet when he describes her as both extremely bold and timid, brazen and infantile, and concludes that her power emanated from some deep dark place that he calls her "innata aristrocracia," Bianco also epitomizes an ambivalence toward this powerful female figure, an ambivalence that is detectable even in the comments of her most sympathetic memorialists:

> No quiero decir que en la vida real Victoria fuera menos persuasiva que cuando escribía, pero entonces su persuasión no provenía de las palabras. Provenía de su innata aristocracia, de su porte, de su presencia. No necesitaba hablar para traslucir inteligencia.[5]

[I don't mean to say that in real life Victoria was less persuasive than when she wrote, but then, her persuasiveness did not come from words. It came from her innate aristocracy, from her conduct, from her presence. She didn't have to talk to show her intelligence.]

Recently remembered as "la mujer más hermosa de este lado de la Garbo y la Crawford que el Río de la Plata habia visto en cuerpo y alma"[6] [the most beautiful woman besides Garbo and Crawford that the Río de la Plata had ever seen in flesh and spirit], she is most often portrayed as a woman who, mysteriously, conveyed her power by being, rather than through her actions or literary production. Such commentaries suggest the myth and ambivalence that surround her public image and the difficulty of assessing her autobiographical writings as literature.

In 1952, when Victoria Ocampo resumed writing her *Autobiografía*, she was 62 years old (she was born in 1890) and already a polemical figure in Argentina. She continued to revise this work until shortly before her death in 1979. The *Autobiografía* seems meant to supply the background—and the last word—for reading Ocampo's collected work, which she began to publish timidly in the 1920s, but which burst forth in the 1930s and continued in a steady flow for the following four decades. More than any text published during her lifetime, the *Autobiografía* provides vital glimpses into the clash of influences, messages, and goals she established for herself as an Argentine woman of letters. This text provides a provocative point of departure from which to examine the paradoxical literary identity of Ocampo—a woman divided between allegiance to her sex and a conflicting attachment to the privileges of her class.

By focusing on Ocampo's posthumous autobiography, this discussion will analyze Ocampo's attempt to reconcile through the autobiographical writing the contradictions she displays as a woman and a self-avowed feminist who also championed the patriarchal values of the ruling class. In this primary step toward re-vision[7] of Ocampo's life and work and the myth surrounding both, she is most informatively considered in her various roles as a writer, publisher, and social figure who was torn between adherence to male models and the need for self-affirmation in each sphere. By its posthumous publication and contents, the *Autobiografía* represents the nexus between three interrelated facets of her literary career. In its exploration of the contradictions of the "blood ties" that defined her femininity as well as her birthright in the patriarchal ruling class, the *Autobiografía* provides an essential link between the testimonial essays, in which she focuses her experience through the works and lives of others, and her role as director of *Sur*, where she sponsored and coordinated the texts of others (mostly men) who shared her belief in the immutability of high artistic standards, but not her search for a language that would break the bonds of patriarchy.

This reading is concerned with a primary task of gynocentric criticism as described by Elaine Showalter: "to plot the precise cultural locus of female literary identity and to describe the forces that intersect an individual woman writer's cultural field.[8] In this exploration of the "vexed relation" to male literary culture which Ocampo shares with many women writers, it is assumed that "gender both informs and complicates both the reading and writing of texts."[9] The case of this woman of letters who composed in the "personal" genres of autobiography and memoir while maintaining a strong profile as a cultural businesswoman poses a challenge to the traditional marginalization of women's autobiographical writing and the role of businesswomen of letters who have managed publishing empires that have shaped the course of cultural debate. By analyzing the ways in which her literary language and multifaceted cultural project both trapped and liberated her, I hope to contribute to the demystification of this important female figure in modern Latin American cultural history, whose portion and profile were exceptional in her environment but by no means unique to it. In the unexplored space between her image as a public figure—"la parte visible del iceberg Ocampo"[10] [the visible part of the iceberg Ocampo]—and the lesser-known private self revealed through the autobiographical writings, there lies a striking example of the paradoxes of female literary accomplishment.

## "LA [OTRA] MITAD DE LA VERDAD"

Cada autor, grande o pequeño, genial o mediocre, escribe un solo libro a lo largo de su vida, aun cuando cambie de título y de tema.[11]

[Every author, great or small, brilliant or mediocre, writes a single book during his lifetime, though its title or theme may change.]

Lo cierto es que no conozco *por dentro* ninguna materia fuera de la que usaba [Montaigne]: 'Je suis moy mesme la matière de mon livre.'[12]

[It is certain that I know no other material than that used by Montaigne: 'I am myself the material of my book.']

Ocampo's six-volume *Autobiografía* is remarkable for its prehistory of the author. Obviously foreseen for posthumous publication (and prepared by the author with complete photo-inconography, it traces her ancestry, childhood, adolescence, and young adulthood through the first three decades of the twentieth century and stops with the inauguration of *Sur* in 1931. In references sprinkled throughout her work, Ocampo says she began composing her "memorias" (memoirs) in the 1930s; she continued to work on them until shortly before her death in 1979. She undertook the major revisions in 1952–1953.

The years from puberty in the early 1900s through first great love lost in 1929 are the focal points of the narrative. These three decades are characterized by a seemingly endless series of rites of passage; anecdote and confession are accompanied by letters written and received from key personal friends and correspondence between historic ancestors central to the story. In the *Autobiografía*, unlike the *Testimonios*, the history of her family which grounds the story and the rites of passage and existential crises which punctuate it all take her body and female sexuality as their explicit battleground.

The focus on her corporality as the point of integration and conflict is a remarkable departure from the typically disembodied and ethereal discussion of her self which permeates the testimonial essays published during her life. The story is built around moments of crisis and transition: she is portrayed as a sexual being coming of age in a patriarchal ruling-class environment and forced to confront rigid Victorian codes of behavior. Key stages in her sexual coming of age—menstruation, rejection of her maternal instincts—form the base of the personal, social, and professional choices she says she made in the first forty years of life. The tale culminates in the founding of *Sur*, the work she considered her greatest achievement.

Ocampo depicts herself in the decades that preceded the founding of *Sur* as an initially timid rebel victimized by a complex system of double standards that held her prisoner—first in her father's house, then in her husband's—until she rebelled, first into passionate adultery and then into the world of literary production. The *Autobiografía* must be considered as a parallel text, for it was composed over the same forty-year period in which the *Testimonios* and volumes of *Sur* established Ocampo's reputation and kept her relentlessly in the public eye. Given the magnitude of her published work and the dearth of critical consensus about its import in Argentine letters, this *Autobioqrafía* raises particular questions. The first concerns Ocampo's exclusive choice of focus upon her early years from the vantage point of the 1950s. What image of her formative years did she compose in the last three decades of her life for publication after her death? From a writer whose "yoismo" was legendary for over half a century, and whose entire corpus constitutes an exercise in autobiographical form, does this work represent "la [otra] mitad de la verdad," as she insisted, or is it merely the concluding chapter of her official history, filling in the early years before she became a public figure and entered the world of international personalities? What, finally, did she hope to add to—or change in—the reading of her life story by this posthumous pubication?

Purposely withheld from publication until her death (although she circulated versions of the manuscript among friends), the six volumes were released at regular intervals of about one year from 1980 to 1985. The spiciest parts of the narrative—especially the account of her illicit love affair with "J" in the 1920s, described in passionate if abstract terms—have been excerpted by Argentine equivalents of *Life*, *Time*, and *Cosmopolitan* to form the basis of continuing "human interest" stories in the popular press.[13] But neither the sensational reproduction of photoessays nor her continued presence in the book review pages of the Buenos Aires press has provoked the serious reconsideration of her life or work called for by this posthumous publication. The *Autobiografía* gives impetus to a rereading of Ocampo as a woman and literary personality whose public image as "Señora cultura"[14] approaches mythic status, but whose self-image and consciousness as a woman remain surprisingly guarded by the author (although amply debated by acquaintances).

What seems to have concerned her most is the revelation of her emotional and physical development as a woman—important grounding for her identity as writer, publisher, journalist, or society matron, but never focused on in her other writing on its own terms. Describing the *Autobiografía* as a "documento"—"cualquier cosa que sirve para ilustrar o comprobar algo" (1:60) [whatever works to illustrate or prove something]—Ocampo states her intention to tell the truth about her coming of age as a member of one of Buenos Aires's first families at the height of the Victorian era:

> No me cabe duda de que se podrá pensar, con todas las apariencias de la razón, que el único drama sufrido, las únicas dificultades vencidas en mi adolescencia y juventud, eran de la índole del desayuno que no llegó a hora fija, o del baño sin agua caliente por una momentánea descompostura de la caldera. Sin embargo, esto que parecería ser la verdad no es toda la verdad, ni siquiera la mitad de la verdad (2:9–10).

> [I have no doubt that one could think, with all apparent justification, that the only traumas I suffered, the only difficulties I overcame in my youth and adolescence, were along the lines of a breakfast that wasn't served on time or having to take a cold bath because of a temporary loss of hot water. Nonetheless, that which would appear to be the truth is not the whole truth, not even half the truth.]

She envisioned this work as a means to self-discovery ("alumbramiento") and thus a liberation from the sense of feeling so different from others that plagues her. Through the process she hopes to give birth to herself. At the same time, by reconciling who she was with who she wishes she had been (6: 11–13), she will also exonerate herself in the eyes of present and future critics:

> Hay dos sentimientos diferentes que me llevan a escribir estas Memorias. Uno es esa necesidad de alumbramiento, de confesión general; es el más importante. El otro es el deseo de tomar la delantera a posibles biografías futuras, con una autobiografía explícita (6: 13).

> [There are two different sentiments that motivate me to write these memoirs. One is the necessity for enlightenment, for a general confession; this is the most

important. The other is the desire to get a jump on possible future biographies with an explicit autobiography.]

Her final choice of the title *Autobiografía* for the posthumous volumes (as opposed to the *Testimonios*, memoirs published during her life) signals a bold distinction between this autobiographical "tale of becoming" and previously published memoirs of "the outer world for people and events."[15] Until the late 1970s Ocampo intended to title the autobiography "Memoirs," indicating a paradoxical resistance to validating the work as more than occasional writing, the shield she used to defend the *Testimonios*. As she considers the applicability of terms like "confession" and "document" in her autobiography, her dual purpose of vindication in the public eye and self-revelation takes clear shape.

In the *Autobiografía*, Ocampo's story is framed as a classic case of feminist consciousness-raising. The story outlines a conflict between who she is and who others want her to be, and offers a justification for who she became. By its posthumous publication, Ocampo offers this text as the concluding installment in a fifty-year project to balance official history and intimate memoirs in all her literary activities.

It is hardly a coincidence that she resumed this project in 1952—the year in which Eva Perón died and Juan Perón began his second term as president. Eva Perón's autobiography *La razón de mi vida* was published in 1951 and helped inscribe her permanently in Peronist hagiography.[16] Eva's presentation of her public persona in the Peronist Party, with almost no mention of her origins, family, or career before she met Juan, could not contrast more with the blood legacy Ocampo retraces so painstakingly. When spoken of together, Ocampo and Eva Perón are usually placed at opposite ends of the Argentine feminist spectrum, yet these autobiographical texts illustrate the straddling of traditions—male/female, national/international, contemporary/historical—and the conflict between class and sex which are central to rereading the lives of and myths surrounding both.

Eva's autobiography seeks to strengthen the official history of the Peronist Party: it is the story of Eva's self-sacrifice to her mission to serve the people, and a song of praise to Juan Perón, the figure who subsumes all other points of reference in her personal and political history. An iconoclastic figure, she presents herself as an exceptional but at heart conventional woman. Ocampo, by contrast, steeps herself in the oligarchic, patriarchic tradition into which she was born, loudly proclaiming her unconventionality and iconoclastic tendencies. Yet Ocampo's autobiography is as distinct from those of her male oligarchic forefathers and peers as it is from the officialist memoir of Evita couched in working-class, saintly, and feminine terms. Ocampo demonstrates the problematic position of female members of the Argentine elite: clearly at odds with the male autobiographical and literary traditions, they have been accorded no similarly stable position in the elite mythology, yet they continue to claim it as their own. Both Eva Perón and Ocampo present their life stories in forms that expose the paradoxical status of their positions in Peronist and anti-Peronist mythology.

In the 1950s, Ocampo was increasingly defensive about her own brand of feminism (women's suffrage was granted in 1947 through Eva's decisive influence), and *Sur*'s standards of "culture" were constantly under attack from Peronists and the anti-Peronist left (*Contorno*, for example, was initiated in 1953). *Sur* celebrated its twentieth anniversary in 1952 with the most deluxe issue of its history; yet recent historians mark this period as the beginning of its decline.

The three major phases in the dramatic (melodramatic?) story of Ocampo's coming of age take her body as their central battleground and metaphor. A detailed outline of her lineage in volume 1, recognizable from Argentine history books and her own writings, sets the stage for her struggle to reconcile an imposing family heritage with the double standard applied to female children's birthright, a conflict that permeates the *Autobiografía* from beginning to end. The menstrual blood, which comes as a terrible shock, symbolizes her exclusion from the "derecho de primogenitura" she had never questioned (as the oldest of six female children) but which her parents had never considered. But primogeniture refers to the right of the eldest son to inherit the property of his father, and was not understood to apply to female children. The sexual difference became clear to Ocampo only when she began to menstruate:

> Un dia al abrocharme al calzón en el cuarto de baño ví que tenía una mancha roja. . . . Era sangre. . . . Me sentí de pronto como aprisionada por una fatalidad que rechazaba con todas mis fuerzas. ¡Huir! Pero como huir de mi propio cuerpo. . . . Me sentía presa . . . de mi cuerpo que odiaba (1: 146).

> [One day while fastening my pants in the bathroom, I saw a red stain. . . . It was blood. . . . Immediately I felt imprisoned by a fate that I rejected with all my strength. Flee! But how to flee from my own body. . . . I felt trapped . . . by my body that I despised.]

Her upbringing is depicted as only apparently privileged; emphasis is placed on her attempts to evolve her own code of ethics among hypocrites and tyrants (family members) while avoiding open rebellion. Expressions of anger and regret punctuate accounts of the paltry formal education— primarily studies in French and English literature—given young girls of the upper class. Educated by tutors at home with only her sister Angélica as classmate, she was never supposed to make history on her own: "La educación que se daba a las mujeres era por definición y adrede incompleta, deficiente. 'Si hubiera sido varón, hubiera seguida una carrera,' decía mi padre de mi, con melancolia probablemente" (2: 16) [The education given to girls was by definition and on purpose incomplete and deficient. 'If she had been a boy, she would have pursued a career,' my father said of me, probably with regret].

The record of four generations of ancestors paraded before the reader in volumes 1 and 2, buttressed by genealogical research Ocampo conducted in the 1960s, serves as much to set the stage for who she is not as for who she is. The elaborate backdrop of forebears serves primarily to focus the most alienating experience in the early years—the onset of menstruation and first incontrovertible evidence of her femininity. She depicts herself as a "prisoner" in her female body, marginal to this impressive patriarchal heritage.

Apparently unlike the writers and characters discussed by Sandra Gilbert and Susan Gubar who name women's names in order to construct "grandmatologies" that reclaim their female heritage, Ocampo seems to seek shelter in the traditional family name.[17] The *Autobiografía* is an attempt to ground her female experience in a family name that is both overwhelming and nullifying. Yet the ambition to expose her femininity and confront the patriarchal traditions is complicated by the same patriarchal (and particularly Victorian) conventions that govern personal writing by women. She relegates all boys and men with whom she had romantic liaisons or sexual relations to an anonymous system of initials (for example, "J"), a practice that contrasts sharply with her obsession with naming names of ancestors in the same text.

How are we to judge, for example, the bold iconography of photographs and reproductions of herself (on the cover of each volume and spread throughout the volumes) and of selected central figures (family members, ancestors, and "great" men like Tagore), when contrasted with the use of initials for *all* of the men toward whom she acknowledges a series of childhood crushes? The use of initials at first seems to parody the openness she claims to demonstrate by revealing the evolution of her experience in love. Most of all, it contrasts curiously with the obsession with naming family members and friends of historical importance which permeates most of the autobiography.

This contrast between personal/sexual expression and the weight of family tradition is extended and reinforced by the bold photo-iconography that runs throughout the volumes, which were printed exactly as they were composed. Pictures of four generations of Aguirres and Ocampos are distributed throughout volumes 1 and 2, along with a photograph of Domingo Sarmiento dedicated to her great-grandfather, Manuel Ocampo. Famous friends and mentors, such as Marguerite Moreno (the diva who was Ocampo's voice teacher), Keyserling (two pictures), Ernest Ansermet, and Tagore, are also represented by imposing photographs. Naturally, numerous full-page photographs of herself grace the pages, as well as two portraits of her by well-known artists of the day—Helleu (1909, a drypoint done in Paris) and Troubetskoy (1913)—and the classic photograph by Gisèle Freund. Most are head-and-shoulder portraits of her alone; thus they do not convey a sense of her imposing height or size—she was over six feet tall. All are of herself as a young woman; none brings her beyond the early 1930s. Again, the body is suppressed. Yet the uniformity in size of most of the photographs of herself and others (mostly single shots of single figures which cover a full page) manages to convey the grandeur of her project by other means. The cover of each volume is dominated by a large photograph of the author; only volumes 1 and 4 vary from the format of the elegant young face in a designer hat, with the body cut off at the shoulders. The cover photograph of volume 1 depicts her as a small child on the knee of her imposing father; volume 3 (which contains the story of her romance with "J") departs from the other likenesses with a highly stylized oil painting of a full-body pose.

Even while she refers to her lovers by initial only, the tactic of hiding their identity reaches its contradictory height when she reproduces a photograph of "J" (3: 32–33) and of a statue of Joan of Arc, which is labeled as a likeness of "L. G. F.," the focus of an adolescent crush nipped by her elders (volume 1). Possible reasons for such tactics abound—irony, modesty, flaunting of tradition as she breaks it, respect for the families of these men. But in view of the flaunting of famous names and their photographic likenesses, the refusal to name these three symbols of her social development as a sexual being— the men involved in her first romantic fantasy, her ill-fated first marriage, and her first love affair—is remarkable indeed. Such differing treatments of two central facets of her life before *Sur* signals a lasting division in her attempts to reconcile personal aspirations and emotions with the weight of official family history.

In volumes 2 and 3 she passes from prisoner in the house of her parents to passionate adulteress in the house of her husband. Likening her world of the 1910s to that of García Lorca's *Casa de Bernarda Alba* and the nineteenth-century "esclavitud tremenda" of Charlotte Brontë or Elizabeth Barrett, she depicts the impossibility of directly confronting the intransigent moral code imposed by her family on her relations with men or her professional aspirations. In her discussion of her long-term clandestine love affair with "J" during the height of her childbearing years, she explains that maternal instincts were overshadowed, with regret and resignation, by the stigma of illegitimacy of any offspring (divorce was illegal in Argentina until very recently). Forever the outsider, Ocampo thus transformed the "curse" of menstruation into a symbol of a unique "women's privilege" now forbidden her.

In volumes 4, 5, and 6, the dramatic conflict is focused on her passion for ideas and those who generate them, and her keen disappointment with their passion for her body, not her mind. The disintegration of her love affair with "J" combined with disappointing experiences with better-known intellectual jet-setters to provoke an identity crisis. She depicts the existential dilemma that peaked in 1929 as the inspiration to give birth to *Sur*, a literary endeavor more ambitious than she had imagined.

The 1920s represent years of critical turning points in her life, the years between her break from both parents and husband and the publication of the first issue of *Sur*. This was the decade in which her two greatest passions and ambitions—for love and for literature—sought their meshing points and in which her search for a self was a graphic struggle to reconcile body, mind, and spirit. These 1910s and 1920s barely hint at the political turmoil sweeping Argentina—the anarchist movement and struggles for workers' rights, women's rights, university reform. Nor does she mention avant-garde projects in the arts, for she took little part in any of these. This is a private drama, whose historical background comprises her own blood relatives (and their close friends), whose literary and spiritual guides are English and French writers like Proust, Montaigne, George Sand, Henri Bergson, and Stendahl, and whose characters are a batch of foreign intellectuals—Keyserling, Ortega y Gasset, Tagore, Waldo Frank—whom she was to cultivate first in Buenos Aires, then in Europe and the United States.

Yet both the Argentine blood heritage and the European intellectual one provide a plethora of mixed messages and apparent contradictions. Ocampo seems to promise their resolution through her own writing and magazine endeavors (announced in volume 6), but she appears more often strung between these two sets of antecedents than at peace with either. Speaking of the early 1930s, she claims discomfort with her dual role in the magazine: as beneficent *mecenas* she feels at home, but as literary editor/publisher soliciting and judging others' literary production she feels inadequate (6: 69).

What is the overall picture the reader draws of the young (aged twenty to forty) Victoria Ocampo? A rich young woman who does not fit; deeply alienated, but tied to the primary representatives (both family and mentors) of the system of values that provoke her alienation. A young woman who first intuitively, then with forethought, creates from this alienated body a literary corpus and offensive. Though Ocampo capitalizes on class privilege, unlike her forefathers she battles the internal and external cultural expectations imposed on her sex.

## "YO SOY LO OTRO, PERO, ¿QUÉ?"

[Autobiography] is the most self-assertive and self-revealing of genres.[18]

To understand one's life as a story demands that one perceive that life as making sense; autobiographies record the sense their authors hope their lives make.[19]

As the picture of a young Argentine woman of the upper class coming of age in the early part of the twentieth century, Ocampo's work differs dramatically from the nineteenth-century male testimonial/autobiographical tradition of the founding fathers of Argentina, in whose company she is usually placed by dint of class. Indeed, her work is more accurately inserted in the "autogynographical" company of nineteenth- and twentieth-century European and American women writers.[20]

As much recent study of women's autobiography reveals, no matter how traditional critics and theorists of autobiography define the genre, women who dare to take themselves as the primary focus of their own first-person narratives have generally been considered either arrogant and self-centered (thereby offending accepted codes of women's behavior) or trivial, since the "private" life of even a "public" woman is traditionally devalued when judged by the standard of autobiographies of men of accomplishment. Female autobiographers who try to bridge the gap between public images and private lives have often found themselves in a paradoxical double bind: efforts to reveal their "true" self throw them into direct confrontation with critical expectations of trained readers and social expectations for women's propriety. Telling the truth becomes even harder than it first appeared.

Nancy Miller attributes some nineteenth-century writers' hesitancy to name names of lovers to the backlash against Jean-Jacques Rousseau's "tell-all stance—especially in the area of the sexual connection, the erogenous zones of the self." In her study of George Sand, Simone de Beauvoir and others, she shows that "full disclosure" is obviously not the aim of male or female autobiographers, but that the issue poses a special problem for women autobiographers even when they are distinguished writers and "already figures of public fiction." For women autobiographers, "the concern of notoriety, then, functions as an additional grid or constraint placed upon the truth." For women, the self's being justified is "indelibly marked by what Simone de Beauvoir calls 'feminitude,' a culturally determined status of difference and oppression."

Like the works of the writers in Miller's study, Ocampo's work presents an "official *reconstructed* personality" while it also broaches the author's "'submerged core,' [and] the 'sexual mystery that would make a drama.'" The difference between women's autobiography and that of men, according to Miller, is located in "the 'I' of the beholder, in the *reader's* perception and identity": although both male and female writers inscribe their sexuality on a literary text, male gender "is given and received literally as a mere *donnée* of personhood." Thus Miller proposed the notion of gender-bound reading, "a practice of the text that would recognize the status of the reader as differentiated subject . . . named by gender and committed in a dialectics of identification to deciphering the inscription of the female subject."[21] The intertextual self-examination in which Ocampo engages in *Testimonios*, the *Autobiografía*, and *Sur* is significantly informed by such gender-bound reading.

The consistently peculiar vision of women's autobiography in discussions among traditional (male) critics of the genre (and critics reading male texts) has drawn the attention of feminist critics rereading these works. Although critics of male texts share only a basic consensus about the definition of autobiography, their consistent lack of attention to the voluminous personal writing by women is striking.[22] When Domna Stanton began in the early 1980s to trace the history of women's autobiographical production in literature, she was mystified by the plethora of autobiographies by men listed under the catalog heading and the "ghostly absence" of titles by women:

> Even in phallocratic terms, it made no sense. How could that void be reconciled with the age-old, pervasive decoding of all female writing as autobiographical? One answer . . . was that "autobiographical" constituted a positive term when applied to Augustine and Montaigne, Rousseau and Goethe, Henry Adams and Henry Miller, but that it had negative connotations when imposed on women's texts. It had been used, I realized, . . . to affirm that women could not transcend, but only record, the concerns of the private self; thus, it had effectively served to devalue their writing.[23]

In the lengthy debate about the relative merits of and distinctions between various forms of personal narrative, critics have generally tended to privilege "autobiography" above all others. As Ocampo's avoidance of this term until the last years of her life shows, she also believed in this hierarchy. In the context of her collected work, the *Autobiografía* is, then, the boldest possible affirmation of self-narration: it represents an attempt to lay down the shield of the mirrored reflections of her self through others which she has used in the testimonial project. Ironically, the title also suggests that the taboo against discussing her body explicitly can be broken only after her death.

Stanton, Estelle Jelinek, and other feminist theorists point consistently to the need to read the difference in self-fashioning in women's autobiographies; they call for dispensing with polemics among critics eager to limit discussions to genre and focusing instead on the gender of self-representation. It is in this context that Ocampo's very different emphasis on her corporality and female sexuality can best be understood.

In her groundbreaking studies of women's autobiography, Jelinek is not interested in the traditional male critical tendency to "legitimize autobiography as an aesthetic genre in order to distinguish it from mere historical document" or to perpetuate a hierarchy among autobiographical forms which privileges autobiography over memoirs, testimonies, or diaries. Jelinek terms this tendency an "autobiographical fallacy" and examines the problems such reading has posed for women autobiographers.[24]

According to Jelinek's hypothesis of differences between male and female autobiography, Ocampo's work combines primary features of both male and female autobiographies: it displays "a unity [and unidirectionality] that betokens a faith in the continuity of the world and [her] own self-image," while in narrative form and organization it reveals much of the "disconnectedness" and "fragmentation" traditionally linked to women's autobiographical writing.[25] The *Autobiografía* combines various forms—from historical summary and fragments of childhood memories to previously published material and letters, inserted in groups or singly, sometimes with little introduction. Transitions between these parts can be loose, tight, or not initially apparent.

Ocampo was as familiar through her reading with the European and American traditions of women's autobiography—from Sor Juana Inés de la Cruz and St. Teresa de Ávila to George Sand, Mme de Stael, Colette, and Virginia Woolf—as she was with the Argentine male "generación del ochenta" of Domingo Sarmiento and Manuel A. Pueyrredon (1802–1865) through her family connections. She combined facets of both traditions in her own testimonial and autobiographical works, just as she struggled in her life to reconcile her sexuality and feminism with her oligarchic class connections. Ocampo belonged to the upper class by dint of family heritage, but her sex and experience determined a unique evolution. She was not a player in the political world of her forefathers, but rather combined the role of female salon leader with extensive writing and the direction of an important literary magazine—a combination of roles not shared exactly by any of her contemporaries, male or female, in Argentina.

In a study of five activist women autobiographers born in the nineteenth century—Emmeline Pankhurst, Emma Goldman, Dorothy Day (founder of the *Catholic Worker*), Eleanor Roosevelt, and Golda Meir—Patricia Meyer Spacks characterizes their accounts as "female variants on the high tradition of the spiritual autobiography." Although only Day could be said to adhere to a formal tradition, Spacks compares the "certainty" characteristics of spiritual autobiographies (which "draw energy and conviction from the affirmation of transcendent meaning") to the "rhetoric of *uncertainty*... about the self, about the value of womanhood, about the proper balance of commitments" evident in these modern women's autobiographies.

The women in Spacks's study possess two traits in common with Ocampo: they all "describe themselves, implicitly or explicitly, as gaining identity from their chosen work," and yet "all won not only fame but notoriety, each the object of bitter attack for her public achievements." Ocampo always explained her commitment to *Sur* in terms of its "spiritual meaning" (Spacks's term), often to the dismay of friends and foes alike.[26] She also characterized her own story as a "proclamation of faith" (1: 59) in the confessional tradition of Catholic mystics like St. Teresa (1515–1582) and Sor Juana (1648/51–1695).[27]

Argentine critics of Ocampo's *Testimonios* such as Blas Matamoro and Juan José Sebreli have positioned her in the tradition of the male "generación del ochenta" [the generation of 1880], describing testimonial writers of the oligarchy who make "el inventario de sus posesiones, hablando sobre sus parientes, sus amigos, sus casas, sus viajes, sus libros"[28] [the inventory of their possessions, and speak about their relations, friends, houses, travels, and books]. She demonstrates the tendency that Adolfo Prieto identifies within "buena parte de la literatura autobiográfica [masculina] argentina durante el siglo XIX: el actitud del hombre que necesita justificarse ante la opinión pública"[29] [a good portion of Argentine (male) autobiographical literature in the nineteenth century: the attitude of the man who must justify himself to the public], yet the "triviality" for which she is criticized by Matamoro and Sebreli only highlights the difference in social experience, expectations, and self-perception of female members of the same class.

In discussing the problematic relation of literate women in history to "the culture of the alphabet," Gilbert and Gubar concur with Claude Lévi-Strauss that "writing may always have been associated with class oppression." Yet they distinguish the literary production of women, regardless of class affiliation, from that of men: "as feminist theorists from Woolf to Beauvoir have argued, the situation of women goes beyond class: no matter what their socioeconomic status, those who reproduce the species have never controlled the production of culture."[30] The undifferentiated classification of Ocampo's autobiography and collected work still maintained by critics of the Argentine male oligarchy ignores the sexual difference central to a full understanding of her self-image and the cultural myth that surrounds her. The unresolved search for an identity as female oligarch which lies at the center of Ocampo's collected work and represents the explicit focus of the *Autobiografía* raises questions about the role of women in propagating high culture. Ocampo's identification with the patriarchal legacy of Argentina's founding fathers constitutes the dilemma at the core of her cultural ideology and her sexual identity.

Argentine women writers roughly contemporary to Ocampo such as Delfina Bunge de Galvez, Norah Lange, Silvina Bullrich, María Rosa Oliver, and Carlotta Garrido de la Peña have also written autobiographical accounts that provide a challenging basis for comparison with Ocampo's *Autobiografía*.[31] Unlike these women, however, Ocampo wrote exclusively in explicitly autobiographical forms. Also unlike her female contemporaries in Argentina, she was a businesswoman of letters. Acknowledged as a central figure in the production of high culture, she was not only mistress of her own texts but also editor and coordinator of others' literary production.

Elizabeth Winston's study of autobiographies by North American and British women writers published after 1920 helps to place Ocampo's among the unprecedented number of autobiographies written by women and men in the Americas and Europe in the 1930s:

Women who published autobiographies after 1920 . . . no longer apologized for their careers and successes, though a few still showed signs of uneasiness at having violated cultural expectations for women. . . . This change in the autobiographer's relation to her readers reflects an important change in the writer's self-image and the kinds of autobiographical intentions she exhibited. That is, the more confident these women became of the legitimacy of their way of life, the more freely they used autobiography for explicitly personal and, thus, more self-validating reasons—to express strongly held beliefs, explore and understand the self, or experiment with the conventions of the genre.[32]

Winston summarizes common reasons given by women like Gertrude Stein, Edith Sitwell, and Harriett Monroe for writing autobiographies: "to inform or exhort their readers, to clarify the past for themselves, . . . to experiment with the autobiographical form, or to assert their personal superiority." A recurring conflict in these works also seems to apply to Ocampo:

> Yet, even in these vigorously self-affirming narratives, especially in Sitwell's angry autobiography, one detects the signs of struggle, the force spent in challenging criticism and fighting restriction. One gets a glimpse, in other words, of the price of success for a woman writing.[33]

The posthumous publication of the *Autobiografía* reinforces a reading of Ocampo's entire testimonial and autobiographical opus as a lifelong struggle to shape an integrated persona. Although the *Autobiografía* suggests that her disappointment in love and doubts about her own talent as a writer in the 1920s would be assuaged by the founding of *Sur*, like the *Testimonios*, this account rather emphasizes a series of dilemmas that she seemed never to resolve. Her primary adherence to French as a literary language in her own writing conflicted with her commitment to publish in Spanish for Argentine readers, causing a sense of linguistic displacement in more than metaphoric terms. As a woman, she was torn between adherence to male models and the need for self-affirmation. And in her search to define her self, she was torn between dependency on patriarchy and defense of her own autonomy.

Ocampo's *Autobiografía* betrays a self as divided and disparate as those of the women writers who served as her literary models. Yet, as Nancy Miller has explained in her study of French women autobiographers, the exercise of justifying an unorthodox life by writing about it is an assertion of power which must also be understood as a reviolation of masculine turf. Ocampo's *Autobiografía* is also "a defense and illustration, at once a treatise on overcoming received notions of femininity, and a poetics calling for another, freer text."[34] Though Ocampo's work displays the prejudices of her class and economic status, as does that of her male predecessors, the subject of her autobiography is similar to that of other women: "a self both scotomized and overexposed by the fact of her femininity as a social reality."[35] In *Sur y Cía* [Sur & Company], the last volume of the *Autobiografía*, Ocampo promises to resolve the conflict of her dual identity through the founding and directing of *Sur*, undoubtedly the literary project for which she is best known. On the last page of her narrative (6: 86) she declares that the story of her life was melded with that of the magazine from the day it was born in 1931, thus justifying the closure of this *Autobiografía*.

In an essay commemorating Ocampo in 1979, Emir Rodríguez Monegal called for a rereading of her *Testimonios* and suggests her problematic position in the modern literary history of Argentina: "Se va a necesitar mucho tiempo para que [*Los testimonios*] sean leídos como lo que son: la crónica de una mujer que en país de machos condescendientes se atrevió a pensar y a sentir y amar como se le dió la gana" [much time will need to pass before the *Testimonios* will be read for what they are: the chronicle of a woman who dared to think, to feel, and to love exactly as she pleased in a country of condescending machos]. And he disagrees with Borges's cavalier assessment of Ocampo as impervious to social convention and the judgment of others—"'Victoria siempre hizo lo que quiso, *and she got away with it*'" [Victoria always did what she wanted. . . . ]. In his epitaph he responds to Borges—"Si, se salió con la suya, pero a que precio"[36] [yes, she always got her way, but at what price]— and signals both the problem and the solution for it.

Elaine Showalter has argued that "the specificity of female writing will emerge . . . from the study of the woman writer's interaction with both her male and female literary heritages." It is precisely this combination of traditions which Ocampo straddled so uncomfortably throughout five decades of autobiographical production and editorial involvement. Like other "women writing," Ocampo is not "*inside* and *outside* of the male tradition," but rather "inside two traditions simultaneously."[37] Despite the impressive volume of her literary production, she made an uneasy peace with the two "traditions." Ocampo's work represents a challenge to accepted theories of literary influence and to conventional role divisions in the business of letters. The "price" she paid for her accomplishments is reflected in the persistent disparity between her public image and the private self which emerges from an integral reading of her collected work.

Ocampo determined *Sur*'s official policy and was called to account for it publicly, but she was marginalized as a writer and a woman when she applied these ideals within the very pages of the magazine. While she might have wished that the story of her life were contained in *Sur*, only the official half of it can be read there. The unofficial one is better reconstructed through the ensemble of testimonial and autobiographical writings.

In the *Autobiografía*, Ocampo presents a previously unarticulated look at her struggles to conquer expectations to which she was intuitively and intellectually opposed. Though it is a provocative picture, unique in modern Argentine letters, of a young woman coming of age in the early part of the twentieth century, it also has the air of official epitaph. The work reveals in one bold, consolidated text both the extent of Ocampo's feminist rebellion and the restrictions imposed on it by her loyalty to the upper class into which she was born.

## NOTES

1. John King, "Towards a Reading of the Argentine Literary Magazine *Sur*," *Latin American Research Review* 16, 2 (1981): 57–78. For the most extensive study of *Sur*,

see John King, "*Sur* and Argentine Culture: 1931–1970" (Ph.D. diss., Oxford University, 1982).

This question is discussed in the context of Ocampo's collected work in Janet Greenberg, "The Divided Self: Forms of Autobiography in the Writings of Victoria Ocampo" (Ph.D. diss., University of California, Berkeley, 1986).

2. Of particular note is Sylvia Molloy's upcoming book on autobiography in Argentina which contains a significant rereading of Victoria Ocampo's autobiography.

3. Although Ocampo had been writing her "Memorias" since the 1930s, the version finally published was composed in 1952–1953 and revised continuously until shortly before her death.

The *Autobiografía* has been published in six volumes by Ediciones Revista Sur (Buenos Aires): Volume 1: *El archipiélago* [the archipelago], 1979; 2: *El imperio insular* [the insular empire] (1980), 1982; 3: *La rama de Salzburgo* [the Salzburg branch] (1981), 1982; 4: *Viraje* [changing direction], 1982; 5: *Figuras simbólicas—Medida de Francia* [symbolic figures—using France as a measure], 1983; VI: *Sur y Cía* [Sur & Company], 1984. All dates in parentheses refer to the latest editions.

4. John King, "Towards a Reading."

5. "Victoria" (1981), rpt. in *Páginas de José Bianco* (Buenos Aires: Editorial Celtia, 1984), 184–185.

6. Emir Rodríguez Monegal, "Victoria Ocampo," *Vuelta* 3, 30 (May 1979): 45.

7. A term given its current meaning in feminist context by Adrienne Rich, "When We Dead Awaken: Writing in Re-Vision", in *On Lies, Secrets, and Silence: Selected Prose, 1966–1978* (New York: W. W. Norton, 1979). Rich defines the critical "re-vision" of literature from a feminist perspective as "the act of looking back, of seeing with fresh eyes, of entering an old text from a critical direction." This process "is for women more than a chapter in cultural history—it is an act of survival"(35).

8. Elaine Showalter, "Feminist Criticism in the Wilderness," in *Writing and Sexual Difference*, special issue of *Critical Inquiry* 8, 2 (Winter 1981): 202–203. Showalter also describes two distinct varieties of feminist criticism—the first is concerned with "woman as reader," the second with "woman as writer"—in "Toward A Feminist Poetics," in *The New Feminist Criticism: Essays on Women, Literature and Theory*, ed. Elaine Showalter (New York: Pantheon Books, 1985).

9. Elizabeth Abel, "Editor's Introduction," in *Writing and Sexual Difference*, 173.

10. Emir Rodríguez Monegal, "Victoria Ocampo," 47.

11. "Carta al lector a propósito del título," *Testimonios III* (Buenos Aires: Editorial Sudamericana, 1946), 8.

12. "Mujeres en la Academia," *Testimonios* 10 (Buenos Aires: SUR, 1977), 19.

13. See, for example, María Núñez, "Me casé para darle el gusto a mi padre" (the last part in a series of excerpts from the *Autobiografía*), *Para ti* (Buenos Aires) 28 December 1980; and Ernesto Schoo, "La vida de Victoria Ocampo," pt. 3, *Revista Siete Dias* 9 (July 1980): 99–102. Prepublication excerpts were also published in *La Nación* and the Spanish edition of *Life* (exact dates unavailable).

A new wave of essays in homage to Ocampo also appeared in popular magazines after her death, some with extravagant photographs. See, for example, Luis Mazas, "Victoria Ocampo: La señora cultura," *Somos* 2, 64 (December 9, 1977); and María Ester Vázquez, "Homenaje a Victoria Ocampo: Una argentina universalita," *Brigitte* (Buenos Aires), 7 January 1980.

14. One of many flattering titles coined by the popular press. This appears in Luis Mazas, "Victoria Ocampo: La señora cultura," *Somos* (roughly equivalent to *Time* or *Newsweek*), 2, 64 (December 9, 1977).

15. Marcus K. Billson and Sidonie A. Smith discuss the distinction between women's autobiography and memoirs in "Lillian Hellman and the Strategy of the 'Other,'" in *Women's Autobiography: Essays in Criticism*, ed. Estelle C. Jelinek (Bloomington: Indiana University Press, 1980), 163.

16. On Eva Perón's autobiography, see especially Marysa Navarro, "Of Sparrows and Condors: The Autobiography of Eva Perón," in *The Female Autograph*, ed. Domna Stanton (New York: Literary Forum, 1984), 205–211.

17. Sandra Caruso Mortola Gilbert and Susan Dreyfuss David Gubar, "Ceremonies of the Alphabet: Female Grandmatologies and the Female Autograph," in *The Female Autograph*, ed. Domna C. Stanton, 25–26. The title plays on Jacques Lacan's term from *Of Grammatology*.

18. Elizabeth Winston, "The Autobiographer and Her Readers: From Apology to Affirmation," in *Woman's Autobiography: Essays in Criticism*, ed. Estelle Jelinek, 95.

19. Patricia Meyer Spacks, "Selves in Hiding," in *Women's Autobiography: Essays in Criticism*, ed. Estelle Jelinek, 131.

20. This term was coined by Domna Stanton in "Autogynography: Is the Subject Different?" in *The Female Autograph*, ed. Domna Stanton.

21. Miller, "Women's Autobiography in France: For a Dialectics of Identification," in *Women and Language in Literature and Society*, ed. Sally McConnell-Ginet, Ruth Borker, and Nelly Furman (New York: Praeger, 1980), 267. Miller expands on the distinction made by Helene Cixous in *The Laugh of the Medusa* of a "marked" masculine form of writing to include a "masculine mode of reception."

22. See, for example, Philippe Lejeune's definition of "the autobiographical pact," first in *L'autobiographie en France* (Paris: Armand Colin, 1971) and then in *Le pacte autobiographique* (Paris: Seuil, 1975) and "Le pacte autobiographique (bis)," *Poétique* 56 (November 1983): 416–434. In "Women and Autobiography at Author's Expense," his only treatment of women's autobiography (in *The Female Autograph*, ed. Domna C. Stanton), Lejeune concludes that "what women are undoubtedly trying to gain through the tool of autobiography is equality in the expression of unhappiness" (259).

Also see Roy Pascal's influential study, *Design and Truth in Autobiography* (Cambridge, Mass.: Harvard University Press, 1960).

23. Domna Stanton, "Autogynography," 6–7.

24. Estelle Jelinek, "Introduction: Women's Autobiography and the Male Tradition," *Women's Autobiography*, 10. Other important studies of women, autobiography, and memory include Estelle C. Jelinek, *The Tradition of Women's Autobiography: From Antiquity to the Present* (Boston: Twayne, 1986); Dale Spender, ed., *Personal Chronicles: Women's Autobiographical Writings*, special issue of *Women's Studies International Forum* 10, 1 (1987); Margaret A. Lourie, Domna Stanton, and Martha Vicinus, eds., *Women and Memory*, special issue of *Michigan Quarterly Review* 36, 1 (Winter 1987).

25. Jelinek, *Women's Autobiography*, 10.

26. Patricia Meyer Spacks, "Selves in Hiding," 113. For a provocative discussion of variations on "confessional" and "spiritual" autobiographies by politically engaged women of the nineteenth century, see also Estelle Jelinek, "The Paradox and Success of E. Cady Stanton," *Women's Autobiography*.

27. In Emilie Bergmann's essay in the present volume, Sor Juana is treated as a central precursor to feminist consciousness and autobiographical practice. Also see Electa Arenal, "The Convent as Catalyst for Autonomy: Two Hispanic Nuns of the Seventeenth Century," in *Women in Hispanic Literature: Icons and Fallen Idols*, ed. Beth Miller (Berkeley, Los Angeles, London: University of California Press, 1983), 174.

28. Juan José Sebreli, "Victoria Ocampo" (1975), rpt. in *De Buenos Aires y su gente: Antología* (Buenos Aires: Centro Editor de América Latina, 1982), 144. Also see Blas Matamoro, *Oligarquía y literatura* (Buenos Aires: Libros del Tercer Mundo, 1975), with scathing chapters on Victoria and Silvina Ocampo, Manuel Mújica Lainez, and others. Variations on this line of criticism continue to be published regularly in the Argentine press.

29. Adolfo Prieto, *La literatura autobiográfica argentina* (Buenos Aires: Centro Editor de América Latina, 1982), 50, 21. Prieto does not mention Ocampo, since she falls outside the chronological boundaries of his study. The memoirs and letters of Mariquita Sánchez (who does fall within the period) are mentioned only in passing; Prieto offers little apparatus for analyzing the memoirs of women or others who did not figure in the central military and political events of the period.

30. Gilbert and Gubar, "Ceremonies," 25.

31. See especially Delfina Bunge de Galvez, *Viaje alrededor de mi infancia* (1938) and *La vida en los sueños* (1951); Norah Lange, *Cuadernos de infancia* (1937); Carlotta Garrido de la Peña, *Mis recuerdos* (1935); María Rosa Oliver's three-volume autobiography, *Mundo, mi casa: Recuerdos de infancia* (1965), *La vida cotidiana* (1969), and *Mi fé es el hombre* (1981, published posthumously); and Silvina Bullrich, *Mis memorias* (1980).

32. Elizabeth Winston, "The Autobiographer and Her Readers," 94–95.

33. Ibid., 95.

34. Nancy K. Miller, 262–263.

35. Ibid., 270–272. See also Germaine Brée's essay on George Sand, "The Fictions of Autobiography," *Nineteenth Century French Studies* 4 (Summer 1976): 438–449.

36. Rodríguez Monegal, "Victoria Ocampo," 47.

37. Elaine Showalter, "Feminist Criticism in the Wilderness," 203.

# NINE

# Sor Juana Inés de la Cruz: Dreaming in a Double Voice

*Emilie L. Bergmann*

## LITERARY STATUS AS OBSTACLE TO FEMINIST READINGS

Sor Juana Inés de la Cruz (1648–1695)[1] was already recognized during her lifetime as Colonial Latin America's greatest poet, and she has been triply canonized as an origin for Latin American literature, as the epitome of Baroque literature in Spanish, and as the first feminist writing in the New World. It is of obvious importance to study Sor Juana's work from a feminist perspective in order to examine the interrelationships between these potentially conflicting canonical categories. The picture we have of Sor Juana as woman is blurred by the self-imposed images of her as poet and scholar, eluding and parodying the gender categories of her time, by means of intricate and absorbing webs of rhetorical structure and erudite allusion that were accessible to few of her contemporaries. Since her tercentenary in 1951, her work has become the focus of increasingly serious and detailed critical attention, which forms an even more imposing edifice of authority and prestige. While Latin American women readers and writers are drawn to Sor Juana's image as precursor, the dense erudition that has been the object of recent critical attention can prove culturally alien to the female reader of the twentieth century.

The problems that need to be addressed in feminist readings of Sor Juana's works are not those of rediscovery or restoration of prestige but questions of the conditions of her prestige and the ways in which she may be read. These are questions of feminist methods of reading and uncovering the roots of gendered literary consciousness on the part of a brilliant and self-aware female writer.

Sor Juana continues to appear as the larger-than-life protagonist in the drama of readers' and critics' responses to her secular and religious writing, a drama of which she appears to have been acutely aware. The court of the viceroys of Mexico bestowed upon her at the age of thirteen a double-edged social role as a prodigy, which meant that while she was respected for her intellectual accomplishments, she was also marginalized as a freakish phenomenon and kept on display as another treasure in the viceroys' collection. She was aware of her exceptional position in society, beginning with her illegitimate birth to a Spanish-born nobleman and a Mexican-born mother of Spanish ancestry, her studious childhood, and her reception as a prodigy at the court of Colonial Mexico, through her chosen existence as a nun who contributed to but could not participate in the elaborate cultural life of the city surrounding her Jeronymite convent, and in her eventual renunciation of the intellectual pursuits for which she had chosen convent life, to devote herself to asceticism and finally to die in her mid-forties while caring for the victims of a plague. Subsequent generations of readers have continued to redefine her anomalous role as a learned woman and productive writer in an environment that singled her out but had no place for her.

For women readers in the twentienth century, and particularly for writers in search of inspiring role models, Sor Juana has become an icon of female intellectual independence. In *Mujer que sabe latín* (1973), the Mexican feminist writer Rosario Castellanos lists examples of pre-twentieth-century women who broke with traditional roles and managed to "attain their authentic image and . . . choose themselves and prefer themselves over all others."[2] At the head of Castellanos's list is Sor Juana, but she is followed by a collection of fictional characters distinguished for their abandonment of everything, including sanity and life, to the cause of antisocial passion: Melibea, "Dorotea," "Amelia," Ana Ozores, Anna Karenina, Hedda Gabler, and "La Pintada," whose nickname seems the final reduction of woman as literary character to the level of caricature. In this company of the imaginary creations of male writers, Sor Juana exists as legend, as phenomenon but not as woman in the imagination of the Mexican woman writer in search of a female tradition.[3]

As twentieth-century readers and critics reread the works of this woman canonized by her editors as the "Tenth Muse," and as critics explicate the complexity and subtlety of her classical allusions and scientific knowledge, the overwhelming impression is of her status as an exception in terms of sex and geographical distance from the European center of culture. Seen in her context by feminist readers in the twentieth century, she is an example of the necessity of special privilege in order for a talented woman to develop and exercise her talents in a culture that limits women's options, and her life is an illustration of the precariousness of that position.

What is remarkable about Sor Juana's writing is her clear awareness of her decisions to depart from the norm, and her unflinching confrontation with the consequences of those decisions. In her prose, poetry, and drama,

Sor Juana voices her protest against the injustice of women's place in her hypocritical society and of her own emblematic position of privilege at an impossible price. She defends herself and women in general in direct, first-person statements in her prose, through irony in her poetry, and through the character of Doña Leonor in her play *Los empeños de una casa* [*The Trials of a Household*]. Leonor is extraordinarily beautiful and learned, but because she has no personal autonomy even in the choice of a husband, these attributes have been her misfortune, attracting multitudes of suitors from among whom her father will choose. Once she has voiced her obligatory lamentations, Leonor departs from the female norm for Spanish drama of the time by affirming her exceptional learning and describing the man she loves in a tone and in detail ordinarily reserved for men regarding women. Leonor's self-depiction as brilliant scholar could easily be applied to Sor Juana herself. Most important is an awareness of the price of her accomplishment and renown, with no false modesty or regret.

> Inclinéme a los estudios
> desde mis primeros años
> con tan ardientes desvelos,
> con tan ansiosos cuidados,
> que reduje a tiempo breve
> fatigas de mucho espacio.
> .................................
> Era de mi patria toda
> el objeto venerado
> de aquellas adoraciones
> que forma el común aplauso.
> (2:2. 305–324)

[From my earliest years I was inclined toward study, with such burning sleeplessness and such anxious devotion that I reduced long tasks to a short space of time. . . . Throughout the country I was the venerated object of that adoration constituted by common applause.][4]

*Los empeños de una casa* departs from the norm of *comedia* plots in which intellectual women are subdued through marriage. Here, the woman is not blamed for choosing to realize her intellectual potential; instead, the *vulgo*, the "superstitious" throng, are blamed for simultaneously exalting their idol to the status of a deity and depriving her of her freedom. Leonor's marriage to a man she has chosen is both a concession to comic convention—the only ending possible for a work belonging to such a public genre as theater—and a symbolic resolution to the problem of female autonomy.

Sor Juana herself knew that there were no such felicitous reconciliations in the lives of learned women. In her autobiographical account in defense of her scholarly pursuits, the *Respuesta a Sor Filotea*, she explains that she rejected marriage and chose the convent so that she could continue to study. Since the purpose of the *Respuesta* was in part an apologia, her self-portrayal is both honest and calculated to show her courage and ingenuity in confronting a paucity of options in her youth.

## THE AUTOBIOGRAPHICAL PROJECT AS SELF-DEFINITION

Born Juana Ramírez de Azbaje, the illegitimate child of a Mexican-born mother, she began life on the margins of the rigidly hierarchical Counter-Reformation culture of Nueva España. In a society that was itself in a process of transition and self-definition, separated as it was from the European centers of the dominant culture, Sor Juana defined herself, and determined the course of all but the last two years of her life, within the possible modes of existence. She devoted much of her life to writing secular and religious poetry and to the study of theology, speculative philosophy, and natural science, all unusual for a woman and dangerous even for male writers in a Counter-Reformation Hispanic environment. The contradictions and silences in her writing are indications of the tensions generated by her confrontations with Counter-Reformation doctrines of humility, obedience, and ignorance as preferable to heresy. Sor Juana's self-definition extends even to the fact that most of the biographical details we have come from her own account in the *Respuesta a Sor Filotea* [response to Sor Filotea]. This is her view of herself, her self-portrait created in the image by which she chose to be remembered, written between the lines of an erudite letter defending her right to study and to make her work available to others.

Aware of how potentially disruptive a self-defined and articulate woman could be, Sor Juana's confessor, Antonio Núñez de Miranda, "having recognized her singular erudition together with her not inconsequential beauty . . . used to say that God could not send a greater scourge to Mexico than if he had allowed Juana Inés to remain in the public and secular world."[5] The term Father Núñez de Miranda used was "la publicidad del siglo," and the theological debate in which the nun engaged in 1690 did bring her into the public sphere, not completely by her own choice.

Ironically, the confrontation with the church hierarchy ensuing from this particular debate began with the apparent encouragement of her superiors in 1690, when she wrote a critique of a sermon by the Portuguese Jesuit Antonio de Vieyra on Christ's greatest gift to mankind. Where her pursuits in the enclosed convent world intersected with the politicized sphere of theological discourse outside, the nun found herself trapped in a public light that, for a woman in her context, meant scandal. Her critique came to the attention of Manuel Fernández de Santa Cruz, Bishop of Puebla, who published it without the nun's knowledge under the title *Carta Atenagórica*, meaning "worthy of Athena." At the same time he criticized Sor Juana for her participation in theological debates, in a letter signed "Sor Filotea," applying St. Paul's prescription that women should keep silent and study only for the sake of learning, not with the purpose of teaching others. He advised Sor Juana to abandon secular studies for theology.

Sor Juana's defense, the well-known *Respuesta a Sor Filotea* (1691), confronts the issue of women's right to study and courageously affirms her scholarly dedication. Her clarity of reasoning, eloquence, and erudition are evident in this defense. But she also renounced her scholarly pursuits soon after writing the *Respuesta* and dispersed her library, one of the most extensive in the Americas at the time. The reasons for this renunciation are not clear, but most probably were a combination of pressure from ecclesiastical authority and a change in the power structure that had previously supported her work. Although the *Respuesta* was not published, only circulated, during Sor Juana's lifetime, her confessor Father Núñez withdrew his support from Sor Juana soon afterward.

Sor Juana's self-depiction and justification in the *Respuesta* is itself daring and dangerous, and each representation of her choices has a purpose. For example, she says that she was willing to dress as a boy in order to go to school and learn Latin. Latin was not only the language of learning but also the language of power, and her erudition won her entrance into the court of the viceroy and his wife, who became her patrons. While she was learning Latin at home, she says, she cut off an inch of her beloved hair each time she did not progress sufficiently: her perception of the relationship between female identity and access to power is evident. She was acclaimed and welcomed in the secular world, but decided to enter the convent because, as she says, given the "total antipathy she felt for marriage," convent life seemed "the least unsuitable and the most honorable" way of life she could choose. As the title of Electa Arenal's study of Sor Juana and other nuns of the period indicates, the convent was a "catalyst for autonomy," an environment in which, at least for a time, she could engage in intellectual work.[6]

But in her self-representation, Sor Juana also depicts herself as defiant and unable to repress her intellectual curiosity. Having chosen religious life as a setting for intellectual work, she found that the church objected to her studies in natural science, the secular area of speculative philosophy that could not be controlled by theological doctrine and would eventually challenge it openly. When ordered to renounce her studies for a few months, Sor Juana says, she was unable to resist the pursuit of knowledge and made inadvertent scientific observations in the cooking of an egg or the contemplation of perspective in a convent dormitory. She jokingly speculates on how much more Aristotle would have written had he entered the kitchen.[7] Her intellectual activity, ranging from the everyday to the most esoteric areas of theology, astronomy, mathematics, and speculative philosophy, brought her into areas the church hierarchy considered dangerous and potentially

heretical. Thus, there could be no adequate rebuttal to the implicit accusa-
tions in the letter by "Sor Filotea"; the nun's obedience to the church meant
renunciation of the very intellectual work that had motivated her decision to
renounce the "world" and enter the convent.

The interaction of the "world" and the convent in Sor Juana's life was
complex and multidimensional. All her work, with the exception of the
*Primero Sueño* [*First Dream*], as she explains in the *Respuesta a Sor Filotea*, was
written on commission for religious or court festivities. Like most writers of
her time, she was dependent upon the benevolence of her patrons, in her case
patrons in the highest secular and religious positions. Unlike that of her male
counterparts, her very writing—even her popular *villancicos* written for ecclesiastical festivities—was an act of defiance. She was a nun of the Jeronymite
order, which allowed her the time and freedom to study and to receive educated and powerful visitors in her "salon," in the convent's public *locutorio*,
where she could discuss intellectual and artistic questions. Nonetheless, her
vows ultimately bound her to obedience to her superiors. When she was
accused by the bishop of Puebla, disguised as a sisterly adviser, of devoting
herself too much to worldly pursuits, the offense was clearly not her love
poetry or her commissioned works for public ceremonies but her theological
writing, her participation in an area where women as scholars were not permitted, and the accusation served as a warning that ultimately silenced her.

She refers to silence, and the dangers of misunderstanding its meaning, in
her *Respuesta*, leaving the perceptive reader to wonder what she left unsaid:

> . . . casi me he determinado a dejarlo al silencio, pero como éste es cosa negati-
> va, aunque explica mucho con el énfasis de no explicar, es necesario ponerle
> algún breve rótulo para que se entienda lo que se pretende que el silencio diga;
> y si no, dirá nada el silencio, porque ése es su oficio: decir nada.

She then refers to St. Paul's experience of hearing words that he could not
repeat:

> No dice lo que vio, pero dice que no lo puede decir; de manera que aquellas
> cosas que no se pueden decir, es menester decir siquiera que no se pueden
> decir, para que se entienda que el callar no es no haber qué decir, sino no caber
> en las voces lo mucho que hay que decir.

> [I . . . was sorely tempted to take refuge in silence. But as silence is a negative
> thing, though it explains a great deal through the very stress of not explaining,
> we must assign some meaning to it that we may understand what the silence is
> intended to say, for if not, silence will say nothing, as that is its very office, *to say
> nothing*. . . . [St. Paul] does not say what he heard; he says that he cannot say it.
> So that of things one cannot say, it is needful to say at least that they cannot be
> said, so that it may be understood that not speaking is not the same as having
> nothing to say, but rather being unable to express the many things there are to
> say.][8]

## SOR JUANA IN THE GENDERED IMAGINATION

Recent critics have tried to explain the renunciation and silence at the end of Sor Juana's life. Her renunciation was emblematic for Latin American women writers of the twentieth century, whose careers may not have been marked by such dramatic changes from public acclaim to confrontation with and censure by the authorities, but who still encountered social obstacles to their writing and publication. Hispanic women writers regard her as a kind of patron saint. Rosario Castellanos's significant inclusion of Sor Juana in a list of fictional characters is symptomatic of the place of women intellectuals in Hispanic society. Women writers and critics continued to be excluded from the mainstream of cultural life, and separated from a significant role model by her distortion as legend during the three centuries following her birth.

Not surprisingly, among the first major studies on Sor Juana's work were those by men like Ludwig Pfandl, who explained her unique intellectual accomplishments as resulting from a biological aberration combined with a narcissistic fixation on her father: if she could not be denied her intellectual accomplishments, she must be denied her identity as a woman, thereby depriving other women of the possibility of recognizing themselves in her writing.[9] Octavio Paz claims that women were "slow" to bring their critical talents to bear on her work, and yet it was the research of Dorothy Schons in the 1920s that revealed Sor Juana's illegitimacy and supplied essential material for Paz's rewriting of Pfandl's thesis concerning Sor Juana's relationship to her father.[10]

Since Sor Juana's tercentenary in the 1950s, studies (including Paz's) have focused on her erudition in the context of the dominant European culture that she seems to have assimilated, transformed, and in some cases perhaps anticipated—in particular, Cartesian philosophy of mind. Recent studies of Sor Juana's polemical letters, the *Carta Atenagórica* and the *Respuesta a Sor Filotea*, as well as her long epistemological poem, the *Primero Sueño*, illuminate the intellectual subtleties of these texts. It is necessary, however, to bring this erudition into the perspective of Sor Juana's self-identity as female writer and find the radical difference evident in each of her assumptions of the mask of seventeenth-century European culture, particularly since her *Sueño* addresses the question of knowledge itself. Paz admits that his subtitle, *Las trampas de la fe* [*The Traps of Faith*], applies only to Sor Juana's self-accusation before the ecclesiastical authorities, but it emphasizes the hopelessness of her attempt at intellectual freedom within the convent and as a woman manipulating discourse in a setting where discourse could be effectively distorted or contradicted by the men in power.

Sor Juana's intellectual energy—her ability to deploy the arguments of Scholastic theology and surpass the subtle intertextual complexity of Spain's

most challenging Baroque poet, Luis de Góngora—placed her in the Hispanic literary canon, but under conditions that denied the importance of
gender and her relationship to her racially and hierarchically complex society. Thus, the Chicana playwright Estela Portillo Trambley's dramatization
of Sor Juana's life contributes to a feminist reading by representing her close
spiritual relationships with her Jeronymite sisters and a painful separation
from Juana, the mulatto slave who was reared with Sor Juana and sent with
her to the convent as a servant.[11] Trambley indicates the direction for feminist reading of Sor Juana by populating the stage with human relationships.
She dramatizes the loyalties, conflicts, and self-awareness that animated Sor
Juana's life and have spoken to generations of women readers in search of
verification of their experience.

Painted portraits of Sor Juana show her wearing a large oval medallion
depicting the Annunciation, sometimes nearly covering her chest—an image
appropriate to her Jeronymite order but also symbolic of the poet's paradoxical status. Through the process of her literary canonization, the image
of her as exceptional—chosen like the Virgin for special honors and trials,
singled out first by her gifts and then by the viceroys—obscures her multidimensional being as a woman, and her being in the world. She herself
alluded to the sufferings of Christ in her *Respuesta*, choosing an even more
daring symbol for her unique status.

As an illegitimate and unmarried female outsider, Sor Juana exposes contradictions in contemporary Hispanic culture, particularly and obviously in
the popular *redondilla* "Hombres necios" [foolish men], mocking men's condemnation of prostitution as immoral when they are themselves the eager
beneficiaries and the essential mechanism for its perpetuation:

> Hombres necios que acusáis
> a la mujer sin razón,
> sin ver que sois la ocasión
> de lo mismo que culpáis:
>
> ...........................
>
> ¿O cuál es más de culpar,
> aunque cualquiera mal haga:
> la que peca por la paga
> o el que paga por pecar?
>
> [You foolish men, who accuse
> Women without good reason,
> You are the cause of what you blame,
> Yours the guilt you deny.
>
> ...........................
>
> When each is guilty of sin,
> Which is the most to blame:
> She who sins for payment,
> Or he who pays for the sin?][12]

## DOUBLE-VOICED DREAMING IN THE
## DISCOURSE OF THE BAROQUE

Sor Juana exposes the contradictions more subtly in the last line of her philosophical reflection on knowledge, the *Sueño*, whose last line, "y yo despierta" [and I, awake], introduces for the first time in this 975-line poem the identity of the speaker as female. The gendered "despierta" appearing at the end invites a rereading of the encyclopedic and apparently universalizing exploration of macrocosm and microcosm. The dream of comprehensive knowledge from which she awakens is a dream of intellectual freedom in which she can represent her subjectivity as consciousness. The representation of mental exploration is her clearest, most universalized, and thus most ambitious self-portrait.

The criticism of the 1970s and 1980s has placed the *Primero Sueño* in the tradition of dream and visionary literature. A typical example is Cicero's *Somnium Scipionis*, in which the structure of the universe as concentric spheres moving in harmony is revealed to the dreaming narrator by an ancestor. What is unique about the *Sueño* is the absence of a guiding spirit upon whose authority the dreamer can depend, and the failure of the dream to reveal a cosmic system by which all things can be understood.[13] The Olympian gods wander throughout the poem, but the Christian God is mentioned only indirectly in a reference to the Eucharist. This particular absence is not so surprising, given Sor Juana's professed fear of heresy in a misinterpretation of doctrine, voiced specifically in the *Respuesta*. The dreamer's autonomy and the pagan cosmology are radical departures from tradition and evasions of Inquisitorial objections. In light of these absences, Sor Juana's audacity can be appreciated.

Sor Juana's constituting herself as subject challenges the gender system. She undermines the self-justifying intellectual theory of the gender system in her defense of her right to study theology in her *Respuesta a Sor Filotea*. She exposes the social practice of objectifying women as prostitutes (in "Hombres necios") and as objects of desire in her poems on her own portrait and in verbal portraits of other women. The *Sueño*, with its implicit and explicit valorization and universalization of her mental activity and, not incidentally, of her unconscious physical processes, refutes both the theory and the practice of objectifying women.

Sor Juana transforms many of the traditions in which she participates, thus surpassing her models. This emulation is not mere stylistic bravura or aesthetic virtuosity, but rather an active engagement with the texts and the ideology they embody. An awareness of this engagement as an exceptionally brilliant and marginalized subject can lead to a useful approach to the *Sueño*. Sor Juana's stylistic complexity is clearly inspired by Góngora's dynamic interrelationships of the conceptual and mythological, with imagery interwoven so densely that his contemporaries often complained of deliberate obscurity and, worse, that in his *Soledades* there was no meaning, only a chaos of words and seductive images. The "Homero español" replied that there was embedded in the complexity of the text a philosophical meaning, but it has only been in recent criticism that an underlying structure has been explained in terms of the networks of mythological allusions.[14] One of the submerged themes of these systems of mythological allusion is the transgression of human and divine law through violence, incest, homoerotic lust of deities for mortals, and attempts by mortals to surpass the gods: the *Soledad primera* opens with an allusion to Zeus's rape of Europa and his abduction of Ganymede, and the *Polifemo* describes Sicily as tomb of the Titans, destroyed in their attempt to scale the heavens. Implicit is the image of the poet, surpassing his models to push his linguistic play beyond the known limits of poetic creation. Sor Juana employs this theme of transgression for her own purposes.

One of the rare seventeenth-century readers able to appreciate the significance of Góngora's allusions, Sor Juana uses similarly transgressive and sacrilegious figures from classical mythology in the *Sueño*. More important than the sensory or emotional impact of imagery is the metarepresentation of the poet's attempt to transgress the limits of everyday reality. She begins with allusion to arcane knowledge, the "pyramid" that is more than a simple geometrical figure or a reference to astronomical models. She intensifies the sense of mystery with an allusion to Nictymene, whose incest was punished by her transformation into an owl, here depicted as blasphemously drinking the oil from the sacred lamps of day.[15] Scattered throughout the poem are mythological figures who were destroyed in their vain attempts to cross the boundaries between human and divine—Icarus, Phaeton, Actaeon—and imagery of shipwrecks, all metaphors for the failure of the envisioned modes of knowledge, whether intuitive, visionary, or logical. The suggestively arcane pyramid and the owl (with her triple identity as the incestuous Nictymene, Ascalaphos the underworld betrayer of Persephone, and the bird of Minerva) are grouped with the main light-source of the night, the triform moon-goddess Hecate, who has no dependable and authoritative shape and is a traditional symbol of the mysterious changes in women's bodies, never stable or law-abiding.

The soul's partial liberation from the body in sleep makes this dream vision possible, but the body's processes in sleep are described in scientific detail: the furnace of digestion, the bellows of the lungs, and the mechanism of hunger that awakens the sleeper. It has been suggested that the description of landscape in lines 97–100 represents the hidden darkness and concavities of the female body:

> En los del monte senos escondidos,
> cóncavos de peñascos mal formados

—de su aspereza menos defendidos
que de su obscuridad asegurados—,

[In forest lap and hidden mound
and hollow less by bristling thicket
than by dark defended—somber lairs
where even noon seems night—][16]

The lyric voice, however, until line 975, conveys a conviction that its "digo yo" carries the weight of the patriarchal texts it echoes, and the representation of sleeping microcosm and macrocosm seems gendered only on the level of mythology rather than physiology or metaphorical geography. More significant than the landscape in lines 97–100 are the references to female sexuality, among the deities later in the poem. The sea-goddess Thetis, with her "fértiles pechos maternales" [fertile maternal breasts], figures in a cosmogony: "los dulces apoyó manantïales / de humor terrestre" (lines 628–632) [from which all earthly life in bounty flows]. Her role as a source of vital energy is linked directly with the poem's search for a method of knowing the universe, proceeding along the Great Chain of Being. Ironically, this maternal image of the unity of the world with its source is articulated just after the dreamer has accepted the painful method of separating each element of the cosmos from the others in order to study, classify, and categorize it. The dream enacts the tensions and contradictions surfacing in seventeenth-century philosophy, and it demonstrates the close interaction between philosophical and poetic method.

Knowledge and female sexuality are again conceptually linked through mythology and with the recognition of the futility of trying to know one of nature's most basic secrets, beauty and reproductive powers. These powers are embodied in an elaborate image in the *Sueño*, an exploration of plant reproduction in a flower that is a clear metaphor for the female body in cycles of virginity, sexual blossoming, and motherhood:

quien de la breve flor aun no sabía
por qué ebúrnea figura
circunscribe su frágil hermosura:
mixtos, por qué, colores
—confundiendo la grana en los albores—
fragrante le son gala:
ámbares por qué exhala,
y el leve, si más bello
ropaje al viento explica,
que en una y otra fresca multiplica
hija, formando pompa escarolada
de dorados perfiles cairelada,
que—roto del capillo el blanco sello—
de dulce herida de la Cipria Diosa

los despojos ostenta jactanciosa,
si ya el que la colora,
candor al alba, púrpura al aurora
no le usurpó, y, mezclado,
purpúreo es ampo, rosicler nevado:
tornasol que concita
los que del prado aplausos solicita:
preceptor quizá vano
—si no ejemplo profano—
de industria femenil que el más activo
veneno, hace dos veces ser nocivo
en el velo aparente
de la que finge tez resplandeciente.

                                    (730–756)

[nor yet, how the brief flower
blooms, frail chalice, in
ivory beauty circumscribed;
nor how, assorting colors—
scarlet tones with pale—
its fragrance it displays;
nor how, when lightest clad,
in flimsiest garment,
sweetest ambers it exhales,
and by the wind, ethereal,
multiplied, time and again,
produces offspring laced
with its same golden tints,
as delicately fringed,
from close protected bud,
unsealed—Venus's sweet wound—
blossoming forth in full array,
dawn's blush and pallor
borrowing to combine
the snowflake and the rose,
with rainbow hues soliciting
and glorying in Nature's applause;
mistress of vanity, perhaps,
profane example of feminine art,
which mixing sublimates and leads
to dress appearances,
deceitful, in bright veils,
turns deadliest poison
to even deadlier effect.][17]

The mingling of white and red in the description of female beauty was a commonplace of Renaissance poetry, and the terms "purpúreo" and "rosicler nevado" were typical of Góngora, but the delicate eroticism combined with scientific investigation and its failure before such miracles transforms poetic cliché and redirects the tradition. The transition to a condemnation of the use of cosmetics is not simply a distraction from the sensual impact of the preceding verses, but serves rather to confirm the suspicion that the reference has been to human, rather than floral, sexuality throughout the passage.

## POETIC PORTRAIT, EPISTEMOLOGICAL SELF-PORTRAIT

The *Primero Sueño* explores the available modes of human knowledge from the geometrical movements of celestial bodies to the intricate workings of the human body, using induction, logic, and intuition, all revealed as inadequate in the waking world. The poem is shaped by the limits of human knowledge. Sor Juana's poetic portraits and self-portraits confront and are shaped by the limits of female identity. They are also shaped by and confront the literary conventions of the time.

Although the terms "verbal portrait" and "self-portrait" suggest analogies with the visual arts, it is only the verbal portrait, as in the medieval *blason* or the Petrarchist representation of the lady's attributes, that enumerates physical attributes. Literary self-portraiture, a mode distinct from verbal portraiture as well as from autobiography, is a representation of the subject's consciousness—not how the writer appears to others, nor the events in her life, but what she knows and how she explains her knowing it. The exploration of human knowledge, ranging from the relationships of the stars and the shadow of the earth on the moon to the internal processes of the body in sleep, in the *Sueño*, exemplifies self-portraiture as an epistemological and encyclopedic mode.[18] This is a mode distinct from Sor Juana's autobiographical narrative in her *Respuesta a Sor Filotea*, although her self-representation in the letter goes beyond the narration of experience.

The vast epistemological vision of the *Sueño* is given the greatest latitude within contemporary poetic conventions through the metrical form of the *silva*, irregularly rhymed, having no fixed stanzaic form, and through the generic classification of "dream vision." But if this kind of dream need not be gendered until the moment of waking, in which the dreamer's voice is identified, the poet cannot so easily suppress her female perspective in verbal portraits describing other women, for example her patroness the Condesa de Paredes in the *romance decasílabo* "Lámina sirva el cielo al retrato" [may heaven serve as the plate for the engraving]. The traditional medieval *blason* and, later, the Petrarchan portrait objectify the woman in terms of her physical attributes from head to toe, attaching metaphysical attributes through metaphor to each detail of her body but explicitly rejecting any inherent value in the object chosen for contemplation. Sor Juana's verbal portraits of her patronesses expose the contradictions of neoplatonic love poetry. If it is only the soul's correspondence to spiritual values that is represented in the metaphorical representation of physical beauty, and the poetic portrait is truly devoid of the erotic intent that physical description seems to imply, then it should not matter whether the subject contemplating and describing a woman's physical beauty is male or female. But desire is the central issue of Renaissance secular poetry, and it was a bold aesthetic departure for a female subject to enter the closed system of male observers and speakers, each outdoing the other's verbal representations of female objects.

There are cultural barriers to the female poet's inscribing her gaze on the female body as well as barriers to her inscribing her own body, and those cultural barriers are products of the prohibition of female desire. Courtly love conventions position the beloved as dominant and denying her favors to the devoted male lover, whose description of her beauty has the literary function of substituting for his control of her body. The women Sor Juana describes and to whom she dedicates much of her secular poetry were in fact in positions of real power; they were her patrons. The poems cast an ironic light on the claims of Renaissance poetry, a kind of irony possible only in a poem signed by a woman.

The potential for mockery of the spiritual intentions of the lyric voice in Renaissance poetry had been exploited by some of Sor Juana's male predecessors. Petrarchist poetry, abounding in lexicalized metaphors of hair as gold, eyes as suns, lips of coral, complexion of marble or crystal, teeth as pearls, inspired Francisco de Quevedo to explode the conventions and ironically consider how much the metaphorical jewels and gold would fetch on the market. The terms of the metaphor—the corporeal beauty and the precious metals and stones to which it is compared—are equally physical and lacking in transcendent value. The function of the precious objects, to elevate physical beauty to a metaphysical realm, is debased as the poet converts them into market value and calls attention to the objectification of the beloved.

In her *romance decasílabo* "Lámina sirva el cielo al retrato," Sor Juana uses a more subtle approach to the exploitation and parody of conventional poetic portraiture. Her female identity creates a witty tension between eroticism and intellectualization. She asserts that only the heavens can serve as a surface on which to inscribe this portrait ("lámina," in Trueblood's translation, a plate for engraving rather than canvas) and requests that the stars compose "syllables" to represent her. By textualizing the female body, Sor Juana challenges the objectification of women in Renaissance portraiture and affirms herself as writer.

She chooses erudite images from a wide range of classical and contemporary contexts: the Condesa de Paredes's face is compared to that of "Hécate," her waist to the Bosporus, her legs to Doric or Ionian columns, her grace to a banana tree. Sor Juana restores some value to the endeavor of representing her patroness by transferring the imagery of the complexion from the realm of pure sensory delight to that of intellect, in a personification reminiscent of Góngora's image of straw in Polyphemus's overflowing shepherd's pouch, as "pálida tutora" [pale governess] dutifully carrying out the responsibility of ripening fruit. In Sor Juana's poem,

> Cátedras de abril, tus mejillas,
> clásicas dan a mayo, estudiosas:
> métodos a jazmines nevados,
> fórmula rubicunda a las rosas.[19]
>
> (25–28)

[Your cheeks are April's lecture halls, / with classic lessons to impart to May: / recipes for making jasmine snowy, / formulas for redness in the rose.][20]

Thus, Sor Juana's wit is based on a metaphorical and authoritative structure of pedagogy and of plays on the classical etymologies of words themselves. As *ingenio*, wit itself represents the processes of consciousness and of poetic creation.

Sor Juana renews the old metaphors of feminine beauty, even in a poem that purports to participate in a traditional mode of depicting women as passive and as metaphorical possessions through contemplation in terms of objects of value. This project is not without ambivalences and contradictions. The poet constitutes the female as a culturally created object while she defiantly affirms her own legitimacy as female subject, participating in that culture and inscribing the female body into culture rather than nature as poetic symbol of transcendent value and theological symbol of inherent female sinfulness. Thus, by textualizing the female body in the *romance decasílabo* Sor Juana rejects the division of nature from culture and the corresponding gender categories.

Sor Juana portrays herself as literary creator and mocks the conventions of verbal portraiture in her "Ovillejos," a conscious imitation of Jacinto Polo de Medina's "Fábula burlesca de Apolo y Dafne" in its skeptical attitude toward the possibility of portraying "Lisarda" in words.[21] Polo began with the feet instead of the head in his description of purely literary beings; Sor Juana does not even begin her description of Lisarda until line 229, and she does not in fact portray anything but the endeavor of verbal portraiture itself. To emphasize the burlesque nature of this portrait, Sor Juana refers to an anecdote cited twice by Cervantes in part 2 of *Don Quijote*, concerning the bad painter Orbaneja, whose anarchic aesthetic motto was "Dé donde diere" (2.3 and 71). Sor Juana claims to paint

> dé donde diere,
> salga como saliere,
> aunque saque un retrato,
> tal que, después, le ponga: *Aquéste es gato*.
>
> (19–22)

[haphazardly; let the picture come out as it will, even if it produces a portrait on which afterwards a label will have to be attached: "This is a cat."]

While the medium of forms and colors should be sufficient for the painter to convey his meaning without the assistance of another art, the poet who is already working with words playfully suggests the need for a clarifying label borrowed from writing, a medium that is in fact not outside her activity but already inscribed within it.

Amid descriptions of the difficulties of poetic creation, the lyric speaker makes a pointed observation about the vanity of traditional love poetry:

> ¿Pues qué es ver las metáforas cansadas
> en que han dado las Musas alcanzadas?
> No hay ciencia, arte, ni oficio
> que con extraño vicio
> los poetas, con vana sutileza,
> no anden acomodando a la belleza;
> y pensando que pintan de los cielos,
> hacen los retablos de sus duelos.
>
> (95–102)

[What are all the tired metaphors with which poets have overtaken the Muses? There is no science, art, or profession the poets have not, with strange malice and vain subtlety, accommodated to beauty, and thinking that they paint the heavens, they paint altarpieces to their sufferings.]

The conventions of courtly love, she points out, verge on masochistic idolatry.

The creative voice and a critical one engage in a dialogue that culminates in the attempted affirmation, "Es, pues, Lisarda; es, pues . . ." [Lisarda is, well, she is . . . ]. In response, the internal "critic" complains that this poem is a painting and not a definition. Considerable energy is spent on the attempt to rhyme with "Lisarda"; the poet struggling with the unwieldy medium of language in poetic form is the true object of representation in this verbal portrait. The closing line of the poem affirms that the "Ovillejos" represent poetic process and do not create a static visual image: "Juana Inés de la Cruz la retrataba" [Juana Inés de la Cruz was portraying her].

It is not only Sor Juana's verbal portraits of other women that challenge the objectification of women. The *Sueño* and her defense of female intellectual activity in the *Respuesta* establish the validity of the female subject. In Sor Juana's poems, this female subject is inseparable from her self-contemplation and contemplation of other women. Her sonnet "Este, que ves, engaño colorido," a meditation on her painted portrait as a deception, confronts and demystifies the enigmas of time and desire in the tradition of *carpe diem* poetry, traditionally urging the lady to enjoy her transitory beauty by yielding to her suitor's desires. The clarity of the lyric voice deflects the possessive gaze from her own image and instead turns a mirror toward the male observer, as Diego Velázquez's Venus challenges the expected view of herself and, if the visual logic of the painting is followed, contemplates the voyeur in her mirror.

While Velázquez's mirror shows only an enigmatic face and reveals nothing of what is seen by the woman, Sor Juana's poetic voice interprets the image of feminine beauty as a symbol of mortality, the ostensible theme of all seductive *carpe diem* poetry. But it is the profound and almost violent irony with which she exposes the irrationality of the traditional appeal to yield to fleshly temptation because of one's mortality that is striking in the sonnet. Although Sor Juana echoes Luis de Góngora's sonnet "Mientras por competir con tu cabello," in her poem the female speaker, whose face is the object portrayed in the painted representation of beauty, reveals the irrationality of the genre. Her representation of the true nature of mortal beauty is shocking: "es cadáver, es polvo, es sombra, es nada" [it is a cadaver, it is dust, it is shadow, it is nothing]. She dramatically transforms her poetic models and renders Góngora's "en sombra, en polvo, en tierra, en humo, en nada" [into shadow, dust, earth, smoke, nothing] a euphemistic evasion.

Sor Juana's female perspective illuminates the contradictions of time and desire inherent in the *topos* of *carpe diem* in its Counter-Reformation theological context. The speaking subject explores the questions of being in the world, being for oneself, being in relation to God—questions that require a valuing of the subject and not her painted representation. The terms are reversed, as in any mirror, by the gender difference in the speaking subject, from temporal pleasure to eternal salvation.

Sor Juana confronted questions of female perspective that cannot be isolated from the aesthetic and philosophical questions implicit in each literary work. When one addresses the specific problems of literary portraiture in Sor Juana's work, the paradoxes and contradictions apparent in the polemical letters and the daring *Sueño* are necessary points of reference. The audacity of a woman poet's usurpation of the male role of observer of women is the first obvious confrontation of the poet with the limitations imposed by gender as defined by her society. But this is only a single image in the mirror she holds up to gender (as in her sonnet on her portrait, "Este, que ves . . ."), to the codes of behavior for nuns, and to the definitions of theological and secular knowledge in her time. Her female identity combined with her erudition made it possible for her to equal and often exceed the expertise of her hierarchical superiors in terms of the systems of knowledge of the times. She manipulated these codes in the defense of women's learning, seeming to reproduce them, but with a baffling difference that astounded by its ingenuity but could not, ultimately, protect her from those in power. In her polemical letters, she cites Scripture and interprets it historically to defend women's right to study, if not to preach or take a public role in the religious hierarchy, but ultimately Scripture belonged to the bishop of Puebla, and to more powerful enemies of an autonomous female subject. While the *Respuesta* was written in a mode of scholarly discourse the bishop would recognize as his own—a mask donned by the female writer to gain entrance into male realms of theological debate—the bishop had condescendingly or ironically affirmed Sor Juana's female identity as the writer of her *Carta Atenagórica*, by signing his reply "Sor Filotea," as if it were undignified for a male superior to engage in intellectual debate with a female inferior.

## FEMALE SUBJECT, FEMALE GAZE

Despite his professed disagreement with Ludwig Pfandl's thesis concerning Sor Juana as psychological aberration, Octavio Paz's puzzlement at the phenomenon of the female gaze in Sor Juana's portraits causes him to devote a disproportionate part of his study to determining the nature of Sor Juana's sexuality. He vacillates between the ideology of courtly, neoplatonic, intellectual, and spiritual friendship and the anachronism of "lesbian" or "sapphic" overtones of the relationship between the nun and her patroness, the Condesa de Paredes.[22]

A more productive question than the nature of the poet's unknowable "sentimientos" would be the significance of her act of writing the transgressive female gaze. Her writing is a direct confrontation with the cultural constitution of the female as the passive object of contemplation. She constructs a trap of her own for the patriarchal reader, accustomed to the bad faith of Renaissance poetics of desire, taken for granted in its gendered standard of discourse. The female object of desire, treated as a passive statue in male poetic discourse, is revealed in Sor Juana's poetry to have been listening all along, and to be capable of mimicking the same discourse in a disconcerting way. Paz constructs a labyrinthine history of Western love leading occasionally through strictly male-defined Greek homosexuality, but he does not address the disruption caused by Sor Juana's writing about the female body from the point of view of the female gaze. Hardly another woman poet would write again so consciously of a named female body until the twentieth century, when the significance of such inscription would be inextricable from personal confession.

To Paz the central purpose of Sor Juana's life was knowledge, but in her cultural context knowledge was not neutral or merely acquired with no relationship to the structures of power. Learning Latin was a preliminary to the inscription of herself as subject in the structure of power. The search for knowledge was inextricably bound up with the mechanisms of power, and the modes of operation of these mechanisms in Sor Juana's life were linked directly to the act of writing. She represents herself as a questing mind, and in her portraits there are books, but there is also the hand holding the pen, a means of participation in theological debate and courtly ceremonies. In her *Respuesta*, Sor Juana argues that well-educated older women should teach girls on a level higher than the "Amiga," and it seems clear that Sor Juana would have taught, had the conditions existed for her to do so.[23]

In her *villancico* "Víctor, víctor Catarina," Sor Juana praises the erudite St. Catherine not only for her knowledge but also for her use of it to confound the patriarchs and convince them that "el sexo / no es esencia en lo entendido" [to be female does not mean to lack wisdom]. Catherine, like Sor Juana, served the Church by defying the command to keep silent:

> Estudia, arguye y enseña,
> y es de la Iglesia servicio,
> que no la quiere ignorante
> El que racional la hizo.

> [She studied, taught, and argued,
> and thereby served the Church,
> for He who created her a rational being
> did not want her ignorant.]

Her writings in ink have been lost ("¡oh dolor!"), but her example has been inscribed in blood.[24] Sor Juana's praise of St. Catherine is another self-portrait, conscious of its significance.

## REWRITING THE FEMALE SCRIPT

In the dangerous project of constituting a female subject in the context of Counter-Reformation Hispanic discourse, who are Sor Juana's precursors? Her point of view as the illegitimate child of a Mexican-born mother and her position outside the institution of marriage, chosen to enable her to pursue her intellectual interests, place her on the margins of the culture whose discourse she so expertly manipulated, and this point of view makes her in some senses unique. In her *Respuesta* she cites biblical heroines in the defense of women's right to intellectual development, but a key precursor is St. Teresa of Ávila, who never claimed the right to study and who sought anonymity as a solution to her problems with the religious authorities of the late sixteenth century. Teresa did not write until her fifties, when she could no longer be accused, like so many other women mystics who were discredited, of being a hysterical female. When she did write about her mystical experiences, Teresa attributed them to "una persona que conozco," someone she happened to know. She constitutes herself invisibly as the "persona," a valid subject whose experience is an example of the relationship of the soul to God or of spiritual methods others can imitate. And yet, the presence of the nun speaking from experience to her religious sisters is unmistakable in Teresa's oral style.

In her *Sueño*, Juana's solution was androgyny rather than anonymity. It is the only poem she claims to have written for her own pleasure. The *Sueño*'s development is ultimately toward an exaltation of the range and power of human knowledge, followed by the simultaneous recognition of the limits of possible modes of that knowledge and the reawakening to the dreamer's female identity. Androgynous and freely exploring the microcosm and macrocosm, the self can only temporarily transcend the limits of knowledge, just as Sor Juana's transcendence of gender in the poem, as well as in life, was only temporary. Juana refers to her own futile attempts at anonymity, "veiling the light of her name," in her *Respuesta*, but the continuation of her intellectual life depended in part upon the recognition and protection of important public figures. She had chosen to reflect on the very problems of self-depiction that were a major philosophical preoccupation of her male contemporaries. Her poetry defies the traditional objectification of women by constituting herself as subject, and as subject and object of a dream that fuses a poetic voice with a philosophical vision. Her affirmation of the validity of her life and thought inspired generations of Hispanic women to look for innovative depictions of woman as subject, to depict the conflict between her vision of herself and the appealing portraits painted to silence the expression of that vision.

## NOTES

1. Sor Juana's birthdate is disputed. In his biography of Sor Juana (1700), Father Diego Calleja gives her birthdate as November 12, 1651. Since the celebration of her tercentenary in 1951, a certificate of baptism has been found to support her birthdate as 1648, which Octavio Paz regards as "almost certain." Octavio Paz, *Sor Juana Inés de la Cruz; O, Las trampas de la fe* (Barcelona: Seix Barral, 1982), 96–97.

2. Rosario Castellanos, *Mujer que sabe latín* (Mexico: Fondo de Cultura Económica, 1973, rpt. 1984), 19–20: "Para elegirse a sí misma y preferirse por encima de los demás se necesita haber llegado, vital, emocional o reflexivamente a lo que Sartre llama una situación límite. Situación límite por su intensidad, su dramatismo, su desgarradora densidad metafísica.

"Monjas que derriban las paredes de su celda como Sor Juana y la Portuguesa; doncellas que burlan a los guardianes de su castidad para asir el amor como Melibea." (Throughout this essay, English paraphrases are mine unless otherwise indicated.)

3. Both Rosario Castellanos and Marie-Cécile Bénassy-Berling cast Sor Juana in the role of Virginia Woolf's imaginary "Shakespeare's sister." Bénassy-Berling, however, compares the Mexican nun, with her unique and irresistible vocation for learning, to other successful women writers of the period: Christine de Pisan, María de Zayas, and Aphra Behn. See Castellanos, *Mujer que sabe latín*, 43; Bénassy-Berling, *Humanisme et religion chez Sor Juana Inés de la Cruz: La femme et la culture au XVIIᵉ siècle* (Paris: Publications de la Sorbonne, Editions Hispaniques, 1982), 74.

4. Sor Juana Inés de la Cruz, *Obras completas*, ed. Alfonso Méndez Plancarte (Mexico: Fondo de Cultura Económica, 1951–1957), Vol. 4, *Comedias, sainetes, y prosa*, ed. Alberto G. Salceda (1957), 37–38.

5. "Habiendo conocido [. . .] lo singular de su erudición junto con su no pequeña hermosura, atractivos todos a la curiosidad de muchos, que desearían conocerla y tendrían por felicidad el cortejarla, solía decir que no podía Dios enviar azote mayor a aqueste reino que si permitiese que Juana Inés se quedase en la publicidad del siglo." Cited in Paz, *Sor Juana Inés de la Cruz*, 12.

6. Electa Arenal, "The Convent as Catalyst for Autonomy," in *Women in Hispanic Literature: Icons and Fallen Idols*, ed. Beth Miller (Berkeley, Los Angeles, London: University of California Press, 1983). See also: Electa Arenal and Stacey Schlau, *Untold Sisters: Hispanic Nuns in Their Own Works* (Albuquerque: University of New Mexico Press, 1989).

7. Sor Juana Inés de la Cruz, *Obras completas* 4: 458, 460.

8. *Obras completas*, 4: 441–442. Translation by Margaret Sayers Peden in *A Woman of Genius: The Intellectual Autobiography of Sor Juana Inés de la Cruz* (Salisbury, Conn.: Lime Rock Press, 1982), 18–20. Josefina Ludmer also addresses the permutations of "callar" and "decir" in this passage in "Tretas del débil," in *La sartén por el mango: Encuentro de escritoras latinoamericanas*, ed. Patricia Elena González and Eliana Ortega (Río Piedras, Puerto Rico: Ediciones Huracán, 1984), 47–54. See also Paz, *Sor Juana*, 16–17.

9. Paz, *Sor Juana*, 12, 92–95, 172–173.

10. Ibid., 91, citing Dorothy Schons, "Some Obscure Points in the Life of Sor Juana Inés de la Cruz," *Modern Philology* 24, 2 (1926): 141–162.

11. Estela Portillo Trambley, *Sor Juana and Other Plays* (Ypsilanti, Mich.: Bilingual Press/Editorial Bilingue, 1983). Also, Electa Arenal, *This Life Within Me Won't Keep Still*, a play based on the lives and works of Sor Juana and Anne Bradstreet, performed in New York, fall 1979 and spring 1987.

12. Sor Juana Inés de la Cruz, *Obras completas*, vol. 1, *Lírica personal*, 228. Translation by Muriel Kittel in Angel Flores and Kate Flores, eds., *The Defiant Muse: Hispanic Feminist Poems from the Middle Ages to the Present* (New York: Feminist Press, 1986), 21–23.

13. Paz, *Sor Juana*, 472–486; Georgina Sabat-Rivers, *El "Sueño" de Sor Juana Inés de la Cruz: Tradiciones literarias y originalidad* (London: Tamesis, 1976); and Luis Harss's introduction and commentary in *Sor Juana's Dream* (New York: Lumen Books, 1986), 23.

14. John Beverley, *Aspects of Góngora's "Soledades"* (West Lafayette, Ind.: Purdue University Press, 1979).

15. Jean Franco, "Sor Juana Explores Space," in *Plotting Women: Gender and Representation in Mexico* (New York: Columbia University Press, 1989), 33–38.

16. *Obras completas*, 1: 337; translation by Luis Harss, *Sor Juana's Dream*, 32, commentary 76.

17. *Obras completas*, 1: 353–354; translation by Luis Harss, *Sor Juana's Dream*, 60–62.

18. Michel Beaujour, *Miroirs d'encre: Rhétorique de l'autoportrait* (Paris: Seuil, 1980), 7–23.

19. *Obras completas*, 1: 171–173.

20. Alan S. Trueblood, *A Sor Juana Anthology* (Cambridge, Mass.: Harvard University Press, 1989), 51.

21. *Obras completas*, 1: 320–330.

22. Paz, *Sor Juana*, 136–138.

23. Bénassy-Berling, *Humanisme et religion*, 97, takes issue with Pfandl's depiction of Sor Juana's pursuit of knowledge as self-contained and devoid of any interest in teaching. Trueblood, *A Sor Juana Anthology*, 6, says she taught in a school associated with the convent.

24. *Obras completas*, vol. 2, *Villancicos y letras sacras*, 170–172; translation by Kate Flores, *The Defiant Muse*, 24.

# TEN

# Toward a History of Women's Periodicals in Latin America: Introduction

*Seminar on Women and Culture in Latin America*

The history of women's participation in journalism is a study yet to be written. Such a study would undoubtedly force a rewriting of the history of Latin American culture. For Latin American women, periodical literature has constituted the chief form of participation in public dialogue, in contrast with women in the United States, who drew upon their Protestant heritage and the precedent of abolitionists such as the Grimke sisters to claim access to the public podium. This bibliography, compiled by Janet Greenberg, while making no claim to encyclopedic coverage, is intended to indicate the scope of this vast and vital subject.

As summarized in the table on page 184, our research so far shows that the most consistent production of periodicals by and for women has occurred in Mexico, Argentina, and Brazil. Indeed, the publication of women's magazines has been consistent in Argentina in every decade since the 1830s and in Brazil since the 1840s. By the early 1920s every country in South America, with the apparent exception of the Guayanas, supported at least one women's magazine. The greatest burst of feminist magazine activity in any period excluding the 1980s was in the 1920s and 1930s. Over fifty magazines on this list appeared in these decades. In the 1980s, with the rebirth of significant feminist movements, production has again skyrocketed all over Mexico, Central and South America, and the Caribbean. Though the data presented here are impressive, our efforts to trace the production in the Andean region have so far yielded only limited results from which no conclusions should be drawn. Indeed, at this preliminary stage, no conclusions should be drawn about the existence or nonexistence of women's periodicals in areas that have so far yielded no records.

The earliest evidence of women's involvement in print journalism in Latin America uncovered by this project is the work of Señora de Bernardo Calderón, listed by Lola Anderson ("Mexican Women Journalists," *Pan American Bulletin* 68 [May 1934]: 315–320) as the first woman printer-journalist in Mexico. Her name first appeared on a newssheet in 1641; she wrote and published *hojas volantes* from a printing press that she continued to operate until 1684. Subsequent generations of her family included several other women printer-journalists. Women writers are credited with having worked on one of the earliest periodicals published in New Spain, the *Gazeta de México y Noticias de Nueva España* (1722). There is evidence that in 1800 María Fernández de Jauregui inherited her husband's printing press and used it, among other purposes, for periodical publishing.

For most of the nineteenth century, women's writings, like those of men, belonged almost exclusively to an elite culture. In the early decades of independence, even before the democratization of education and the impact of late-nineteenth-century social movements, a transnational, often multilingual network of print culture blossomed among elite and educated women of the Americas and Europe. Literate women from Peru to Paris, from the Southern Cone to the Caribbean to the United States, were brought into dialogue in the public arena of periodical literature. Starting in the early years of independence, Spanish American and Brazilian women forcefully entered the debate about women's role in politics and culture. Editors of pamphlets and periodicals, frequently writing under pseudonyms, often defended the political power of domesticity. They insisted on the rights of women to better education or to be heard in the public sphere; they expanded the definition of motherhood to include devotion to the pen; they opened discussions with influential women in other nations.

Juana Manuela Gorriti, the Argentine writer exiled in Peru in the 1840s, established communication between Lima and the women of her native country by founding a magazine. Returning to Argentina in the 1850s, she initiated a literary journal, *La Alborada del Plata*, that carried international debates on women's role in modernity. In that same decade, another Argentine woman, Juana Manso, founded *O Jornal de Senhoras* while living in Brazil. Returning to Argentina in 1854, she began the *Album de Señoritas*. Cuban Gertrudis Gómez de Avellaneda, who moved readily between Spain and Cuba, published the *Album del Bello Sexo* in Spain in the 1840s and the *Album Cubano de lo Bueno y lo Bello* in Havana in the 1860s. The journalistic career of Bolivian Carolina Freyre de Jaimes (b. 1835) spanned four countries and over fifty years of publishing activity in major newspapers and women's magazines. After establishing her career as a journalist in Peru at a very young age, she directed the women's magazine *El Album* (Lima and Bolivia, 1860s–1870s), to which such figures as Juana Manuela Gorriti regularly contributed. She founded and directed *La Columna del Hogar* (Buenos Aires, 1898/99–1902) and cofounded *La Revista Argentina* in Santa Fe, with the express goal of publishing a feminist magazine for the provinces. Her leadership among women activists and feminists is suggested by the records uncovered of decades of collaboration with Gorriti and Clorinda Matto de Turner from the 1840s to the early 1900s.

The existence of this women's print network challenges assumptions about the supposed isolation, parochialism, and triviality of women's culture in the nineteenth century. Such assumptions are often anchored in an uncritical acceptance of ideologies that identify men with production and a public sphere and women with consumption and a domestic sphere. The image of women as readers seems to pose little threat to this configuration: reading counts as a form of consumption in bourgeois terms. The image of women writing, on the other hand, can be threatening. It involves women producing in the public sphere, often from within the domestic center, who introduce domestic issues into the place of public discussion and insist on making visible the activity of women in workplaces, politics, and commercial and social life. Once the literary-journalistic activity of women is examined, cherished boundaries between public and domestic instantly blur.

The increasing presence of women in networks of print culture can be measured both by women's own journalistic production and by the proliferation of masculine productions directed at women readers. It is no surprise that so many publications in the nineteenth century (some of them listed below) were devoted to women's interests: fashion, cosmetics, and serialized novels were stock elements of popular journalism from the middle years of the century. Indeed, as numbers of female readers increased, the kinds of publications destined for a female audience proliferated. The circulation of women's periodicals in Mexico in the mid-1800s compares with that of independent feminist periodicals today: *La Semana de las Señoritas Mejicanas* (Mexico City, 1851–1852) lists almost 1,400 subscribers, of whom only 200 resided in Mexico City, *El Semanario de las Señoritas Mejicanas* (1841–1842) lists a high of 1,020 subscribers, only 196 in Mexico City. Such evidence may point to an international readership for these magazines.

The mid-nineteenth century saw two kinds of "women's" periodicals: the ladies' magazine, a publication typically edited by men and devoted heavily to changing styles and fashions for women, and the liberal republican periodical edited by women, devoted principally to demands for female emancipation and a voice in national debate. The latter type often met with strong reactions. Male opponents to these conspicuous female interventions fired strongly satirical rejoinders. In Argentina, journals titled *La Matrona Comentadora* or *El Hijo de Su Madre* played on misogynist images of women as libertines or unrestrained gossips.

One early and dramatic example of a masculinist attack on women's journalism was effected by Don Manuel Irigoyen, the anonymous publisher of *La Argentina* (1830–1831), the earliest Argentine magazine pretending to be written by and for women. In its pages Irigoyen waged a slanderous campaign against a rival magazine really founded and edited by a woman, *La Aljaba*, published by Petrona Rosende de Sierra, an advocate of women's rights. Advertised before the appearance of *La Argentina*, and inaugurated a month later, *La Aljaba* was driven out of business after eighteen issues: the editor of *La Argentina* accused it of plagiarism. As the pun in its title suggests (*aljaba* means both "fuschia" and "quiver for arrows"), *La Aljaba*'s radical message was that "nos libraremos de las injusticias de los demás hombres, solamente cuando no existamos entre ellos."

At the same time that the female voice was attacked by men, it was also appropriated by them. During the political upheavals of the first half of the nineteenth century, the female voice and female print context were not infrequently usurped to express a masculine critique of society and government in times of censorship and surveillance.

It was in the latter half of the nineteenth century, with the widespread educational reform movements and the formation of activist women's groups, that women's print culture became more visible. The rights of women and workers were important concerns within the emerging political groups that would change society in much of Latin America. In the Southern Cone these groups owed much of their force to the waves of immigration and to the rapid urbanization of the period. In the north, activist women participated in the Cuban Independence movement and the Mexican Revolution, incorporating urgent programs of political and moral reform into the national agenda. Beginning in 1870, Mexican poet and educator Rita Cetina Gutiérrez collaborated with other women teachers to publish *La Siempreviva*, a newspaper dedicated to overcoming women's unequal status, improving hygiene, and educating mothers in nutrition and childcare. Brazilian Francisca Senhorina da Motta Diniz cast her arguments for women's equality in terms of progressivism and the moral superiority of the New World, invoking the national pride of the Brazilian politicians whom she addressed. The first issue of her journal *O Sexo Feminino* appeared on September 7, 1873, the fifty-first anniversary of Brazilian independence from Portugal, with the assertion that "the Americas will give the cry of independence for women."

The combination of greater access to basic education for women in many regions of Latin America, and therefore a wider reading public, the centralization of population in cities, European immigration, and the entrance of women into the wage labor force gave rise to a general acceleration of periodical literature by and for women at the turn of the century. Socialist and anarchist newspapers written for and directed by women coexisted with types of popular romance like the serialized novels of the beginning of the twentieth century.

In Brazil, the literate population of São Paulo and Rio de Janeiro grew tenfold between 1890 and 1920. Women incorporated urgent programs of moral reform tied to social change. Formulating demands for legislation

against child labor, campaigns against prostitution, and civil rights for disfranchised groups of society, female political organizing found its most effective voice in periodicals of all kinds. The *Revista Feminina*, published and
edited by Virgilina de Souza Selles in São Paulo from 1914 to 1927, printed
between 20,000 and 25,000 copies of each issue in 1918. It was hailed by
Brazilian women as "the first great work of our sex" and "an organ for intellectual communication" (Susan Besse, "Freedom and Bondage: The Impact
of Capitalism on Women in São Paulo, Brazil, 1917–1937" [Ph.D. diss., Yale
University, 1983], 32).

Nearly a century of women's publishing in the anarchist and socialist
press can be traced through the career and writings of Dr. Alicia Moreau de
Justo. A feminist trained in France as a gynecologist, she emigrated to
Argentina at the turn of the century. A leader in the Socialist Party from its
founding by her husband, Juan B. Justo, Moreau directed and contributed to
numerous feminist, anarchist, and socialist journals published from 1900 to
the 1970s. Her work appeared, for example, in the anarchist *Nuestra Causa*
(1910s) and the sophisticated, international *Vida Femenina* (a publication of
the Socialist Party in the 1920s), and she served for many years as director of
*La Vanguardia*, the major national newspaper of the Socialist Party. While she
was director of *La Vanguardia*, the magazine published a regular women's
supplement, *La Vanguardia Femenina*, which entertained the complex debates
surrounding women's suffrage in the 1940s.

At the same time that some women were actively organizing for radical
social protest, there emerged opposing currents espoused by traditionalist
and right-wing groups. These too had their own periodical literature (well
represented in this bibliography). What is most fascinating about this coexistence is that many groups with very different aims shared similar rhet-
orics about the special place and rights of women in society.

The visibility and partial success of the feminist and women's rights agenda forced its inclusion in male-dominated forms of journalism as well. Likewise, the potential of the female readership was not lost on the editors of the
large daily and weekly publications. Popular Brazilian magazines of general
interest such as *A Cigarra* vied to capture the female audience with features
on fashion, sketches of prominent women in the professions and performing
arts, articles on love, marriage, and feminism, and write-in advice columns.
The work of women contributors began to appear in mainstream newspapers. Carolina Freyre published regularly in the Argentine daily *La
Nación* while it was edited by her husband in the 1890s. Victoria Ocampo
published her first essay (a commentary on Dante written in French) in the
same daily in 1920. Feminist labor activist Juana María Beggino published
in the general daily *La Capital* in Rosario, Argentina, in the 1910s. It is clear
that by the end of World War I most major newspapers and journals recognized the existence of their female audiences. "Women's sections" appeared,

covering the most diverse topics, as did women contributors, altering the nature of mass periodical literature.

The magazines and periodicals listed below attest not only the reality of women's writing but also women's editing, printing, selling advertisements and subscriptions, planning, fighting censorship, and spending money— their own and other people's. (Victoria Ocampo and Clorinda Matto de Turner both founded publishing houses.) Little magazines everywhere are characterized by brief lifespans. Nevertheless, the short lives of most of the entries included here attest the hostile environment in which these activities were often carried out. The ephemeral character of many of the publications listed here should thus be read as a sign of struggle and scarcity; at the same time, the continuity of production and the reappearance of the same names on different mastheads bear witness to the steadiness and determination with which the work was carried on.

Unquestionably, these texts constitute an uninterrupted tradition of cultural practice. For women like Gorriti, Manso, Matto de Turner, and Storni, magazine work was an integral part of life as an intellectual and activist. Today, journalistic work remains an important activity for many women writers. Isabel Allende, for example, speaks of finding her comic voice writing a women's column titled "Civilice su troglodita." Women poets and novelists are main contributors to *fem*, the Mexican periodical founded in 1976 and the most prominent representative of the contemporary feminist magazine. Its continuous publication since that date, its wide range of Latin American and international contributors, and its commitment to controversy have won it particular distinction. Where women have not controlled their own presses and magazines, they have gained access to political and cultural periodicals of general interest published by men. Progressive periodicals in most countries and periods are important sources for tracing women's writing and debates on women's rights. In Cuba, for example, research indicates that since the revolution in 1959 the most detailed sources for information on feminism and the status of women are the general periodicals *Revolución* and *Bohemia*.

While the history of women's periodical literature differs at many points from that of its male counterpart, other continuities are shared. Both developed in relation to a growing reading public, the emergence of new political ideologies, the spread of mass education, and the professionalization of the writer. We know that the first novel in Latin America, *El periquillo sarniento*, was written by a journalist. The development of the essay as a literary form is especially crucial in the study of Latin American thought and letters, and this is mainly a result of the large numbers of writers and statesmen who found their widest audiences and greatest source of financial support through the periodical.

For lettered members of both genders, journalism played an important role in unifying different areas of Latin America. As the major poles of urban culture in the late nineteenth century, Mexico City, Rio de Janeiro, and Buenos Aires served as magnets attracting contributors and publications of all kinds. Literary journals like *Revista Azul* and *Revista de América*, though devoted almost solely to belles lettres, showed the high impact that specialized journals could achieve in unifying literary culture. A major newspaper, *La Nación* of Buenos Aires, showed its range by employing as correspondents the Cuban José Martí and the Nicaraguan Rubén Darío. The impact of journalism on the shaping of genres (for example, the essay, the *crónica*, the serial, the short story) cannot be underestimated. As a means of support for the intellectual, whether female or male, journalism had no peer, especially once the role of the writer was no longer systematically linked to a directive role in political or economic affairs.

In the twentieth century, journals such as *Amauta* in Peru and the *Revista de Avance* in Cuba show the workings of the intelligentsia as a force for social change. It is with *Sur*, founded by Victoria Ocampo in Argentina, that one can perhaps best measure the intense impact of a long-lived literary journal in Latin America. Testimonials from many writers attest the influence that this journal, under Ocampo's direction, had in the Spanish-speaking world. What is less widely recognized, however, is that Ocampo was an inheritor of a tradition of women's as well as men's journalistic participation. Her work, while certainly the best known by a woman, has a long heritage in Latin America, one inspired by the most diverse of causes.

A relevant counterpoint to the materials presented here is found in the history of women's periodicals and feminist journalism in Iberia. Here Spain's long tradition of conservative, Catholic ideology weighs heavily. During the enlightened mid-eighteenth century, a distinct protest against women's oppression was voiced in *La Pensadora Gaditana* (1768), a weekly twenty-four-page essay by Beatriz Cienfuegos. With the return to despotism, Madrid's flourishing periodical literature was decimated in 1823–1824, just as Spain's newly independent colonies were beginning to explore the possibilities of the secular, liberal state. The "first" Spanish women's magazine, *Correo de las Damas* (1833), was an adaptation of a French publication. Journals advocating women's political participation and emancipation through education did not reappear until 1841, when the monthly *Gobierno Representativo y Constitución del Bello Sexo* began appearing in Madrid. Cádiz, a port city in contact with Europe and Latin America and site of the liberal constitution of 1812, was a center for Fourierist feminism. There, socialist feminism found its first clear expression in *El Pensil Gaditano*, which later became *El Pensil Ibérico* (1857–1859). This pioneering publication compared the mechanisms of women's oppression with those of class.

*El Pensil* was shut down by the Church, and the journal *Ellas: Órgano Oficial del Sexo Femenino* (1851) capitulated to misogynist pressures. But direct repression was not the worst obstacle to feminist publication in Spain. Elite women's periodicals advocated the education of women only in the interest of upper-class women's conformity to the role of nurturer of Christian citizens. They disclaimed any challenge to orthodox class structure and gender roles. The Church and women of the Castilian aristocracy and the Catalan industrialist bourgeoisie combined forces to publish and organize paternalistic efforts such as the promisingly titled *La Mujer Que Vive de Su Trabajo* (1906). This publication was devoted to moral and religious education aimed at controlling the increasingly dangerous class of female industrial and domestic workers. The conservative, antisuffragist Asociación National de Mujeres Españolas (1918) claimed to speak for "los intereses feministas de España," despite the dissent of other feminists. In addition, Catalan regionalism, which became a nationalist movement at the turn of the century, was reflected in conservative women's journals like *Or i grana: Setmanari autonomist per les dones, propulsor d'una lliga patriotica de damas* (1906).

Some well-known nineteenth-century feminists published in journals of their own, such as Gertrudis Gómez de Avellaneda's *La Ilustración: Album del Bello Sexo* (1845) and Emilia Pardo Bazán's *Nuevo Teatro Crítico* (1891–1893). In the 1870s and 1880s, women's publications such as *Ilustración de la Mujer* (1882–1887) and liberal publications reflected Krausist support of women's education for emancipation and social change. Likewise, during the Second Republic and the Civil War, women on the left like Dolores Ibarruri (La Pasionaria) participated in socialist, communist, and anarcho-syndicalist organizations and their publications. They also addressed specifically female audiences in journals affiliated with a range of political organizations, including Pasionaria's *Mujeres: Órgano de la Agrupación de Mujeres Antifascistas* (1936). In 1936 the autonomous anarchist women's organization Mujeres Libres was founded. Its collectivized publication *Mujeres Liberes*, studied by Mary Nash, reflects anarchist theory and practice in its focus on the necessity of women's education not only as mothers but also as cultural and political participants.

From 1939 to 1976 little feminist activity surfaced in Spain, but immediately following the establishment of the elected government, Lidia Falcón and other feminists began such publications as *Vindicación Feminista*. Basic research on Spanish women's periodicals can be found in María Isabel Marrades and Adolfo Perinat, *Mujer, prensa, y sociedad en España, 1800–1939* (Madrid: Centro de Investigaciones Sociológicas, 1980); Mary Nash, *"Mujeres Libres," España, 1936–39* (Barcelona: Tusquets, 1976); Geraldine Scanlon, *La polémica feminista en la España contemporánea (1868–1974)* (Madrid: Siglo XXI, 1976); and Isabel Segura and Marta Selva, *Revistes de dones, 1846–1935* (Barcelona: Edhasa, 1984). An important research project that remains to be undertaken is an investigation of the connections and lines of communication between Spanish and Portuguese feminist movements and their Latin American counterparts.

Study of the history of Latin American periodical literature is increasing. In relation to the interaction of male-dominated journalism with literary culture, scholars such as Boyd Carter and Aníbal González have traced this role for the high-culture literary movements of the late nineteenth century. Angel Rama's *La ciudad letrada* is a fundamental source on the general history of print culture in Latin America. A number of feminist scholars have recently been engaged in the study of women's periodicals, and their work has opened doors to areas of research unheeded by mainstream historiographers. Early critics such as Lily Sosa de Newton of Argentina or Jane Herrick of the United States have set the course for the study of periodicals in Argentina and Mexico City, respectively. Susan Kent Besse's study of women's movements in early twentieth century São Paulo contains a wealth of information on women's periodical writings. The massive bibliographical compilation of Meri Knaster has been of capital importance to us in this study. Knaster's annotated bibliography, while designed to cover all aspects of women's social existence in Spanish America, grants considerable attention to literary periodicals. We are indebted to Silvia Arrom, June Hahner, and Asuncion Lavrín, all of whom have compiled considerable data about the publications of Latin American women. In their independent research projects, these scholars have earned distinction for stimulating what will certainly be a vast and fruitful terrain for future scholarship.

Though our research makes clear that literate women have not been nearly so isolated from one another as scholars and historians have often assumed, it is equally true that their dialogue remains largely hidden to us. Feminist historians have used some of the magazines as resources, but little attention has been paid to them as historical and cultural artifacts. The magazines themselves are often inaccessible—found, when they can be traced at all, in rare book rooms or private collections in Latin America, Europe, and the United States. They have not been microfilmed and are usually printed on paper that disintegrates rapidly. They constitute a critical, and often missing, link in the documentation of women's thoughts and actions, a link that not only can clarify the evolution of feminist thought and practice in modern history but also could provide a stronger basis from which to build contemporary feminism. In presenting this working bibliography we seek to open yet another route to reconstructing ideas, strategies, goals, and achievements that may until now have been lost to women working for social justice.

ELEVEN

# Toward a History of Women's Periodicals in Latin America: A Working Bibliography

*Janet Greenberg*

This list is intended as a research tool useful in the growing efforts of researchers working toward a more complete awareness of women's history in Latin America. As the variety of periodicals included attests, the scope of women's participation in print journalism is vast and continuous: research so far has revealed evidence of nearly four hundred periodicals published and written by or for women in Latin America since the eighteenth century. There are over two hundred entries in the period 1722–1979, and almost two hundred women's magazines—many of them feminist—have been published since 1980. Titles include periodicals from Central and South America and the Spanish Caribbean and span the former colonies of Spain, Portugal, and France. (Research also revealed three feminist journals published in the 1980s in Barbados and one in the Netherlands Antilles, not included here.) In addition, a limited number of periodicals published in the United States and Europe and by international organizations like the United Nations and the Organization of American States are included, where evidence shows that their primary direction is toward women in Latin America. Chicana magazines published in the United States have not been included. We have included early general-interest magazines for women discovered so far, but we have not attempted to provide comprehensive coverage of mass-circulation magazines for women in the late twentieth century. In the contemporary period, the emphasis is on feminist magazines instead.

Data have been collected from a wide range of sources and have yielded some conclusive records and much information that must be filled in and verified by future investigators. As is evident from the list, all sources are not equally detailed; in some cases, complementary information about an entry was gleaned from multiple sources. Information has been gathered from archival research in South America; discussions with women publishers and journalists and with librarians about records they remember but can no longer trace; private magazine collections on both continents; primary materials in North American libraries; and numerous secondary bibliographic sources. Though this list represents the fullest compilation of periodicals by and for women in Latin America to date, it is necessarily incomplete and open to corrections. In the meantime, it is hoped that information supplied in it will aid researchers in uncovering the hidden threads of women's continued activity in public and private spheres, and that it will serve as a point of departure for tracing the consistent participation of women in print journalism.

## NOTES ON THE ENTRIES

When information regarding an entry was supplied by a written source other than the periodical itself—for example, a library catalog or a published secondary source—the reference is noted in brackets after the entry. A complete bibliography of the references follows the magazine list. If information was culled from more than one reference, others are also cited.

Due to often incomplete and sometimes conflicting information about entries, the reader will find this list punctuated with question marks. For example, a *publication date* such as "1860s (?)" means that circumstantial evidence indicates the 1860s as the probable publication period, but no specific dates were traced. Likewise, a *publication period* listed as "[?–1899]" indicates that the date of the first issue is unknown and that there is evidence to show that the last known year of publication was 1899. A publication date such as "[?–1890–1892–?]" means that beginning and end dates are unknown, but that evidence shows the publication was in print during 1890–1892 and existed before and after those dates. Question marks referring to *cities or countries* of publication or *names of editors* are used in a similar way.

In all cases, an effort has been made to indicate the maximum amount of information available regarding publication period, director(s), place of publication, and other pertinent points without making assumptions not specifically supported by primary or secondary sources.

1. *La Abogada Internacional.* USA. [1980] Special volume of *The International Woman Lawyer* (late 1960s–1980–?). *La Abogada Newsletter.* USA. [?–Feb–Sept 1979 (12, 1–4)–Jan 1982–?] Both are publications of the International Federation of Women Lawyers.
   [Schlesinger Library]
   /USA/

2. *Acción.* Lima, Peru. [?–1981–?] Publication of Acción para la Liberación de la Mujer Peruana (ALIMUPER). Three times/year.
   [Women's period 81–82]
   /Peru/

3. *Acción Femenina: Revista del Consejo Nacional de Mujeres de Uruguay.*

## Summary Of Publication Information
### 377 women's Periodicals—Latin America, 1722–1988[a]

| | Before 1800 | 1800–1839 | 1840–1869 | 1870–1890 | 1891–1899 | 1900–1920 | 1921–1940 | 1941–1960 | 1961–1979 | 1980–1988 | No date available | Total by country |
|---|---|---|---|---|---|---|---|---|---|---|---|---|
| Argentina | | 3 | 6 | 4 | 12 | 7 | 16 | 4 | 3 | 17 | 1 | 73 |
| Belize | | | | | | | | | | 1 | | 1 |
| Bolivia | | | | | | | 3 | 11 | 2(1) | 5 | 2 | 23 |
| Brazil | | 1 | 5 | 10(2) | 2 | 1 | 1 | | 2 | 18 | | 40 |
| Chile | | | | 1 | | | 2 | | 6 | 15 | 6 | 30 |
| Colombia | | | 1 | 2 | | | 1 | 3 | 1 | 11 | | 19 |
| Costa Rica | | | | | | | | | 1 | 8 | | 9 |
| Cuba | | 1 | | 1 | | | 4 | 2 | 1(1) | 1 | 2 | 12 |
| Dominican Republic | | | | | 1 | | 1 | 2 | | 5 | | 9 |
| Ecuador | | | | | | | | 1 | 1 | 9 | 1 | 12 |
| Europe[b] | | | 1 | | | | | 1 | 3 | 3 | | 8 |
| Guatemala | | | | | | | 1 | | 1 | | | 2 |
| Honduras | | | | | | | 1 | | 1 | | | 2 |
| Mexico[c] | 1+ | 4 | 9 | 2 | | 2 | 9 | 2 | 9 | 14 | 3 | 55 |
| Nicaragua | | | | | | | | | | 3 | | 3 |
| North America: USA & Canada | | | | 2 | | 1 | | | 9 | 5 | | 17 |
| Panama | | | | | | | | | | 1 | | 1 |
| Peru | | | | 1 | 1 | | | | 1(1) | 18 | | 21 |
| Puerto Rico | | | 1 | 1 | 1 | 1 | | | 1 | 5 | | 10 |
| El Salvador | | | | | | | | | | 2 | | 2 |
| UN, OAS, etc. | | | | | | | | | 3 | 1 | | 4 |
| Uruguay | | | 2 | | 1 | 3 | 3 | 3 | | 5 | | 17 |
| Venezuela | | | | | | | 2 | | 2 | 4 | | 8 |

| Total by period | 1+ | 9 | 26 | 25 | 18 | 15 | 45 | 27 | 46 | 151 | 15 | 378 |
| --- | --- | --- | --- | --- | --- | --- | --- | --- | --- | --- | --- | --- |

[a] In general, each periodical is recorded once, in the earliest known year or period of publication. Thus, a magazine that began in 1922 but continued publication for twenty-five years is registered in the period "1921–1940," the period on the chart corresponding to its initial date. When there are no data indicating publication period or century, individual titles are recorded in the category "No date available." In the rare case that a periodical was published in more than one country it is recorded in each country.

Numbers noted in parentheses on the chart reflect periodicals published in another country with a focus on women in this one. For example, two Brazilian women's magazines were published in the USA in the 1870s–1890s; they are recorded under "North America" under that period and noted in parentheses under "Brazil." Other instances of this practice include magazines published by expatriate or exile communities in Paris, Mexico, and the like.

[b] "Europe" indicates variously Italy, France, Britain, and Sweden. No publications from Spain are included in this bibliography or under this heading.

[c] In the category "Mexico, Before 1800" the entry "1+" reflects evidence of women's ownership and participation in print media in the period, but only one actual title of such a publication has been discovered.

Montevideo, Uruguay: Imp. El Siglo Ilustrado. [July 1917 (1, 1)–
Dec 1925 (8, 51)] Director: Paulina Luisi. Monthly, 24cm. Suspended publication in 1921, resumed 1922. 7, 51 (Dec 1925) is
"Homenage a Paulina Luisi."
[Uruguay National Library; Schlesinger Library; *Mujer* (Montevideo) Sept 1986 with picture of 1, 1]
/Uruguay/

4. *La Acción Femenina.* Buenos Aires. Argentina. [1920s–1930s(?)] Covered activities of women socialists in Argentina.
[Knaster]
/Argentina/

5. *La Acción Femenina.* Chile. [?–1936 (5)–?]
[UC]
/Chile/

6. *Adelante.* Quito, Ecuador. [Nov 1976 (1)] "Voz oficial de las Brigadas Femeninas Universitarias, Quito, Universided Central."
[Ramírez Bautista, 355]
/Ecuador/

7. *El Adelanto.* Buenos Aires, Argentina. [1897 (1)–1899–?] "Periódico
Educacionista, Literario y Social." Director: Pascuala Cueto. Administrators: Justa Ramos, Aurelia Wasserzug, María V. Repetto.
[*La Mujer* 31 (1899)]
/Argentina/

8. *Agitación Femenina.* Colombia. [1944–1946] Founded, edited,
directed, and distributed by Ofelia Uribe de Acosta, Colombian suffragist.
[Gloria Velasco, *mujer/fempress* Sept 1988, 11]
/Colombia/

9. *El Águila Mexicana.* Mexico. [1823] "The first periodical to make a
definite attempt to appeal to women readers." Daily newspaper published for a few months.
[Anderson, 319; Herrick, 137, citing Fortino Ibarra de Anda in "Las
mexicanas en el periodismo," *El periodismo en México*, Mexico, 1935]
/Mexico/

10. *Al Margen.* Lima, Peru. [?–1986–?] Published by Grupo de Autoconciencia Lesbianas Feministas (GALF), Apdo. 11789, Lima 11, Peru.
[ISIS 5 (1986)]
/Peru/

11. *La Alborada.* Chile. [?] Labor newspaper focused on women.
[Lavrin]
/Chile/

12. *La Alborada del Plata.* Buenos Aires, Argentina. [1877 (1st series)–
1880 (2d series)–?] Newspaper. Editors: Juana Manuela Gorriti and

(later) Lola Larrosa. Founder: Josefina Pelliza de Sagasta.
/Argentina/

13. *El Album.* Lima, Peru, and Bolivia. [1860s–1870s(?)] Editor: Carolina Freyre de Jaimes. Juana Gorriti, frequent contributor.
[*Búcaro Americano* 1896, 11; O'Doyley]
/Peru/

14. *El Album.* Matanzas, Cuba. [1882] Director: Catalina Rodríguez de Morales. Biweekly.
[Knaster #397]
/Cuba/

15. *Album Cubano de lo Bueno y lo Bello.* Havana, Cuba. Published by La Antilla. [1860] Director: Gertrudis Gómez de Avellaneda. Biweekly; twelve issues. "Directed solely at women."
[Knaster #398; O'Doyley]
/Cuba/

16. *El Album de la Familia.* Mexico. [1839]
[Arrom, 356]
/Mexico/

17. *El Album de la Mujer.* Mexico. [1883–1990] Editor: Concepción Gimeno de Flaquer (a Spaniard). 34–42 cm.
[Knaster #399; Herrick, 135]
/Mexico/

18. *Album de las Damas.* Matanzas, Cuba. [1894–1895] Publication of Galería Literaria. Editor: Pablo Peniche. Weekly.
[Knaster #400]
/Cuba/

19. *El Album de las Niñas.* Buenos Aires, Argentina. [1877] "Published semi-serious literary pieces." Weekly.
[Knaster #401]
/Argentina/

20. *Album de Señoritas.* Buenos Aires, Argentina. [1 Jan 1854–17 Feb 1854] Founder and director: Juana Paula Manso de Noronha. "Periódico de Literatura, Modas, Bellas Artes y Teatros."
/Argentina/

21. *El Album de las Señoritas Potosinas.* San Luis Potosí, Mexico. [1865 (last issue: 14 Oct 1865, forty-five pages)] "Periódico de literatura y variedades." Each issue four pages. Listed circulation in the third week at 124 subscriptions.
[Herrick, 135]
/Mexico/

22. *El Album Mexico.* Mexico City. [1849] 2 vols.
[Herrick, 135]
/Mexico/

23. *Alfonsina.* Buenos Aires, Argentina. [Oct 1953 (1, 1)–?]

24. *Alfonsina.* Buenos Aires, Argentina. [1983–1984] Monthly feminist newspaper.
/Argentina/

25. *La Aljaba.* Buenos Aires, Argentina. [16 Nov 1830–14 Jan 1831] Eighteen issues in all. Director: Petrona Rosende de Sierra. Motto: "Nos libraremos de las injusticias de los demás hombres, solamente cuando no existamos entre ellos."
/Argentina/

26. *Alondras.* Ciudad Bolívar, Venezuela. [1934 (1)–?] Director: Anita Ramírez.
[*Mujeres de América* May/June, 1934]
/Venezuela/

27. *Alternativa Feminista.* Buenos Aires, Argentina. [8 March 1985 (1)–?] Bimonthly; irregular.
[RLIN]
/Argentina/

28. *Alternativas.* Lima, Peru. [?–1986–?] Serie "Mujer" and Serie "La Prostitución." Publication of Creatividad y Cambio (address: Jr. Quilca 431, Lima, Peru).
[ISIS 5 (1986)]
/Peru/

29. *AMMPE folios.* Mexico. [1971 (?)–?] Publication of Asociación Mundial de Mujeres Periodistas y Escritoras.
[Schlesinger Library]
/Mexico/

30. *Anales de la Educación Común.* Buenos Aires, Argentina. [1850s] Director (2d series): Juana Paula Manso de Noronha (with support from Sarmiento).
[Sosa de Newton (2)]
/Argentina/

31. *Anales Neuro-psiquiátricos del Frenocomio de Mujeres de Bogotá/Asistencia Social de Cundinamarca.* Bogotá, Colombia: Editorial Kelly. [1942 (1)–?]
[RLIN]
/Colombia/

32. *Los Andes.* Lima, Peru. [?–1895–?] Editor and director: Clorinda Matto de Turner. A general-interest publication that also published material on women.
[*Búcaro Americano*, 154: Matto mentions this publication]
/Peru/

33. *Anhelos.* Cochabamba, Bolivia. [Aug 1929 (1, 2)] Directors: María

Quiroga de Montenegro and Mercedes Anaya de Urquidi. Motto on the masthead: "Por la elevación material y cultural de la mujer."
/Bolivia/

34. *Anima Vita.* Brazil. [1910 (1)] Labor and women's rights topics.
[Lavrin]
/Brazil/

35. *Anuario Cultural e Informativo del Consejo Nacional de Mujeres de Guatemala.* Guatemala City. [?–1973–1976–?]
[RLIN]
/Guatemala/

36. *Argentina: Oficina Nacional de la Mujer.* Buenos Aires, Argentina. [1968–?] Continued as *Argentina: Departamento de la Mujer.* Bimonthly; irregular. Topics on employment.
[RLIN]
/Argentina/

37. *La Argentina.* Buenos Aires, Argentina. [31 Oct 1830 (1, 1)–3 July 1831 (1, 24); July 1831 (2, 1)–17 July 1831 (2, 6)] This is the first known publication that pretends to be written by a woman for women, but no authors or publishers are named in its pages. A. Zinny (*Efimeridografía Argirometropolitana hasta la caída del gobierno de Rosas,* Buenos Aires: Imprenta del Plata, 1869) lists the publisher and editor as don Manuel Irigoyen.
/Argentina/

38. *Asociación de Mujeres de El Salvador: Boletín.* San José, Costa Rica/ Mexico City. [Sept 1981 (1)–?] First issue subtitled: "In winning rights for women and the family, we build a new society."
[Women's period 81–82]
/El Salvador/Costa Rica/Mexico/

39. *Aspiración.* La Paz, Bolivia. [?–1950s–?] Founder: Matilde Carmona De Busch.
[Dicc . . . Boliviana, 73–74]
/Bolivia/

40. *Átomos.* Buenos Aires, Argentina. [?–1898–?] Director: V. French Matheu. Described as "bella revista de recreo."
[*Búcaro Americano* 15 Nov 1898, 449]
/Argentina/

41. *Athenea.* Potosí (?), Bolivia. [1930s–1940s(?)] Founder: María Gutierrez de Medinaceli, under the auspices of Liceo de Señoritas.
[Dicc . . . Boliviana, 135]
/Bolivia/

42. *Aurora Brasileira.* Ithaca, New York. [22 Oct 1873–20 May 1875] "Periódico litterario e noticioso." Published by Cornell University

students from Brazil. Editor: H. de Aguino. Generally monthly; eight pages; 8 × 12 in.
[Hahner, 282]
/Brazil/USA/

43. *La Avispa.* Caracas, Venezuela. [1970s (?)]
[Ramírez Bautista, 355]
/Venezuela/

44. *La Azucena.* Puerto Rico. [1870–1877] Editor: Alejandro Tapia y Rivera.
[Knaster #403]
/Puerto Rico/

45. *Bahóruco.* Santo Domingo, Dominican Republic. [?–1934–?]
[*Mujeres de América* May/June 1934]
/Dominican Republic/

46. *La Batalla.* Montevideo, Uruguay. [1915–1927] "Periódico de Ideas y de Críticas, dirigido por Maria Collazo, anarquista y feminista. Predica la participación social activa de las mujeres y denuncia sistematicamente su marginación y la violencia de que era objeto."
[*Mujer* (Montevideo) Sept 1986]
/Uruguay/

47. *Bello Sexo.* Rio de Janeiro, Brazil. [21 Aug 1862–28 Sept 1862] "Periódico Religioso, de Instrucção e Recreio, Noticioso e Crítico." Editor-in-chief: Julia de Albuquerque Sandy Aguiar. Weekly; four pages; 7 × 10$\frac{1}{2}$ in.
[Hahner, 281]
/Brazil/

48. *Biblioteca de Señoritas.* Bogotá, Colombia. [1858–1859] Regular columnist: Soledad Acosta de Samper.
[Knaster #404]
/Colombia/

49. *Blanco y Azul.* Santa Fe, Argentina. [?–1898–?] Director: Amadeo Gómez. This magazine seems to be for "the fair sex." Described as "lectura agradable," "delicadamente impresa, como para las manos enguantadas de las señoritas."
[*Búcaro Americano* 15 Nov 1898, 449]
/Argentina/

50. *Boletím.* Rio de Janeiro, Brazil. [?–1986–?] Publication of the Movimiento de Mujeres 8 de Marzo (address: Rua Esmeraldino Bandeira 120, 20961 Estação de Riachuelo).
[ISIS 5 (1986)]
/Brazil/

51. *Boletím.* Rio de Janeiro, Brazil. [?–1986–?] Publication of the Asso-

ciação Libertade Mulher (ALM/RJ) (address: Rua Valparaiso 22, Apto. 405, Tijuca).
[ISIS 5 (1986)]
/Brazil/

52. *Boletím CIM.* Mato Grosso, Brazil. (?–1986–?] Published by Centro de Informação da Mulher (address: Caixa Postal 5, 78730 São Felix do Araguaja). "Feminist bulletin." This magazine is possibly the same as *CIM.* [1980s–present (?)] "Feminist bulletin." Women's Information Center (address: Caixa Postal 11.399, 154099 São Paulo, Brazil). [*Connexions* (1985)]
[ISIS 5 (1986)]
/Brazil/

53. *Boletín Cívico-Cultural: Órgano del Comité Sampedrano de Mujeres.* San Pedro Sula, Honduras: El Comité. [Early 1960s–1966–? (vol 27, Apr 1966)]
[UC]
/Honduras/

54. *Boletín de la Alianza Nacional Feminista.* Havana, Cuba. [?–1934–?]
[*Mujeres de América* May/June 1934]
/Cuba/

55. *Boletín Diálogo Mujer.* Bogotá, Colombia. [May 1987 (1)] "Este boletín es el órgano informativo de la Fundación Diálogo Mujer" (address: Equipo Diálogo Mujer, Apdo. Aéreo 43061, Bogotá). Twelve pages.
[*mujer/fempress* Feb/Mar 1988]
/Colombia/

56. *Boletín Documental Sobre las Mujeres* (title varies slightly). Cuernavaca, Mexico: Coordinación de Iniciativas para el Desarrollo Humano de América Latina. [15 Aug 1970 (1)–1976–?] Special anthology issue of English translations also published.
[UC; RLIN]
/Mexico/

57. *Boletín Igualdad.* Santo Domingo, Dominican Republic. [1987–?] Publication of the Centro de Servicios Legales para la Mujer (CENSEL; address: Benigno de Castillo, No. 28 altos, Santo Domingo). 1987 issue has sixteen pages.
[*mujer/fempress* Feb/Mar 1988, 52]
/Dominican Republic/

58. *Boletín Internacional de AMES.* El Salvador. [1980s–present (?)] "Bimonthly bulletin of the Women's Association of El Salvador promoting national liberation and women's role."
[*Connexions*]
/El Salvador/

59. *Boletín Manuela Ramos*. Lima, Peru. [?–1986–?] Publication of Movi-
    miento Manuela Ramos (address: Av. Bolivia 921, Brena, Lima 14,
    Peru).
    [ISIS 5 (1986)]
    /Peru/

60. *Boletina feminista*. Lima, Peru. [1988 (1)] Published by Movimiento
    Feminista Mayo (address: c/o Ana María Portugal, Aptdo. 110245,
    Lima). Issue 1 nine pages.
    [*mujer/fempress* Sept 1988, 26]
    /Peru/

61. *Brujas*. Buenos Aires, Argentina. [1980s(?)–present] "Feminist
    quarterly." Publication of Asociación Trabajo y Estudio Sobre la
    Mujer (address: Calle Venezuela 1288, Buenos Aires).
    [*Connexions*]
    /Argentina/

62. *Brujas: Las mujeres Escriben*. Medellín, Colombia. [1980s–?] "Femi-
    nist monthly." Publication of Centro de Estudios de Investigaciones
    de la Mujer (address: Apdo. Aéreo 49105, Medellín).
    [*Connexions*; RLIN; *Mujeres en Acción*]
    /Colombia/

63. *El Búcaro Americano*. Buenos Aires, Argentina. [1896–1908] Director:
    Clorinda Matto de Turner. 1st series: 1, 1–6, 42: 1 Feb 1896–25 Mar
    1901. 2d series: 6, 43–8, 65: 15 June 1906–15 May 1908.
    /Argentina/

64. *La Cacerola*. Montevideo, Uruguay. [1983 (1)–present] "Feminist
    bimonthly." Publication of Grupo de Estudios Sobre la Condición
    de la Mujer en el Uruguay (GRECMU; address: Miguel del Corro
    1474, Montevideo, Uruguay). Irregular; seven issues in all by 1987.
    GRECMU also publishes "Serie de Documentos Ocasionales"
    [1984–?]; *La Cacerola–La Tribuna* [1980s–1988], coproduced with
    Centro de la Tribuna Internacional de la Mujer (issue 34, 1988,
    titled *Mujer y Conciencia*).
    [RLIN; *mujer/fempress* Oct 1988, 28]
    /Uruguay/

65. *Cadernos de Pesquisa*. [1980s(?)] Journal of research on women; one of
    the publications of the Fundação Carlos Chagas.
    [Women's period 81–82]
    /Brazil/

66. *La Camelia*. Buenos Aires, Argentina. [11 April 1852 (1)–20 June
    1852 (31)] Motto: "Libertad y no licencia; igualdad entre ambos
    sexos." Founders and directors: Rosa Guerra and Juana Manso.
    Weekly.
    /Argentina/

67. *La Camelia*. Mexico City, Mexico: Imprenta de J. R. Navarro. [1853] (illus. and music) "Semanario de literatura, variedades, teatros, modos, etc., dedicado a las señoritas mejicanas." Volume 1 447 pages. [Knaster #405; Herrick, 135]
/Mexico/

68. *El Canelo*. Santiago de Chile. [1987 (1)] "Editada por el Centro El Canelo de Nos, sede del Consejo de Educación de Adultos de América Latina (CEAAL; address: Diagonal Oriente 1604, Santiago, or Casilla 6257, Santiago 22). Covers topics such as "derechos humanos, redes de mujeres, educación, tecnologías campesinas." Bimonthly.
[*Mujeres en Acción*]
/Chile/

69. *CAPIDE, Informativo*. Temuco, Chile. [Mar 1987 (1); May 1987 (2)] "Boletín interno de información y comunicación de grupos de mujeres (fundamentalmente indígena) que trabajan con el programa." Publication of Programa de Educación con Mujeres, CAPIDE (address: Casilla 739, Temuco).
[*mujer/fempress* Feb/Mar 1988]
/Chile/

70. *La Capital*. Rosario, Argentina. [Late 1910s] General daily newspaper. Regularly published work of Juana María Beggino, feminist labor activist.
[Sosa de Newton, unpub.]
/Argentina/

71. *Caracolas*. Santiago de Chile. [?–1986–?] Published by Mujeres Zona Oriente (address: Los Alerces 2900, Santiago de Chile).
[ISIS 5 (1986)]
/Chile/

72. *El Cardello de las Mujeres*. Mexico: Oficina del Ciudadano Alejandro Valdes. [dates?] Twenty-three issues published.
[RLIN]
/Mexico/

73. *Cartillas: Documentos de Trabajo*. Santiago de Chile. [?–1986–?] Publication of Instituto de Estudios Democráticos de la Mujer (address: Casilla 16901, Correo 9, Santiago de Chile).
[ISIS 5 (1986)]
/Chile/

74. *Cartillas de Capacitación para Mujeres*. Mexico City, Mexico. [?–1986–?] Publication of Equipo de Mujeres en Acción Solidaria (EMAS; address: Apdo. Postal 21-318, 04000 Mexico DF).
[ISIS 5 (1986)]
/Mexico/

75. *Centro para Mujeres: Boletín.* Mexico City. [?–1981–1982–?] Publication of the Center, focused on health and labor rights.
[Women's period 81–82]
/Mexico/

76. *Cepamujer.* Quito, Ecuador. [?–1986–?] Publication of Centro Ecuatoriano para la Promoción de la Mujer (CEPAM; address: Apdo. 182-C, Sucursal 15, Quito).
[ISIS 5 (1986)]
/Ecuador/

77. *Chana com Chana.* São Paulo; Brazil. [?–1982–?] Experimental lesbian journal. Publication of Grupo de Acção Lesbico-Feminista (address: Caixa Postal 62–618, CEP 01000 São Paulo, SP).
[Women's period 81–82]
/Brazil/

78. *La Chancleta.* Serie "Cuadernos de Trabajo." Rosario, Argentina. [?–1986–?] Publication of INDESO MUJER (address: Montevideo 2303, Rosario).
[ISIS 5 (1986)]
/Argentina/

79. *CHANGE International Reports: Women and Society.* London, England. [1980-1981–?] Publication of CHANGE (address: Parnell House, 25 Wilton Rd., London SWIVIJS). "CHANGE is a nonprofit, independent organization founded to research and publish reports on the condition and status of women all over the world. . . ; where possible reports are written by women indigenous to the area." Issue 4: *Military Ideology and the Dissolution of Democracy—Women in Chile.* Issue 5: *Women in Peru.*
[ILET]
/Britain/

80. *Chicana Service Action Center News.* Los Angeles, Calif., USA [1973–1977–?]
[Schlesinger Library]
/USA/

81. *Chichamaya.* Barranquilla, Colombia. [?–1987–?] "Revista que reaparece y registra diversos temas como 'la mujer negra y su papel en la historia,' 'el sexo como mercancía,' 'mujer vivienda,' etc." (Address: Apdo. Aéreo. 3611, Barranquilla.)
[Manzana 1987]
/Colombia/

82. *CIDHAL Noticias: Boletín Informativo de CIDHAL* (Comunicación, Intercambio y Desarrollo Humano en América Latina). [1980s; no. 10 Apr/June 1984] Quarterly. (Address: Apdo. 5779, Cuernavaca 6000, Morelos, Mexico.) Before 1982 this publication was known as *Boletín*

*Documental Sobre las Mujeres.* In late 1970s this center also published an English newsletter, *CIDAL NEWS.*
[*Connexions*; Women's period 81–82; Ramírez Bautista]
/Mexico/

83. *CIHUAT/Voz de la Coalición de Mujeres.* Mexico City, Mexico. [May 1977 (1)–?]
[Ramírez Bautista]
/Mexico/

84. *Cine-Video-Mujer: Boletín Informativo.* Ottowa, Canada. [1987 (1)–1988] Focus is on "la labor que las mujeres latinas y caribeñas realizan en el campo audio-visual." Publication of Film Studies Department, Carleton University (address: c/o Suzana Pick, Ottawa, Ontario K15 5B6). Issue 1 has four pages.
[*mujer/fempress* June 1988, 28]
/Canada/

85. *Círculo de la Mujer: Boletín Informativo y Formativo.* Santiago de Chile: Academia de Humanismo. [1979–(?)]
[Women's period 81–82]
/Chile/

86. *El Clamor... (?) de la Mujer.* Argentina. [Mid or late 1800s(?)] Catalog entry found in the Colegio Nacional Library in Buenos Aires (1984), but no further information available.
/Argentina/

87. *Claridad.* Potosí (?), Bolivia. [1930s–1940s(?)] Founded by María Gutiérrez de Medinaceli, under the auspices of the Liceo de Señoritas.
[Dicc... Boliviana, 135]
/Bolivia/

88. *Claudia.* Buenos Aires, Argentina. [1957 (1)–present (1987)] Publication of Ryela, SA. Mass circulation women's magazine.
[Ulrich]
/Buenos Aires/

89. *Claudia.* São Paulo, Brazil. [1961 (1)–present] Editor: Victor Civitá. Circulation (1986): 274,000.
[Ulrich]
/Brazil/

90. *Claudia.* Mexico City; Mexico: Editorial Mex Ameris S. A. [1965 (1)–present] Editors: Mely Perales, Beatriz Marti, Bona Campillo. Covers art, fiction, cooking, fashion, biographies.
[Madison]
/Mexico/

91. *Colección Comunicación Alternativa de la Mujer Presenta...* Morelia, Mexico. [1980(?)–present] One publication of ISIS through ILET:

Unidad de Comunicación Alternativa de la Mujer. Each issue has distinct title. Coordinator: Adriana Santa Cruz. Several issues per year. SEE ALSO: *ISIS*.
[*Connexions*; RLIN]
/Mexico/

92. *Colección Mujeres del Ecuador*. Guayaquil, Ecuador: Editorial Jouvin. [dates?]
[RLIN]
/Ecuador/

93. *La Columna del Hogar*. Buenos Aires, Argentina. [1898 OR 1899 (1)– 1902(?)] Founder and director: Carolina Freyre de Jaimes. *Búcaro Americano* (15 Apr 1899, 498) says director was "Madame Viviane en colaboración de ilustradas señoras."
[Sosa de Newton, unpub.; *Búcaro Americano*]
/Argentina/

94. *COMAI*. [1980s–present(?)] "Bimonthly feminist bulletin focusing on health." (Address: Apdo. 2172, Estación Metropol Shopping Center, 00919 Hato Rey, Puerto Rico.)
[*Connexions*]
/Puerto Rico/

95. *Comisión Interamericana de Mujeres (CIM)*. [1970s–1980s] Publication of the Inter-American Commission of Women. This specialized organization of the OAS publishes periodic reports on women's status, *CIM News Bulletin* and *Informe Presentado a la Reunión de la Comisión de la Condición Jurídica y Social de la Mujer de las Naciones Unidas* (Washington, D.C.: Unión Panamericana). Annual. Issued in Spanish and English.
[RLIN]
/OAS/

96. *Compañeras*. Mixcoac, Mexico. [?–1986–1987–?] "Revista trimestral editada por Mujeres para el Diálogo, dirigida a los vastos sectores populares mexicanos." (Address: Apdo. Postal 19-493, Mixcoac, 13910).
[Manzana 1987; ISIS 5 (1986)]
/Mexico/

97. *Congreso Nacional de Mujeres (Cuba)—Memoria*. Havana: Imp. y Papelería La Universal. [dates?] Organized by the Federación Nacional de Asociaciones Femeninas. Annual?
[RLIN]
/Cuba/

98. *Consejo Nacional de Mujeres del Uruguay: Boletín Informativo*. Montevideo, Uruguay. [?–1982–?] SEE ALSO: *Acción Femenina*.
[Women's period 81–82]
/Uruguay/

99. *Correio das Modas.* Rio de Janeiro, Brazil. [5 Jan 1839–31 Dec 1840]
    Male publisher. "Jornal Crítico e litterario das modas, bailes, thea-
    tros, etc."
    [Hahner, 283]
    /Brazil/

100. *El Correo de las Señoras.* Mexico. [1883–1893] Director: José Adrián
    M. Rico. Weekly; sixteen pages.
    [Herrick, 137; Knaster #406]
    /Mexico/

101. *El Correo de los Niños.* Mexico. [1813]
    [Arrom, 356]
    /Mexico/

102. *Cotidiano Mujer.* Montevideo, Uruguay: Colectivo Editorial Mujer.
    [1985 (1)–1986–?] Monthly. (Address: Ana Monterroso de Laval-
    leja 2010, C. C. 10649, D-1 Montevideo.)
    [UC; RLIN; ISIS 5 (1986)]
    /Uruguay/

103. *Cuaderno de Existencia Lesbiana.* Buenos Aires, Argentina. [1988 (1)]
    (Address: Ilse Kornreich, C. C. 3904 Correo Central, 1000, Buenos
    Aires.)
    [*mujer/fempress* June 1988, 27]
    /Argentina/

104. *Cuadernos de Comunicación Alternativa.* La Paz, Bolivia. [?–1987–?]
    Publication of Centro de Integración de Medios de Comunicación
    Alternativa (CIMCA; address: Apdo. 5828, La Paz) and Centro de
    Promoción de la Mujer "Gregoria Apaya." "Ambas instituciones
    han trabajado en los últimos años en la ciudad de La Paz con mu-
    jeres de sectores populares fundamentales."
    [*mujer/fempress* Sept 1987]
    /Bolivia/

105. *Cuadernos de la Mujer.* Quito, Ecuador. [1986 (1)–present] Occasional
    series published by Centro de Planificación y Estudios Sociales
    (CEPLAES), "un grupo de trabajo sobre el tema de la mujer."
    Issue 1: *Aportes para el Debate Sobre Marxismo y Feminismo*; 2: *Mujer y
    Política*; 3: *Mujer y Violencia*; 4: *No Sé Quién Nos Irá a Apoyar: El Voto de
    la Ecuatoriana en Mayo de 1984.* (Address: Casilla 6127 CCI, Quito).
    [*mujer/fempress* May 1987 and Feb/Mar 1988]
    /Ecuador/

106. *Cuadernos de la Mujer del Campo.* Santiago de Chile. [dates?] Publica-
    tion of the Programa de Estudios y Capacitación de la Mujer Cam-
    pesina de Indígena, Academia de Humanismo Cristiano.
    [RLIN]
    /Chile/

107. *Cuadernos de Liberación de Liberación y Vida.* Santiago de Chile. [1987–

present] Publication of the Agrupación "Mujeres de Viña del Mar" (AMUDEVI).
[*mujer/fempress* Sept 1987]
/Chile/

108. *Cuadernos de Nueva Mujer.* Quito, Ecuador. [Jan 1984 (1)–?] Illus., 28 cm.
[UC; RLIN]
/Ecuador/

109. *Cuadernos de Ventana.* San José, Costa Rica. [March 1988 (1, 1)] A less expensive continuation of this group's previous *Ventana.* (Address: Alda Facio, Colectivo "Ventana," Apto. 230, San Pedro Montes de Oca, San José.)
[*mujer/fempress* May 1988]
/Costa Rica/

110. *Cuadernos Feministas.* Buenos Aires, Argentina. [1988 (1)] Issue 1: *Sexualidad, Anticoncepción, Maternidad.* Forty-four pages. (Address: ATEM, Salta 1064, 1081 Buenos Aires.)
[*mujer/fempress* July 1988]
/Argentina/

111. *Cuéntame Tu Vida.* Cali, Colombia. [1977–present(?)] "Feminist magazine on women, creativity and culture." By 1982, five issues had been produced; irregular. (Address: Apdo. Aéreo 3021, Cali.)
[*Connexions*; Women's period 81–82]
/Colombia/

112. *Cunhary.* São Paulo, Brazil. [Mar 1988 (1)] "Informativo de la Red Mujer." "Diario que pretende colaborar en la articulación de los más diversos grupos de mujeres de sectores populares en todo el país." (Address: Moema Viezzer, Rede Mulher, Caixa Postal 1803, 015051 São Paulo, SP.)
[*mujer/fempress* July 1988]
/Brazil/

113. *Despertar.* Bolivia. [1940s or 1950s(?)] Editor-in-chief: Elvira Delgado Mantilla de Bedregal, a feminist activist who published works on women's rights.
[Dicc. . . Boliviana, 92]
/Bolivia/

114. *El diario.* Bolivia. [1943–?] A mass circulation daily. Daily Women's Section includes columns "La Crónica Social" and "La Página Femenina" by Elena Jahnsen de Carrasco.
[Dicc. . . Boliviana, 147]
/Bolivia/

115. *El Diario de las chicas.* San José, Guaymallén, Argentina. [Sept 1987 (5)] "Boletín de mujeres." Publication of Secretaría de la Mujer, Fundación Ecuménica de Cuyo (address: María E. José/Sofía Vega,

Pedernerea 1291, 5519 San José, Guaymallén). Issue 5 eight pages.
[*mujer/fempress* Feb/Mar 1988]
/Argentina/

116. *Diario de los Niños*. Mexico. [1839–1940]
[Arrom, 356]
/Mexico/

117. *O Direito das Damas*. Rio de Janeiro, Brazil. [Jan 1882] Owner: Ida-
lina d'Alcantara Costa & Comp. Four pages; 9 × 12 in.
[Hahner, 283]
/Brazil/

118. *Documentos Sobre la Mujer*. Managua, Nicaragua. [Oct–Dec 1987 (1)]
Publication of Centro de Investigación de la Realidad de América
Latina (CIRA) (address: Ciudad Jardin A-22, Apto. 814, Mana-
gua). Issue 1 fifty-two pages.
[*mujer/fempress* Apr 1988]
/Nicaragua/

119. *O Domingo*. Rio de Janeiro, Brazil. [23 Nov 1873–9 May 1875] "Jornal litterario e recreativo." Editor and owner: Violante A. Ximenes
de Bivar e Vellasco. Weekly; four pages; $8\frac{3}{4} \times 12\frac{1}{4}$ in.
[Hahner, 281]
/Brazil/

120. *Eco das Damas*. Rio de Janeiro. [8 Apr 1879–1880; then 1885–26 Aug
1888] Owner: Amelia Carolina da Silva & Comp. Generally semi-
monthly or monthly: four to eight pages; from $10\frac{1}{4} \times 13\frac{3}{4}$ to $14\frac{1}{2} \times 21\frac{3}{4}$
in.
[Hahner, 281]
/Brazil/

121. *El Eco de las Niñas*. Montevideo, Uruguay. [Feb–Apr 1887]
[Lavrin #2]
/Uruguay/

122. *Ecos de Gloria*. Caracas, Venezuela. [1931 (1)–1935–?] Director
(1935): Valentina Méndez Loynaz.
[*Mujeres de América* Jan–Feb 1935]
/Venezuela/

123. *La Educación*. Buenos Aires, Argentina. [1854] Founder and editor:
Rosa Guerra.
[Sosa de Newton, Las args, 191]
/Argentina/

124. *La Elegancia*. Buenos Aires, Argentina. [Late 1890s] An elegantly
produced and illustrated fashion magazine for women. Reviewed by
Clorinda Matto de Turner.
[*Búcaro Americano* 15 Nov 1898, 449]
/Argentina/

125. *Ellas*. Santiago de Chile: Editorial Nacional Gabriela Mistral. [Feb–

May, July–Dec 1981–?] "Suplemento femenino de *Hoy*" (major daily newspaper).
[UC]
/Chile/

126. *Ellas*. Cuba. [1934 (1); also 1950s–?] Women's Magazine.
[Valdés]
/Cuba/

127. *Las Entendidas*. San José, Costa Rica. [1988 (1)] Publication of Grupo Lésbico Feminista Costarricense (address: c/o Alda Facio, Apdo. Postal 230, San José). Issue 1 two pages.
[*mujer/fempress* June 1988, 28]
/Costa Rica/

128. *Entregas de la Licorne/La Licorne*. Montevideo, Uruguay/Paris, France. 1st series: nos. 1–3, 1947–1948 (title *La Licorne*), Paris; text in French. 2d series: vols 1–6, nos. 1–12, Nov 1953–1959, Montevideo; Spanish text. 3d series: 1961, Montevideo; Spanish text. Publisher and editor: Susana Soca (Uruguayan).
/Uruguay/

129. *Escalada*. Escalada (suburb of Buenos Aires?), Argentina. [?–1931–?] "Órgano de la Sala de Primeros Auxilios de Remedios de Escalada." Director (1931–?): Margarita del Campo, a feminist leader.
[¡*Mujer!* 1, 2 (1931)]
/Argentina/

130. *La Escoba*. La Paz, Bolivia. [1986 (1)–present] "Boletín del Centro de Información y Desarrollo de la Mujer (CIDEM)." 22 cm.
[*Connexions*; RLIN]
/Bolivia/

131. *Escobas, Manzanas, y Hadas*. Santiago de Chile. [June 1988 (1)] Directors (?): Betty Salomon and Lucía Villagran. Publication of Centro Ecuménico Diego de Medellín (address: Casilla 386-V, Santiago 21). Pretende ser un boletín que recoja la voz, las esperanzas, las alegrías de muchas mujeres cristianas que buscan encontrarse a sí mismas como personas y comprometerse con este propósito liberador de Dios." Issue 1 eighteen pages.
[*mujer/fempress* Aug 1988, 27]
/Chile/

132. *La Escuela Costarricense*. San José, Costa Rica. [?–1934–?] Pedagogical magazine with focus on women's fashion and appearance.
[*Mujeres de América* May/June 1934]
/Costa Rica/

133. *Esporádica*. Mexico City, Mexico. [Oct 1987 (0–2)–Summer 1988] Editors and publishers: Adriana Batista and Ana Luisa Barreto. "Una revista de historietas." Illustrated comic books, in color.

Thirty-two pages. Subtitle: "Un punto de vista desde las enaguas."
/Mexico/

134. *"Esse Sexo que a Nosso": Serie.* [?–1986–?] Publication of Proyecto Mujer, Fundacāo Carlos Chagas (address: Morato 1565. 05513 São Paulo, SP).
[ISIS 5 (1986)]
/Brazil/

135. *A Estação.* Oporto, Brazil. [15 Jan 1879–15 Feb 1904] "Jornal illustrado para a familia." Male publisher. Brazilian edition of Portuguese journal.
[Hahner, 283]
/Brazil/

136. *Estudios de Población.* Bogotá, Colombia. (?–1981–1982–?] Publication of the Asociación Colombiana para el Estudio de la Población (ACEP). Original articles and translations from *Studies in Family Planning.* Some feminist material.
[Women's period 81–82]
/Colombia/

137. *Excelsior.* Mexico City. [1933–?] Major daily newspaper. Dramatic editor and writer: Catalina D'Erzell.
[Anderson, 317]
/Mexico/

138. *A Familia.* São Paulo, Brazil. [1888–1889]; Rio de Janeiro, Brazil [1889–perhaps 1897]. "Jornal litterario dedicado a educação da mae de familia." Editor: Josephina Alvares de Azevedo. Generally weekly; four or eight pages; 9 × 13 in.
[Hahner, 283]
/Brazil/

139. *La Familia.* Bogotá, Colombia: Imp. La Luz. [1884—?] Editor: Soledad Acosta de Samper (mostly written by herself).
[Knaster #407]
/Colombia/

140. *La Familia.* Santiago de Chile. [1890–1892] "Periódico Quincenal de Ciencias, Artes, Modas i Conocimientos Útiles."
[Lavrin #2]
/Chile/

141. *fem.* Mexico City, Mexico. "Publicación Feminista" [1976 (1)–Jan–Mar 1977 (1, 2)–present] Editor: Elena Urrutia. Publication of Difusión Cultural Feminista AC. Continuous: quarterly/bimonthly/monthly. 1986 circulation: 15,000.
[Ulrich; UC; Cx]
/Mexico/

142. *Fémina.* Montevideo, Uruguay. [1939–1945] "Revista Uruguaya

para la Mujer, dirigida por Mirta Garmendia, con notas de apoyo a los aliados durante la guerra de 1939–45 y modas."
[*Mujer* (Montevideo) Sept 1986]
/Uruguay/

143. *Fémina.* Santo Domingo (San Pedro de Macoris), Dominican Republic. [?–1934–?] Material on "sus ideales en pro de la mujer."
[*Mujeres de América* May/June 1934]
/Dominican Republic/

144. *Fémina Sapiens.* Bogotá, Colombia. [?–1986–?] Publication of Centro de Documentación y Comunicación Feminista (address: Apdo. Aéreo 25922, Bogotá).
[ISIS 5 (1986)]
/Colombia/

145. *Feminaria.* Buenos Aires, Argentina. [June 1988 (1, 1)–present] Excerpt from statement of purpose: "*Feminaria* quiere compartir teoría feminista de alto nivel producida fuera y dentro del país, posibilitando así un debate amplio de experiencias ya vividas . . . que aportan a la definición de estrategias propias." Director: Lea Fletcher. (Address: Casilla de Correo 402, 1000 Buenos Aires.) Quarterly; vol 1, no. 1 forty-eight pages.
/Argentina/

146. *FMC: Boletín de la Federación de Mujeres Cubanas.* Havana, Cuba. [date?] In Spanish, English, and French.
[RLIN]
/Cuba/

147. *Gazeta de México y Noticias de Nueva España.* Mexico. [1722 (1)–?] "Several women were concerned with the publication of the first real periodical published in New Spain."
[Anderson, 319]
/Mexico, 18th c./

148. *Güemes.* Salta, Argentina. [c. 1905–1907–c. 1925] Founder: Benita Campos.
[Sosa de Newton, Las args, 192]
/Argentina/

149. *La Guirnalda Puerto-Riqueña.* Puerto Rico. [1856–1857] Director: Ignacio Guaso ("male feminist").
[Knaster #408]
/Puerto Rico/

150. *El Heraldo.* Cochabamba, Bolivia. [1950s–1960s] Major daily newspaper. "Jefe de Redacción y Colaboradora": Julia Loayza y L., who also collaborated in many mainstream publications.
[Dicc . . . Boliviana, 155]
/Bolivia/

151. *Heraldo de la Mujer*. Humacao, Puerto Rico. [20 Mar 1918–June 1919]
[RLIN]
/Puerto Rico/

152. *El Hogar*. Mexico City. [13 Sept 1913(1)–1934–?] Publisher and editor: Emilia Enriquez de Rivera. Began as a small sheet; by 1934 issues averaged fifty pages with staff of sixty.
[Anderson, 315]
/Mexico/

153. *El Hogar*. Buenos Aires, Argentina. [current(?)] "Ilustración argentina para la mujer, la casa y el niño." Weekly.
[RLIN]
/Argentina/

154. *Hogar Linqueño*. Lincoln, Provincia de Buenos Aires, Argentina. [?–1934–?]
[*Mujeres de América* May/June 1934]
/Argentina/

155. *Hojas Poéticas: Poesía en Voces de Mujer*. Tucson, Ariz., USA: Scorpion Press. [1976 (1)–?]
[UC]
/USA/

156. *Ideal Femenino*. La Paz (?), Bolivia. [1940s–1950s–1960s(?)] Founder: Matilde Carmona De Busch, feminist activist and wife of Bolivian president, 1938.
[Dicc. . . Boliviana, 73–74]
/Bolivia/

157. *Ideas: Revista de Mujeres de México*. [1945 (2–3)–1946]
[UC]
/Mexico/

158. *Ideas y Acción*. Montevideo, Uruguay. [?–1930s–?] Director: Sara Alvarez Rey. "Feminist magazine." Newspaper of the Partido Independiente Democrático Femenino.
[Lavrin; Lavrin #2]
/Uruguay/

159. *Impressoes*. Rio de Janeiro, Brazil. [Dec 1987 (0)] Publication of Rede de Artes e Literatura Feminista (address: C.P. 70176, Ag. Ipanema, 22422, Rio de Janeiro). Ninety-four pages.
[*mujer/fempress* Feb/Mar 1988]
/Brazil/

160. *Impulsamos Microempresarios*. Cali, Colombia. [?–1987–?] "Única revista colombiana dedicada al sector informal de la economía y en el cual la mujer juega un papel fundamental. Trabaja en un progama llamado 'Mujer Comunitaria' que orienta e informa a las interesadas

en como constituir una empresa comunitaria." (Address: Apdo. Aéreo 3346, Cali.)
[Manzana 1987]
/Colombia/

161. *Informativo CENDOC—Mujer*. Lima, Peru. [?–1987–?] Publication of Centro de Documentación Sobre la Mujer. "Registra todo lo que escriben las mujeres, 'todo tiene importancia, todo significa un paso hacia un futuro diferente para la mujer.'" (Address: Av. Arenales 2626, Lima 14.)
[Manzana 1987]
/Peru/

162. *Inquietudes de la Lucha*. . . [?–1986–?] Santiago de Chile. Publication of MOMUPO (address: c/o Marina Valdes, José Santiago Aldunate 2842, Población Bulnes, Renca, Santiago de Chile).
/Chile/

163. *Interamerican Commission on Women: Publications* (Organization of American States). SEE *Comisión Interamericana de Mujeres*.

164. *ISIS Boletín Internacional de las Mujeres/ISIS International Women's Journal*. Santiago de Chile and Rome, Italy. [1976–present] "International feminist networking publication." Publication of ILET: Unidad de Comunicación Alternativa de la Mujer. Quarterly; Spanish and English editions. Other publications of ISIS: *Mujeres en Acción/Women in Action*, a quarterly pamphlet supplement in Spanish and English; *Boletín de la Red de Salud de las Mujeres Latinoamericanas y del Caribe*; and *Colección Comunicación Alternativa de la Mujer* (SEE separate entry).
/Chile/Italy/

165. *IXQUIC Boletín*. Mexico City, Mexico. (Subject: Guatemala). [1980s–?] Publication of Centro de la Investigación de la Mujer en Guatemala (address: Apdo. Postal 27008, CP 06760, Mexico DF).
[*Connexions*]
/Guatemala/Mexico/

166. *Jornal das Familias*. Rio de Janeiro, Brazil/Paris, France. [1863–1878] Male publisher.
[Hahner, 283]
/Brazil/France/

167. *O Jornal das Senhoras*. Rio de Janeiro. [1 Jan 1852–30 Dec 1855] "Modas, Litteratura, Bellas-Artes, Teatros e Crítica." Weekly; eight pages; $8 \times 11\frac{1}{4}$ in.
[Hahner, 280]
/Brazil/

168. *Justicia y Paz*. Mexico City, Mexico. Aug 1987 special issue: *Revista de Derechos Humanos*. "Este número está dedicado a los derechos de la

mujer." Publication of Justicia y Paz (address: Centro Universitario Cultural, Odontología 35, Copilco, Universidad, 04360 México DF). Illus.; seventy-two pages.
[*mujer/fempress* Feb/Mar 1988]
/Mexico/

169. *Killa.* Huancayo, Peru. [Aug/Sept 1987 (13)] "Boletín de Filomena, Mujer Minera, Comités de Amas de Casa; de circulación interna, fotocopiado." (Address: Calle Real 536, 67.305, Huancayo, Peru.) Issue 13 twelve pages.
[*mujer/fempress* Feb/Mar 1988]
/Peru/

170. *LADOC.* Lima, Peru. [1980s–?] "Bimonthly publication of Latin American documentation" with women's focus. (Address: Apdo. 5594, Lima).
[*Connexions*]
/Peru/

171. *Leque.* São Paulo, Brazil. [1886–1887] "Organo litterario, dedicado ao bello sexo." Male publisher.
[Hahner, 283]
/Brazil/

172. *Letras de Buenos Aires.* Buenos Aires, Argentina. [Oct–Dec 1980 (1, 1)–May 1984 (4, 11)–?] Director: Victoria Pueyrredon.
/Argentina/

173. *Letras Femeninas.* Beaumont, Tex., USA. [Spring 1975 (1)–1980s] Publication of Asociación de Literatura Femenina, Dept. of Modern Languages, Texas A&M University. Semiannual.
[UC]
/USA/

174. *Letras Femeninas en Uruguay.* Montevideo, Uruguay. [dates?] Publication of the Asociación de Literatura Femenina Hispánica.
[UC]
/Uruguay/

175. *La Licorne.* SEE *Entregas de la Licorne.*

176. *Lo que Todo Marxista Debe Saber Sobre Feminismo, Machismo, y Aborto: Diez Prejuicios Sobre el Feminismo...* Santo Domingo, Dominican Republic. [?–1987–?] A pamphlet series published by Editorial Alas (address: Calle 1, No. 3 Urb. Mari-Pili, sector Honduras, Santo Domingo). "Editorial que publica diversos y ágiles folletos que tienen como misión difundir ideas en torno a problemas como la relación hombre-mujer y tópicos de comunicación colectiva."
[Manzana 1987]
/Dominican Republic/

177. *La Lucha Obrera.* Montevideo, Uruguay. [1884] "Semanario de los

Obreros Internacionalistas. Desde una columna permanente se tra-
taban temas como: participación de la mujer en la vida colectiva,
necesidad de formar una sección de mujeres en la Asociación Internacional de Obreros."
[*Mujer* (Montevideo) Sept 1986]
/Uruguay/

178. *Luna Nueva.* Río Piedras, Puerto Rico. [8 Mar 1988 (1, 1)] "Boletín
del colectivo 'Feministas en Marcha'" (address: Apdo. 21939, Estación UPR, Río Piedras, P.R. 00931).
[*mujer/fempress* May 1988]
/Puerto Rico/

179. *Luz.* Mexico City. [1929 (1)] Publisher: Guadalupe Ramirez and
"five other cultured and serious-minded women." Editor-in-chief:
Guadalupe Ramírez.
[Anderson, 316]
/Mexico/

180. *Madrugada, Nuestras Vidas.* La Paz, Bolivia. [?–1986–1987–?] One of
a number of publications of the Centro de Promoción de la Mujer
"Gregoria Apaza" (address: Casilla 21170, La Paz).
[ISIS 5 (1986); Manzana 1987]
/Bolivia/

181. *La Maga.* Guayaquil, Ecuador. [1988 (1, 0)] Publication of Centro
Acción de la Mujer (address: Casilla Postal 10201, Guayaquil).
Thirty-two pages.
[*mujer/fempress* June 1988]
/Ecuador/

182. *La Mala Vida.* Caracas, Venezuela. [?–1986–?] Publication of Colectivo La Mala Vida (address: Apdo. Postal 54028, Caracas
1051-A).
[ISIS 5 (1986)]
/Venezuela/

183. *La Manzana de la Discordia.* Cali, Colombia. [1980s–?] "Irregularly
published feminist bulletin." Publication of the Grupo Amplio por la
Liberación de la Mujer (address: Apdo. Aéreo 20527, Cali).
[*Connexions*]
/Colombia/

184. *María, Liberación del Pueblo.* Cuernavaca, Morelos, Mexico. [1980s–
present] "Feminist monthly bulletin for and by working class and
peasant women." (Address: Apdo. 158-B, Avenida Morelos 714,
Cuernavaca, Morelos).
[*Connexions*]
/Mexico/

185. *María, María.* Salvador, Bahia, Brazil. [?–1986–?] Publication of
Brasil Mulher/Salvador (Address: Caixa Postal 4062, CEP 40000
Salvador, BA).
[ISIS 5 (1986)]
/Brazil/

186. *MAYAM 85: Boletín Internacional de la Mujer Argentina y Americana 85.*
Mendoza, Argentina. [?–1986–?] Quarterly. (Address: Gutiérrez
650, 4° Piso Apto. 29, 5500 Mendoza).
[*Index of Women's Media 1986*]
/Argentina/

187. *A Mensageira.* São Paulo, Brazil. [15 Oct 1897–15 Jan 1900] "Revista
literaria dedicada a mulher brasileira." Director: Presciliana Duarte
de Almeida. Semimonthly; sixteen pages; 10 × 13 in.
[Hahner, 283]
/Brazil/

188. *Micaela.* Spanga, Sweden. [1980s(?)–present] "Bimonthly feminist
publication about Latin American affairs and exiled Latin American
women in Sweden." Publication of ALAM (address: Box 5099, 6305
Spanga).
[*Connexions*]
/Sweden/

189. *Miscelanea de Damas.* Buenos Aires, Argentina. [1833 (1 issue only?)]
[Sosa de Newton (2)]
/Argentina/

190. *Movimiento Nacional de Mujeres Newsletter.* Mexico City, Mexico.
[?–1981–?] Advocates integration of women as equals in all activities social, economic, political; presses campaigns against
discriminatory laws; analysis of textbooks, etc.
[Women's period 81–82]
/Mexico/

191. *¡Mujer! (Tribuna Femenina).* Buenos Aires, Argentina. [July 1931
(1, 2)–1932–?] Director: Lola López Blanco. Seems to be an independent socialist feminist magazine.
/Argentina/

192. *La Mujer.* Havana, Cuba. [?–1934 (73)–?] Director (1934): Maria
Collado y Romero.
[*Mujeres de América* May/June 1934]
/Cuba/

193. *La Mujer.* Buenos Aires, Argentina. [1860s–1870s(?)] "Revista feme-
nina." Contributor: Carolina Jaimes de Freyre (b. 1849).
[Dicc . . . Boliviana, 120]
/Argentina/

194. *La Mujer*. Buenos Aires, Argentina. [1899 (1, 31)–several years?]
Male publisher.
/Argentina/

195. *La Mujer*. Puerto Rico. [1910 (1)] Founder: Luisa Capetillo (1880–
1922). "Feminist magazine founded by one of the first Puerto Rican
feminist labor activists/journalists."
[*Women's World Records*]
/Puerto Rico/

196. *La Mujer*. Bogotá, Colombia: Imp. de Silvestre y Cía. [1878–1881]
Tome 1: "Segunda edición abreviada," 1880; 5 tomes in all. Other
title: *Lectura para las Familias*. "Revista quincenal exclusivamente re-
dactada por señoras y señoritas." Director: Soledad Acosta de Samper (1833–1903). Biweekly; 26cm.
[Knaster #409; Melvyl; RLIN]
/Colombia/

197. *La Mujer*. Mexico City, Mexico. [no. 1 before 1933] Founder: María
Rios Cárdenas. "Short lived and unpopular owing to its theme."
[Anderson, 317]
/Mexico/

198. *La Mujer*. Buenos Aires, Argentina. [1982 (1)–1986] Regular supple-
ment (weekly/biweekly?) of the daily tabloid *El Tiempo Argentino*
(circulation 40,000–50,000). By 1986, grew to twelve pages. Editor:
Nelly Casas. Regular columnist: Liz Spett.
[ILET (1982)]
/Argentina/

199. *La Mujer*. Curico, Chile. [founded 1897] "Revista quincenal, órgano
de la Academia Mercedes Marin del Solar." Clorinda Matto wrote:
"Su programa es el mismo que el *Búcaro*, con referencia a la ilustración de la mujer como base del progreso universal; su índole literaria
y su ideal la confraternidad americana entre los escritores del habla
española."
[*Búcaro Americano* 15 Sept 1897, 281]
/Chile/

200. *La Mujer*. Quito, Ecuador. [?–1986–?] Publication of the Instituto de
Estudios de la Familia (address: Robles 850, Quito).
[ISIS 5 (1986)]
/Ecuador/

201. *Mujer*. San José, Costa Rica. [1980s (no. 2 Aug 1985)] Publication of
the Centro Feminista de Información y Acción.
[RLIN]
/Costa Rica/

202. *Mujer: Revista Feminina por Excelencia*. Villahermosa, Mexico. [15 Dec

1935 (1, 1)–?]
[UC]
/Mexico/

203. *Mujer Cefémina*. San José, Costa Rica. [1980s(?)–present] Monthly thematic feminist bulletin.
[*Connexions*]
/Costa Rica/

204. *Mujer Centroamericana*. Guatemala. [dates?] Monthly.
[RLIN]
/Guatemala/

205. *Mujer Combatiente*. Bucaramanga, Colombia. [?–1987–?] "Órgano de expresión del grupo femenino 8 de marzo registra las actividades políticas de las mujeres."
[Manzana 1987]
/Colombia/

206. *Una Mujer Cualquiera*. Caracas, Venezuela. [?–1981–?] Publication of the Grupo Feminista la Conjura. Two to three issues/year (irregular).
[Women's period 81–82]
/Venezuela/

207. *La Mujer de Hoy*. Mexico City, Mexico. [?–Apr 1963 (3, 32)–?]
[Schlesinger Library]
/Mexico/

208. *La Mujer en el Mundo*. Mexico City, Mexico. [Aug 1982 (1)–?] Regular section (two times/week) in the mass circulation daily *El Día*. Coordinator: Patricia Esquenazi.
[ILET]
/Mexico/

209. *La Mujer en la Historia/Cuadernos Culturales*. Peru. [?–1987–?] Publication of the Centro de Documentación Sobre la Mujer (CENDOC). A pamphlet series; 1987 titles include *Mercedes Cabello: O, El riesgo de ser mujer* by Ana María Portugal, sixteen pages.
[*mujer/fempress* Sept 1987]
/Peru/

210. *mujer/fempress*. Santiago de Chile. [1982(?)–present] Publication of the Unidad de Comunicación Alternativa de la Mujer (ILET) (address: Casilla 16637, Correo 9, Santiago de Chile). Monthly collection of clippings (and original articles by own journalists) from Latin American press (mainly) concerning women. ILET also publishes monographic special thematic supplements, *Especial Mujer*.
/Chile/

211. *Mujer Levántate*. Lima, Peru. [?–1981–?] Bulletin of the Frente

Socialista de Mujeres.
[Women's period 81–82]
/Peru/

212. *La Mujer Mexicana.* Morelia, Mexico. [1901 (1)–1908] "Publicación mensual dedicado al bello sexo." Written and published by Mariano de Jesús Torres. Monthly. Paged continuously; issues unnumbered. 1901 issue: 148 pages, 24 cm.
[Lavrin; RLIN]
/Mexico/

213. *La Mujer Moderna.* Mexico. [date?] Weekly.
[RLIN]
/Mexico/

214. *Mujer, Mujer.* Santo Domingo, Dominican Republic. [Jan 1984 (1, 1)–current] Publication of the Círculo de Estudios de la Mujer. Monthly; 22 cm. Beginning with Boletín 2 (Feb 1984), year numbering is dropped.
[RLIN]
/Dominican Republic/

215. *La Mujer Nueva.* Santiago de Chile. [1935–1936; Nov 1935 (1, 1)–Dec 1936 (1, 12)] Feminist magazine; mouthpiece of the Movimiento Pro-Emancipación de la Mujer de Chile (MEMCH).
[Lavrín; Lavrín #2]
/Chile/

216. *Mujer y Desarrollo.* Santo Domingo, Dominican Republic. [Apr 1978 (1, 1)–1979–?] Publication of Mujeres en Desarrollo. Quarterly. (Spanish and English: Apr–Dec 1978; Spanish only: Mar 1979.)
[RLIN]
/Dominican Republic/

217. *Mujer y Educación.* Santiago de Chile. [Winter 1987 (1)] "Revista del colectivo 'Mujer y educación'" (address: Gladys Guzmán, 7ª Línea 1247, piso 4, Santiago de Chile). Issue 1 sixteen pages.
[*mujer/fempress* Apr 1988]
/Chile/

218. *Mujer y Familia.* San José, Costa Rica. [1987–1988] "Boletín informativo." Publication of the Centro Nacional para el Desarrollo de la Mujer y la Familia (CMF), del Ministerio de Cultura, Juventud y Deportes (address: Apdo. 10227, 1000 San José).
[*mujer/fempress* July 1988]
/Costa Rica/

219. *Mujer y Hogar.* San José, Costa Rica. [1943 (1)] Director: Carmen Cornejo. (address: Apdo. 89, San José.) Weekly.
[Ulrich; RLIN]
/Costa Rica/

220. *Mujer y Salud: Serie.* Bolivia. [?–1986–?] Publication of CIDEM.
   [ISIS 5 (1986)]
   /Bolivia/

221. *Mujer y Sociedad.* Lima, Peru. [15 July 1980 (1)–present] "Revista
   Feminista Peruana de Actualidad y Análisis." Publication of Editora
   Ital Peru. Bimonthly publication of the Centro de Comunicación
   e Investigación Aplicada, a women's collective. Publication possibly
   suspended in 1982. (address: Jr. Trujillo 678, Lima 17.)
   [*Connexions*; UC; Women's period 81–82; *Mujeres en Acción*]
   /Peru/

222. *Mujeres.* Lima, Peru. [Dec 1987 (1, 1)] Publication of the Instituto de
   la Mujer Peruana "María Jesus Alvarado," MUJERES (Pablo Ber-
   mudez 214, Of. 605, Lima 11, Jesus María). Quarterly. Issue 1 is
   four-page tabloid.
   [*mujer/fempress* Feb/Mar 1988]
   /Peru/

223. *Mujeres.* Buenos Aires, Argentina. [Nov 1981 (1)–?]
   [UC; RLIN]
   /Argentina/

224. *Mujeres.* Buenos Aires, Argentina. [1987 (1, 1)] "Revista de la Secretaría de la Mujer del Partido Justicialista de la Capital Federal"
   (address: Mujeres, Ayacucho 915, Capital Federal, Argentina).
   Issue 1 eight pages.
   [*mujer/fempress* Apr 1988]
   /Argentina/

225. *Mujeres.* Mexico. [date?] Title varies slightly. Monthly; 31 cm.
   [RLIN]
   /Mexico/

226. *Mujeres.* Havana, Cuba. [1959 (1)–1986(?)] Publication of the Fe-
   deración de Mujeres Cubanas. Editor (1986): Hortensia Gómez.
   Circulation in 1986: 150,000.
   [Valdés; Melvyl; Ulrich; Women's period 81–82]
   /Cuba/

227. *Mujeres.* Santo Domingo, Dominican Republic. [?–1986–1987–?]
   Publication of the Círculo de Estudio Feminista. "Periódico mensual
   con noticias sobre salud, actividades diversas y cotidianas de las
   mujeres. Incluyen una fotonovela vista desde la óptica femenina y
   con ánimo cuestionador." (address: Apdo. Postal 2793, Santo
   Domingo.)
   [ISIS 5 (1986); Manzana 1987]
   /Dominican Republic/

228. *Mujeres Adelante*. Panama. [1984 (1)–Jan/Mar 1985 (2)] Quarterly; 28cm.
[RLIN]
/Panama/

229. *Mujeres Campesinas*. La Paz, Bolivia. [dates?] Publication of the Facultad Latinoamericana de Ciencias Sociales. (Paper series?)
[RLIN]
/Bolivia/

230. *Mujeres de América*. Buenos Aires, Argentina. [Jan–Dec 1933 (1)–Jan/Feb 1935 (3, 13)] Director: Nelly Marino Carvallo. Motto: "Revista del pensamiento y vinculación femenina en los países Ibero-Americanos."
[UC]
/Argentina/

231. *Mujeres del Cusco/Serie Mujer*. Cuzco, Peru. [?–1981–1982–?] Publication of the Asociación Amauta in conjunction with the Centro de Publicaciones Educativas TAREA. Issue 1 (1981?): 1: Trabajo y Vida Cotidiana"; 2 (May 1982): "Su Participación Social y Política." 29 cm.
[*Connexions*; RLIN]
/Peru/

232. *Mujeres en Espejo*. Mexico City, Mexico. [1983–1985–?] Folios Ediciones.
[UC]
/Mexico/

233. *Mujeres en Lucha*. Caracas, Venezuela. [?–1986–?] Publication of Círculos Femeninos Populares (address: Apdo. 4240, Caracas 1010-A).
[ISIS 5 (1986)]
/Venezuela/

234. *Mujeres en Movimiento*. Buenos Aires, Argentina: Agencia Periodística CID. [Mar 1986 (0)–?]
[RLIN]
/Argentina/

235. *¡Mujeres!* Guatemala. [date?] Publication of the Alianza Femenina Guatemalteca. 31 cm.
[RLIN]
/Guatemala/

236. *Mujeres Organizándonos*. Lima, Peru. [Feb 1983 (1, 1)– present] Occasional folio on working-class and peasant women. Publication of the Instituto de la Mujer Peruana María Jesús Alvarado. 20 cm.
[*Connexions*; RLIN]
/Peru/

237. *Mujeres y Medicina*. Mexico City, Mexico. [1987 (3)] Compiler: Dora

Cardaci. Publication of the División de Ciencias Biológicas y de la Salud, Departamento de Atención a la Salud, Area Educación y Salud, Universidad Autónoma Metropolitana (address: Unidad Xochimilco, México DF). Issue 3 sixty-five pages.
[*mujer/fempress* Nov 1988]
/Mexico/

238. *A Mulher*. New York, USA. [Jan 1881–June 1881] Editors: Josepha A. F. M. de Oliveira and María A. G. Estrella. "Periódico illustrado de litteratura e Bellas Artes consagrada aos interesses e direitos da Mulher Brazileira." Monthly; eight pages; $8\frac{1}{2} \times 11\frac{3}{4}$ in.
[Hahner, 283]
/Brazil/USA/

239. *Mulher e Saude*. Cuiba, MT, Brazil. [?–1986–?] Publication of the Associação de Mulheres de Mato Grosso (address: Rua Baltazar Navarro 321, Bairro Bandeirante, 78000 Cuiba, MT).
[ISIS 5 (1986)]
/Brazil/

240. *Mulher em Vida*. São Paulo, Brazil. [?–1986–?] Publication of the Organização Autonoma das Mulheres (address: Rua Ribeiro de Lima 344, CEP 01122, Sao Paulo, SP).
[ISIS 5 (1986)]
/Brazil/

241. *Mulher Noticias*. Minas Gerais, Brazil. [Dec 1987/Jan 1988 (1, 0)] Publication of the Conselho Estadual da Mulher de Minas Gerais (address: Av. Augusto de Lima, 276, Minas Gerais). Focuses on the role of women in national politics.
[*mujer/fempress* June 1988]
/Brazil/

242. *Mulherio*. São Paulo, Brazil. [?–1981–1988] Publication of the Nucleo de Comunicaçoes Mulherio. Formerly published by the Fundação Carlos Chagas. Bimonthly newspaper (1981–1982); monthly thereafter. See *Nexo* for continuation of this journal, 1988–?.
[*Connexions*; ISIS 5 (1986)]
/Brazil/

243. *Mundo Femenino*. Montevideo, Uruguay. [1923] "Para mujeres." Director: Edgar Lund-Lloyd.
[*Mujer* (Montevideo) Sept 1986]
/Uruguay/

244. *El Nacional Revolucionario*. Mexico. [?–1933–?] General daily. Editor of Women's Page: Mario Río Cárdenas (former publisher of *La Mujer*), who wrote regular feminist editorials.
[Anderson, 318]
/Mexico/

245. *Naciones Unidas/United Nations Publications: Noticiero sobre la Condición de la Mujer.* New York, USA: UN Subdivisión de Promoción de la Igualdad del Hombre y la Mujer/UN Section on the Status of Women. [June 1974–?] Title changed to *Noticiero Sobre la Condición Jurídica y Social de la Mujer* (date?).
[RLIN]
/UN/

246. *Nervio.* Buenos Aires, Argentina. [May 1931 (1, 1)–Nov 1936 (4, 48)–?] Not specifically a feminist magazine. Regular contributors of feminist material: Alfonsina Storni, Herminia Brumana, María Lacerda de Moura.
[*¡Mujer!* 2 (1931)]
/Argentina/

247. *Network.* Belize. [?–1981–?] Quarterly journal of the Belize Committee for Women and Development.
[Women's period 81–82]
/Belize/

248. *Nexo.* São Paulo, Brazil. [1988 (1, 1)] Renamed and reconceived continuation of *Mulherio.* Publication of the Nucleo de Comunicaciones Mulherio (address: Rua Cunha Gago, 704, Pinheiros, 05421, Sáo Paulo, SP). Issue 1 twenty-seven pages.
[*mujer/fempress* Sept 1988]
/Brazil/

249. *Nos Mulheres.* Sáo Paulo, Brazil. [June 1976 (1)–?] Publication of the Associação de Mulheres.
[Ramírez Bautista]
/Brazil/

250. *Nosotras.* Montevideo, Uruguay. [1945–1949] "Revista mensual de las Mujeres Comunistas al Servicio de la Patria, dirigida por Julia Arévalo. De orientación política y sindical."
[*Mujer* (Montevideo) Sept 1986]
/Uruguay/

251. *Nosotras.* La Paz (?), Bolivia. [1939 (1)–?] Founders: Marina Lijerón Baldivia de Betachini and Elvira Llosa de Salmón. "Revista femenina."
[Dicc...Boliviana, 153, 158]
/Bolivia/

252. *Nosotras.* La Paz (?), Bolivia. [1950s–1960s(?)] (Could be same as *Nosotras* above.] Founder: Matilde Carmona de Busch.
[Dicc...Boliviana, 73–74]
/Bolivia/

253. *Nosotras*. Valparaiso, Chile. [Early twentieth century?] "Feminist magazine."
[Lavrin]
/Chile/

254. *Nosotras*. Guatemala. [1932/1933 (1)–1935/1936–?]
[*Mujeres de América* May/June 1934 and Jan/Feb 1935]
/Guatemala/

255. *Nosotras*. La Plata, Argentina. [?–1903–Aug 1904 (3, 63/64)–?] Director: María Abella de Ramírez (Uruguayan). Subdirector: Justa Burgos Meyer. Subtitle: "Revista Feminista, Literaria y Social." Motto: "Ayudémonos las unas a las otras: la Unión hace la fuerza." Contains articles on the Centro Socialista Femenino de Buenos Aires, contributions from Fenia Chertkow de Repetto, etc.
/Argentina/

256. *Nosotras*. Paris, France. [Jan 1974–1976–?] "Bulletin bilingue d'un groupe de femmes latinoamericaines à Paris."
[Ramírez Bautista]
/France/

257. *Nosso Boletím de Campanha*. Rio de Janeiro, Brazil. [?–1986–?] Publication of the Colectivo de Mulheres (address: Caixa Postal 33114, CEP 22.442, Rio de Janeiro, RJ).
[ISIS 5 (1986)]
/Brazil/

258. *Noticias/News*. San Juan, Puerto Rico. [?–1986–?] Publication of Casa Protegida Julia Burgos (address: GPO Box 2433, San Juan 00936).
[ISIS 5 (1986)]
/Puerto Rico/

259. *Novo Correio de Modas*. Rio de Janeiro, Brazil. [1852–1854] Male publisher. "Novellas, poesias, viagens, recordाçãos, historias, anecdotas, e charadas."
[Hahner, 283]
/Brazil/

260. *Nuestra Causa*. Buenos Aires, Argentina. [1910s(?)–1930s–?] Feminist socialist/anarchist magazine published by Unión Feminista Nacional. Directors included Adela García Salaberry. Writers included Alicia Moreau de Justo and Elisa Bachofen.
[Sosa de Newton, unpub.; Henault, 63; Lavrin #2]
/Argentina/

261. *Nuestra Revista*. Buenos Aires, Argentina. [1931(1)] Director: Leonor Real. A children's publication?
[*¡Mujer!* 2 (1931), 25]
/Argentina/

262. *Nuestra Revista*. La Paz (?), Bolivia. [1960s] Director and owner: Elsa
     Paredes de Salazar. "Publicación que difunde las aspiraciones feme-
     ninas, difunde los Derechos de la Mujer e impulsa el conocimineto
     de Bolivia y de sus valores en el exterior."
     [Dicc. . . Boliviana, intro.]
     /Bolivia/

263. *Nuestra Tribuna*. Necochea, Argentina. [1922–1925] "Primer periódi-
     co anarquista internacional escrito por mujeres y para mujeres."
     Quincenario. Director: Juana Rouco Buela. Full title(?): *Nuestra Tri-
     buna Quincenario Feminina de Ideas, Arte, Crítica, y Literatura.*
     [Sosa de Newton; Lavrin #2]
     /Argentina/

264. *Nueva Acción Femenina*. Montevideo, Uruguay. [1968 (1–15)–1972]
     "Periódico mensual independiente." Editor: Q. F. Ana María Re-
     dondo. "Dirigido por Ofelia Machado." Microfilm: Herstory.
     [UC; RLIN; Madison; *Mujer* (Montevideo) Sept 1986]
     /Uruguay/

265. *Nueva Dimensión*. Mar del Plata, Argentina. [1988 (1, 1)] Director:
     María Ridao Mendez. "Informa sobre las actividades del Grupo
     Nueva Dimensión" (address: Moreno 3215, 7-A, 7600 Mar del Pla-
     ta). Issue 1 eight pages.
     [*mujer/fempress* Sept 1988]
     /Argentina/

266. *Nueva Mujer*. Quito, Ecuador. [?–1981–?] Frequency unknown. Pub-
     lisher: Magdalena Adoum (address: Toledo 1455 y Coruna, Quito).
     "News, feature articles on feminism, women's status, etc."
     [Women's period 81–82]
     /Ecuador/

267. *La Nueva Mujer*. Buenos Aires (?), Argentina. [1910 (1)] Founder:
     María Abellade Ramírez. Publication of the Liga Feminista
     Nacional.
     [Sosa de Newton, unpub.]
     /Argentina/

268. *Nueva Mujer*. Quito and Guayaquil (?), Ecuador. [Dec 1980–June
     1981 (1st series, 3 issues); Mar 1982–? (2d series)] Director: Mag-
     dalena Adoum. Average issue length: seventy pages; 5,000 copies.
     Formerly *Nueva* (1970–1979), then *Cuadernos de Nueva* (1979–1980).
     [ILET]
     /Ecuador/

269. *Nueva Senda*. Argentina. [1909–?] Anarchist magazine founded by
     Juana Rouco Buela.
     [Sosa de Newton]
     /Argentina/

270. *Nueva Sociedad*. Caracas, Venezuela. [?–Jan/Feb 1988 (93)–?] Special issue 93, Jan/Feb 1988, *Ser Mujer en America Latina*. Publication of Nueva Sociedad (address: Apdo. 61712, Caracas 1060-A).
[*mujer/fempress* Apr 1988]
/Venezuela/

271. *Nuevos Horizontes*. Guayaquil, Ecuador. [?–1934–?] Publication of the Legión Femenina de Educación Popular. Contributors included Gabriela Mistral.
[*Mujeres de América* May/June 1934]
/Ecuador/

272. *Nzinga Informativa*. Rio de Janeiro, Brazil. [?–1986–?] Published by NZINGA/Colectivo de Mulheres Negras (address: Caixa Postal 2073, 20,000 Rio de Janeiro, RJ).
[ISIS 5 (1986)]
/Brazil/

273. *8 de marzo*. Lima, Peru. [Mar 1988 (1, 1)] "Boletín mensual de la mujer trabajadora, responsabilidad del equipo de Capacitación Mujer y Trabajo del Centro Flora Tristan." (address: Centro de la Mujer Peruana "Flora Tristan," Parque Ilernan Velarde No. 42, Lima.) Issue 1 five pages.
[*mujer/fempress* July 1988]
/Peru/

274. *Opinión Nacional*. Bolivia. [Founded 1929] General publication. Director: Corral Zambrana de Sánchez (1940s–1950s).
[Dicc . . . Boliviana, 82–83]
/Bolivia/

275. *La Ondina del Plata*. Buenos Aires, Argentina. [1875–1879] "The most distinguished and articulate of the profeminist writers was María Eugenia Echenique from Córdoba."
[Lavrin #2]
/Argentina/

276. *Orientación Femenina*. Mexico. [1955 (1, 1)] Publication of the Grupo de Orientación Femenina.
[RLIN]
/Mexico/

277. *Ormiga*. Santiago de Chile. [?–1981–?] Published by "a group of university students"; "used for discussion with women in the poblaciones (slums)." Monthly.
[Women's period 81–82]
/Chile/

278. *O.S.F.A.* Buenos Aires, Argentina. [1930s(?)–May/June 1945 (64)–?] Publication of the Organización Sionista Femenina en la

Argentina. Monthly.
[RLIN]
/Argentina/

279. *Pachamama*. Bogotá, Colombia. [Mar 1988 (1)] "Boletín del Taller
de Recursos para la Mujer que circulará por toda Colombia en la red
de Organizaciones de Mujeres de Sectores Populares" (Address: Taller de Recursos para la Mujer, Apdo. Aéreo 5732, Bogotá).
[*mujer/fempress* July 1988]
/Colombia/

280. *La Palanca*. Chile. [date?] Labor newspaper focused on women.
[Lavrin]
/Chile/

281. *Panorama de las Señoritas*. Mexico. [1842–?] Publisher: Vicente García
Torres.
[Knaster #410; Arrom]
/Mexico/

282. *Para Ti*. Buenos Aires, Argentina. [16 May 1922 (1)–continuous(?)
to present] Motto: "Todo lo que interesa a la mujer." Director
(1925–1934?): Matilde Velas Palacios. Director (after 1935–c.
1950): María Morrison de Parker.
[Sosa de Newton, unpub.]
/Argentina/

283. *Participación de la Mujer: Boletín bimestral*. Caracas, Venezuela.
[1981(?) (1)–?] Publication of the Ministry of State for Women's
Participation in Development.
[Women's period 81–82]
/Venezuela/

284. *Patlatolli: Palabra Lesbiana*. Jalisco, Mexico. [Oct 1987 (1)] "Boletín
del Movimiento de Lesbianas Mexicanas." Publication of the Grupo
Patlatolli (address: Apdo. Postal 1–623, 44100 Guadalajara, Jalisco). Issue 1 twelve pages.
[*mujer/fempress* Feb/Mar 1988]
/Mexico/

285. *Pensamiento*. Santa Fe, Argentina. [Founded June 1895; ended before
Mar 1896] Founder and director: Carlota Garrido de la Peña. Garrido de la Peña wrote that she founded it with the idea of publicizing
"el peso de la sabiduría femenina," and to reinforce women's efforts
toward education and good ways to make careers and independent
livings.
[*Búcaro Americano* (1896), 100]
/Argentina/

286. *Persona*. Buenos Aires, Argentina. [Oct 1974 (1)–1981–?] Publica-

tion of the Organización Argentina (Feminista). Bimonthly.
[Women's period 81–82; Ramírez Bautista, 357]
/Argentina/

287. *Piguep̈*. Piguë (?), Argentina. [Early 1920s (?)] Founder: Herminia Brumana.
/Argentina/

288. *Pinocho*. Mexico. [Founded 1925 or 1926] A children's magazine published for one year. Editor and publisher: Juana Manrique de Lara. Contained English translations, stories, etc.
[Anderson, 316]
/Mexico/

289. *El Plata Ilustrado*. Argentina. [?–1871–1872–?] A general magazine that published much writing by women in this period. Eduarda Mansilla de García published "Notas" under pseudonym "Alvar."
[Sosa de Newton, unpub.]
/Argentina/

290. *Por la Raza*. Cochabamba, Bolivia. [1930s–?] Publication of the Cruz Roja Departamental de Cochabamba. Director (1930s–?): Corral Zambrana de Sánchez.
[Dicc . . . Boliviana, 82–83]
/Bolivia/

291. *Porto Rico*. Paris, France. [May 1977–?] Publication of the Collectif de Femmes Portoricaines.
[Ramírez Bautista, 357]
/France/Puerto Rico/

292. *La Prensa*. Sucre, Bolivia. [1940s(?)–1960s(?)] General daily. Director: Adriana Oropeza V. de Penaranda ("en ausencia de su esposo [Adriana Oropeza] se hacía cargo de la Dirección del periódico"; "luchó por los Derechos de la Mujer").
[Dicc . . . Boliviana]
/Bolivia/

293. *Prensa de Mujeres*. Buenos Aires, Argentina. [Aug 1983 (0)–Oct 1983 (2)–?] Monthly. Editors: Leonor Calvera, Mirta Henault, Marta Remolar.
/Argentina/

294. *Prensa Popular*. La Paz, Bolivia. [?–May 1987–?] "Boletín de información interna de los Centros de Madres de la Fundación San Gabriel" (address: Voz de los Centros de Madres, c/o Magali Vega, Casilla 3652, La Paz). May 1987 issue eight pages (mimeographed).
[*mujer/fempress* Feb/Mar 1988]
/Bolivia/

295. *Presencia da Mulher*. São Paulo, Brazil. [Mid-1986–present] Bimonthly magazine produced by a group of women. Editor: "Libertade

Mulher Ltda." Goal: "difundir las aspiraciones de la nueva mujer-
. . .destruyendo los mitos sobre su . . .inferioridad." (Address: Ana
María Rocha, R. dos Bororos, 5–1 andar, Bela Vista–CEP 01320,
São Paulo).
[*Mujeres en Acción*]
/Brazil/

296. *El Presente Amistoso Dedicado a las Señoritas Mexicanas*. Mexico. [1847–
     1852] Editor: Ignacio Cumplido. Literary annual.
     [Herrick, 135; Arrom; Knaster #411]
     /Mexico/

297. *Primaveira*. Rio de Janeiro, Brazil. [29 Aug 1880–31 Oct 1880] direc-
     tor: Francisco Senhorihna da Motta Diniz. "Revista semanal in-
     structiva noticiosa." Weekly; four pages; $9\frac{1}{4} \times 12\frac{3}{4}$ in.
     [Hahner, 282]
     /Brazil/

298. *Programa de Información para la Mujer en Costa Rica*. San José, Costa
     Rica. [May 1988 (1)] "Primer boletín de avances bibliográficos."
     Publication of Red Nacional de Información para la Mujer (address:
     Mafalda Sibille, Apdo. 484, Moravia, San José). Issue 1 seventy-two
     pages.
     [*mujer/fempress* Aug 1988]
     /Costa Rica/

299. *Protagonista, la Mujer*. San José, Costa Rica. [1986(?) (1, 1–4)] Pub-
     lication of the Asociación de Mujeres, Trabajo y Cultura. Continues
     as *Protagonistas*. (Some issues lack volume numbering and date.)
     [RLIN]
     /Costa Rica/

300. *Quehaceres*. Santo Domingo, Dominican Republic. [Jan–July 1981
     (1)–1987–?] Newsletter of CIPAF, Centro de Investigación para la
     Acción Femenina of the Universidad Autónoma de Santo Domingo.
     Bimonthly (?); monthly (in 1987). CIPAF also publishes pamphlet
     series, "Ediciones Populares Feministas," and book series, "Teoría
     Feminista."
     [Manzana 1987; Women's period 81–82; ISIS 5 (1986)]
     /Dominican Republic/

301. *La Rezón Mestiza*. San Francisco, Calif., USA. [Mar 1974 (1, 1)–Feb
     1975 (2, 1)] Publication of Concilio Mujeres.
     [Schlesinger Library]
     /USA/

302. *Recreio de Bello Sexo*. Rio de Janeiro, Brazil/Paris, France. [1852–
     1856] "Modas, litteratura, bellas artes e theatro." Male publisher.
     [Hahner, 283]
     /Brazil/France/

303. *El Recreo*. Lima (?), Peru. [1860s or 1870s(?)] The first magazine founded by Clorinda Matto de Turner. Described in an essay about her in 1898: "*El Recreo*, con lo que se dió a conocer a los hombres de letras de su país."
[*Búcaro Americano* 15 Sept 1898, 421 (essay about her reprinted from *Revista de Buenos Aires*)]
/Peru/

304. *Regeneración y Prosperidad: Órgano de la Liga Antialcohólica de Mujeres Hondureñas*. Tegucigalpa, Honduras. [1931 (1)–1932–?]
[UC]
/Honduras/

305. *La Revuelta*. Mexico. [Sept 1976 (1, 1)]
[Ramírez Bautista (1978)]
/Mexico/

306. *La Revista Argentina*. Coronda, Santa Fe, Argentina. [1902–1905] Founders and directors: Carlota Garrido de la Peña and Carolina Jaimes de Freyre. (Goal: to publish a feminist magazine for the provinces.)
[Sosa de Newton, unpub.]
/Argentina/

307. *Revista de la Asociación Femenina de Camaguey*. Cuba. [1921 (1)–1926] Editor: Isabel Esperanza Betancourt. Monthly (poetry, fiction).
[RLIN; Madison; Schlesinger Library]
/Cuba/

308. *Revista de la Secretaría Nacional de la Mujer*. Santiago de Chile. [June/July 1976 (1)–?]
[UC]
/Chile/

309. *Revista de Mujeres*. Havana, Cuba. [1980s(?)]
[UC]
/Cuba/

310. *Revista del Consejo Nacional de Mujeres*. Buenos Aires, Argentina. [Sept 1930 (1)–May/June 1933 (17)–?]. Bimonthly.
/Argentina/

311. *Revista del Hogar*. Puebla, Mexico. [?–1934–?]
[*Mujeres de América* May/June 1934]
/Mexico/

312. *Revista Femenina*. Medellín, Colombia. [Oct 1938 (1)–?] (19 volumes?) Irregular. Publication of the Instituto Central Femenino. 25 cm.
[RLIN]
/Colombia/

313. *Revista Femenina*. Montevideo, Uruguay. [?–1934–?]
     [*Mujeres de América* May/June 1934]
     /Uruguay/

314. *Revista Femenina*. São Paulo, Brazil. [?–1934–?]
     [*Mujeres de América* May/June 1934]
     /Brazil/

315. *Revista Médico-Quirúrgica de Patología Femenina*. Buenos Aires, Argen-
     tina. [1932 (1)–1946–?] Irregular some years. Publication of the
     Hospital Rivadavia.
     [UC; RLIN]
     /Argentina/

316. *Revista Mujeres*. Santa Cruz, Calif., USA. [Jan 1984 (1, 1)–?] Text
     in Spanish and English. Publication of Las Mujeres, University of
     California, Santa Cruz.
     [UC]
     /USA/

317. *Rumbos*. Bolivia. [Founded 1943] "desde donde [Alfonsina Paredes
     Larrea] inició una campaña feminista en pro de la emancipación de
     la mujer boliviana." Weekly.
     [Dicc . . . Boliviana, 199]
     /Bolivia/

318. *Salud Cam: Serie*. Guayaquil, Ecuador. [?–1986–?]
     Publication of Centro de Acción de la Mujer (address: Casilla 10201,
     Guayaquil).
     /Ecuador/

319. *La Semana de las Señoritas*. Mexico. [1850–1852]
     [Arrom, 356]
     /Mexico/

320. *La Semana de las Señoritas Mejicanas*. Mexico City, Mexico. [1851–
     1852] Five volumes. The magazine is said to have had the largest
     circulation of any women's magazine. Vol 1 lists 1,116 subscriptions
     (146 in Mexico City); vol 2 lists 1,383 (196 in Mexico City). Dedi-
     cated to the "fair sex"; translations, recipes, etc.
     [Herrick, 135, 144; Knaster #412]
     /Mexico/

321. *El Semanario de las Señoritas Mejicanas*. Mexico City, Mexico: Imprenta
     de Vicente G. Torres. [1841–1842(?)] Three volumes. Editor: Isidro
     Rafael Gondra. Four divisions in each issue: "bellas artes, física,
     literatura, moral." Vol 1 lists 1,020 subscribers; vol 2 lists 886.
     [Herrick, 135, 137; Anderson, 319; Knaster #413]
     /Mexico/

322. *Sembrador*. Mexico City, Mexico. [Founded before 1929 (?)] Short

lived. Founder: Guadalupe Ramírez.
[Anderson, 316]
/Mexico/

323. *Semillas para el Cambio*. San Juan, Puerto Rico. [?–1986–?] Publication of Centro de Ayuda a Víctimas de Violación (address: Call Box 70184, San Juan 000936).
[ISIS 5 (1986)]
/Puerto Rico/

324. *Ser Mujer*. Buenos Aires, Argentina. [1974–?(1–75)] Publisher: Abril Educativo y Cultural 1974. "Enciclopedia femenina en fascículos coleccionables."
[RLIN]
/Argentina/

325. *Ser Mujer*. Montevideo, Uruguay. [1983–1986–?] Publication of AUPFHIR, Asociación Uruguaya de Planificación Familiar e Investigaciones Sobre Reproducción (address: Br. Artigas 1550, Montevideo). Quarterly.
[ISIS 5 (1986); *Mujer* (Montevideo) Sept 1986]
/Uruguay/

326. *Serie Estudios de Promoción Femenina*. La Paz, Bolivia. [date?] Publication of the Centro de Investigaciones Sociales.
[RLIN]
/Bolivia/

327. *Serie Experiencia con Grupos de Mujeres*. Santiago de Chile. [date?] Publication of the Programa de Estudios y Capacitación de la Mujer Campesina e Indigena, Academia de Humanismo Cristiano.
[RLIN]
/Chile/

328. *Serie Mujer y Producción*. Santiago de Chile. [date?] Publication of the Centro de Estudios de la Mujer.
[RLIN]
/Chile/

329. *Serie Mujer y Sociedad*. Bogotá, Colombia. [1981–?] Publication of the Servicio Colombiano de Comunicación Social. 23–28 cm.
[RLIN]
/Colombia/

330. *Serie Mujeres*. Lima, Peru. [1980s–?] Publication of the Movimiento Feminista Creatividad y Cambio. "Occasional thematic folios focusing on the situation of women."
[*Connexions*]
/Peru/

331. *Sexo Explícito*. [?–1986–?] Rio de Janeiro, Brazil. Publication of the

Casa da Mulher (address: Rua Debret 23, sala 1316, CEP 20030, Rio de Janeiro, RJ).
[ISIS 5 (1986)]
/Brazil/

332. *O Sexo Feminino.* 1st series: Campanha, Minas Gerais, Brazil. [7 Sept 1873–7 Sept 1874] Weekly; four pages; $6\frac{3}{4} \times 9\frac{1}{4}$ in. Rio de Janeiro. [22 July 1875–2 Apr 1876] Generally semimonthly; four pages; $8\frac{3}{4} \times 12\frac{1}{4}$ in. 2d series: [2 June 1889–probably 1896] Title changed to *O Quinze de Novembro do Sexo Feminino* after Nov 1889. Weekly, then generally semimonthly; four pages; from $8\frac{3}{4} \times 12\frac{1}{4}$ in. to $12 \times 17$ in. Principal editor: Francisca S. da M. Diniz.
[Hahner]
/Brazil/

333. *La Siempreviva.* Yucatán, Mexico. [1870–1880] "Founded, edited and staffed by early feminist society in Mérida, Mexico; dedicated to the education of women."
[Knaster #414]
/Mexico/

334. *Somos.* Managua, Nicaragua. [1980s–present(?)] Publication of the Asociación de Mujeres Nicaragüenses Luisa Amanda Espinoza (AMNLAE). Bimonthly bulletin.
[*Connexions*]
/Nicaragua/

335. *Superación.* La Paz (?), Bolivia. [Founded 1960] Director: Elsa Paredes de Salazar. "Revista femenina."
[Dicc . . . Boliviana, intro]
/Bolivia/

336. *Sur.* Buenos Aires, Argentina. [1931–1970: regular quarterly, monthly, bimonthly; 1970–1986: biannual] Founder and publisher: Victoria Ocampo.
/Argentina/

337. *Tabasco Feminista.* Villahermosa, Mexico. [Mar 1933 (1)] "Órgano del partido Feminista Revolucionario de Tabasco. Adherido al Partido Nacional Revolucionario."
[UC; RLIN]
/Mexico/

338. *Tacón de la Chancleta.* Río Piedras, Puerto Rico. [Jan 1975 (1)– 1978–?] Publication of the University of Puerto Rico in Río Piedras. Monthly.
[Knaster LARR 1976, 8; Ramírez Bautista 1978]
/Puerto Rico/

339. *El Tacora.* Bolivia (?). [Late 1800s(?)] Magazine directed by the

father of Carolina Jaimes de Freyre; she published extensively in it.
[Dicc... Boliviana, 120]
/Bolivia/

340. *Taller Cultural de la Mujer.* Chillán, Chile. [Dec 1987 (1)] Bulletin of
the Taller Cultural de la Mujer. "Un nuevo espacio donde la mujer
pueda expresarse...en el proceso de democratización y transfor-
mación del país." (Address: Libertad 820, Chillán.) Issue 1 sixteen
pages.
[*mujer/fempress* July 1988]
/Chile/

341. *Tejemaneje.* Cayey, Puerto Rico. [1988 (1, 1)] Official bulletin of
Proyecto de Estudios de la Mujer del Colegio Universitario de Cayey
(address: Universidad de Puerto Rico, 00633 Cayey).
[*mujer/fempress* June 1988]
/Puerto Rico/

342. *El Tesoro del Hogar.* Peru (?)/Argentina (?). [1890s(?)] Director: Las-
tenia Larriva de Llona (also a novelist).
[*Búcaro Americano* 1896, 12]
/Peru(?)/Argentina(?)/

343. *La Tortuga.* Lima, Peru. [Mar 1982 (1)] Publication of the Asociación Mujer-Mujer (formerly a mimeographed bulletin called *Mujer,
la Tortuga*).
[Women's period 81–82]
/Peru/

344. *La Tribuna.* New York City, USA. [1980s; Mar 1988 (36)] Bulletin
of the Centro de la Tribuna Internacional de la Mujer (address:
777 United Nations Plaza, New York, NY 10017, USA). Issue 36
forty-eight pages.
[*mujer fempress* May 1988]
/USA/

345. *La Tribuna Femenina.* Buenos Aires, Argentina. [1917(?)] Founder
and director: Carolina de Muzilli. Feminist socialist magazine.
[Sosa de Newton, unpub.]
/Argentina/

346. *Triple Jeopardy.* Berkeley, Calif., and New York City, USA. [Sept/Oct
1971 (1, 1)–Summer 1975] Publication of the Third World Women's
Alliance. Bimonthly, with a single summer issue. Undated special
issue with title *La Mujer en la Lucha de Liberación.* Text in English and
Spanish.
[RLIN; microfilm from Harvard Univ. Library (1971–1975)]
/USA/

347. *Tu Voz, Mujer.* Concepción, Chile. [1980s] Publication of the Com-

mittee for the Defense of the Rights of Women (CODEM). "Semi-clandestine bimonthly newsletter to organize poor women."
[*Connexions*]
/Chile/

348. *UMBO*. Paris, France. [May 1977 (1)] Spanish-language bulletin of the Paris chapter of the Unión de Mujeres de Bolivia. Mimeographed.
[Ramírez Bautista 1978]
/France/Bolivia/

349. *Unidas*. Rosario, Argentina. [1980s–1986–?] Publication of the Grupo de Mujeres de Rosario (address: Casilla de Correo 720, 2000 Rosario).
[ISIS 5 (1986)]
/Argentina/

350. *El Universal*. Mexico City, Mexico. [1920s–1933–?] Major daily. Cable editor and country editor: Virginia Huerta.
[Anderson, 317]
/Mexico/

351. *Vamos Mujer*. Santiago de Chile. [1980s–?] "Occasional publication of the Committee for the Defense of the Rights of Women (CODEM)."
[*Connexions*]
/Chile/

352. *Vamos Mujer: Serie "Nuestros Derechos."* Bogotá, Colombia. [1980s–1980–?] Publication of Casa de la Mujer (address: Apdo. Aéreo 36151, Bogotá).
[ISIS 5 (1986)]
/Colombia/

353. *La Vanguardia Femenina*. Buenos Aires, Argentina. [11 June 1946 (1)–?] Monthly women's supplement of *La Vanguardia*, daily(?)/weekly(?) newspaper of the Argentine Socialist Party from the 1910s(?) to the present. Director of *La Vanguardia* (1940s–1960s?): Alicia Moreau de Justo. *La Vanguardia* was also directed by Victoria Gucovsky.
[Sosa de Newton, unpub.]
/Argentina/

354. *VEMEA Informa*. Cuernavaca, Morelos, Mexico. [1980s(?)–present] Publication of Vejez en Mexico, Estudio y Acción (VEMEA; address: Apdo. Postal 1912, Cuernavaca, Morelos 62000).
[ISIS 5 (1986)]
/Mexico/

355. *Ventana: Una Visión Diferente de la Mujer*. San José, Costa Rica.

[1980s(?)–1988] Occasional feminist magazine. See *Cuadernos de Ventana*, its continuation begun Mar 1988.
[*Connexions*, 5 (1986)]
/Costa Rica/

356. *Verdad*. Colombia. [1955–1956 or 1957.] "Semanario integramente escrito y editado por mujeres." Founder: Ofelia Uribe de Acosta (Colombian suffragist).
[*mujer/fempress* Sept 1988]
/Colombia/

357. *Vértice*. Buenos Aires, Argentina. [Dec 1937 (1, 1)–Feb 1942 (5, 7; believed to be complete)] Founder and director: Julia Prilutzky Farny de Zinny.
/Argentina/

358. *Viva*. Lima, Peru. [1980s(?)–present] Publication of the Centro de la Mujer Peruana "Flora Tristán." Regular feminist magazine.
[*Connexions*, 5 (1986)]
/Peru/

359. *La Vida Feminina*. Montevideo, Uruguay. [1917(?)–1926 (9, 86)–1931 (14, 147)–?] A ladies' magazine published and written by men: notes on fashion, home economics, etc.
/Uruguay/

360. *Vida Feminina*. Buenos Aires, Argentina. [Nov 1932 (1)–1941 (probable end date)] A feminist socialist magazine, affiliated with the Argentine Socialist Party. Director: María L. Berronda. Regular contributors: Alicia Moreau de Justo, Nicolas Repetto, etc. Motto: "Revista de la mujer inteligente."
[*Mujeres de América* May/June 1934]
/Argentina/

361. *A Violeta*. São Paulo, Brazil. [1886–1887] "Folha litteraria dedicada ao bello sexo."
[Hahner, 283]
/Brazil/

362. *Voz da Verdade*. Rio de Janeiro, Brazil. [12 May 1885–25 June 1885] Editor and owner: Francisca Senhorinha da Motta Diniz. Each issue four pages, 10 × 13 in.
[Hahner, 282]
/Brazil/

363. *La Voz de la Mujer*. Albuquerque, N.M., USA. [1970–1971–?] Publication continued by New Mexico NOW (National Organization of Women). Monthly. Archived by Herstory.
[UC; RLIN]
/USA/

364. *La Voz de la Mujer*. El Paso, Tex., USA. [28 July 1907 (1, 5)–?]
[UC]
/USA/

365. *La Voz de la Mujer*. Buenos Aires, Argentina. [1896 (1)–1897–1901]
Nine issues in all. Anarcho-feminist magazine.
[Feijóo; Sosa de Newton, unpub.]
/Argentina/

366. *La Voz de la Mujer*. Quito, Ecuador. [1980s(?)–present] Publication
of the Union Femenina de Pichincha (address: Apdo. Postal 155-C,
Sucursal 15, Quito).
[ISIS 5 (1986)]
/Ecuador/

367. *La Voz de la Mujer*. Managua, Nicaragua. [1980s] Publication of the
Asociación de Mujeres Nicaragüenses Luisa Amanda Espinoza
(AMNLAE). Monthly magazine of the Nicaraguan women's asso-
ciation, dealing with issues facing women today.
[Women's period 81–82]
/Nicaragua/

368. *La Voz de la Niñas*. Buenos Aires, Argentina. [?–1898–?] Commentary by Clorinda Matto de Turner: "semanario de pequeño formato
destinado al bello sexo y en cuyas páginas palpita el pensamiento de
la mujer con el vigor impulsivo del progreso."
[*Búcaro Americano* 15 Nov 1898, 449]
/Argentina/

369. *A Woman's Work Is Never Done/Trabajo de Mujer Nunca Se Termina*. Los
Angeles, Calif., USA. [Aug/Sept 1973(?) (1, 1)–?] Publication of the
Los Angeles Women's Liberation Union.
[RLIN]
/USA/

370. *Women: Journal of Liberation*. Baltimore, Md., USA. [Fall 1969 (1,
1)–1974 (3, 4)–?] Cuban feminist magazine.
[Valdés, 16; UC]
/USA/Cuba/

371. *Women's Feature Service* (WFS). Rome, Italy. [?–1987–?] An international news service distributing feature articles by Third World
women journalists from women's perspective with focus on development issues. Established by InterPress Service (IPS). Coordinator of
women, communication and Development Project: Anita Anand.
(Address: Via Panisperna 207, 00184 Rome).
[Women in Action]
/Italy/

372. *Women's World*. See ISIS Publications.

373. *WIRE Service Publications* New York City, USA. [1970s–present] Se-

rial and occasional publications on Latin American women by the Women's International Resource Exchange.
/USA/

## BIBLIOGRAPHIC SOURCES FOR ENTRIES

Following is a list of library catalogs, data bases, and bibliographic essays that provided names of magazines and information on their publication.

In some cases, information on entries was gleaned from contemporary periodicals that have variously advertised, corresponded with, or criticized sister publications from the earliest records here. When a periodical listed as a primary source is also a source for information on another entry, it is noted as a reference for that entry; more complete information can be found under its primary entry in the list.

Anderson = Anderson, Lola. "Mexican Women Journalists." *Pan American Bulletin* 68 (May 1934): 315–20.

Arrom = Arrom, Silvia Marina. *The Women of Mexico City: 1790–1857*. Stanford, Calif.: Stanford University Press, 1985. (Bibliography.)

*Connexions* = magazine resource library list of holdings, 4228 Telegraph Ave., Oakland, CA 94609. [A version of this list is also published as "Resources" in *Connexions: An International Women's Quarterly* 16 (Spring 1985.)]

Dicc . . . Boliviana = Paredes de Salazar, Elsa. *Diccionario biográfico de la mujer boliviana*. La Paz: Ediciones Isla, 1965.

Feijóo = Feijóo, María del Carmen. *Las feministas*. Buenos Aires: Centro Editor de América Latina, 1975.

Hahner = Hahner, June E. "The Nineteenth Century Feminist Press and Women's Rights in Brazil," in *Latin American Women: Historical Perspectives*. Edited by Asunción Lavrin. Greenwood, Conn.: Greenwood Press, 1978.

Henault = Henault, Mirta. *Alicia Moreau de Justo*. Buenos Aires: Centro Editor de América Latina, 1983.

Herrick = Herrick, Jane. "Periodicals for Women in Mexico City during the Nineteenth Century." *The Americas* 14, 2 (October 1957): 18–19. (Published by Academy of American Franciscan History.)

Index = Allen. Martha Leslie, ed. *Index/Directory of Women's Media 1986*. Washington, D.C.: Women's Institute for Freedom of the Press, 1986.

ILET = *Colección Comunicación Alternativa de la Mujer* (various issues, 1982–present.)

ISIS 5 (1986) = *ISIS International Women's Journal* 5 (1986). List of "Women's Centers, Groups and Services" in Central and South America.

Knaster = Knaster, Meri. *Women in Spanish America: An Annotated Bibliography from Pre-Conquest to Contemporary Times*. Boston: G. K. Hall, 1977.

Knaster LARR = Knaster, Meri. "Women in Latin America: The State of Research 1975." *LARR* 11, 1 (1976): 3–74.

Lavrin = Lavrin, Asunción. "Sources for the Study of Women in Latin America." In *Latin American Masses and Minorities: Their Images and Realities*, ed. Dan C. Hazen. Madison, Wis.: SALALM, 1987.

Lavrin #2 = Lavrin, Asunción. *The Ideology of Feminism in the Southern Cone, 1900–1940*. Latin American Program Working Papers 169. Washington, D.C.: Wilson Center, Smithsonian Institution, 1986.

Madison = Danky, James P., et al., eds. *Women's Periodicals and Newspapers: Holdings of the University of Wisconsin, Madison Libraries*. Boston: G. K. Hall, 1982.

Melvyl = University of California systemwide computerized library catalog.

Manzana 1987 = *La Manzana de la Discordia* 8 (1987). A list of magazines received by this Colombian feminist magazine.

Mujeres en Acción = *Mujeres en Acción*, ISIS supplement 7 (1987). (Also used: *Women in Action*, the slightly different English version of same.)

National Union List of Serials = Bound catalogs, beginning around 1910, which list periodicals collected in U.S. libraries (listed under the year they were collected). In some cases, a useful source for verifying publication period of magazines.

O'Doyley = O'Doyley, Enid F. "A Survey of the Critical Literature on Female Feminist Writers of Hispanic America." In *Latin American Masses and Minorities: Their Images and Realities*, edited by Dan C. Hazen. Madison, Wis.: SALALM, 1987.

Ramírez Bautista 1978 = Ramírez Bautista, Elia. *Femmes latino-americaines: bibliographie*. Paris: Université de Paris VIII, Centre de Recherche, 1978. Photocopied manuscript dated 1978; book not updated, 1985.)

RLIN = Research Library Information Network subject search of Spanish-language periodicals with key words like "feminista," "feminina," "femenina," and "mujer" (and plurals).

Schlesinger Library = *Catalog of Arthur and Elizabeth Schlesinger Library on the the History of Women in America*. Boston: G. K. Hall, 1984.

Sosa de Newton = Sosa de Newton, Lily. *Diccionario biográfico de mujeres arguentinas*. Buenos Aires: Editorial Plus Ultra, 1980.

Sosa de Newton, Las args. = Sosa de Newton, Lily. *Las argentinas de ayer a hoy*. Buenos Aires: Ediciones Zanetti, 1967.

Sosa de Newton, unpub. = Sosa de Newton, Lily. "Incorporación de la mujer al periodismo en la Argentina." Paper presented at the International Symposium on Women in Literature, Nicaragua, 1984.

UC = University of California, Berkeley on-line catalogs of holdings; subject searches under Spanish language periodicals with key works like "mujer," " feminista," "femenina," "ella."

Ulrich = *Ulrich's Guide to International Periodicals 1986–87*. (A current list of periodicals in print with several pages on "Women's Interest Periodicals," giving circulation statistics and other useful data.)

Valdés = Valdés, Nelson P. "A Bibliography on Cuban Women in the Twentieth Century." *Cuban Studies Newsletter* 4 (June 1974): 1–31.

Women's period 81–82 = "International Guide to Women's Periodicals and Resources, 1981/82." *Resources for Feminist Research* 10, 4 (December 1981/ January 1982). Section on Latin America and Caribbean.

Women's Records = *Women's Book of World Records and Achievements.* Ed. Lois Decker O'Neill. New York: Da Capo Press, [1983?], c. 1979.

# TWELVE

# Bibliographical Update: Women, Politics, and Culture in Latin America

This bibliography was prepared with the support of a grant from the Hewlett Foundation, and the Center for Research in International Studies at Stanford University. The project was supervised by Mary Pratt. Research and editorial work were done by Kathryn McKnight with assistance from Manley Williams. Logistical support was supplied by the Stanford Humanities Center.

## INTRODUCTORY NOTE

This bibliography of some six hundred entries has two relatively modest aims. First, we have sought to compile a list of bibliographical works relevant to the study of women, politics, and culture in Latin America. Second, we have sought to provide bibliographical updates in several relevant areas, listing works of the past ten to fifteen years that are likely not to have appeared in other sources.

The focus of this book on the history of women in politics, lettered culture, and intellectual life has dictated the priorities of this bibliography. Such emphases correct a conspicuous gap in the existing bibliographical literature. With a few notable exceptions, the intellectual, literary, political, and even pedagogical activity of Latin American women scarcely appear in bibliographical work on women in Latin America. In those few bibliographies that have sections on "culture," the term is generally taken to mean everyday life, domestic activity, manual work, reproduction, the body. Feminism has taught us the importance of these dimensions of women's being and activity. At the same time, to define culture exclusively this way with respect to women is to reproduce a male elitism that elides women's participation in intellectual, artistic, and political life except at the grass-roots and domestic levels. "Third World" stereotypes can also be a factor here: in orthodox social science, Latin America is readily construed as a place without culture. We have not attempted to survey directly the current literature on women and health, reproduction, migration, demographics, and development, but we have included an extensive list of existing bibliographical works on these areas.

The materials assembled here come from several sources: first, our own research files and materials compiled for our study group; second, periodical indexes; and third, computer searches conducted at the Stanford and UC Berkeley libraries. Anyone who has attempted bibliographical work knows the limitations of these resources, in particular with respect to small-circulation, local, and occasional publications. The vital presence of such writings in contemporary Latin American feminism is suggested by the monthly review *mujer/fempress* (Chile), whose final pages each month list new pamphlets, monographs, circulars, and occasional publications. Few such writings appear here, however.

While literary criticism figures prominently in the bibliography, literary scholars will notice that we have chosen not to include studies of individual authors. Only general and comparative studies are included. This choice was the most drastic one we had to face in preparing this bibliography. It means that a great many scholars and colleagues engaged in feminist literary research are not represented or are underrepresented here. Quite simply, our resources were overwhelmed by the volume of work on individual authors in the past decade and by the logistics required for a responsible, comprehensive survey. Fortunately, other work, such as that of Diane Marting in the United States, to some extent corrects this omission. Marting's 1987 bibliography of Latin American literature by women will soon be accompanied by a more detailed volume, *Fifty Spanish American Women Writers*, which will survey criticism on the authors considered.

For similar logistical reasons, this bibliography does not attempt to survey current work on Chicanas, Puertorriqueñas, and Latinas in the United States. This was another difficult choice dictated by our lack of resources and expertise in these areas where current scholarship is extraordinarily rich. A recent bibliographical survey by Karen Lynn Stoner, *Latinas of the Americas* (1989), published by Garland Press, devotes many pages to Latinas of the United States and will, we hope, provide the compilation we could not attempt.

## SUMMARY OF HEADINGS

1. Women: Bibliographies and Bibliographical Essays
    1.1  General and International Bibliographies
    1.2  Latin America—General and Comparative Bibliographies

## I.  WOMEN: BIBLIOGRAPHIES AND BIBLIOGRAPHICAL ESSAYS

### *1.1   General and International Bibliographies*

Ballou, Patricia K. *Women: A Bibliography of Bibliographies.* Boston: G. K. Hall, 1980.

Boulding, Elise, et al. *Handbook of International Data on Women.* New York: Sage Publications, 1976; distributed by Halsted Press.

Byrne, Pamela R., and Suzanne R. Ontiveros, eds. *Women in the Third World: A Historical Bibliography.* ABC-Clio Research Guides 15. Santa Barbara, Calif.: ABC-Clio Information Services, 1986.

Cotera, Martha. *Latina Sourcebook.* Austin: Information Systems Development, 1982.

Delores, Joann et al. *Women and Society: An Annotated Bibliography.* 2 vols. Beverly Hills, Calif.: Sage Publications, 1978.

Ducey, Mitchell F., ed. *Papers of the Women's International League for Peace and Freedom, 1915–1978: A Guide to the Microfilm Edition.* Sanford, N.C.: Microfilming Corp. of America, 1983.

Fenton, Thomas, and Mary J. Heffron, eds. *Women in the Third World: A Directory of Resources.* Maryknoll, N.Y.: Orbis Books, 1986.

———. *Third World Resource Directory.* Maryknoll, N.Y.: Orbis Books, 1984.

Gilbert, V. G., and D. S. Tatla. *Women's Studies: A Bibliography of Dissertations, 1870–1982.* New York: Basil Blackwell, 1985.

Hildenbrand, Suzanne, ed. *Women's Collections: Libraries, Archives, and Consciousness.* New York: Haworth Press, 1986.

Hinding, Andrea et al., eds. *Women's History Sources: A Guide to Archives and Manuscript Collections in the U.S.* 2 vols. New York: R. R. Bowker, 1979.

International Archiefvoor de Vrouwenbeweging. *Catalog of the Library of the International Archives for the Women's Movement, Amsterdam, Holland.* 4 vols. Boston: G. K. Hall, 1980.

Jacobs, Sue-Ellen. *Women in Perspective: A Guide for Cross-Cultural Studies.* Urbana: University of Illinois Press, 1974.

Krichmar, Albert et al. *The Women's Movement in the Seventies: An International English-Language Bibliography.* Metuchen, N.J.: Scarecrow Press, 1977.

Lugo Filippi, Carmen. "Recursos internacionales para la mujer." *fem* 7, 25 (October 1982–January 1983): 43–46.

Oakes, Elizabeth H., and Kathleen E. Sheldon. *A Guide to Social Science Resources in Women's Studies.* Santa Barbara, Calif.: American Bibliography Center–Clio Press, 1978.

Parveen Shaukat, Ali. *Women in the Third World: A Comprehensive Bibliography.* Progressive Series 28. Lahore, Pakistan: Progressive Publishers, 1975.

Resnick, Margery, and Isabelle de Courtivron. *Women Writers in Translation: An Annotated Bibliography, 1945–82.* New York: Garland Press, 1984.

Rosenberg, Marie Barovic, and Len V. Bergstrom, eds. *Women and Society: A Critical Overview of the Literature with a Selected Annotated Bibliography*, vol. 1. Beverly Hills, Calif.: Sage Publications, 1978.

Saulniers, Suzanne Smith, and Cathy A. Rakowski. *Women in the Development Process: A Select Bibliography on Women in Sub-Saharan Africa and Latin America.* Austin: Institute of Latin American Studies, University of Texas, 1977.

Searing, Susan E. *Introduction to Library Research in Women's Studies.* Boulder, Colo.: Westview Press, 1985.

Stineman, Ester, and Catherine Loeb. *Women's Studies: A Recommended Core Bibliography.* Littleton, Colo.: Libraries Unlimited, 1979.

UNESCO. *Bibliographic Guide to the Studies on the Status of Women: Development and Population Trends.* New York: Unipub, 1983.

Williamson, Jane. *New Feminist Scholarship: A Guide to Bibliographies.* Old Westbury, N.Y.: Clearinghouse on Women's Studies, Feminist Press, 1979.

Zavitz, Carol, and Hans Kleipool. "International Guide to Women's Periodicals and Resources, 1981–2. Guide International sur les Resources et Périodiques des Femmes 1981–2." *Resources for Feminist Research/ Documentation sur la recherche féministe* 10, 4 (December 1981–January 1982).

### 1.2   Latin America—General and Comparative Bibliographies

Anrup, Roland. "Feminist Research in Latin America." *Ibero Americana* 13, 2 (1984): 77–83.

Feijóo, María del Carmen. *La mujer, el desarrollo, y las tendencias de población en*

*América Latina: Bibliografía comentada.* Estudios CEDES 3, 1. Buenos Aires: Centro de Estudios de Estado y Sociedad, 1980.

Hahner, June Edith. "Researching the History of Latin American Women: Past and Future Directions." *Revista Interamericana de Bibliografía* 33, 4 (1983): 545–552.

Knaster, Meri. "Women in Latin America: State of Research, 1975." *Latin American Research Review* 11, 1 (1976): 3–74.

————. *Women in Spanish America: An Annotated Bibliography from Pre-Conquest to Contemporary Times.* Boston: G. K. Hall, 1977.

Lavrín, Asunción. "Recent Studies on Women in Latin America (Review Article)." *Latin American Research Review* 19, 1 (1984): 181–189.

————. "Sources for the Study of Women in Latin ·America." In *Latin American Masses and Minorities: Their Images and Realities,* edited by Dan C. Hazen. Madison, Wis.: SALALM, 1987.

Navarro, Marysa. "Review Essay: Research on Latin American Women." *Signs: Journal of Women in Culture and Society* 5, 1 (Autumn 1979): 111–120.

Pan American Health Organization. *Women, Health, and Development in the Americas: An Annotated Bibliography.* Scientific Publication 464. Washington, D.C.: Pan American Health Organization, 1984.

Pescatello, Ann M. "Bibliography." In *Power and Pawn: The Female in Iberian Families, Societies, and Cultures.* Westport, Conn.: Greenwood Press, 1976.

————. "The Female in Ibero-America: An Essay on Research Bibliography and Research Directions." *Latin American Research Review* 7 (Summer 1972): 125–141.

————, ed. "Bibliography." In *Female and Male in Latin America: Essays.* Pittsburgh: University of Pittsburgh Press, 1973.

Soeiro, S. A. "Recent Work on Latin American Women." *Journal of Inter-American Studies and World Affairs* 17, 4 (1975): 497–516.

Stoner, K. Lynn. *Latinas of the Americas: A Source Book.* New York: Garland Press, 1989.

Vidal, Virginia. "Ellas tienen la palabra: Libros sobre mujeres." *Nueva Sociedad* 67 (July–August 1983): 153–157.

## 1.3   Latin America—Bibliographies on Specific Countries

Agramont Virreira, Miriam. *Bibliografía de la mujer boliviana (1920–1985).* La Paz: Ediciones CIDEM, 1986.

Alfaro, Teresa, ed. *Relación bibliográfica: Tesis sobre la mujer peruana.* Lima: Perú-Mujer, 1982.

Bartra, Eli, Elsa Rodríguez, and Nina Torres. *Mujer: Una bibliografía, México.* Xochimilco, Mexico: Universidad Autónoma Metropolitana, 1983.

Bettancourt, Adalzira. *Diccionário Bio-bibliográfico de Mulheres Ilustres, Notáveis, e Intelectuais do Brasil.* 3 vols. (Surnames A-B only.) Rio de Janeiro: Editôra Pongetti, 1969–1972.

Centro de Estudios de Población y Desarrollo. "Bibliografía peruana acerca de la condición social y jurídica de la mujer." In *Diagnóstico social y jurídico de la mujer en el Perú*. Lima: CEPD, 1979.

Centro de Información y Desarrollo de la Mujer (La Paz, Bolivia). *Directorio de instituciones femeninas: La Paz, Sucre, Cochabamba, Potosí, Santa Cruz, y Oruro*. La Paz: Ediciones CIDEM, 1986.

Codex, S. R. L. *Organizaciones de promoción femenina*. La Paz: CODEX, 1973.

Consejo Nacional de Población (México). *Bibliografía sobre la mujer*. 3d. ed. Mexico City: Consejo Nacional de Población, 1986.

Escobedo, Raquel. *Galería de mujeres ilustres* [México]. Mexico City: Editores Mexicanos Univedos, 1967.

Fraire, Osvaldo A. *Diccionario biográfico de la mujer en el Uruguay*. Montevideo: Imprenta Rosgal, 1983.

Fundação, Carlos Chagas. *Mulher Brasileira: Bibliografia Anotada*. São Paulo: Editora Brasiliense, 1979.

Hahner, June Edith. "Recent Research on Women in Brazil." *Latin American Research Review* 20, 3 (1985): 163–179.

Melo Lancheros, Livia Stella. *Valores femeninos de Colombia: Bio-bibliography*. Bogotá: Editorial y Papeleria Carvajal, 1966.

Pérez, L. A. "Women in the Cuban Revolutionary War, 1953–58: A Bibliography." *Science and Society* 39 (Spring 1975): 104–108.

Pérez, Paola. *Diez años de investigaciones sobre la mujer en Nicaragua, 1976–1986*. Managua: Ministerio de la Presidencia, Oficina de la Mujer, 1986.

Paredes de Salazar, Elssa. *Diccionario Biográfico de la mujer boliviana*. La Paz: Ediciones Isla, 1965.

Rojas de Brunicelli, Sonia. *Guía de la mujer*. Caracas: Ministerio para la Participación de la Mujer en el Desarrollo, 1981.

Sosa de Newton, Lily. *Las argentinas de ayer a hoy*. Buenos Aires: Ediciones Zanetti, 1967.

———. *Diccionario biográfico de mujeres argentinas*. Buenos Aires: Editorial Plus Ultra, 1980.

Stuart, Bertie Cohen. *Women in the Caribbean: An Annotated Bibliography*. Leiden, Netherlands: Department of Caribbean Studies, Royal Institute of Linguistics and Anthropology, 1979.

Valdés, Nelson P. "A Bibliography of Cuban Periodicals Related to Women." *Cuban Studies/Estudios Cubanos* 12, 2 (July 1982): 73–80.

———. "A Bibliography on Cuban Women in the Twentieth Century." *Cuban Studies Newsletter* (University Center for International Studies and Center for Latin American Studies, Pittsburgh) 4, 2 (June 1974).

*1.4 Latin America—Bibliographies on Women and Literature*

Correas de Zapata, Cecilia, and Lygia Johnson, eds. "One Hundred Years of Women Writers in Latin America." *Latin American Literary Review* 3 (1975): 7–16.

Cortina, Lynn Ellen Rice. *Spanish-American Women Writers in English Transla-*

*tion: A Bibliography.* Los Angeles: California State University Latin American Studies Center, 1980.

Cortina, Regina. *Spanish Women Writers: A Bibliography.* New York: Garland Publishing, 1983.

Corvalán, Graciela N. V. *Latin American Women Writers in English Translation: A Bibliography.* Los Angeles: California State University Latin American Studies Center, 1980.

Fernández y Fernández, Aurora. *Escritoras de América: Catálogo.* Mexico City: Imprenta Zavala, 1966.

Flori, Mónica. "A Selected and Annotated Filmography on Latin American Women." *Third Woman* 2, 2 (1984): 117–121.

Fox-Lockert, Lucía. *Women Novelists in Spain and Spanish America.* Metuchen, N.J.: Scarecrow Press, 1979.

Lindstrom, Naomi. "Feminist Criticism of Latin American Literature: Bibliographic Notes." *Latin American Research Review* 1 (1980): 151–159.

Marting, Diane. *Fifty Spanish American Women Writers.* Westport, Conn.: Greenwood Press, 1989.

————. *Women Writers of Spanish America: An Annotated Bio-Bibliographical Guide.* Westport, Conn.: Greenwood Press, 1987.

Miller, Beth Kurti, and Alfonso González. *Veintiseis autoras del Méxicoactual.* Mexico City: Costa-Amic, 1978.

Moratorio, Arsinoe. *La mujer en la poesía del Uruguay: Bibliografía, 1879–1969.* Montevideo: Biblioteca Nacional, 1970(?).

## II. LATIN AMERICAN WOMEN AND LITERATURE: RECENT CRITICAL AND SCHOLARLY STUDIES (EXCLUDING SINGLE-AUTHOR STUDIES)

### 2.1  *Edited Collections and Special Issues of Journals*

Alcira Arancibia, Juana, ed. *Evaluación de la literatura femenina de Latinoamérica, Siglo XX: Simposio Internacional de Literatura, Universidad de Costa Rica.* San José, Costa Rica: Instituto Literario y Cultural Hispánico, 1984.

Carmelo, Virgilio, and Naomi Lindstrom, eds. *Woman as Myth and Metaphor in Latin American Literature.* Columbia: University of Missouri Press, 1985.

Chevigny, Bell Gale, and Gari Laguardia, eds. *Reinventing the Americas: Comparative Studies of Literature of the United States and Spanish America.* Cambridge: Cambridge University Press, 1986.

Garfield, Evelyn Picón, ed. *Women's Voices from Latin America: Interviews with Six Contemporary Authors.* Detroit: Wayne State University Press, 1985.

Glantz, Margo et al. *Bordando sobre la escritura y la cocina: Coloquio.* Mexico City: Instituto Nacional de Bellas Artes, 1984.

González, Patricia Elena, and Eliana Ortega, eds. *La sartén por el mango: Encuentro de escritoras latinoamericanas.* Río Piedras, Puerto Rico: Ediciones Huracán, 1984.

Gutiérrez, Daniela, ed. *Mitominas*. Buenos Aires: Municipalidad de la Ciudad de Buenos Aires, 1986.

Meyer, Doris, and Margarite Fernández Olmos, eds. *Contemporary Women Authors of Latin America: Introductory Essays*. New York: Brooklyn College Press, 1983.

Miller, Beth Kurti, ed. *Mujeres en la literatura*. Mexico City: Fleischer Editora, 1978.

————. *Women in Hispanic Literature: Icons and Fallen Idols*. Berkeley, Los Angeles, London: University of California Press, 1983.

Miller, Yvette E., and Charles M. Tatum, eds. *Latin American Women Writers, Yesterday and Today: Selected Proceedings from the Conference on Women Writers from Latin America, March 15–16, 1975*. Pittsburgh: Latin American Literary Review, 1977.

Minc, Rose, ed. *Revista Iberoamericana: Número especial dedicado a las escritoras de la América Hispánica*. University of Pittsburgh, International Institute of Ibero-American Literature, 51, 132–133 (July–December 1985).

Mora, Gabriela, and Karen S. Van Hooft, eds. *Theory and Practice of Feminist Literary Criticism*. Ypsilanti, Mich.: Bilingual Press, 1982.

Pescatello, Ann M., ed. *The Hispanic Caribbean Woman and the Literary Media*. Special issue of *Revista Interamericana* (Inter American University of Puerto Rico, Hato Rey) 4, 2 (Summer 1974).

Pratt, Mary Louise, and Marta Morello-Frosch, eds. *América Latina: Mujer, Escritura, Praxis*. Special Issue of *Nuevo Texto Critico* 4, 2 (Autumn 1990).

Urrutia, Elena, ed. *Imagen y realidad de la mujer*. Mexico City: SEP Setentas, 1975.

Vidal, Hernán, ed. *Cultural and Historical Grounding for Hispanic and Luso-Brazilian Feminist Literary Criticism*. Minneapolis: Institute for the Study of Ideologies and Literature, 1989.

*Women in Latin American Literature: A Symposium*. Latin American Studies Occasional Papers 10. Amherst: International Area Studies Programs, University of Massachusetts at Amherst, 1979.


### 2.2  General, Comparative, and Methodological Studies

Agosín, Marjorie. "Whispers and Triumphs: Latin American Women Writers Today." *Women's Studies International Forum* 9, 4 (1986): 427–433.

Alegría, Fernando. "Aporte de la mujer al nuevo lenguaje poético de Latinoamérica." *Revista/Review Interamericana* 12, 1 (Spring 1982): 27–35.

Alvarez, Griselda. *Diez mujeres en la poesía mexicana del siglo XX: Colección metropolitana*. Mexico City: Complejo Editorial Mexicano, 1974.

Alves, Branca Moreira. *Ideología e Feminismo*. Petrópolis, R.J., Brasil: Vozes, 1980.

Anzaldúa, Gloria. *Borderland/La frontera: The New Mestiza*. San Francisco: Spinsters/Aunt Lute, 1987.

Araújo, Helena. "Escritoras latinoamericanas: Por fuera del 'boom'?" *Quimera: Revista de Literatura* 30 (April 1983): 8–11.

———. "La narradora y la diferencia." *Cuadernos de Marcha*, 3d series 2, 11 (September 1986): 72–77.

———. "Narrativa femenina latinoamericana." *Hispamérica: Revista de Literatura* (Gaithersburg, Md.) 11, 32 (August 1982): 23–34.

Arizpe, Lourdes. "Interview with Carmen Naranjo: Women and Latin American Literature." *Signs* 5, 1 (1979): 98–110.

Basaglia, Franca. "Mujer: El cuerpo como prisión." *Cuadernos de Marcha*, 3d series 2, 8 (June 1986): 69–76.

Bonzini, Silvia, and Laura Klein. "Un no de claridad." *Punto de Vista* 21 (August 1984): 32–38.

Boorman, Joan Rea. "Contemporary Latin American Women Dramatists." *Rice University Studies* 64, 1 (1978): 69–80.

Bradú, Fabienne. *Señas particulares: Escritora*. Mexico City: Fondo de Cultura Económica, 1987.

Brett, Guy. *Through Our Own Eyes: Popular Art and Modern History*. Philadelphia: New Society Publishers, 1987.

Bullrich, Silvina. *La mujer en la literatura argentina*. Buenos Aires: Centro Nacional de Documentación e Información Educativa, 1972.

Bustamante, Cecilia. "Intelectuales peruanas de la generación de José Carlos Mariátegui." *Northsouth* 7, 13 (1982): 111–126.

Carner, Francisco. *Las mujeres y el amor en el Mexico del siglo XIX a través de sus novelas*. Mexico City: Colegio de Mexico, 1975.

Castro-Klarén, Sara. "The Novelness of a Possible Poetics for Women." In *Cultural and Historical Grounding for Hispanic and Luso-Brazilian Feminist Literary Criticism*, ed. H. Vidal. Minneapolis: Institute for the Study of Ideologies and Literature, 1989.

———. "La crítica literaria feminista y la escritura en América Latina." In *La sartén por el mango: Encuentro de escritoras latinoamericanas*, ed. Patricia Elena González and Eliana Ortega. Río Piedras, Puerto Rico: Ediciones Huracán, 1984.

Catalá, Rafael. *Para una lectura americana del barroco mexicano: Sor Juana Inés de la Cruz y Sigüenza y Góngora*. Minneapolis: Prisma Institute and Institute for the Study of Ideologies and Literature, 1987.

Cixous, Hélene. *Vivre l'orange*. Paris: Des Femmes, 1979.

Correas de Zapata, Celia. *Ensayos hispanoamericanos*. Buenos Aires: Corregidor, 1978.

Cuza Male, Belkis, Matilde Daviu, and Rosario Ferré. "No más máscaras: Un diálogo entre tres escritoras del Caribe." In *Literatures in Transition: The Many Voices of the Caribbean*, eds. Linda Gould Levine, G. F. Waldman, and R. S. Minc. Gaithersburg, Md.: Hispamérica, 1982.

Cypess, Sandra Messinger. "Visual and Verbal Distances: The Woman Poet in a Patriarchal Culture." *Revista/Review Interamericana* 12, 1 (Spring 1982): 150–157.

———. "Women Dramatists of Puerto Rico." *Revista/Review Interamericana* 9, 1 (Spring 1979): 24–41.

Dallal, Alberto. *Femina-Danza*. Mexico City: Universidad Nacional Autónoma de México, Instituto de Investigaciones Estéticas, 1985.

Dorn, Georgette M. "Four Twentieth Century Latin American Women Authors." *SECOLAS Annals* 10 (1979): 125–133.

Elu de Leñero, María del Carmen. *Perspectivas femeninas en América Latina*. SEP Setentas 264. Mexico City: SEP, Dirección General de Divulgación, 1976.

Erazo, Viviana, and Adriana Santa Cruz. *Compropolitán: El orden transnacional y su modelo femenino: Un estudio de las revistas femeninas en América Latina*. Mexico City: Editorial Nueva Imagen, 1981.

Erro Orthmann, Nora, and Sylvia Vásquez. *La escritora hispanoamericana*. Mexico City: Joaquin Mortiz.

Franco, Jean. "Apuntes sobre la crítica feminista y la literatura hispanoamericana." *Hispamérica* 15, 45 (1986): 31–43.

———. *Plotting Women*. New York: Columbia University Press, 1989.

———. "Teoría feminista en los ochenta." *fem* 10, 44 (February–March): 52–55.

García, Carola. *Revistas femeninas*. Mexico City: Ediciones El Caballito, 1980.

García-Pinto, Magdalena. *Historias íntimas: Conversaciones con diez escritoras latinoamericanas*. Hanover, N.H.: Ediciones del Norte, 1988.

Garfield, Evelyn Picon. *Women's Voices from Latin America: Interviews with Six Contemporary Authors*. Detroit: Wayne State University Press, 1985.

Garrels, Elizabeth. *Las grietas de la ternura: Nueva lectura de Teresa de la Parra*. Caracas: Monte Avila, 1985.

Gorriti, J. M. et al. *Las escritoras, 1840–1940*. Buenos Aires: Centro Editor de América Latina, 1980.

Gotlib, Nádia Battella. "O Quarto Congresso Interamericano de Escritoras." *Língua e Literatura* 9 (1980): 405–412.

Guerra Cunningham, Lucía. "Algunas reflexiones teóricas sobre la novela femenina." *Hispamérica* 10, 28 (1981): 29–39.

———. "La mujer latinoamericana y la tradición literaria femenina." *fem* 3, 10 (1979): 6–12.

———. "Pasividad, ensoñación, y existencia enajenada: Hacia una caracterización de la novela femenina chilena." *Atenea* 438 (1979): 149–164.

Handelsman, Michael H. *Amazonas y artistas: Un estudio de la prosa de la mujer ecuatoriana*. Guayaquil: Casa de la Cultura Ecuatoriana, Núcleo del Guayas, 1978.

Herrera Zapién, Tarsicio. *López Velarde y Sor Juana, feministas opuestos*. Mexico City: Editorial Porrúa, 1984.

Jehenson, Myriam Yvonne. "Four Women in Search of Freedom: Agustini,

Ibarbourou, Storni, and Mistral." *Hispanic Journal* 5, 1 (Fall 1983): 169–180.

Jordan, Dawn M. "Building a History of Women's Literature in Brazil." *Plaza: Literatura y Crítica* 5–6 (Fall–Spring 1981–1982).

Kamenszain, Tamara. "Género femenino y género poético." *Revista de la Universidad de México*, N.S. 40, 39 (July 1984): 11–14.

Kaminsky, Amy. "Lesbian Cartographies: Body, Text, and Geography." In *Cultural and Historical Grounding for Hispanic and Luso-Brazilian Feminist Literary Criticism*, ed. H. Vidal. Minneapolis: Institute for the Study of Ideologies and Literature, 1989.

LaDuke, Betty. *Compañeras: Women, Art, and Social Change in Latin America*. San Francisco: City Lights Books, 1985.

Lavrin, Asunción. *The Ideology of Feminism in the Southern Cone, 1900–1940*. Latin American Program Working Papers 169. Washington, D.C.: Wilson Center, Smithsonian Institution, 1986.

Lemistre Pujol, Annie. "Los orígenes de la literatura femenina en Latinoamérica y Costa Rica." *Káñina: Revista de Artes y Letras de la Universidad de Costa Rica* 9, 2 (July–December 1985).

Lombardi, Mary. "Women in the Modern Art Movement in Brazil: Salon leaders, Artists, and Musicians, 1917–1930." Ph.D. diss., University of California, Los Angeles, 1977.

López, Ivette. "Puerto Rico: Las nuevas narradoras y la identidad cultural." *Perspectives on Contemporary Literature* 8 (1982): 77–83.

López González, Aralia. *De la intimidad a la acción: La narrativa de escritoras latinoamericanas y su desarrollo*. Mexico City: Universidad Autónoma de Mexico, Ixtapalapa, 1985.

Ludmer, Josefina. "Tretas del débil." In *La sartén por el mango: Encuentro de escritoras latinoamericanas*, ed. Patricia Elena González and Eliana Ortega. Río Piedras, Puerto Rico: Ediciones Huracán, 1984.

Luquc Valderrama, Lucía. "La novela femenina en Colombia" Ph.D. diss., Pontificia Universidad Católica Javeriana (Bogotá) 1954.

Maíz, Magdalena. "Tres escritoras: Garro/Castellanos/Mendoza." *Plural* 12, 142 (July 1983): 62–65.

Masiello, Francine. "Between Civilization and Barbarism: Women, Family, and Literature in Mid-nineteenth-century Argentina." In *Cultural and Historical Grounding for Hispanic and Luso-Brazilian Feminist Literary Criticism*. ed. H. Vidal. Minneapolis: Institute for the Study of Ideologies and Literature, 1989. 517–566.

———. "Discurso de mujeres, lenguaje del poder: Reflexiones sobre la crítica feminista a mediados de los años 80." *Hispamérica* 15, 45 (1986): 53–60.

———. "Subversions of Authority: Feminist Literary Culture in the River Plate Region," forthcoming in *Ideologies and Literatures*.

Mattelart, Michèlle. *La cultura de la opresión femenina.* Mexico City: Era, 1977.
————. *Women, Media Crisis: Femininity and Disorder.* London: Comedia Publishing Group, 1986.
Migdal, Alicia. "Mujeres: Del confort a la intemperie." *Cuadernos de Marcha,* 3d series 2, 14 (December 1986): 67–74.
Miller, Beth Kurti. "Peruvian Women Writers: Directions for Further Research." *Revista/Review Interamericanna* 12, 1 (Spring 1982): 36–48.
Molloy, Sylvia. "Dos lecturas del cisne: Rubén Darío y Delmira Agustini." In *La sartén por el mango: Encuentro de escritoras latinoamericanas,* ed. Patricia Elena González and Eliana Ortega. Río Piedras, Puerto Rico: Ediciones Huracán, 1984.
Mora, Gabriela. "Un diálogo entre feministas hispanoamericanas." In *Cultural and Historical Grounding for Hispanic and Luso-Brazilian Literary Criticism,* ed. H. Vidal. Minneapolis: Prisma Institute, 1989.
Muriel, Josefina. *Cultura femenina novohispana.* Mexico City: Universidad Nacional Autónoma de México, 1982.
Oehmke-Loustanau, Martha. "Mexico's Contemporary Women Novelists." Ph.D. diss., University of New Mexico, 1973.
Ordoñez, Elizabeth J. "The problematical permutations of feminist theory." In *Cultural and Historical Grounding for Hispanic and Luso-Brazilian Feminist Literary Criticism,* ed., H. Vidal. Minneapolis: Institute for the Study of Ideologies and Literatures, 1989.
Ordóñez, Montserrat. "La voz de las poetas latinoamericanas." *Magazin Dominical, El Espectador* (Bogotá) 141 (8 December 1985): 6–8.
Pacífico, Patricia. "A Feminist Approach to Three Latin American Women Writers." In *Una historia de servicio: 66 aniversario de la Universidad Interamericana.* Río Piedras, Puerto Rico: Inter American University Press, 1979.
Percas de Ponseti, Helena. "Reflexiones sobre la poesía femenina hispanoamericana." *Revista/Review Interamericana* 12, 1 (Spring 1982): 49–55.
Peri Rossi, Cristina. "Literatura y mujer." *Eco* 42, 257 (March 1983): 498–506.
Piñeda, Empar. "El discurso de la diferencia y de la igualdad." *fem* 36 (October–November 1984): 7–16.
Poniatowska, Elena. "La literatura de las mujeres es parte de la literatura de los oprimidos." *fem* 6, 21 (February–March 1982): 23–27.
————. "Mujer y literatura en América Latina." *Eco* 42, 257 (March 1983): 462–472.
Resnick, Susan. "Presencias: Latin American Filmmakers in the Feminine Plural." *Women and Performance: A Journal of Feminist Theory* 2, 1 (1984): 32–48.
Rivero, Eliana. "Hacia una definición de la lírica femenina en Hispanoamérica: Voz y trayectoria." *Revista/Review Interamericana* 12, 1 (Spring 1982): 11–26.

———. "Las nuevas poetas cubanas." *Areito* 5, 17 (November 1978): 99–106.

Robles, Marta. *La sombra fugitiva: Escritoras en la cultura nacional.* 2 vols. Mexico City: Universidad Nacional Autónoma de México, 1986.

———. "Tres mujeres en la literatura mexicana: Rosario Castellanos, Elena Garro, Inés Arredondo." *Cuadernos americanos* 246, 1 (January–February 1983): 223–235.

Rocco-Cuzzi, Renata, and Isabel Stratta. "Las escritoras: 1940–1970." In *Historia de la literatura argentina.* Vol. 5, *Los contemporáneos.* Buenos Aires: Centro Editor de América Latina, 1982.

Russotto, Márgara. "No basta un cuarto propio." *fem* 6, 21 (February–March 1982): 13–15.

Saffioti, Heleieth Iara Bongiovani. *Women in Class Society.* New York: Monthly Review Press, 1978.

Santí, Enrico-Mario. "El sexo de la escritura." *Revista/Review Interamericana* 12, 1 (Spring 1982): 146–149.

Sarlo, Beatriz. *El imperio de los sentimientos: Narraciones de circulación periódica en la Argentina, 1917–1927.* Buenos Aires: Catálogos Editora, 1985.

Schipper, Mineke. *Unheard Words: Women and Literature in Africa, the Arab World, Asia, the Caribbean, and Latin America.* London: Allison & Busby, 1985.

Sommer, Doris. "Irresistible Romance: The Foundational Fictions of Latin America." In *Nation and Narration,* ed. Homi Bhabha. London: Methuen, 1988.

———. "Not Just Any Narrative: How Romance Can Love Us to Death." In *The Historical Novel in Latin America,* ed. Daniel Balderston. College Park, Md.: Hispamérica, 1986.

Stycos, Maria Nowakowska. "Twentieth-Century Hispanic Women Poets: An Introduction." *Revista/Review Interamericana* 12, 1 (Spring 1982): 5–10.

Traba, Marta. "Hipótesis sobre una escritura diferente." *fem* 6, 22 (February–March 1982): 9–12.

Valdés, Héctor. *Poetisas mexicanas del siglo XX.* Mexico City: Universidad Nacional Autónoma de México, 1976.

Vallbona, Rima de Kanina. "Trayectoria actual de la poesía femenina en Costa Rica." *Revista de Artes y Letras de la Universidad de Costa Rica* 5, 2 (July–December 1981): 18–27.

Verwey, Antonieta Eva. *Una recapitulación del "punto de vista" como técnica narrativa en vista de una posible diferenciación entre escritura femenina y masculina, 1900–1972, 1972–1987.* Querétaro, Mexico: Universidad Autónoma de Querétaro, 1988(?).

Vidal, Hernán. "La crítica literaria feminista hispanoamericana como problemática de defensa de los derechos humanos: Argumentos en apoyo de una arquetipificación universalista." In *Cultural and Historical Grounding for*

*Hispanic and Luso-Brazilian Literary Criticism*, ed. H. Vidal. Minneapolis: Prisma Institute, 1989.

Young, Dolly J., and William D. Young. "The New Journalism in Mexico: Two Women Writers." *Chasqui: Revista de Literatura Latinoamericana* 12, 2–3 (February–May 1983): 72–80.

Yudice, George. "El asalto a la marginalidad." *Hispamérica* 15, 45 (1986): 45–52.

Zornosa, Anna Lucía. "Collaboration and Modernization: Case-Study of a Transnational Magazine." *Studies in Latin American Popular Culture* 2 (1983): 24–35.

### 2.3 Representations of Women in Literature and Other Media

Asociación Perú-Mujer. *La imagen de la mujer: Seminario Taller, noviembre 1981, Cajamarca, Perú*. Lima: Asociación Perú-Mujer, Frente Democrático de Mujeres de Cajamarca, 1982.

Bazán Montenegro, Dora. *La mujer en las tradiciones peruanas*. Madrid: Maribel, 1967.

Bergueiro, Jesús. *La mujer argentina en la anécdota*. Buenos Aires: Ediciones La Obra, 1959.

Bonilla de Ramos, Elssy. *La mujer y su imagen en los medios*. Bogotá: Centro de Estudios Sobre Desarrollo Económico, Facultad de Economía, Universidad de los Andes, 1981.

Carrera, Magali Marie. "The Representation of Women in Aztec-Mexica Sculpture." Ph.D. dissertation, Columbia University, 1979.

Castro, Rafaela. "Mexican Women's Sexual Jokes." *Aztlán* 13, 1–2 (Spring–Fall 1982): 275–293.

Dapaz Strout, Lilia. "Hacia el hombre nuevo: Una antología del folklore antifeminista; mito y 'mitos' sobre 'el continente negro.'" *Cuadernos Hispanoamericanos* 391–393 (January–March 1983): 653–661.

Dominella, Ana Rosa. *Imagen de la mujer en la narrativa mexicana contemporanea*. N.P., 1977.

Erazo, Viviana, and Adriana Santa Cruz. *Compropolitán: El orden transnacional y su modelo femenino: Un estudio de las revistas femeninas en América Latina*. Mexico City: Instituto Latinoamericano de Estudios Trasnacionales, Editorial Nueva Imagen, 1980.

Fisbach, Erich. "La femme, génératrice de l'univers manichéen du tango." *Les langues Neo-latines: Bulletin trimestrial de la Société de Langues* 79, 3 (1985): 44–53.

Franco, Jean. "The Incorporation of Women: A Comparison of North American and Mexican Popular Narrative." In *Studies in Entertainment*, ed. Tania Modleski. Bloomington: Indiana University Press, 1986.

González Freire, Nati. "La mujer en la literatura de América Latina." *Cuadernos Hispanoamericanos* 414 (December 1984): 84–92.

Guerra Cunningham, Lucía. "El personaje literario femenino y otras mutila-
ciones." *Hispamérica* 15 (April 1986): 3–19.
Herrera-Sobek, María. "The Treacherous Woman Archetype: A Structuring
Agent in the 'Corrido.'" *Aztlán* 13, 1–2 (Spring–Fall 1982): 135–148.
Lafaye, Jacquesa. *Quetzalcóatl and Guadalupe: The formation of Mexican National
Consciousness, 1531–1813.* Translated by Benjamin Keen. Chicago: Uni-
versity of Chicago Press, 1974.
Laguerre, Enrique Arturo. "De Rita Baiana a Teresa Batista: Personajes de
la novela brasileña." *Sin Nombre* 12, 2 (Winter 1982): 25–37.
Lavrin, Asunción. "Unlike Sor Juana? The Model Nun in the Religious
Literature of Colonial Mexico." *University of Dayton Review* 16, 2 (Spring
1983): 75–92.
León-Portilla, Miguel. "Afrodita y Tlazoltéotl." *Vuelta* 6, 71 (October 1982):
4–8.
Magnarelli, Sharon. *The Lost Rib: Female Characters in the Spanish American
Novel.* Lewisburg, Pa.: Bucknell University Press, 1985.
Maza, Francisco de la. *El guadalupanismo mexicano.* Mexico City: Fondo de
Cultura Económica, 1981.
Miguel, María Esther de. "La circunstancia femenina en el hecho literario."
*fem* 6, 21 (February–March 1982): 47–52.
Muñoz Gomá, María Angélica. "La mujer de hogar en *Casa grande* de Orrego
Luco y en documentos históricos de su época." *Historia* 18 (1983): 103–
133.
Pulido, Esperanza. *La mujer mexicana en la música.* Mexico City: Ediciones de la
Revista Bellas Artes, 1958.
Richard, Nelly. "En la masmédula: La femineidad como reverso de lo domi-
nante." *Hueso Húmero* 15–16 (October 1982–April 1983): 218–222.
Sant'Ana, Elma. *O Folclore da Mulher Gaúcha.* Pôrto Alegre, Brazil: Tchê!
Comunicações, 1984.
Villanueva Collado, Alfredo. "Filí-Melé: Símbolo y mujer en la poesía de
Luis Palés Matos e Iván Silén." *Revista Chicano-Riqueña* 10, 4 (Fall 1982):
47–54.
Wong, Oscar. "La mujer en la poesía mexicana." *Plural*, 2d series 11, 131
(August 1982): 54–59.

III. LATIN AMERICAN WOMEN IN SOCIETY, POLITICS,
AND HISTORY:
RECENT CRITICAL AND SCHOLARLY WORK

### 3.1 Feminism in Latin America

Alegría, Juana Armanda. *Mujer, viento, y ventura: La liberación femenina al desnudo . . . un desnudo que duele?* Mexico City: Editorial Diana, 1977.
Alvarez Vignoli de Demicheli, Sofía. *Igualdad jurídica de la mujer: Alberdi, su*

*precursor en América, textos legales vigentes.* Buenos Aires: Depalma, 1973.

Armagno Cosentino, José. *Carolina Muzilli.* Buenos Aires: Centro Editor de América Latina, 1984.

Azize, Yamila. *Luchas de la mujer en Puerto Rico, 1980–1919.* San Juan: Litografía Metropolitana, 1979.

Carlson, Marifran. *Feminismo: The Woman's Movement in Argentina from Its Beginnings to Evita Perón.* Chicago: Academy Chicago Publishers, 1987.

Davis, Mary. "El feminismo de nuestros días: Problemas de organización de las mujeres." *fem* 7, 25 (October 1982–January 1983): 23–26.

Feijóo, María del Carmen. *Las feministas.* Buenos Aires: Centro Editor de América Latina, 1975.

———. "Las feministas." In *La vida de nuestro pueblo.* Buenos Aires: Centro Editor de América Latina, 1982.

———. "Las luchas feministas." *Todo Es Historia* 128 (January 1978): 6–23.

Ferreras, Ramón Alberto. *Historia del feminismo en la República Dominicana.* Santo Domingo: Editorial Cosmos, 1976.

Flora, Cornelia Butler. *Socialist Feminism in Latin America.* Working Paper 14. East Lansing: Michigan State University, 1982.

Foppa, A. "First Feminist Congress in Mexico, 1916." *Signs* 5, 1 (1979): 192–199.

García, Elisabeth Souza-Lobo. "Femmes au Brésil: Mouvement et recherche (Review Article)." *Cahiers des Amériques Latines* 26 (July–December 1982): 149–151.

Hahner, June Edith. "Feminism, Women's Rights, and the Suffrage Movement in Brazil, 1850–1932." *Latin American Research Review* 1 (1980): 65–111.

———. *A Mulher Brasileira e Suas Lutas Sociais e Politicas, 1850–1937.* São Paulo: Editora Brasiliense, 1981.

———. "The Nineteenth-Century Feminist Press and Women's Rights in Brazil." In *Latin American Women: Historical Perspectives,* ed. Asunción Lavrin. Greenwood, Conn.: Greenwood Press, 1978.

Hernández, Zoila. *Movimiento social de mujeres.* Lima: Mujer y Sociedad, 1985.

Inter-American Commission of Women. *Historical Review on the Recognition of the Political Rights of American Women.* Washington, D.C.: Pan American Union, 1965.

———. *Report Presented to the Twenty-eighth Session of the United Nations Commission on the Status of Women.* Washington, D.C.: Organization of American States, 1979.

———. *Special Committee for Studies and Recommendations of the Inter-American Commission of Women for the World Conference of International Women's Year.* Inter American Commission of Women 2. Washington, D.C.: General Secretariat, Organization of American States, 1975.

ISIS International. *Movimiento feminista en América Latina y el Caribe: Balance y perspectivas*. Santiago: ISIS International, 1986. Published in English as *The Latin American Women's Movement: Reflections and Actions*. Special issue of *ISIS International Women's Journal* 5 (1986).

Jacquette, Jane S. "Female Political Participation in Latin America: Raising Feminist Issues." In *Women and the World, 1975–1985: The Women's Decade*, ed. Lynne B. Iglitzin and Ruth Ross. 2d ed. Santa Barbara, Calif.: ABC-CLIO, 1986. (Update of 1976 article, "Studies in International and Comparative Politics.")

Jelin, Elizabeth. *Los nuevos movimientos sociales: Mujeres, Rock nacional*. Biblioteca Política Argentina 124. Buenos Aires: Centro Editor de América Latina, 1985.

Lavinas, Lena, and Helén Le Doare. "Mobilisations et organisations féminines dans les secteurs populaires." *Cahiers des Amériques Latines* 26 (July–December 1982): 39–58.

Lavrin, Asunción. *The Ideology of Feminism in the Southern Cone, 1900–1940*. Latin American Program Working Papers 169. Washington, D.C.: Wilson Center, Smithsonian Institution, 1986.

Leite, M. L. M. "A Brazilian Feminist and Her Contribution to the Pacifist Cause." *Women's Studies International Forum* 6, 4 (1983): 371–373.

Levi Artaza, Sara. *La mujer y sus derechos*. Jesús María, Lima: ADEC, 1985.

Little, Cynthia Jeffress. "Education, Philanthropy, and Feminism: Components of Argentine Womanhood, 1860–1926." In *Latin American Women: Historical Perspectives*, ed. Asunción Lavrin. Westport, Conn.: Greenwood Press, 1978.

Macías, Ana. *Against All Odds: The Feminist Movement in Mexico to 1940*. Westport, Conn.: Greenwood Press, 1982.

Miller, Francesca. "The International Relations of Women of the Americas." *The Americas: A Quarterly Review of Inter-American Cultural History* 43, 2 (October 1986): 171–182.

Molyneux, M. "No God, No Boss, No Husband—Anarchist Feminism in Nineteenth-Century Argentina." *Latin American Perspectives* 13, 1 (1986): 119–145.

Morton, Ward M. *Woman Suffrage in Mexico*. Gainesville: University of Florida Press, 1962.

Navarro, Marysa. "First Feminist Meeting of Latin America and the Caribbean." *Signs* 8, 1 (1982): 154–159.

Perón, Eva. *La mujer puede votar*. Buenos Aires: n.p., 1947.

Portal, Magda. *Hacia la mujer nueva*. Lima: Editorial Cooperativa Aprista Atahualpa, 1933.

Puiggrós, Adriana. "Mariátegui: Lucha de clases y luchas feministas." *fem* 7, 25 (October 1982–January 1983): 9–14.

Quartim de Moraes, Maria Lygia. *Mulheres em Movimento: O Balanço da Década da Mulher do Ponto de Vista do Feminismo, das Religões, e da Política*. São Paulo: Nobel, 1985.

Reddy, Daniel R. "Aspects of the Feminist Movement in Peruvian Letters and Politics." *SECOLAS Annals* 6 (March 1975): 53–64.

Romero R., Carmen María et al. "La investigación de los problemas de la mujer rural." *Revista de Ciencias Sociales* (Costa Rica) 25 (March 1984): 47–58.

Silva-Labarca, Myra. "Féminisme et politique en Amérique Latine." *Amérique Latine* 19 (July–September 1984): 17–21.

Simões, Solange de Deus. *Pátria e Família*. Petrópolis, Brazil: Vozes, 1985.

Venturi, Donatella. *I golpe delle donne: L'uso reazioario della questione femminile in America Latina*. Movimento Operario 48. Bari, Italy: De Donato, 1978.

Vidal, Virginia. *La emancipación de la mujer*. Santiago: Quimantu, 1972.

Villavicencio, Marzita. "Así hacemos nuestra historia." *fem 32 (February– March 1984): 15–16.*

### 3.2 Women and Other Social and Political Movements

Acebey, David, comp. *¡Aquí también Domitila!* Mexico City: Siglo Veintiuno Editores, 1985.

Acevedo, Marta. "El Partido Socialista Unificado Mexicano y las mujeres." *fem* 6, 21 (February–March 1982): 86–88.

Andreas, Carol. *When Women Rebel: The Rise of Popular Feminism in Peru*. Westport, Conn.: L. Hill, 1985.

Ardaya, Gloria. "La mujer en la lucha del pueblo boliviano: Las Barzolas y el Comité de Amas de Casa." *Nueva Sociedad* 65 (March–April 1983): 112–126.

Association of Salvadoran Women (AMES). "Participation of Latin-American Women in Social and Political Organizations—Reflections of Salvadorean Women." *Monthly Review* 34, 2 (1982): 11–23.

Aviel, J. F. "Political Participation of Women in Latin America." *Western Political Quarterly* 34, 1 (1981): 156–173.

Biles, Robert E. *Women and Political Participation in Latin America*. East Lansing: Michigan State University, 1983.

Blay, Eva Alterman. "The Political Participation of Women in Brazil: Female Mayors." *Signs* 5 (Autumn 1979): 42–59.

———. "Social Movements and Women's Participation in Brazil." *International Political Science Review* 6, 3 (1985): 297–305.

Bonafini, Hebe de. *Historias de vida*. Buenos Aires: Fraterna/del Nuevo Extremo, 1985.

Borge, Tomás. *La mujer y la revolución nicaragüense*. New York: Pathfinder Press, 1983.

Borges Costa, Leticia et al. *El rol de la mujer en la iglesia y en la sociedad: Conclusiones y recomendaciones*. Jornadas Ecuménicas Latinoamericanas. Montevideo: UNELAM, 1968.

Burgos Debray, Elizabeth, ed. *Me llamo Rigoberta Menchú y así me nació la conciencia*. Mexico City: Siglo Veintiuno Editores, 1985. (English translation by Ann Wright, *I, Rigoberta Menchú: An Indian Woman in Guatemala*. London: Verso, 1984.)

Carlessi, Carolina. *Mujeres en el origen del movimiento sindical*. Lima: Lilith, 1984.

Castro, Fidel. *Fidel Castro habla a las mujeres de América Latina: Huelga general de deudores contra el F.M.I. Encuentro Sobre la Situación de la Mujer en América Latina y el Caribe Hoy, 7 de junio de 1985*. Colección Sucesos 6. Buenos Aires: Editorial Anteo, 1985. (English translation in *Meeting on the Status of Latin American and Caribbean Women*. Havana: Editora Política, 1985.)

Centro de Estudios Históricos del Movimiento Obrero Mexicano. *La mujer y el movimiento obrero mexicano en el siglo XIX: Antología de la prensa obrera*. Mexico City: Centro de Estudios Históricos del Movimiento Obrero Mexicano, 1975.

Chaney, Elsa. *Supermadre: Women in Politics in Latin America*. Austin: University of Texas Press, 1979.

Chungara, Domitila Barrios de, and Moema Viezzer. *Si me permiten hablar: Testimonio de Domitila, una mujer de las minas de Bolivia*. 2d ed. Mexico City: Siglo Veintiuno Editores, 1978. (English translation: *Let Me Speak!: The Testimony of Domitila, a Woman of the Bolivian Mines*. Translated by Victoria Ortiz. New York: Monthly Review Press, 1978.)

Ciria, Alberto. "Flesh and Fantasy: The Many Faces of Evita (and Juan Perón)." *Latin American Research Review* 18, 2 (1983): 150–162.

Demitrópulos, Libertad. *Eva Perón*. Biblioteca Política Argentina 47. Buenos Aires: Centro Editor de América Latina, 1984.

Dos Santos, Estela. *Las mujeres peronistas*. Biblioteca Política Argentina 23. Buenos Aires: Centro Editor de América Latina, 1983.

Echevarría, Alicia. *De burguesa a guerrillera*. Mexico City: J. Mortiz, 1986.

Feijóo María del Carmen, and Mónica Gozna. "Las mujeres en la transición a la democracia." In *Los nuevos movimientos sociales*, ed. Elizabeth Jelin. Buenos Aires: Centro Editor de América Latina, 1985.

Floria, Carlos Alberto. *La mujer argentina y la política*. Buenos Aires: Centro Nacional de Documentación e Información Educativa, 1972.

Franco, Jean. "Killing Priests, Nuns, Women, and Children." In *On Signs*, ed. Marshall Blonsky. Baltimore: Johns Hopkins University Press, 1985.

"Guatemala: Women in Revolution." *Latin American Perspectives* 10, 1 (Winter 1983): 103–108.

Harris, H. "Women in Struggle: Nicaragua." *Third World Quarterly* 5, 4 (1983): 899–908.

Jaquette, Jane S. "Women in Revolutionary Movements in Latin America." *Journal of Marriage and Family* 35, 2 (1973): 344–354.

Jiménez, Liliam. "La mujer revolucionaria en El Salvador." *Plural* 13, 156 (September 1984): 38–44.

Kirkwood, Julieta. *Ser política en Chile*. Santiago: Facultad Latinoamericana de Ciencias Sociales, 1986.

———. "Women and Politics in Chile." *International Social Science Journal* 35, 4 (183): 625–63.

McGee, Sandra Deutsch. *Counterrevolution in Argentina, 1900–1932: The Argentine Patriotic League.* Lincoln, Nebr.: University of Nebraska Press, 1986.

———. "The Visible and the Invisible 'Liga Patriótica Argentina,' 1919–1928: Gender Roles and the Right Wing." *Hispanic American Historical Review* 64, 2 (May 1984): 233–258.

Mendieta Alatoree, Angeles. *La mujer en la revolución mexicana.* Mexico City: Instituto Nacional de Estudios Históricos de la Revolución Mexicana, 1961.

Movimiento Manuela Ramos. *La mujer, la gran ausente: Elecciones municipales, 1983.* Lima: Ediciones Prensa Manuela Ramos, Taller de Política, 1983.

Navarro, Marysa. *Evita.* Bilbao, Spain: Ediciones Corregidor, 1981.

"Primer Congreso Latinoamericano de Mujeres Socialistas: Respuesta socialista a la opresión de la mujer y la familia." *Nueva Sociedad* 71 (March–April 1984): 93–95.

Puga, Carmela, ed. *La mujer y la revolución: Discursos, entrevistas, artículos, ensayos.* Colección Testimonio. Lima: Editorial Causachun, 1972.

Queiroz Martín, Teresa, "Obstáculos que dificultan la participación político-social de la mujer popular en Costa Rica." *Anuario de Estudios Centroamericanos* 9 (1983): 145–153

Reedy, Daniel R. "Magda Portal: Peru's Voice of Social Protest." *Revista de Estudios Hispánicos* 4, 1 (April 1970): 85–97.

Reif, L. L. "Women in Latin American Guerrilla Movements: A Comparative Perspective." *Comparative Politics* 18, 2 (1986): 147–169.

Rodríguez Villamil, Silvia. *Mujer, estado, y política en el Uruguay del siglo XX.* Montevideo: Ediciones de la Banda Oriental, 1984.

Ruiz, Claudia Ximena. "La comandante Julia." *fem* 34 (June–July 1984): 45–47.

Santos, Estela dos. *Las mujeres peronistas.* Buenos Aires: Centro Editor de América Latina, 1983.

Schmidt, Steffen W. "Political Participation and Development Role of Women in Latin America." *Journal of International Affairs* 30, 2 (1977): 243–260.

Simpson, A. "Women in Struggle: El Salvador." *Third World Quarterly* 5, 4 (1983): 894–899.

Soto, Shirlene Ann. *The Mexican Woman: A Study of Her Participation in the Revolution, 1910 to 1940.* Palo Alto, Calif.: R&E Research Associates, 1979.

Tabak, Fanny. *Autoritarismo e Participação da Mulher.* Rio de Janeiro: Graal, 1983.

———. *Mulher e Política.* Rio de Janeiro: Paz a Terra, 1982.

———. "O Papel da Mulher na Definição das Políticas Públicas no Brasil."

*Revista Brasileira de Estudos Políticos* 54 (January 1982): 107–132.

Vitale, Luis. *Historia y sociología de la mujer latinoamericana.* Colección Ensayo Contemporáneo. Barcelona: Fontamar, 1981.

*Women and Politics in Twentieth Century Latin America.* Studies in Third World Societies 15. Williamsburg, Va.: Department of Anthropology, College of William and Mary, 1981.

Women's International Resource Exchange Service. *Nicaraguan Women and the Revolution.* New York: WIRE Service, n.d.

————. *Women and War: El Salvador.* New York: WIRE Service, n.d.

### 3.3.   Women and Work

Alonso, José Antonio. *Sexo, trabajo, y marginalidad urbana.* Mexico City: Editorial Edicol, 1981.

Arenal, Electa, and Stacey Schlau. *Untold Sisters: Hispanic Nuns in Their Own Work.* Albuquerque: University of New Mexico Press, 1989.

Arizpe, Lourdes, ed. *La mujer y la unidad doméstica: Antología.* Mexico City: SEP Diana, 1982.

Boomen, Josephus van den. *Algunos aspectos de la actividad económica de la mujer en la América Latina.* Santiago: Centro Latinoamericano de Demografía, 1968.

Borges, Wanda Rosa. *A Profissionalização Feminina.* São Paulo: Edições Loyola, 1980.

Bunster, X., and Chaney, E. M. *Sellers and Servants: Working Women in Lima, Peru.* New York: Praeger, 1985.

Chang, Ligia, and María Angélica Ducci. *Temas sobre la formación profesional para la mujer.* San José, Costa Rica: CEDAL, 1978.

Deere, Carmen Diana. "La mujer rural y las reformas agrarias en Perú, Chile, y Cuba." *Revista de Ciencias Sociales* (Costa Rica) 25 (March 1983): 59–73.

————. "Rural Women and State Policy: The Latin American Agrarian Reform Experience." *World Development* 13, 9 (1985): 1037–1053.

Elizaga, Juan Carlos. *Participación de la mujer en la mano de obra en América Latina: La fecundidad y otros determinantes.* CELADE Series D, 95. Santiago: CELADE, 1977.

Feijóo, María del Carmen, and Elizabeth Jelin. *Trabajo y familia en el ciclo de vida femenino: El caso de los sectores populares de Buenos Aires.* Estudios CEDES 3, 8/9. Buenos Aires: Centro de Estudios de Estado y Sociedad, 1980.

Gitahy C., Leda et al. "Luttes ouvrières et luttes des ouvrières á São Bernardo do Campo." *Cahiers des Amèriques Latines* 26 (July–December 1982): 149–151.

Guy, D. J. "Women, Peonage, and Industrialization: Argentina, 1810–1914." *Latin American Research Review* 16, 3 (1981): 65–89.

Jelin, Elizabeth. *Migración a las ciudades y participación en la fuerza de trabajo de las mujeres latinoamericanas: El caso del servicio doméstico.* Estudios Sociales 4. Buenos Aires: Centro de Estudios de Estado y Sociedad, 1976.

———. *La mujer y el mercado de trabajo.* Estudios CEDES 1, 6. 2d ed. Buenos Aires: Centro de Estudios de Estado y Sociedad, 1978.

Jesus, Carolina Maria de. *Diário de Bitita.* Rio de Janeiro: Editora Nova Fronteira, 1986.

Lama, Marta de la. "Secretaría de la mujer." *fem* 8, 31 (December 1983–January 1984): 47–50.

Leitinger, Ilse A. *Women's Legal Status and Role Choices in Six Latin American Societies.* Ann Arbor: Women in International Development, Michigan State University, 1985.

Moser, Anita. *A Nova Submissão: Mulheres da Zona Rural no Processo de Trabalho Industrial.* Pôrto Alegre, Brazil: Edipaz, 1985.

Pantelides, Edith A. *Estudio de la población femenina económicamente activa en América Latina, 1950–1970.* CELADE Series C, 161. Santiago: CELADE, 1976.

Prates, Suzana. *Participación de la mujer en el mercado de trabajo uruguayo.* Montevideo: Centro de Informaciones y Estudios del Uruguay, 1980.

Programa Regional del Empleo para América Latina y el Caribe. *Participación laboral femenina y diferencias de remuneraciones según sexo en América Latina.* Investigaciones Sobre Empleo 13. Santiago: PREALC, 1978.

Rey de Marulanda, Nohra. *Las mujeres jefes de hogar.* Bogotá: CEDE, Facultad de Economía, Universidad de los Andes, 1982.

Robaina, Tomás Fernández. *Recuerdos secretos de dos mujeres públicas.* Havana: Editorial Letras Cubanas, 1984.

Vallens, Vivian M. *Working Women in Mexico During the Porfiriato, 1880–1910.* San Francisco: R&E Research Associates, 1978.

Wainerman, Catalina. *La medición del trabajo femenino.* Cuadernos del CENEP 21. Buenos Aires: Centro de Estudios de Población, 1981.

———. "Women and Work in Argentina from the Perspective of the Catholic Church in the Middle of the Century." *Desarrollo Económico* 21, 81 (1981): 71–92.

Wilson, F. "Women and Agricultural Change in Latin America: Some Concepts Guiding Research." *World Development* 13, 9 (1985): 1017–1035.

Yeager, Gertrude Mary Matyoka. "Women's Roles in Nineteenth-Century Chile: Public Education Records, 1843–1883." *Latin American Research Review* 18, 3 (1983): 149–156.

## 3.4   Women and Education

Alvarez Estévez, Rolando. *La reeducación de la mujer cubana en la colonia.* Havana: Editorial de Ciencias Sociales, 1976.

Argentina, Ministerio de Cultura y Educación. *Conferencia Interamericana Especializada Sobre Educación Integral de la Mujer, Buenos Aires, 21–25 de agosto de*

*1972*. Buenos Aires: Centro Nacional de Documentación e Información Educativa, 1972.

Braslavsky, Cecilia. *Mujer y educación*. Santiago: Organización de las Naciones Unidas para la Educación, la Ciencia, y la Cultura, Oficina Regional de Educación de la UNESCO para América Latina y el Caribe, 1984.

Capizzano de Capalbo, Beatriz. *La mujer en la educación preescolar argentina*. Buenos Aires: Latina, 1982.

Fernández Berdaguer, María Leticia. "Educación universitaria y desempeño profesional: El caso de las mujeres estudiantes de ciencias económicas de la Universidad de Buenos Aires." *Revista Paraguaya de Sociología* 20, 56 (January–April 1983): 75–97.

Fernández Kelly, Patricia. "Alternative Education for 'Maquiladora' Workers: Centro de Orientación de la Mujer Obrera." *Grassroots Development* 6–7, 2–1 (Winter 1982–Spring 1983): 41–46.

Foz y Foz, Pilar. *La revolución pedagógica en Nueva España, 1754–1820: María Ignacia de Azlor y Encheverz y los colegios de la enseñanza*. Mexico City: Instituto de Estudios y Documentos Históricos, 1981.

Galván de Terrazas, Luz Elena. *La educación superior de la mujer en México, 1876–1940*. Mexico City: SEP Cultura, 1985.

Rosemberg, Fúlvia. *A Educação da Mulher no Brasil*. São Paulo: Global Editora, 1982.

Santos Silva, Loreina. *Women in Higher Education in Puerto Rico*. Mayaguez, Puerto Rico: Office of Scientific Research, University of Puerto Rico, Mayaguez Campus, 1982.

*Seminario Regional Sobre la Formación Profesional de la Mujer Trabajadora (*1976, *Bogotá)*. Informe no. 72. Montevideo: CINTERFOR-SENA: 1976.

Sirvent, María Teresa. *La mujer y el proyecto principal de educación en América Latina y el Caribe*. Santiago: Organización de las Naciones Unidas para la Educación, la Ciencia, y la Cultura, Oficina Regional de Educación de la Unesco para América Latina y el Caribe, 1983.

### 3.5   Overviews and Other Topics

#### 3.5.1   General and Comparative

Ander Egg, Ezequiel, Norma Zamboni, Anabelle Teresa Yáñez, Jorge Gissi, and Enrique Dussell. *Opresión y marginalidad de la mujer en el orden social machista*. Buenos Aires: Editorial Humanitas, 1972.

Arboleda Cuevas, Esmeralda. *El tiempo de la mujer*. Bogotá: Instituto Colombiano de Cultura, Subdirección de Comunicaciones Culturales, División de Publicaciones, 1977.

Baez Díaz, Tomás. *La mujer aborigen y la mujer en la colonia: Su participación en la etapa histórica que termina en 1795*. Santo Domingo: Premio Shell, 1977.

Barbieri, Teresita de. "Políticas de población y la mujer: Antecedentes para su estudio." *Revista Mexicana de Sociología* 45, 1 (January–March 1983): 293–308.

Barroso, Carmen, y Albertina Oliveira Costa, eds. *Mulher, Mulheres*. São Paulo: Cortez Editora, Fundação Carlos Chagas, 1983.

Bastide, Roger et al. *La femme de couleur en Amerique Latine*. L'Homme et la Societé. Paris: Editions Anthropos, 1974.

Baxter, Shelly. *Feminist Theory, State Policy, and Rural Women in Latin America: A Rapporteur's Report*. Helen Kellogg Institute for International Studies Working Papers 49. South Bend, Ind.: Notre Dame University, 1985.

Benería, Lourdes. *The Crossroads of Class and Gender*. Chicago: University of Chicago Press, 1987.

Bingham, Majorie Wall, Susan Hill Gross, and Janet Donaldson, eds. *Women in Latin America*. St. Louis Park, Minn.: Glenhurst Publications, 1985.

Bonder, G. "The Study of Politics from the Standpoint of Women." *International Social Science Journal* 35, 4 (1983): 625–637.

Bonilla de Ramos, Elsy. *Memorias del encuentro sobre la Mujer y los Medios Masivos de Comunicación: Trabajos y discusiones*. Documento del Centro de Estudios sobre Desarrollo Económico 58. Bogotá: CEDE, Universidad de los Andes, 1979.

Boxer, C. R. *Women in Iberian Expansion Overseas, 1415–1815: Some Facts, Fancies, and Personalities*. New York: Oxford University Press, 1975.

Braeucker, Sieglinde. *Frauen widerstand in Lateinamerika*. Hamburg: Libertare Assoziation, 1982.

Bronstein, Audrey. *The Triple Struggle: Latin American Peasant Women*. Boston: South End Press, 1983.

Camisa, Zulma C. *La nupcialidad de las mujeres solteras en la América Latina*. Serie A (Centro Latino Americano de Demografía), 1034. San José, Costa Rica: Centro Latinoamericano de Demografía, 1977.

Carroll, Berenice A., ed. *Liberating Women's History: Theoretical and Critical Essays*. Urbana: University of Illinois Press, 1976.

Casas, Nelly. *Compromiso ser mujer*. Buenos Aires: Peña Lillo, 1985.

Castro-Gilbert, Carmen. *Two Thirds* [Women in Latin America]. United Nations document E/CN.6/58. Toronto, Ontario: Institute for Studies in Education, 1979.

CEPAL. *Cinco estudios sobre la situación de la mujer en América Latina: Conferencia sobre la integración de la mujer en el desarrollo económico y social de América Latina* (2d, 1979, Macuto, Venezuela). Estudios e informes de la CEPAL, 16. New York: United Nations, 1982.

———. *La mujer en el sector popular urbano, América Latina y el Caribe* (1983, Santiago de Chile). Santiago: Naciones Unidas, CEPAL, 1984.

———. *Mujeres en América Latina: Aportes para un discusión*. Mexico City: Fondo de Cultura Económica, 1975.

———. *Mujeres jóvenes en América Latina: Aportes para una discusión*. Montevideo: Arca/Foro Juvenil, 1985.

CIDAL, A.C. "An Anthology on Women in Latin America." Special issue of *Boletín documental sobre las mujeres* 1 (1974). (Address: Apdo. Postal 42, Suc. A, Cuernavaca, Morelos, Mexico.)

D'Avila Neto, Maria Inacia. *O Autoritarismo e a Mulher.* Rio de Janeiro: Achiam e, 1980.

Elsasser, Nan. *Las mujeres.* Old Westbury, N.Y.: Feminist Press, 1981.

Elton, Charlotte. *Migración femenina en América Latina: Factores determinantes.* Serie E, 26. Santiago: Centro Latinoamericano de Demografía, 1978.

Encuentro Continental de Mujeres Cristianas por la Paz. *La mujer taller de la vida, constructora de la nueva sociedad.* Matanzas, Cuba: Centro de Información y Documentación Augusto Cotto, 1983.

Farias, Z'aira Ary. *Domesticidade.* Rio de Janeiro: Achiam e/CMB, 1983.

Franco, Afonso Arinos de Melo et al. "Condição política e social da mulher." *Revista de Ciência Política* 25, 25 (January–April 1982): 77–105.

Gabaldón, José Rafael. "Mujeres de América." *Boletín de la Academia Nacional de la Historia* (Venezuela) 66, 261 (January–March 1983): 113–124.

Gagliano, Diana. *¿Qué pasa con la mujer?* Buenos Aires: Ediciones Depalma, 1981.

Galeano, Eduardo H. "Mujeres del XVII." *Plural* 13, 150 (March 1984): 2–5.

Giménez Caballero, Ernesto. *Las mujeres de América.* Colección Ensayo. Madrid: Editora Nacional, 1971.

Grondona, Adela. *La mujer de la independencia y la independencia de la mujer.* Buenos Aires: Editora Teoría, 1982.

Guerra Cunningham, Lucía, ed. *Mujer y sociedad en América Latina.* Irvine: University of California Press, 1980.

Hahner, June Edith, ed. *Women in Latin American History, Their Lives and Views.* Los Angeles: UCLA Latin American Center Publications, 1980.

Harris, Olivia. *Latin American Women: Report.* London: Minority Rights Group, 1983.

Henderson, James D., and L. R. Henderson. *Ten Notable Women of Latin America.* Chicago: Nelson-Hall, 1978.

Inter-American Commission of Women. *Special Committee for Studies and Recommendations of the Inter-American Commission of Women for the World Conference of International Women's Year.* CIM Studies 2. Washington, D.C.: General Secretariat, Organization of American States, 1975.

———. *The Woman in Latin America: Past, Present, Future.* Washington, D.C.: General Secretariat, Organization of American States, 1974.

Kinzer, Nora Scott. "International Department: Women in Latin America." *Journal of Marriage and the Family* 35, 2 (1973): 299–354.

Kuhner, Maria Helena. *O Desafio Atual da Mulher.* Rio de Janeiro: Livraria F. Alves Editora, 1977.

Latin American and Caribbean Women's Collective. *Slaves of Slaves: The Challenge of Latin American Women.* London: Zed Press, 1980.

Latin American Working Group. *Central American Women Speak for Themselves.* Toronto: Latin American Working Group, 1983.

Lavrin, Asunción, ed. *Latin American Women: Historical Perspectives.* Wesport, Conn.: Greenwood Press, 1978.

Leacock, E. et al. *Women in Latin America: An Anthology from Latin American Perspectives.* Riverside, Calif.: Latin American Perspectives, 1979.

Lemos Morgan, Rodolfo. *La mujer nueva.* Buenos Aires: Ediciones Depalma, 1977.

Leret de Matheus, María Gabriela. *La mujer, una incapaz como el demente y el niño: Según las leyes latinoamericanas.* Colección Ciencias Sociales 13. Mexico City: B. Costa-Amic, 1975.

Martorelli, Horacio. *Mujer y sociedad.* Montevideo: CIEDUR-F.C.U., 1979.

Michelena, Margarita et al. *La mujer.* Colección Testimonios del Fondo 26. Mexico City: Fondo de Cultura Económica, 1975.

Miller, Francesca. "The International Relations of Women of the Americas, 1890–1928." *The Americas: A Quarterly Review of Inter-American Cultural History* (Fall 1985): 171–182.

Mujica, Elisa. "La mujer y la alegría." *Boletín de la Academia Colombiana* 32, 136 (April–June 1982): 69–80.

Naranjo, Carmen, ed. *La mujer y el desarrollo: antología.* SEP Diana 322. Mexico City: SEP Diana, 1981–1982.

Nash, June, and Helen Icken Safa, eds. *Sex and Class in Latin America.* 2d ed. New York: J. F. Bergin, 1980.

———. *Women and Change in Latin America.* South Hadley, Mass.: Bergin and Garvey, 1985.

O'Barr, Jean F., ed. *Perspectives on Power: Women in Africa, Asia, and Latin America.* Occasional Papers Series 13. Durham, N.C.: Duke University, Center for International Studies, 1982.

O'Sullivan-Beware, Nancy. *Las mujeres de los conquistadores: La mujer española en los comienzos de la colonización americana: Aportaciones para el estudio de la transculturación.* Madrid: Compañía Bibliográfica Española, 1956.

Orlansky, Dora, and Silvia Dubrovsky. *The Effects of Rural-Urban Migration on Women's Roles in Latin America.* UNESCO Social Science Clearing House Reports and Papers in the Social Sciences 41. Paris: UNESCO, 1978.

Ortiz, B. S. "Changing Consciousness of Central American Women." *Economic and Political Weekly* 20, 17 (1985): 2.

Paredes Vasconez, Irene. *La mujer en la vida social.* Quito: Su Librería, 1982.

Pescatello, Ann. *Power and Pawn: The Female in Iberian Families, Societies, and Cultures.* Westport, Conn.: Greenwood Press, 1976.

———, ed. *Female and Male in Latin America.* 2d ed. Pittsburgh: University of Pittsburgh Press, 1979.

Renshaw, Richard, ed. *Women in the Church*. New LADOC "Keyhole" Series 2. Lima: Latin American Documentation, 1985.

Rogers, Barbara. *The Domestication of Women: Discrimination in Developing Countries*. New York: St. Martin's Press, 1979.

Saffioti, Heleieth I. B. *A Mulher na Sociedade de Classes: Mito e Realidade*. São Paulo: Vozes, 1976. (English translation: *Women in Class Society*. New York: Monthly Review Press, 1978.)

Santarcángelo, Maria Candida Vergueiro. *A Situação da Mulher*. São Paulo: Editora Soma, 1980.

Schmidt, Steffen W. "Women, Politics, and Development." *Latin American Research Review* 18, 1 (1983): 210–227.

Schmukler, Beatriz. *Patriarchy and the Family: Interrelated Changes During Capitalist Development in Europe and Latin America*. East Lansing: Michigan State University, 1984.

Secretaría de Educación Pública. *La mujer en América Latina*. SEP Setentas 211–212. Mexico City SEP, Subsecretaría de Cultura Popular y Educación Extraescolar, 1975.

Signorelli Marti, Rosa. *La Mujer en Latinoamérica*. Buenos Aires: Embajada de Venezuela, 1979.

Steady, Filomena Chioma, ed. *The Black Woman Cross-Culturally*. Cambridge, Mass.: Schenkman, 1981.

Studart, Heloneida. *Mulher: Objeto de Cama e Mesa*. 13th ed. Petrópolis, Brazil: Vozes, 1982.

Suplicy, Mart. *A Condição da Mulher*. São Paulo: Brasiliense, 1984.

Tejeira, Otilia Arosamena de. *La jaula invisible: La mujer en América Latina: Ensayos*. Colección Escritores Hispanoamericanos 10. Mexico City: B. Costa Amic, 1977.

Trapasso, Rosa Dominga. "Patriarcado e iglesia." *fem* 32 (February–March 1984): 8–11.

Trossero, René Juan. *Mujer latinoamericana*. Buenos Aires: Editorial Bonum, 1976.

United Nations. *Five Studies on the Situation of Women in Latin America*. Estudios e Informes de la CEPAL 16. Santiago: United Nations, 1983.

Varela-Cid, Eduardo, and Luis Vicens, eds. *La imbecilización de la mujer*. Córdoba, Argentina: El Cid, Editor, 1984.

Villafañe Casal, María Teresa. *Mujer española en la conquista y colonización de América*. N.P., 1964.

Vitale, Luis. *Historia y sociología de la mujer latinoamericana*. Colección Ensayo Contemporáneo. Barcelona: Fontamara, 1981.

Wasserstrom, Robert. *Grassroots Development in Latin America and the Caribbean: Oral Histories of Social Change*. New York: Praeger, 1985.

Wiarda, Ieda Siqueira, and Judith F. Helzner. *Women, Population, and International Development in Latin America: Persistent Legacies and New Perceptions for the*

1980's. Program in Latin American Studies Occasional Papers 13. Amherst: International Area Studies Programs, University of Massachussetts, 1981.

*Women in Latin America.* LADOC "Keyhole" Series 10. Washington, D.C.: Latin America Documentation, USCC, 1975.

World Conference of the International Women's Year. *Report of the World Conference of the International Women's Year, Mexico City, 19 June–2 July 1975.* New York: United Nations, 1976.


*3.5.2 Southern Cone*

Abeijón, Carlos. *La mujer argentina antes y después de Eva Perón.* Buenos Aires: Editorial Cuarto Mundo, 1975.

Arteaga, Ana María. *La mujer en Chile.* Santiago: Centro de Estudios de la Mujer, 1986.

Cano Roldán, Imelda. *La mujer en el Reyno de Chile.* Santiago: Municipalidad de Santiago, 1981.

Conferencia Nacional de Mujeres Comunistas, 1971. *La Mujer argentina.* Buenos Aires: Editorial Anteo, 1971.

Correa Morande, María. *La guerra de las mujeres.* Santiago: Editorial Universidad Técnica del Estado, 1974.

Demitrópulos Libertad. *Eva Perón.* Biblioteca Política Argentina 46. Buenos Aires: Centro Editor de América Latina, 1984.

Dougnac Rodríguez, Antonio. "Josef de Andia y Varela, 1768–1841: Una mujer de su época." *Revista Chilena de Historia y Geografía* 151 (1984): 7–35.

Dufau, Graciela, ed. *Seminario: La mujer uruguaya hoy.* 2d ed. Montevideo: Editorial Problemas, 1986.

Flusche, Della M. *Forgotten Females: Women of African and Indian Descent in Colonial Chile.* Detroit: B. Ethridge, 1983.

Godoy, Camila. "Argentina en la mira." *fem* 6, 21 (February–March 1982): 76–78.

Guy, D. J. "Lower-class Families, Women, and the Law in Nineteenth Century Argentina." *Journal of Family History* 10, 3 (1985): 318–331.

Machado Bonet, Ofelia, ed. *Status de la mujer en el Uruguay.* 4th ed. Montevideo: Consejo Nacional de Mujeres en el Uruguay, 1986.

Mattelart, Armand, and Michelle Mattelart. *La mujer chilena en la nueva sociedad.* Santiago: Editorial del Pacífico, 1968.

Megliorini, Inés Candelaria. *Los derechos civiles de la mujer en la República Argentina.* Buenos Aires: Centro Nacional de Documentación e Información Educativa, 1972.

Meza, María Angélica, ed. *La otra mitad de Chile.* Santiago: CESOC, Ediciones Chile y América, 1986.

Montecino Aguirre, Sonia. *Quinchamali: Reino de mujeres.* Santiago: Centro de Estudios de la Mujer, 1986.

*La mujer argentina: Ensayos.* Buenos Aires: Consejo de Mujeres de la República Argentina, 1976.

Puz, Amanda. *La mujer chilena.* Santiago: Editora Nacional Quimantu, 1972.

Rodríguez Molas, Ricardo. *Divorcio y familia tradicional: Debate nacional.* Biblioteca Política Argentina 46. Buenos Aires: Centro Editor de América Latina, 1984.

San Miguel, Nélida. *Derechos de la mujer argentina.* Rosario de Santa Fe, Argentina: Editorial La República, 1983.

Santa Cruz, Lucía, ed. *Tres ensayos sobre la mujer chilena: Siglos XVIII–XIX–XX.* Santiago: Editorial Universitaria, 1978.

Sosa de Newton, Lily, *Las argentinas de ayer a hoy.* Buenos Aires: Ediciones Zanetti, 1967.

Taylor, Julie M. *Eva Perón, the Myths of a Woman.* Chicago: University of Chicago Press, 1979.

Valdéz, Adriana. "Una pregunta desde Chile." *fem* 8, 30 (October–November 1983): 49–52.

### 3.5.3  Andean Countries

Andradi, Esther, and Ana María Portugal, eds. *Ser mujer en el Perú.* 2d ed. Lima: TOKAPU Editores, 1979.

Barrig, Maruja. *Cinturón de castidad: La mujer de clase media en el Perú.* 2d ed. Lima: Mosca Azul Editores, 1979.

Bourque, Susan C., and Kay B. Warren. *Women of the Andes: Patriarchy and Social Change in Two Peruvian Towns.* Ann Arbor: University of Michigan Press, 1981.

Chocán, M. Z. "Re-evaluation of Women in Peru." *Convergence* 8, 1 (1975): 41–48.

Dietrich, Luisa. "Frauen in Peru." *Zeitschrift für Lateinamerika, Wien* 25 (1983): 23–32.

Francke, Marfil. *Las mujeres en el Perú.* Lima: Centro de la Mujer Peruana "Flora Tristán," 1985.

Frente Socialista de Mujeres del Perú. *Problemática de la mujer en el Perú: Realidad nacional.* Lima: Editorial Méndez, 1983.

Galvez Barrera, A. "The Historical Status of Women in Peru." *The Impact of Science on Society* 1 (1980): 7–9.

García y García, Elvira. *La mujer peruana a través de los siglos.* 2 vols. Lima: Impresa Americana, 1924–1925.

Guardia, Sara Beatriz. *Mujeres peruanas: El otro lado de la historia.* Lima: Empresa Editora Humboldt, 1985.

LaDuke, Betty. "Women, Art, and Culture in the New Grenada." *Latin American Perspectives* 11, 3 (Summer 1984): 37–52.

Martí, Luis, *Daughters of the Conquistadores: Women of the Viceroyalty of Peru.* Albuquerque: University of New Mexico Press, 1983.

*La mujer en los Andes*. Estudios Andinos 12. Pittsburgh: University of Pittsburgh, 1976.

Ponce, Ana et al. *Hogar y familia en el Perú*. Lima: Pontificia Universidad Católica del Perú, Facultad de Ciencias Sociales, Diploma de Estudios en Población, 1985.

Prieto de Zegarra, Judith. *Mujer, poder, y desarrollo en el Perú*. Callao: Editorial Dorhca Representaciones, 1980.

Reverter-Pezet, Guillermo. *La mujer en el imperio inca*. Lima: Taller Graf. Marin, 1985.

Rodríguez, C. de Munzo, and Roca de Salone E. "Law and Status of Women in Peru." *Columbia Human Rights Law Review* 8, 1 (1976): 207–228.

Velasco, J. A. "The UN Decade for Women in Peru." *Women's Studies International Forum* 8, 2 (1985): 107–109.

Villalobos de Urrutia, Gabriela. *Diagnóstico de la situación social y económica de la mujer peruana*. Lima: Centro de Población y Desarrollo, 1975.

### 3.5.4 Brazil

Alambert, Zuleika. *A Situação e Organização da Mulher*. São Paulo: Global Editora, 1980.

Barroso, Carmen. *Mulher, Sociedade, e Estado no Brasil*. São Paulo: Editora Brasiliense, 1982.

Besse, Susan Kent. "Freedom and Bondage: The Impact of Capitalism on Women in São Paulo, Brazil, 1917–1937." Ph.D. diss., Yale University, 1983.

Carneiro, Sueli. *Mulher Negra*. São Paulo: Nobel, 1985.

*A Condição Feminina no Rio de Janeiro, Sécuilo XIX*. São Paulo: Editora Hucitecém, Instituto Nacional do Livro, Fundação Nacional Pró-Memória, 1984.

Da Fonseca, R. M. "Law and the Condition of Women in Brazil." *Columbia Human Rights Review* 8, 1 (1976): 11–33.

Hahner, June Edith. *Poverty and Politics: The Urban Poor in Brazil, 1870–1920*. New Mexico: University of New Mexico Press, 1986.

———. *Women in Brazil: Problems and Perspectives*. Albuquerque: Latin American Institute, University of New Mexico, 1984.

———. "'Women's Place' in Politics and Economics in Brazil Since 1964." *Luso Brazilian Review* 19, 1 (Summer 1982): 83–93.

Horta, Elisabeth Vorcaro. *A Mulher na Cultura Brasileira*. Belo Horizonte, Brazil: Imprensa Oficial, 1975.

Leite, Miriam Moreira. *A Mulher no Rio de Janeiro no Século XIX*. São Paulo: Fundação Carlos Chagas, 1982.

Oliveira Costa, Albertina de et al., eds. *Memórias das Mulheres do Exílio: Obra Coletiva*. Rio de Janeiro: Paz e Terra, 1980.

Rosen, B. C., and Laraia, A. L. "Modernity in Women: An Index of Social

Change in Brazil." *Journal of Marriage and Family* 34, 2 (May 1972): 353–360.

Russelwood, A. R. J. "Women and Society in Colonial Brazil." *Journal of Latin American Studies* 9 (May 1977): 1–34.

Saffioti, Heleieth Iara Bongiovani. *Mulher Brasileira.* Rio de Janeiro: Achiam e, 1984.

Silva, Maria Mendes da. *Vida de Mulher.* Rio de Janeiro: Editora Marco Zero, 1981.


*3.5.5    Central America and the Caribbean (including Colombia and Venezuela)*

Acosta-Belén, Edna, ed. *La mujer en la sociedad puertorriqueña.* Río Piedras, Puerto Rico: Ediciones Huracán, 1980. (Translated as *The Puerto Rican Woman: Perspectives on Culture, History, and Society.* 2d ed. New York: Praeger, 1986.)

Benglesdorf, Carollee et al. *Women in Transition.* Special issue of *Cuba Review* 4, 2 (September 1974).

Castro, Fidel. *Women and the Cuban Revolution.* New York: Pathfinder Press, 1981.

Foro de la Mujer Colombiana (1st, Bogotá, 1977). *Documento final.* Bogotá: División de Comunicaciones del SENA, 1978.

González, Vinicio. "Diferencia e igualdad en la situación de la mujer: Una aproximación a su estudio en Costa Rica." *Revista de Ciencias Sociales* (Costa Rica) 25 (March 1983): 91–105.

Holt-Seeland, Inger. *Women of Cuba.* Translated by Elizabeth Hamilton Lacoste, with Mirtha Quintanales and José Vigo. Westport, Conn.: L. Hill, 1982.

Marcucci Vera, César R. *Bolivar, 1783–1830–1980, y la mujer costeña en la independencia.* Bogotá: Editorial ABC, 1980.

Osorno Cardenas, Marta Cecilia. *La mujer colombiana y latinoamericana, la pareja y la familia: Status, situación histórica y actual, dificultades, realización integral.* Medellín: Tip. Italiana-Impresos Marín, 1975.

Randall, Margaret. *Women in Cuba: Twenty Years Later.* New York: Smyrna Press, 1981.

Rubio Sánchez, Manuel. *Status de la mujer en Centroamérica.* Guatemala: Editorial José de Pineda Ibarra, 1976.

Schmidt, Steffen W. "Women in Colombia." In *Women in the World, 1975–1985: The Women's Decade,* ed. Lynne B. Iglitzin and Ruth Ross. Studies in International Comparative Politics 16. 2d ed. Santa Barbara, Calif.: ABC-CLIO, 1986.

———. "Women in Colombia: Attitudes and Future Perspectives in Political Systems." *Journal of Inter-American Studies and World Affairs* 17, 4 (1975): 465–489.

Séjourne, Laurette. *La mujer cubana en el quehacer de la historia*. Mexico City: Siglo Veintiuno, 1980.

Solle, D. "Women in Nicaragua." *Das Argument* (Berlin) 28 (September 1986): 672–677.

Stone, Elizabeth, ed. *Women and the Cuban Revolution*. New York: Pathfinder Press, 1981.

Wagenheim, Olga Jiménez de. "The Puerto Rican Woman in the Nineteenth Century: An Agenda for Research." *Revista/Review Interamericana* 11, 2 (Summer 1981): 196–203.

Wasmer Miguel, Guillermo, ed. *La mujer en Cuba socialista*. Havana: Orbe, 1977.

### 3.5.6 Mexico

Arrom, Silvia Marina. *The Women of Mexico City, 1790–1857*. Stanford, Calif.: Stanford University Press, 1985.

Bénnassy-Berling, Marie-Cécile. *Humanisme et religion chez Sor Juana Inés de la Cruz: La femme et la culture au XVIIe siècle*. Paris: Sorbonne, Editions Hispaniques, 1982.

Bartra, Eli et al. *La Revuelta: Reflexiones, testimonios, y reportajes de Mujeres en Mexico, 1975–1983*. Mexico City: Martín Casillers Editores, 1983.

Benítez, Fernando. *Los demonios en el convento: Sexo y religión en la Nueva España*. Mexico City: Era, 1985.

Bravo, Dolores, and Alejandra Herrera, eds. *Ana Rodríguez de Castro y Aramburu, ilusa, afectadora de santos, falsos milagros, y revelaciones divinas: Proceso inquistorial en la Nueva España (siglos XVIII y XIX)*. Mexico City: Universidad Autónoma Metropolitana, 1984.

Couturier, Edith. "Women and the Family in Eighteenth Century Mexico, Law and Practice." *Journal of Family History* 10, 3 (1985): 294–304.

Franco, Jean. *Plotting Women*. New York: Columbia University Press, 1989.

———. "Women, Fashion, and the Moralists in Early Nineteenth-Century Mexico." In *Homenaje a Ana María Barrenchea*, eds. Isaias Lerner and Lia Lerner. Madrid: Gredos, 1983.

Ladd, Doris M. *Mexican Women in Anahuac and New Spain*. Austin: Institute of Latin American Studies, University of Texas, 1979.

Lomnitz, Larissa. *Networks and Marginality: Life in a Mexican Shantytown*. New York: Academic Press, 1977.

Muriel de la Torre, Josefina. *Los recogimientos de mujeres: Respuesta a una problemática social novo hispana*. Mexico City: Universidad Nacional Autónoma de México, Instituto de Investigaciones Históricas, 1974.

Myers, Kathleen Ann. "Becoming a Nun in Seventeenth Century Mexico: An Edition of the Spiritual Autobiography of Maria de San Joseph (Volume 1)." Ph.D. diss., Brown University, 1986.

O'Quinn, Kathleen Helen. *A Cultural Portrait of Women in Mexico*. Columbia, S.C.: N.P., 1974.

Parcero, María de la Luz. *La mujer en el Siglo XIX en México*. Mexico City: Instituto Nacional de Antropología e Historia, 1982.

Solange, Alberto. "La sexualidad manipulada en Nueva España: Modalidades de recuperación y de adaptación frente a los tribunales eclesiásticos." In *Procedimientos del Primer Simposio Sobre la Historia de Mentalidades, Familia, y Sexualidad en Nueva España*. Mexico City: N.P., 1982.

Tutino, John. "Class and Family: Men and Women in the Mexican Elite, 1750–1810." *The Americas* 39, 3 (January 1983): 359–381.

# INDEX

Designer:   U.C. Press Staff
Compositor:   Asco Trade Typesetting Ltd., Hong Kong
Text:   10/12 Baskerville
Display:   Baskerville
Printer:   Edwards Brothers
Binder:   Edwards Brothers